ABORTION PILLS

ABORTION PILLS

US HISTORY AND POLITICS

CARRIE N. BAKER

Amherst College Press

Copyright © 2024 by Carrie N. Baker
Some rights reserved

This work is licensed under the Creative Commons Attribution-NonCommercial-NoDerivatives 4.0 International License. To view a copy of this license, visit http://creativecommons.org/licenses/by-nc-nd/4.0/ or send a letter to Creative Commons, PO Box 1866, Mountain View, California, 94042, USA.

Note to users: A Creative Commons license is valid only when it is applied to the person or entity that holds rights to the licensed work. This work contains components (e.g. poetry quotations, song lyrics, and/or images) that have been published with permission from their respective rightsholders and to which the rightsholders of this work cannot apply the license. It is ultimately your responsibility to independently evaluate the copyright status of any work or component part of a work you use, and if necessary, seek permission from the appropriate rights holders, in light of your intended use.

The complete manuscript of this work was subjected to a partly closed ("single-anonymous") review process. For more information, visit https://acpress.amherst.edu/peerreview/.

Published in the United States of America by Amherst College Press
Manufactured in the United States of America
Library of Congress Control Number: 2024933972

DOI: https://doi.org/10.3998/mpub.14469549

ISBN 978-1-943208-85-2 (paper)
ISBN 978-1-943208-86-9 (open access)
ISBN 978-1-943208-87-6 (hardcover)

Table of Contents

Acronyms   vii

    Introduction: Kelly's Story   1

        What Are Abortion Pills? Terms and Definitions   5
        Methods and Sources   6
        The Story of Abortion Pills in a Nutshell   7
        Book Outline   9

1   "Medical McCarthyism": RU 486 Development and the Fight
      for FDA Approval, 1980–2000   11

        Anti-Abortion Campaign to Block RU 486 from the US Market   17
        The Feminist Campaign to Bring RU 486 to the United States   22
        FDA Approval of Mifepristone   38

2   "Thankful for Crumbs": The Fight to Expand Abortion
      Pill Access, 2000–2019   55

        FDA Risk Evaluation and Mitigation Strategy (REMS) and
            Mifepristone Research   62
        Self-Induced Abortion?   66
        Campaign to Remove FDA Restrictions   78
        Political Shifts and Movement Mobilization   84

3   "Greased the Wheels": COVID-19 Pandemic and the Rise of
      Telemedicine Abortion   95

        Virtual Abortion Clinics   103
        Organizing to Support Increased Access to Abortion Pills Outside of the
            Medical System   108
        Supreme Court Stops Telemedicine Abortion   110
        The Pendulum Swings: Biden Administration Expands Abortion Pill Access   115

4 **"Trying to Shake Abortion Pills Free from the Gatekeepers":**
Eroding Abortion Rights and Expanding Self-Managed Abortion   121

Texas Bans Abortion: S.B. 8 Spurs Self-Managed Abortion   121
New Research Supports the Safety of Telemedicine and
   Self-Managed Abortion   128
FDA Loosens REMS Restrictions on Mifepristone   132
Spreading the Word About Abortion Pills   136
Legal Risks of Self-Managed Abortion   139

5 **"Mail Those Pills No Matter What": The End of *Roe* Spurs Efforts**
to Expand Abortion Pill Access   149

The Immediate Aftermath of Roe's *Fall*   150
The Push for Telemedicine Abortion Provider Shield Laws   155
Litigation and Legislation to Expand Abortion Pill Access
   at the State Level   161
Federal Initiatives to Expand Abortion Pill Access   167
Expanding Abortion Pill Access Outside of the Medical
   System and the Law   172
Reframing Abortion Pills and Early Abortion   179

6 **"Putting the Genie Back in the Bottle": Post-*Dobbs* Attempts**
to Block Mifepristone   185

Abortion Pill Disinformation   187
Anti-Abortion Campaign to Remove Mifepristone from the Market   194

Conclusion: "Putting Pills Directly in the Hands of Those Who
Need Them"   215

Appendix A: Abortion Pill Timeline   239
Appendix B: Glossary   241
Appendix C: Interviews   243
Acknowledgments   247
Endnotes   249

Acronyms

AAP	Abortion Access Project
ACLU	American Civil Liberties Union
ACOG	American College of Obstetricians and Gynecologists
ADF	Alliance Defending Freedom
AHT	Advances in Health Technology
ANSIRH	Advancing New Strategies in Reproductive Health
ARM	Abortion Rights Mobilization
CPC	crisis pregnancy center
CRR	Center for Reproductive Rights
EMAA	Expanding Medication Abortion Access
ETASU	Elements to Assure Safe Use
FDA	US Food and Drug Administration
FMF	Feminist Majority Foundation
FRC	Family Research Council
FTC	Federal Trade Commission
GLC	Generative Learning Community for self-managed abortion
HHS	Department of Health and Human Services
HIS	Indian Health Service
IND	Investigational New Drug
M+A Hotline	Miscarriage and Abortion Hotline
NAF	National Abortion Federation
NARAL	National Abortion Rights Action League
NAWHERC	Native American Women's Health Education Resource Center
NDA	New Drug Application
NOW	National Organization for Women
NRLC	National Right to Life Committee
NWHN	National Women's Health Network
OARS	Online Abortion Resource Squad

REMS	Risk Evaluation and Mitigation Strategy
RHEDI	Reproductive Health Education in Family Medicine
RHTP	Reproductive Health Technologies Project
SASS	Self-Managed Abortion. Safe and Supported
SHERo	Sisters Helping Every Woman Rise and Organize
SIA Legal Team	Self-Induced Abortion Legal Team
S.T.O.P.	Surveillance Technology Oversight Project
WRRAP	Women's Reproductive Rights Assistance Project

Introduction: Kelly's Story

In early February of 2022, a young Latina named Kelly living in Texas found out she was pregnant. The previous September, Texas had banned abortion at six weeks of pregnancy. At the time she found out she was pregnant, Kelly had just started a new job, didn't have health insurance, and couldn't take time off to travel out of state for an abortion. She googled "affordable ultrasounds" and found a clinic offering free ultrasounds. It had positive reviews, so she gave them a call and made an appointment. When she got there, they were very friendly. She filled out a form, giving her medical history and the reason she was there. She checked the box for abortion. Unbeknownst to Kelly, she was at an anti-abortion "crisis pregnancy center." "Being in Texas, I probably should have been a little more careful," Kelly later said. "They could have easily reported me."[1]

Kelly believed she was at a medical clinic. "At least that's how they portrayed themselves on Google," she later reported. A woman gave her a pregnancy test, which was positive, then asked her if she wanted to go through with the pregnancy. Kelly was honest. "I don't want this pregnancy, I can't have this pregnancy," Kelly told her. "I've been with my partner for only a year. And we're not ready financially. It's just out of the question. I honestly don't see myself being ready to be a mother." The woman asked Kelly whether she had considered adoption. Kelly responded, "There's nothing to consider for me. I've thought about it thoroughly. I stand by my decision." The woman then told her that abortion could kill her. She said abortion pills were especially dangerous.

After waiting about thirty minutes, Kelly received an ultrasound from another woman dressed in scrubs, who told her she was eight weeks pregnant. This woman pressured Kelly not to have an abortion. "I probably told her four or five times as nicely as I could. 'No, I do not want to go through with this pregnancy.' Of course, they don't come off as aggressive, but it did seem pushy, like they're really forcing this down your throat. But they're doing it in the nicest way possible. She had a tone in her voice, like, 'I'm here to take care of you, don't worry.' At the end of the ultrasound, they offered to pray for me." The woman warned Kelly that abortion could cause breast cancer, infertility, and depression.

Still believing the center was an abortion provider, Kelly made an appointment for the following week, hoping to get abortion medications. "I was really distracted by the very motherly, homey feeling from them, the welcoming, 'It's okay, we're here to help you' type of vibe I was getting. That's what really made me think, 'Okay, they're here to help.'" At her next visit, the woman told her they did not provide abortion medications. They insisted on making another appointment for Kelly, but she didn't return. She later found out the center she went to was an anti-abortion organization funded by a Christian church.

Kelly went on Google again and this time located a real medical clinic with affordable ultrasounds. She found out she was ten weeks and three days pregnant, and that Texas did not allow abortion after six weeks. She was told she would have to travel out of state for an abortion. "I was just freaking out. I was just trying to find answers," said Kelly. She absolutely couldn't take time off from her new job during the work week for the eight-hour drive to a clinic out of state. Desperate, she went on Reddit and found an abortion forum where women shared information and answered each other's questions about abortion. That's where she read about the organization Plan C, which shares information about how people can get abortion pills no matter where they live. "I looked up Texas for telehealth and thankfully they gave a very thorough example of what to do for a Texas resident," said Kelly. "I followed every step."

At the time, she was around eleven weeks pregnant, so she had to move quickly. On the Plan C website, Kelly read about how to obtain abortion pills from a US-based telehealth provider located in another state, using mail forwarding. She rented a box in a state where the telehealth provider practiced and had the pills sent overnight to the box, then had the pills forwarded to her home in Texas. The pills arrived in a discreet package within five days of when she first spoke to the telehealth provider. She took them right away, just one day before she reached twelve weeks of pregnancy—the outer limit of what her doctor recommended for the medication dosage that was sent. "I felt super comfortable with the provider I found. She answered all my questions. I got thorough answers. I got the help that I truly needed. She lifted a huge weight off my shoulders," said Kelly. The abortion process took about four hours and felt like a heavy period with pain and some nausea. "This was a really positive experience for me. I felt really safe and I felt assured. I was just so grateful that I was able to succeed with this," Kelly later reported.

When Kelly had her abortion, the US Food and Drug Administration (FDA) had only recently allowed medical providers to offer telehealth abortion with pills. The FDA first approved a combination of two medications for abortion in 2000—mifepristone and misoprostol. Mifepristone, originally known as RU 486, blocks the pregnancy-sustaining hormone progesterone, which loosens pregnancy tissue from the uterine wall. Then misoprostol, taken twenty-four to forty-eight hours later, causes uterine contractions to expel pregnancy tissue. For decades, the FDA only allowed doctors registered with the drug maker to dispense the medication in person. Reproductive health advocates campaigned for years to loosen these restrictions. In December of 2021, shortly before Kelly ordered her medications, the FDA permanently removed the requirement that healthcare providers dispense mifepristone in person, opening the door to telemedicine abortion. The COVID-19 pandemic spurred this shift in policy. As a result, healthcare professionals could consult with their patients by videoconference, telephone, or online forms, and then mail abortion pills to them for use at home.

But then in June 2022, just a few months after Kelly got her abortion, the Supreme Court reversed the constitutional right to abortion established in *Roe v. Wade* in the case of *Dobbs v. Jackson Women's Health Organization*. States throughout the South and Midwest quickly banned healthcare professionals from offering abortion services. As a result, abortion pills and the telehealth infrastructure that advocates had created during the pandemic became a critical option for people seeking to end a pregnancy. Reproductive health advocates fought for new telemedicine provider shield laws that enabled clinicians in states allowing abortion to serve patients in states with bans. Meanwhile, abortion outside of the formal medical system increased dramatically. Drawing on knowledge and practices developed in Latin America and used globally in countries banning abortion, US activists created community networks that mailed free abortion pills to people in states with bans. Websites selling pills also proliferated and prices dropped. Finally, activists developed organizations to share information and provide medical, legal, and emotional support to people using abortion pills outside of the formal medical system.

The overturn of constitutional abortion rights and state bans on abortion, however, was not enough for some abortion opponents. In November 2022, a group of anti-abortion doctors and a dentist sued the FDA in an attempt to remove mifepristone from the market nationwide. In April 2023, a lower court judge in Amarillo, Texas, stayed the FDA's approval of mifepristone and ordered the medication off the US market nationwide. On appeal, the Fifth Circuit reversed in part, allowing mifepristone to stay on the market, but sustained significant limitations on distribution of the medication, including re-imposing the medically unnecessary in-person distribution requirement. The FDA appealed to the Supreme Court. As America waited on pins and needles for a decision, Plan C posted on social media, "No matter how the ruling comes down, people who want to self-manage their abortions will continue to have options through the robust alternative supply systems that now exist in the U.S." They recommended that people order abortion pills in advance to have on hand just in case. "The ecosystem of support—ways people are accessing pills, free hotlines, and community networks—is crucial info to know and repost right now," said Plan C on Instagram the evening before the Supreme Court stayed the Texas court's ruling until a final resolution of the case.[2] Meanwhile, pills kept flowing through legal and extralegal channels.

To fully understand what led to Kelly's ultimately successful journey to abortion and what future "Kellys" may face, this book examines the battle to establish, expand, and maintain legal access to abortion pills in the United States over the last thirty-five years, as well as the story of activists' campaigns to support people using abortion pills outside of the formal medical system. Scholars have documented a long history of abortion practice, politics, and law in the United States, including pre-*Roe* practices of abortion outside of the formal medical system,[3] and scholarship has documented the global feminist movement for self-managed abortion and the global politics of abortion pills,[4] but no one has told the full story of abortion pills in the United States. Scholarship on the *Roe* period has focused primarily on abortion within the formal medical system and the legal regulation and restriction of access to this form of abortion, which has obscured the continued existence of self-managed abortion after *Roe v. Wade* legalized abortion in all fifty states in 1973 and the growing importance of abortion pills, especially for self-managed abortion as reproductive freedom has diminished in recent years.

The goal of this book is to tell the story of abortion pills in the United States and how increasing access to these medications has been a key strategy of women's resistance to attempts by politicians, religious leaders, medical professionals, intimate partners, and others to control women's bodies and lives. I tell this story from my position not only as a feminist legal scholar, but also as a journalist who has closely covered this issue for *Ms.* magazine since 2018, and as a participant in the movement to increase access to abortion pills. As a result, I will focus on the story of abortion pills rather than on abortion historiography or scholarly debates on abortion. I will focus on what happened in the political campaigns for and against access to abortion pills, the laws and policies restricting or promoting access to these medications, and the ways activists expanded access both within the formal medical system and extra-legally outside of it.

In telling this story, I will explore the role science played in abortion politics, the varied strategies and tactics used by abortion pill advocates, disagreements among these advocates, and how the intersections of sex, race, and class impacted abortion pill access and politics. In this book, I will examine how resistance to increasing abortion pill access not only came from the anti-abortion movement and Republican politicians, but also resulted from a combination of FDA conservativism and cautiousness, the market-oriented pharmaceutical, health care, and insurance industries, mainstream medicine's abandonment of abortion care, physician gatekeeping, Democrats' lukewarm support for abortion, the influence of philanthropy in abortion health care and activism, and the cautious approaches of some abortion rights supporters.

In the rest of this introduction, I will first define important terms and concepts used throughout the book, then describe my methods and sources, provide a short summary of the story of abortion pills, and then provide an outline of the chapters.

WHAT ARE ABORTION PILLS? TERMS AND DEFINITIONS[5]

Abortion pills are not common knowledge to most people, so this section will explain what they are and how they are used. The FDA has approved the use of two medications to end an early pregnancy: mifepristone and misoprostol. The recommended regimen is to take one 200-milligram mifepristone pill followed twenty-four to forty-eight hours later with four 200-microgram misoprostol pills through ten weeks of pregnancy (counting from the first day of the last menstrual period).[6] The World Health Organization has approved this regimen for up to twelve weeks after the last menstrual period, including self-administration with no clinician involvement.[7] Abortion pills are effective later in pregnancy under different regimens.[8] Misoprostol taken alone can also end a pregnancy. The World Health Administration recommends three 800-microgram doses taken vaginally, under the tongue, or in the cheek pouch (buccally), three hours apart, with repeat doses if necessary.[9] Mifepristone and misoprostol are commonly referred to as "abortion pills," although both medications have other uses. Mifepristone was called RU 486 when it was first developed in the 1980s by the French pharmaceutical company Roussel Uclaf for the initials of the company and the number assigned to the substance developed. The FDA-approved cancer drug methotrexate is also used off label in combination with misoprostol for treatment of ectopic pregnancies.

People choose medication abortion for a number of reasons, including because they think it is more natural (more like a miscarriage), more private (done at home), more convenient and accessible, more affordable, and less invasive than procedural abortion. Telemedicine abortion is when a clinician screens a patient by videoconference, telephone, or online form, then prescribes abortion pills to be mailed to the patient. Telemedicine abortion is more private, convenient, and accessible than in-clinic abortion for many people.[10]

Abortion pills are safe and effective. Serious adverse events occur in less than one-third of one percent of medication abortions and abortion pills are over 95 percent effective when used within the first ten weeks of pregnancy.[11] They are slightly less effective later in pregnancy. Using these pills in combination is preferable, but misoprostol alone is also safe and effective to end a pregnancy.[12]

Abortion pills are prescription medications in the United States. Misoprostol is a widely available ulcer medication, but mifepristone is tightly controlled by the FDA, which allows only certified healthcare professionals to prescribe the medication and only certified providers and pharmacies to dispense it. As states adopted burdensome restrictions or bans on abortion, and as a result of the high cost of abortion care in states that allowed it, people began buying abortion pills from websites without a prescription or found other ways to access these pills. Finding and using pills without consulting a medical provider is one form of self-managed abortion (also called self-induced abortion). Other forms involve manual vacuum aspiration of the contents of the uterus, or other substances to cause a miscarriage such as herbs.[13]

As of 2020, medication abortion comprised over half of abortions in the United States. The alternative is procedural abortion (often called surgical abortion), which involves the removal of the contents of the uterus either by suction (called aspiration abortion) or manually removing fetal tissue. Procedural abortion in the first trimester takes five to ten minutes and is very safe and effective. Abortion pills are different than Plan B, which is an emergency contraceptive pill used to prevent pregnancy up to five days after intercourse. Abortion pills end a pregnancy and are used after a missed period and/or pregnancy confirmation.

Mifepristone has uses beyond elective abortion. Some physicians use mifepristone off label for miscarriage treatment and during childbirth to soften the cervix. The FDA has approved mifepristone to treat Cushing syndrome. The agency has also approved the use of mifepristone for treating meningioma (a non-cancerous tumor in the membranes around the brain and spinal cord) through a compassionate use program administered by the nonprofit Feminist Majority Foundation. Research has demonstrated that mifepristone is effective at treating a range of other conditions, including fibroids, endometriosis, postpartum depression, and breast cancer, and can act as a contraceptive, but the FDA has not approved the medication for these uses.[14]

METHODS AND SOURCES

This book draws on interviews with over eighty people, including activists, abortion providers, researchers, and people who have used abortion pills (see Appendix C for a list of people interviewed). I quote my sources generously throughout the book in order to give readers a sense of the range of perspectives, contributions, and experiences in the movement to expand access to abortion pills over the last thirty-five years. While many people and organizations have talked about abortion pills over the years, in this book I focus on the people and organizations that took actions to increase access to abortion pills. I also conducted research in several archives, including the papers of Lawrence Lader, Planned Parenthood, and the National Women's Health Network at Smith College, the papers of the Reproductive Health Technologies Project at Schlesinger Library at Harvard University, and the private collections of several activists, including Marie Bass, Francine Coeytaux, and others. This book pays particular attention to the medical research conducted on mifepristone—and how advocates used this research to achieve FDA approval of mifepristone and to push the FDA to lift its restrictions on the medication. This research also advanced the movement toward self-managed abortion by reassuring advocates of the safety of medication abortion outside of a clinical setting. Finally, I have conducted research into the government records and legal cases relating to RU 486/mifepristone. As a legal and social movement scholar, I focus on how activists have shaped the evolution of law and policy, as well as opportunities for extralegal access to abortion pills in the United States. The bulk of the book (Chapters 3 to 6) focuses on the critical period between 2020 and 2024 when activists revolutionized abortion in America by shifting people's understanding of and access to abortion pills and removing and/or bypassing years of political and medical barriers to mifepristone.

While most people seeking abortion are cisgender women, nonbinary people and trans men also become pregnant and need abortions. This book will at times use gendered language to emphasize the gendered dynamics of abortion pill politics.[15]

THE STORY OF ABORTION PILLS IN A NUTSHELL

The French pharmaceutical company Roussel Uclaf developed mifepristone in 1980 and the French government approved use of mifepristone for abortion in 1988, but the battle for FDA approval in the United States lasted decades. Beginning in the 1980s, US women's health advocates collaborated with researchers, healthcare providers, and public health experts to push for FDA approval of mifepristone. When Roussel Uclaf and other drug companies refused to develop the medication for the US market for fear of boycotts and threats of violence from abortion opponents, reproductive health advocates did it themselves, as their predecessors had done with birth control pills in the 1950s.[16] They raised money from wealthy individuals and foundations to conduct the necessary research, found investors willing to create a company to market mifepristone in the United States, and applied for and finally achieved FDA approval of mifepristone. But the FDA placed severe restrictions on mifepristone and doctors required expensive medical tests for people to obtain the medication, making it inaccessible to many people. Meanwhile, women in immigrant communities were sharing knowledge about how to use misoprostol, bringing to the United States grassroots self-managed abortion accompaniment practices that were widespread throughout Latin America, and later elsewhere, after women in Brazil figured out that the widely available and low-cost ulcer medication misoprostol could be used for abortion.[17]

After the FDA approved mifepristone in 2000, reproductive rights advocates urged a wide range of healthcare providers to offer abortion pills, conducted ongoing research to support a less burdensome medical protocol for accessing pills, and worked to remove the FDA restrictions on the medication. The approval of a generic version of mifepristone in 2019 increased access by bringing down the price of the medication. But as abortion restrictions increased over time, particularly in the 2010s, advocates began meeting to discuss the use of misoprostol alone for people who could not access abortion within the medical system. Later, anticipating the fall of constitutional abortion rights established in *Roe v. Wade*, advocates and entrepreneurs built "alternative supply systems" to provide abortion pills to people living in states banning medical providers from offering abortion services. Meanwhile, all along the way, abortion opponents worked to block access to abortion pills, challenging the FDA approval of mifepristone with false claims about the dangers of what they called "chemical abortion," and spreading misinformation about abortion pills through a nationwide network of anti-abortion "crisis pregnancy centers" like the one that obstructed Kelly's access to abortion.

After *Dobbs*, abortion pills meant that women faced a very different set of options when seeking to end a pregnancy than they had experienced before the Supreme Court decided *Roe* in 1973. Whereas before *Roe*, illegal abortion posed significant health risks, post-*Roe*, abortion pills provided a safe and accessible way to end an early pregnancy outside of the formal medical system. Before *Roe*, women often had difficulty finding information about how to obtain a safe abortion. By the time *Roe* was overturned, information about abortion pills was widely available on the internet. Before *Roe*, the legal risks of providing and receiving abortion varied over time, but illegal abortion was often tolerated by authorities.[18] Post-*Roe*, concerns about the legal risks of abortion in states with restrictions were high in the context of a vastly expanded prison-industrial complex. Some anti-abortion prosecutors targeted people using abortion pills and those supporting them.[19] Despite these risks, telemedicine abortion providers offered medication abortion to people in all fifty states, operating both from within the country and from abroad, despite the law. Moreover, activists operated alternative supply networks for people to access abortion medications for free through grassroots accompaniment networks or for low prices through online websites in all fifty states, with free medical, emotional, and legal support services available via hotlines as well. In this way, abortion pills have played a critical role in maintaining access to abortion for many people living in America after the *Dobbs* decision in June 2022. In fact, the year after *Dobbs*, the number of abortions in the United States increased, which experts attributed in part to increased abortion access in states maintaining legal abortion, including telemedicine abortion.[20]

Not everyone was unanimous in their support for creating these alternative pathways for accessing abortion pills, however. Some brick-and-mortar abortion clinic owners expressed the fear that telemedicine abortion providers would drive them out of business by offering a less expensive alternative to patients seeking abortion pills. Some providers didn't believe that women could use abortion pills safely on their own or did not want other providers taking any legal risks. Reproductive justice advocates, whose activism centered the lives and experiences of women of color,[21] warned about state surveillance and criminal prosecution of people ordering and using abortion pills outside of the formal medical system, fearing police would target low-income women and women of color in particular. Some advocates focused on fighting to keep abortion legal, while many worked to transport women to states where abortion health care was still legal. But a small and determined group of reproductive healthcare advocates and clinicians believed that abortion pills were safe and that women were fully capable of using these pills outside of the formal medical system. These advocates believed people should be able to make their own decisions about the risks and benefits of using abortion pills outside of the formal medical system. They also believed that clinicians should be able to make their own risk assessments and provide these services if they chose to as a matter of conscientious provision, the opposite of conscientious objection. This book explores these conflicts, as well as the broader politics of abortion pills in the United States over the last several decades, to understand how the anti-abortion movement, the FDA, the medical system, and the incrementalism of many reproductive health advocates limited access to mifepristone for over two decades, but how COVID-19 and *Dobbs* drove some activists to break through longstanding political and medical barriers and finally place abortion pills directly in the hands of people who needed them.

BOOK OUTLINE

This book is arranged chronologically.[22] Chapter 1 explains the development of RU 486 in 1980 in France and the years-long battle to win FDA approval in the United States. Chapter 2 traces how reproductive rights advocates worked to increase access to mifepristone and misoprostol over the first two decades of the twenty-first century, and anti-abortion attempts to block access. Chapter 3 describes the development of telemedicine abortion during 2020 and 2021, spurred by the COVID-19 pandemic. Chapter 4 documents the erosion of abortion rights and the rise of self-managed abortion in the second half of 2021, including the development of support systems for people self-managing their abortions. Chapter 5 recounts how reproductive rights advocates organized before and after the overturning of *Roe* in June 2022 to make abortion pills accessible to more people by increasing access to telemedicine abortion providers and developing alternative supply networks for abortion pills. Chapter 6 chronicles anti-abortion strategies to restrict abortion pills and discourage people from using them post-*Dobbs*, including criminal prosecution of people for self-managing their abortions, the spread of disinformation about the safety of abortion pills through "crisis pregnancy centers," and a lawsuit filed in a Texas federal court attempting to remove mifepristone from the market nationwide and revive the nineteenth-century Comstock Act prohibiting mailing abortifacients. The conclusion will reflect on the factors that have influenced the expansion or contraction of access to abortion pills at different points in time, as well as what this past means for the future of abortion pill access in the United States.

Understanding the history of abortion medications as well as the ongoing political and legal battles over abortion pills in the United States is important for understanding the future of abortion access in the United States. With the rise of telemedicine abortion in 2020, abortion pills posed a fundamental threat to the longstanding anti-abortion strategy of limiting abortion to brick-and-mortar clinics and then targeting these clinics with excessive regulation as well as protests, blockades, and violence. Post-*Dobbs*, abortion pills became a critical avenue for ending unwanted pregnancies for people living in states banning abortion.

Medication abortion advocates imagined a world of increasing access to abortion pills, including outside of the formal medical system. They imagined a world where women could access safe and supported abortion health care without ever leaving their homes. In this world, after completing an online form or a video conference with a healthcare professional, women could promptly receive abortion pills in the mail, which they could take safely in the privacy of their own homes under the supervision of a clinician, if they so chose. No invasive, time-consuming pelvic exams or blood tests. No state-mandated ultrasounds or waiting periods requiring multiple clinic visits. No walking past lines of screaming anti-abortion protesters. No driving long distances, having to find and pay for childcare, or taking time off from work. No exposure to COVID-19.[23] But some advocates had even more ambitious dreams. The co-founders of Plan C, Francine Coeytaux and Elisa Wells, who advocated for increased access to abortion pills, imagined a world where abortion pills were available on the pharmacy or grocery store shelf next to condoms and pregnancy tests and available without a prescription. They imagined a world where these medications cost very little, and women could buy them to put in their underwear drawer in case they missed a period and did not want to be pregnant. In 2014, Coeytaux and Wells traveled to Ethiopia and saw that abortion pills were available from pharmacies over the counter for just a few dollars.[24] "The discrepancy between what I knew was possible and what was happening here in the U.S. motivated us to found Plan C," said Coeytaux.[25]

The United States is still a long way from over-the-counter abortion pills, and abortion opponents are dead set on banning these medications altogether and criminalizing anyone who uses them. The future is uncertain, but understanding the past is an important step toward building a world where women can control their fertility and their lives.

CHAPTER 1

"Medical McCarthyism": RU 486 Development and the Fight for FDA Approval, 1980–2000

> RU-486 will make its American entrance: science, good sense, and freedom will triumph.
>
> Étienne-Émile Baulieu, 1991[1]

In November 2022, a group of anti-abortion doctors and a dentist calling themselves the Alliance for Hippocratic Medicine filed a lawsuit challenging the FDA's approval of mifepristone that had happened over two decades before. They argued that approval of mifepristone was rushed and that the FDA did not have adequate clinical evidence to support the drug's approval. This chapter goes back to the beginning to trace the development of mifepristone, the years of scientific research showing its safety and effectiveness, and the political wrangling that delayed FDA approval of mifepristone. This chapter will show that, contrary to the claims of the Alliance for Hippocratic Medicine, the FDA took years to approve mifepristone and the approval was based on plenty of scientific evidence to support its safety and effectiveness. This chapter will show that the FDA, in fact, placed unusual restrictions on access to mifepristone, not for scientific reasons, but because of anti-abortion political pressure, harassment, and threats of violence that made the FDA overly cautious. This chapter also shows how the profit-driven pharmaceutical industry refused to take on mifepristone to develop it for the market, leaving this task to a nonprofit reliant on foundation and private money to fund clinical trials and a small startup to take on distributing the medication in the United States, which also contributed to delays in bringing the medication to market.

The story of abortion pills begins with a young French doctor, Étienne-Émile Baulieu, who helped develop mifepristone and would become a tireless advocate for increasing access to abortion pills. In 1962, while pursuing a PhD in biochemistry at Lycée Pasteur in Paris, Baulieu worked with the US researcher Dr. Gregory Pincus, who had helped develop the birth control pill in the 1950s. Pincus first envisioned a molecule that could block the action of the hormone progesterone. Baulieu—later known as the "father of the abortion pill"— took Pincus's idea back to France and helped to develop it into a medication that could end an unwanted pregnancy or complete a miscarriage.

After graduating in 1963, Baulieu was named director of the French National Institute of Health and Medical Research in Paris. He studied hormones and began brainstorming a way to block the hormone progesterone, which prepares the uterus to receive a fertilized egg and then signals the uterus to hold the fertilized egg and sustain the pregnancy after implantation. In 1970, while conducting research on guinea pigs, Baulieu and his team of researchers at the National Institute identified the receptor molecules within uterine cells that receive messages from the hormone progesterone.

Baulieu and other scientists then began searching for a substance—an antiprogesterone—that would latch onto the receptor molecules, occupy them, and block progesterone from delivering its message that enables the uterus to retain the pregnancy. In a 1989 *New York Times* article, Baulieu explained: "The receptors are like a keyhole, and we were trying to produce a false key."[2] He characterized the process as "jamming a radio signal."[3]

Baulieu later said he wanted to find an alternative to the abortion procedures that were available at that time, which were removing a pregnancy by either scraping or suctioning out the contents of the uterus. "Rather than disrupt a pregnancy with a sharpened spoon or a suction tube, why couldn't the natural process be reversed by altering the balance of the same hormone that caused it to begin? My intention was to give women a choice that, through a pill, respects their privacy and physical integrity and allows them to totally avoid the aggression of surgery."[4] He called it an "unpregnancy pill" and a "contragestive" because it countered gestation.[5]

At the time, Baulieu was a part-time consultant at the French pharmaceutical company Roussel Uclaf. Baulieu worked with chemists at the company to develop a compound to block progesterone by grafting a complex atom cluster onto a progesterone-like molecule to make it chemically different from progesterone but similar enough to bond with the receptor molecule. Roussel Uclaf's chief chemist, George Teutsch, led a team of researchers that tried over nine hundred substances to find one with the highest binding qualities.[6] "Whereas Teutsch and his group were making a fake key that would fit the lock, Baulieu's work was defining the shape of the lock," National Abortion Rights Action League (NARAL) founder Lawrence Lader later explained.[7] Lader described how the medication worked in his 1995 book: "by occupying the space in the progesterone receptor without activating it, RU 486 impedes progesterone from entering the receptor. Instead of inducing the usual hormone responses, RU 486 stops them."[8] In 1980, Teutsch's team synthesized a compound that worked. The company named the compound RU 486 for the initials of Roussel Uclaf and the lab serial number of the compound—it was the 38,486th compound synthesized by Roussel Uclaf. The company applied for a patent for RU 486 in 1980 and received it the next year.

Baulieu then recruited an old friend, the Swiss doctor Walter Hermann at Geneva's University Hospital, to test the compound. In the first human trial, RU 486 ended early pregnancies in nine of eleven patients. Baulieu joined with Roussel Uclaf's CEO Dr. Edouard Sakiz to publish these results in 1982. In a larger trial in 1986, Hermann found that RU 486 ended pregnancies in eighty-five out of one hundred women. Other scientists began running tests of RU 486's safety and effectiveness. A doctor in Stockholm, Marc Bygdeman, tested RU 486 in combination with a synthetic prostaglandin, which stimulated uterine contractions, decreased bleeding, and sped up the pregnancy termination.[9] This combination of medications proved to be more than 96 percent effective.[10] Scientists at the World Health Organization and elsewhere began extensively testing RU 486's safety and effectiveness. In 1985, the National Institutes of Health in the United States began to support research on RU 486 for non-abortifacient applications, including contraception and as a treatment for breast cancer, endometriosis, glaucoma, Cushing syndrome, and other disorders.[11] Roussel Uclaf ran clinical trials consisting of two multicenter studies, with twenty-four locations and over two thousand participants. These studies showed a 95.5 percent success rate in the first seven weeks of gestation.[12] After worldwide clinical trials involving twenty thousand women, Roussel Uclaf applied to the French government for approval to market the drug for abortion in October 1987.

In response, Catholic fundamentalists in France led by the president of the French Bishops Conference Msgr. Albert Decourtray organized a campaign to pressure Roussel Uclaf and one of its major shareholders Hoechst AG in Frankfurt, Germany to withdraw the application.[13] They attended shareholders' meetings in large numbers and made inflammatory parallels between RU 486 and cyanide gas used in Nazi concentration camps. Baulieu, who is Jewish, was accused of being a Nazi. At one meeting, an anti-abortion protester yelled, "You are turning the uterus into a crematory oven," reported Dr. Baulieu.[14] US anti-abortion activists such as Judie Brown of the American Life League and John Willke of the National Right to Life Committee (NRLC) supported the protests. In an attempt to pressure Hoechst, they published a story in the *National Right to Life News* inaccurately claiming that a predecessor of Hoechst had manufactured the poison gas used by the Germans during World War II.[15]

Abortion opponents targeted much of their ire at Dr. Edouard Sakiz, the CEO of Roussel Uclaf. At the time, Sakiz received as many as twenty-five threatening letters a day and had to endure protesters yelling outside his office. "Your pill kills babies, and you will suffer the consequences," wrote one letter. Another charged, "Assassins, stop your work of death!"[16] Hundreds of anti-abortion protesters showed up at the company's annual meeting on June 23, 1988, where one protester, anatomy professor and abortion opponent Xavier Dor, screamed at Sakiz for twenty minutes straight.[17] In a *New York Times* article, Sakiz said, "It's impossible to discuss things with these people. When you try arguments, all they say is you're killing babies."[18]

Under anti-abortion pressure, Roussel Uclaf almost withdrew its application, but Sakiz had personal and professional reasons for staying the course. On the personal side, Sakiz was indebted to Baulieu, who helped him get his initial position as director of biological research at Roussel Uclaf in 1966. Baulieu pressed Sakiz and others at the company not to withdraw the application for RU 486 approval. Professionally, Sakiz did not want to repeat the mistake made by Roussel Uclaf in the 1960s of declining to produce the contraceptive pill for fear of offending the Catholic Church in France. "We lost the market for contraceptives even though we were the most important steroid company in the world. And now contraceptives are considered natural; they aren't controversial at all," Sakiz later explained.[19]

In addition to targeting Roussel Uclaf and Hoechst AG, abortion opponents put pressure on the French government to deny the companies' RU 486 application, writing letters to French embassies around the world, threatening to boycott French wine and other products if the government approved RU 486. Despite this pressure, the French government approved the medication under the brand name Mifegyne in September 1988. The protocol they approved was 600 milligrams of RU 486 administered in person, followed within two days with the injectable prostaglandin sulprostone administered in person, and then a follow-up visit two weeks later to confirm successful completion of the abortion. The government approved this regimen through forty-nine days of pregnancy and limited the procedure to hospitals and clinics.[20] The same month, China also approved RU 486.[21]

To protest the approvals, Catholic bishops organized a march through Paris, drawing around two thousand people, and anti-abortion protesters picketed both Roussel Uclaf offices and the French Ministry of Health. US-based NRLC threatened a boycott of Roussel Uclaf in the United States.[22] In the early 1980s, NRLC had threatened to boycott the pharmaceutical company Upjohn for researching the prostaglandin meteneprost, which Upjohn later discontinued.[23] Roussel Uclaf had only 7 percent of its $1.7 billion of sales in the United States, but the company hoped to expand there. Hoechst AG, on the other hand, had 25 percent of its $23 billion in sales in the United States. The company's CEO, Wolfgang Hilger, was Catholic and opposed abortion.[24] Hoechst AG, which owned 54.5 percent of Roussel Uclaf shares, reportedly put pressure on Roussel Uclaf to withdraw the medication from the market.[25] Roussel Uclaf's five-person executive committee was divided, with two older members wanting to withdraw the medication. When an ambitious young vice-president, Alain Madec, announced he was against RU 486, Sakiz worried that Madec might be trying to get Hoechst AG to appoint him CEO.[26] Meanwhile, personal threats by abortion opponents to Roussel Uclaf officials continued unabated and expanded to their spouses and children as well.[27]

Then anti-abortion extremists turned violent. In October of 1988, extremists tear-gassed a theater screening the Claude Chabrol film *Une Affaire de Femmes*, about the 1943 guillotining of Marie-Louise Giraud for performing twenty-seven abortions. Shortly after, Catholic extremists firebombed a Paris movie theater showing Martin Scorsese's film *The Last Temptation of Christ*, purportedly because of a scene depicting Jesus and Mary Magdalene having sex.[28] Three days later, under the pall of religious extremists' violence, Roussel Uclaf's board of directors voted sixteen to four to withdraw RU 486 from the market—just one month after its approval. The company announced they were withdrawing the drug not because of any side effects, but because of anti-abortion protests and threats of violence.[29] Baulieu confronted Sakiz, who told him, "You're independent. You can go out and speak freely."[30]

Within days, Baulieu showed up at the World Congress of Gynecology and Obstetrics in Rio de Janeiro, Brazil,[31] where nearly ten thousand physicians and researchers were gathered. Baulieu and others at the conference spoke out about the withdrawal of RU 486 from the market, generating widespread condemnation. Baulieu called for a "public mobilization to demand RU 486 be made available."[32] Attendees at the conference denounced Roussel Uclaf's decision to withdraw RU 486 from the market. Baulieu called it "morally scandalous," while the dean of Columbia University School of Public Health Allan G. Rosenfeld called it "a tragic decision."[33] Over two thousand attendees signed a petition organized by Rebecca Cook, a professor and attorney for women's rights, objecting to Roussel Uclaf's actions.[34] A Paris gynecologist, Elisabeth Aubény, delivered the petition to Roussel Uclaf. According to surveys at the time, 64 percent of French people supported legal access to RU 486.[35]

Many others protested the withdrawal as well. University professors from the United States and Europe asked physicians to boycott Roussel Uclaf's products and placed advertisements in newspapers calling for people to contact Hoechst AG to protest the withdrawal. The French Family Planning Association national coordinator, Catherine Lesterpet, stated, "we're worried about the rise of Catholic fundamentalism and the blackmail exercised against Roussel."[36] US-based pro-choice groups, including NARAL and Planned Parenthood Federation, denounced Roussel Uclaf's decision to withdraw RU 486 from the market as well.

But the decisive push came when the French government, which owned 36 percent of Roussel Uclaf stock, threatened to transfer the patent to another company in the interest of public health. French Health Minister Claude Évin famously explained at the time, "I could not permit the abortion debate to deprive women of a product that represents medical progress. From the moment government approval for the drug was granted, RU 486 became the moral property of women, not just the property of a drug company."[37] Later, Évin said, "I was doing what I could to make sure France did not surrender to pressure groups animated by archaic ideologies."[38] In response, Roussel Uclaf reversed its decision and put RU 486 back on the market. The company's vice-chairman, Pierre Joly, stated, "We are relieved of the moral burden weighing on our group. For us, the problem is now solved."[39] Since that decision in the fall of 1988, French women have had access to the abortion pill mifepristone.

The initial medical protocol for medication abortion in France involved three appointments. At the first appointment, patients took 600 milligrams of RU 486. At the second appointment two days later, patients received the injectable prostaglandin sulprostone and remained in the clinic in their own clothes the entire time, wearing a sanitary napkin, until they completed the abortion. If the medication did not work, then patients received an aspiration abortion. A follow-up exam was required two weeks later. In 1992, France approved the use of the prostaglandin Cytotec—the brand name for misoprostol—for use with RU 486 and French doctors substituted a 400-microgram oral dose of Cytotec at the second appointment.[40] Cytotec was preferable to the injectable prostaglandin because it came in tablet form to be taken orally, did not need refrigeration, and was much less expensive.[41] To control RU 486 and prevent the development of a black market, each package of RU 486 was labeled with three stickers: one for factory records, one for the hospital or pharmacy records, and the third for the patient's medical charts.[42]

In December 1988, under pressure from Hoechst AG, Roussel Uclaf suspended all other plans to market the drug themselves in other countries, halting distribution of RU 486 in China and stopping plans to distribute the medication in Great Britain, Sweden, and the Netherlands, which were in the process of approving the drug. China, which did not recognize international patent law, synthesized its own version of RU 486 in 1988 and began manufacturing the medication.

In early 1989, leaders at Roussel Uclaf met with the executive director of Planned Parenthood of America, Faye Wattleton, to discuss granting them an exclusive license to distribute RU 486 in the United States. Wattleton traveled to Paris three times to discuss this possibility, but the company eventually declined to move ahead with Planned Parenthood.[43] The same year, the Supreme Court issued a decision in *Webster v. Reproductive Health Services*, which upheld a Missouri law that imposed restrictions on abortion and barred the use of public hospitals or clinics for abortion services.[44] This case, along with anti-abortion actions of the Bush administration and conservative members of Congress, alerted Roussel Uclaf to the hostile political environment for abortion in the United States.

In 1991, Roussel Uclaf and Hoechst issued a joint statement that they would only consider licensing RU 486 to companies in countries "where abortion is tolerated by society," where there was an "advanced medical infrastructure," and where the government had made a written request for the licensing of the medication.[45] In the United States, such an invitation was not forthcoming under Republican President George H.W. Bush. Other countries, however, moved forward. In 1990, Roussel Uclaf resumed marketing the drug in Great Britain, which approved the medication in 1991, and in

Sweden, which approved the medication in 1992.[46] Despite concerns about the United States, Roussel Uclaf's CEO Edouard Sakiz met with the Population Council's president George Zeidenstein in 1991 to discuss the distribution of the medication in the United States.[47]

Meanwhile, anti-abortion extremists continued to stalk and harass Baulieu. When he gave a talk on RU 486 in Toronto in 1991, abortion opponents plastered the streets with posters saying "Wanted, Etienne Baulieu for Genocide" with his photograph.[48]

ANTI-ABORTION CAMPAIGN TO BLOCK RU 486 FROM THE US MARKET[49]

By the late 1980s, the FDA had already approved two medications with abortifacient effects. In 1961, Wyeth Labs obtained approval for methotrexate as an anti-cancer drug, but the medication also stopped fetal cells from growing by blocking the folic acid needed to maintain an early pregnancy.[50] In 1988, over the objections of abortion opponents, the FDA approved an application, from the pharmaceutical company Searle, for a new prostaglandin called misoprostol under the brand name Cytotec to treat ulcers, but the medication also induced labor and could safely end a pregnancy in the first twelve weeks.[51] Methotrexate used in conjunction with misoprostol became commonly used to end ectopic pregnancies, a life-threatening condition where a fertilized egg grows outside the uterus. These medications were not labeled for this use, but doctors used them off label, a common practice for many drugs.

US scientists began studying RU 486 in the early 1980s. In 1983, Roussel Uclaf agreed to provide the US-based Population Council with the right to import RU 486 into the United States for testing.[52] The Population Council, a nonprofit research institution that developed new forms of contraception, obtained an Investigational New Drug (IND) permit from the FDA in 1983 to test the safety and efficacy of RU 486. Between 1984 and 1990, University of Southern California professor of obstetrics and gynecology Dr. David Grimes conducted studies to determine the safety and efficacy of RU 486 for early abortion, finding in one study a 90 percent success rate after administration of 600 milligrams of RU 486 alone.[53] The FDA also issued IND permits to ten research groups to investigate other clinical applications of RU 486, including for Cushing syndrome, meningioma, contraception, breast cancer, and endometriosis.

Abortion opponents mobilized to block RU 486 in the United States in 1988, even before France approved it. NRLC, the United States Conference of Catholic Bishops, the Fundamentalist Crusade Against Abortion, and Robins Carbide Reynolds Fund led the campaign against RU 486 in the United States, calling it a "death drug," a "human pesticide," and a form of "chemical warfare against unborn babies."[54] NRLC's education director Richard Glasow argued that RU 486 "kills an unborn baby whose heart has started to beat and kills and injures women."[55] Other groups organizing against RU 486 included Phyllis Schlafly's Eagle Forum, Focus on the Family, Knights of Columbus,

Concerned Women for America, the Southern Baptist Convention, the International Right to Life Federation, and the Family Research Council. Abortion opponents argued that abortion pills might encourage sexual irresponsibility, teen pregnancy, and infidelity.[56] The anti-abortion movement used two primary strategies to block RU 486 from coming to the United States: boycott threats against drug companies that might market the medication, and calls for the government to stop research on RU 486 and impose an import ban—both of which occurred in a context of increasing violence directed toward abortion clinics and providers.

RU 486 threatened the anti-abortion movement's central strategy of symbolically framing abortion as ending a human life. By enabling people to obtain very early abortions, RU 486 undercut the anti-abortion movement's use of graphic fetal imagery. In a 1986 *Washington Post* article, NRLC's president John Willke explained how RU 486 could undermine efforts to ban abortion: "If what [abortions] destroy in there doesn't look human, then it will make our job more difficult."[57] In 1988, Glasow said, "It's more difficult to make the case that this is a developing baby if you don't have pictures of the fetus. If you can show people fingers and toes, it's dynamite...the abortion debate won't go away, but we'd lose some of our best arguments."[58] Polls at the time showed that Americans looked significantly more favorably on abortion early in pregnancy than in later pregnancy.[59] NRLC also feared they would lose credibility if they were seen as opposing contraception. Glasow warned, "if RU 486 becomes identified in the public's mind with contraception, then right-to-life opposition to the drug could be portrayed as 'reactionary' and 'out of touch' with the mainstream of Americans."[60]

RU 486 also had the potential to undermine one of the anti-abortion movement's primary tactics: protesters blocking clinic access. The medication could allow an increasing number of doctors to offer abortion services, thereby decentralizing abortion care and making it harder for protesters to target doctors and interfere with patient access to clinics by using intimidation and threats of violence.[61] Abortion supporters, on the other hand, argued that, in addition to its other virtues, RU 486 could de-escalate clinic violence by dispersing abortion health care to a wider number of clinicians and locations.[62]

Anti-abortion terrorism played a central role in French RU 486 politics, but it played an even greater role in the United States, where extremists regularly vandalized and destroyed clinics, and harassed, assaulted, and sometimes even murdered clinic employees. In France, England, and Sweden, abortion services were integrated into the public healthcare systems, but in the United States, the medical system had refused to integrate abortion health care into the mainstream. Therefore, abortion services were primarily offered at stand-alone clinics where abortion was the main service provided. As a result, the anti-abortion movement could more easily target abortion health care with protests and violence. Between 1977 and 1988, anti-abortion extremists committed

110 cases of arson, firebombing, and bombing at abortion clinics, involving facilities in twenty-eight states and the District of Columbia. Authorities convicted thirty-three people for this violence.[63]

Anti-abortion violence escalated in the 1990s. Thousands of incidents occurred, including blockades, invasions, chemical attacks, arsons, bombings, death threats, shootings, sniper attacks, and cold-blooded murder. In 1991, a masked gunman shot and paralyzed a clinic worker and wounded a second person in Springfield, Missouri, and a doctor was shot and wounded in Houston, Texas. In 1993, anti-abortion extremist Michael Griffin shot and killed Dr. David Gunn in Pensacola, Florida; Rachelle "Shelley" Shannon shot Dr. George Tiller at point-blank range in Wichita, Kansas; and Dr. George Patterson was shot to death in Mobile, Alabama. In 1994 in Pensacola, Paul Hill shot and killed Dr. John Bayard Britton and a volunteer clinic escort, Lt. Col. James Barrett, injuring another volunteer escort as well. Then in December of that year, John Salvi shot and killed Planned Parenthood receptionist Shannon Lowney in Brookline, Massachusetts, and then shot and killed receptionist Leanne Nicholas at a second clinic, wounding five other people in the attacks. In addition to extreme violence, tens of thousands of protesters blocked access to abortion clinics.[64]

In response, Congress passed the Freedom of Access to Clinic Entrances Act in 1994, creating civil and criminal penalties for blocking access to abortion clinics.[65] But the violence continued. In 1995 in St. Louis, Missouri, Dr. C. Jackson was brutally stabbed fifteen times outside his clinic, then the next year Eric Robert Rudolph detonated two bombs at the Northside Family Planning clinic in Atlanta, Georgia, destroying the clinic and injuring seven people. In Rochester, New York, Dr. David Gandell was wounded by flying glass when a sniper with a high-powered rifle shot into his home. In 1998 in Birmingham, Alabama, Eric Rudolph detonated a bomb packed with nails at the New Woman, All Woman clinic, killing a security guard and maiming a nurse. In Amherst, New York, in 1998, James Charles Kopp shot and killed Dr. Barnett Slepian with a high-powered rifle while he stood with his wife and children in the kitchen of his home.[66]

Anti-abortion violence negatively impacted the willingness of drug companies to market mifepristone in the United States. Anti-abortion extremist groups Operation Rescue, Pro-Life Action League, Rescue America, and Advocates for Life Ministries organized protests at French consulates and embassies as well as at the offices of Hoechst subsidiaries, and threatened violence against Roussel Uclaf officials and physicians conducting trials of the drug. The threats of violence dissuaded researchers from studying RU 486, even for non-abortion applications, and created concern at the FDA about the safety of employees involved in the approval process. Abortion rights supporters argued that anti-abortion violence was a reason *to approve* RU 486 so that it could be offered in any doctor's office, making abortion services less concentrated in discrete, easily targetable clinics.

In addition to violence, harassment, and threats, abortion opponents found political support in the administration of Republican President George H.W. Bush and in members of Congress, who took steps to block US scientists from studying RU 486. In 1986, Senator Robert Dornan (R-CA) circulated a "Dear Colleague" letter about the French "death pill" and threatened to wage a fight against federal research. Dornan warned that RU 486 could mean "taking of a pre-born life will be as easy and trivial as taking aspirin."[67] In March of 1987, Senator Gordon Humphrey (R-NH) wrote a letter to the director of the National Institutes of Health requesting a detailed report of how the drug was being tested and expressing concern that RU 486 was being tested as a contraceptive that might take effect post-fertilization.[68] In 1987 and every year after, Dornan introduced legislation to block federal funds for research on RU 486 and deny FDA authority to permit testing of the drug.[69] In response, the American Public Health Association adopted a resolution to support research on RU 486 in 1988.[70]

Anti-abortion conservatives in Congress also pressed the FDA for an import ban. The FDA had authority under the Food, Drug and Cosmetic Act to permit importation of unapproved drugs for personal use on a discretionary basis and in the interest of compassion.[71] On June 6, 1989, at the request of anti-abortion members of Congress, including Representatives (Reps.) Jesse Helms (R-NC) and Henry Hyde (R-IL), Bush's FDA Commissioner Frank Young imposed Import Alert 66–47 on RU 486, directing customs officials to "automatically detain all shipments of unapproved abortifacient drugs." Without evidence, Young stated RU 486 could present an unreasonable safety risk. The alert prohibited people from bringing RU 486 into the country and had the effect of halting all clinical trials on RU 486 in the United States.[72] After the Bush administration imposed an import alert on RU 486, Roussel Uclaf stopped supplying the medication to the Population Council. Their tests ended in 1990 when the Council ran out of medication. The import alert stymied research on use of RU 486 for other medical conditions as well.[73] In 1991, Bush appointed the first woman to head the National Institutes of Health, Dr. Bernadine Healey, who opposed RU 486 research.

At the time the import ban was imposed, women were a small minority in Congress—only twenty-five women in the House and two in the Senate in 1989, and none occupied positions of leadership—but they spoke out in support of RU 486. Supporters asked the Congressional Caucus on Women's Issues to press for ending the import alert. The Caucus Chair, Representative (Rep.) Patricia Schroeder (D-CO), urged members to send letters to the president and the FDA asking them to reconsider the import alert. They asked to meet with President Bush about the issue, but he refused.[74] In July of 1990, Rep. Barbara Boxer (D-CA) organized seventy members of the House of Representatives to sign a joint letter to the president of Roussel Uclaf requesting the company to market RU 486 in the United States.[75]

Outside the halls of Congress, abortion opponents threatened drug companies with economic harms. Virginia minister Kevin Dubin created the Robins Carbide

Reynolds Fund—named after three pharmaceutical companies sued by patients for harmful drugs. Dubin threatened to organize national boycotts and block investment in companies involved with RU 486. He encouraged product liability lawsuits against Roussel Uclaf and Hoechst, called for legislation to ban the companies from bidding on government contracts, and delivered a twenty-page declaration threatening to boycott Hoechst AG.[76] In 1991, NRLC called for a boycott of the US-based subsidiary of Hoechst AG called Hoechst Celanese. In early 1992, the president of Hoechst Celanese, Ernest Drew, reportedly persuaded Hoechst AG to halt plans to allow the Population Council to renew its clinical testing of RU 486 in the United States.[77] Nevertheless, in 1993, NRLC picketed Hoechst Celanese in several states and later threatened to boycott Copley Pharmaceuticals in Massachusetts after Hoechst Celanese purchased the company. Following NRLC's lead, Catholic hospitals, which controlled one-third of hospital beds in the United States at the time, threatened to boycott pharmaceuticals produced by Roussel Uclaf and Hoechst AG.[78] Abortion opponents also tried to mobilize women against Hoechst by stoking safety fears about RU 486 and calling attention to the absence of women in senior management positions at the company.

In response to these political pressures, Roussel Uclaf set out five criteria for introducing RU 486 to a new country: 1) abortion must be legal; 2) the political climate must be accepting of abortion; 3) an appropriate prostaglandin must be available; 4) the medical services system must be able to carefully monitor patients and the drug supply; and 5) informed consent procedures must be strictly followed.[79] Due to anti-abortion pressure, Roussel Uclaf did not seek FDA approval to market RU 486 in the United States. Newspapers at the time attributed their reluctance to fear of anti-abortion boycotts and violence, as well as the Bush administration's hostility to abortion. Roussel Uclaf also feared the United States Supreme Court would overturn or weaken *Roe v. Wade*, leading to abortion restrictions and bans.[80] They also attributed this decision to economic factors, including the unlikely profitability of the medication along with the difficulty and expense of obtaining FDA approval (which can take five to ten years and cost $70–100 million or more), the potential cost of product liability claims, and the potential loss of public good will.[81]

Some leaders at Roussel Uclaf, however, supported bringing RU 486 to the US market, including former CEO Edouard Sakiz and the Director of Communications and Scientific Relations, Catherine Euvrard, who both supported women's rights. But Hoechst AG's CEO, Wolfgang Hilger, opposed bringing RU 486 to market in the United States. In a *San Francisco Examiner* article, Euvrard criticized the men in power at Hoechst AG for being "afraid of controversy, afraid to fight" and for always seeing RU 486 as a problem of "politics, money and corporate image" rather than a women's health issue. In the same article, Roussel Uclaf's medical director, André Ulmann, described Hoechst's leadership as "men who are often aged men, elderly men who know nothing about birth control and abortion" and "are convinced it is going to bring a lot of trouble" and "jeopardize their market if there is a boycott."[82]

THE FEMINIST CAMPAIGN TO BRING RU 486 TO THE UNITED STATES

In response to the reluctance of Roussel Uclaf and Hoechst AG to market the medication in the United States, a range of feminist organizations organized campaigns to bring RU 486 to the United States, including the Reproductive Health Technologies Project (RHTP), Feminist Majority Foundation (FMF), Abortion Rights Mobilization (ARM), Planned Parenthood Federation of America, the Population Council, and NARAL. Beginning in 1988, these groups worked to generate public understanding and support for RU 486, as well as support from the scientific and medical communities in order to pressure Roussel Uclaf and Hoechst AG to release the patent rights to RU 486 so it could be sold in the United States. "Roussel Uclaf is not convinced that there is public support for RU 486 in the United States," said FMF's Jennifer Jackman in 1991. "The sense we got from them is that the more public support we could demonstrate, the more willing Roussel Uclaf would be to make it available in the United States."[83]

Abortion opponents weren't the only ones wary of RU 486. Some in the feminist health community were hesitant about RU 486 due to the history of medical and pharmaceutical companies promoting medications without adequate testing and warnings. The "father of modern gynecology," J. Marion Sims, performed brutal experimental surgeries on enslaved women without anesthesia in the mid-nineteenth century.[84] A century later, Gregory Pincus and John Rock tested birth control pills on women in Puerto Rico without allowing them to make an informed decision on whether they wanted to serve in the trials.[85] The long history of coercive sterilization and imposition of dangerous contraceptives on women of color made many skeptical toward new technologies.[86]

In 1991, University of Massachusetts Women's Studies professor Janice G. Raymond, along with Renate Klein and Lynette J. Dumble, published a book, *RU 486: Misconceptions, Myths and Morals*, arguing that RU 486 and prostaglandins were "fraught with risk and problems" and endangered women's lives and health.[87] They questioned the women's groups who worked alongside population control groups and pharmaceutical and medical researchers to promote RU 486, noting the contradiction of arguing that medication abortion protects women's privacy while also requiring that the drug be used only under close medical supervision. They warned that Margaret Sanger and others in the early twentieth century had "succumbed to the pressure of promoting physician control and the strict medicalization of birth control" to obtain legalization. Instead, they proposed the de-medicalization of women's health. They pointed to the Jane Collective, which offered safe abortion before *Roe v. Wade*, and to the self-help menstrual extraction movement in the 1960s.[88] They argued, "the feminist critique knew the difference between a procedure which gave women real control of their bodies and a chemical cocktail attended by all the accoutrements of extensive medical-technical intervention."[89] Further, they questioned the impact of abortion medications on the sexual politics of women's lives and their right to refuse sex. They expressed concern that "RU 486 may absolve men of any future contraceptive commitment since the drug has been promoted as 'safe and easy' for women."[90] They concluded, "no procedure requiring medical supervision and involving a host of risks and complications will help provide sexual and reproductive self-determination for women."[91] These concerns seemed to be confirmed when the Population Council—an organization founded in 1952 by prominent eugenicists—was later chosen to conduct the clinical trials of RU 486. The leader of the American Eugenics Society, Frederick Osborn, served as both vice-president and president of the Population Council until 1959.[92] Anti-abortion groups stoked fears about potential dangers of RU 486 by claiming the drug had been inadequately tested, and making parallels to previous controversial products, such as the injectable contraceptive Depo-Provera and the Dalkon Shield, which caused bacterial infections and severe injuries to many women. They also claimed RU 486 would be used to exploit women in developing countries by tricking or coercing them into abortion.[93] In 1993, *Ms.* magazine published side-by-side articles on RU 486 arguing for and against it. Raymond, Klein, and Dumble argued against it,[94] while Janet Callum and Rebecca Chalker argued in favor of RU 486.[95]

To build consensus and support for RU 486, reproductive health advocates Marie Bass and Joanne Howes, who ran a public policy and public affairs consulting firm focused on health issues, formed the Reproductive Health Technologies Project. Bass had worked with NARAL's Political Action Committee in 1982 and 1984, where she had heard about RU 486. Howes had been a Washington lobbyist for Planned Parenthood. In 1986, Bass met in Paris with Dr. André Ulmann, the medical director at Roussel Uclaf, and Étienne-Émile Baulieu to learn about RU 486. Bass and Howes then decided to conduct research on what it would take to bring RU 486 to the United States. They interviewed researchers, medical professionals, and women's health advocates about their views on RU 486 and the possibilities for bringing the medication to the US market. In 1987, with the support of a grant from the Sunnen Foundation in St. Louis, Bass, Howes, and Nanette Falkenberg published "A Report on RU 486 and Its Prospects for Use in the United States." The authors recommended a three-part strategy: increase medical research, find a drug company to distribute the drug, and run a public education campaign to increase awareness of, and demand for, RU 486. "Growing public support will be necessary to convince drug companies to invest their financial resources, and the research community to continue its quest for a safe and effective progesterone antagonist," they argued.[96] They emphasized the potential difficulties of finding a drug company willing to develop and market RU 486, especially in light of the "politicized environment surrounding the rejection of Depo-Provera, and the criticism of the approval and marketing of oral contraceptives before they had been fully tested and understood."[97] They reported that doctors, drug companies, and researchers perceived that feminist women's health groups had blocked FDA approval of Depo-Provera and therefore were hesitant to invest in another reproductive drug. Women's health groups, they found, preferred independent research to drug-company-sponsored research, and were likely to oppose any type of "chemical contraception."[98]

The report rejected Baulieu's strategy of framing RU 486 as a "contragestin" rather than an abortifacient because of the "complexity of trying to change the popular understanding and definition of 'birth control,' abortion and pregnancy."[99] It did, however, note that the National Institutes of Health was testing RU 486 as a contraceptive. They also noted that Roussel Uclaf at the time had an international marketing plan that included the United States and that they were willing to invest significant money to market the drug in the United States. The report predicted that many companies may be interested in developing the drug and recommended "in-depth discussions with the Population Council and Roussel." It concluded, "the potential of RU 486 or a similar drug is very exciting, but it will become a reality only if a concerted effort is organized to make it happen."[100] Bass, Howes, and Falkenberg expressed hope that RU 486 "could fundamentally alter the politics of the abortion issue as we know it today—perhaps even end the issue."[101]

Bass and Howes distributed the report widely to their political contacts, drawing significant attention to the issue. When Planned Parenthood hired Bass and Howes to coordinate a series of ten conferences around the country on new birth control technologies, they included RU 486 in the program, which generated more awareness of the medication. They also worked with Kathy Bonk at the Communications Consortium Media Center to generate media coverage of RU 486. When Roussel Uclaf withdrew the medication from the market in France in 1988, Howes traveled to Brazil to attend the global conference of obstetricians and gynecologists, meeting people and making contacts in the United States and abroad. But Howes and Bass were not able to get mainstream women's organizations interested. "At the end of 1987 and during 1988, pro-choice and women's rights groups were consumed by their efforts to defeat the nomination of Robert Bork to the Supreme Court and, following that victory, by the coming November elections," said Bass. "Their agenda was overcrowded as it was, and their resources were limited. RU 486 was not a priority."[102]

After the fall elections in 1988, Bass and Howes convened a group of about forty representatives of women's health, family planning, pro-choice, and international population organizations on November 21. They shared the science of RU 486 and created space for people to discuss their concerns about the safety of the medication. Judith Norsigian of the Boston Women's Health Book Collective expressed concerns about the effect of the drug on women of color and about access to hospital care in the case of emergencies. Several people recalled that "drugs and devices that were once highly touted had turned into disasters for women—diethylstilbestrol (DES), thalidomide, the Dalkon Shield."[103] Norsigian later said: "We wanted to tread carefully because we had seen so many medical advances that did not pan out well for women. We were cautious and wanted to wait till better research was in before we embraced it completely. But we also recognized that in countries where abortion was illegal, this might be like exactly what was needed, because it could come under the radar screen."[104] Cynthia Pearson of the National Women's Health Network remembered that she wondered why anyone would want to go through a medication-induced miscarriage when they could get an aspiration abortion. "Who would want to go through hours or days of cramps and bleeding?" asked Pearson.[105] Pearson also wanted assurances about the safety of mifepristone before supporting it. After seeing the research from France, and hearing reports from French women who had used the medication, Pearson was reassured about the safety and acceptability of mifepristone. These conversations helped build trust among different constituencies and were critical to achieving strong support for RU 486 in the women's health community, which later facilitated FDA approval of the medication and acceptance of medication abortion, particularly among communities of color. By the end of the daylong meeting, most participants agreed to a special project on RU 486 managed by Bass and Howes.

For the next two years, Bass and Howes convened periodic meetings to keep people informed about the progress of RU 486 around the world and "develop common messages and themes."[106] According to Bass, the meetings became a "forum for listening and learning, for establishing consensus, painstakingly but genuinely."[107] This hard work "defanged a lot of the skeptics who might have said, 'Why do we need a drug? We've got other ways to have an abortion,'" said Amy Allina, who was at the National Women's Health Network (NWHN), which was founded by people who raised questions about the safety of birth control pills. "They looked at the data and they were like, yeah, this is safe. The research has been done in a rigorous way. We've looked for the problems we might worry about, and we think this is an important new option."[108]

Many feminists distrusted mainstream, male-controlled medicine because researchers had ignored women's reports of dangerous side effects of the birth control pill.[109] They preferred what they saw as more natural methods for abortion, such as manual vacuum aspiration controlled by women themselves.[110] In 1989, the Feminist Women's Health Center federation raised funds to send self-help advocate Carol Downer to France to speak with clinic directors, staff, and women who had used the pill. The visits were arranged by another self-help advocate Claudine Serre. "We were very skeptical. We left no stone unturned. We asked every question," recalled Downer. "The thing that jumped out was that all of them had a very positive reaction to experiencing this process." The women said the process felt very natural, similar to a spontaneous miscarriage. "We realized this was a momentous discovery, and once unleashed into the world at large, it would affect millions of women's lives," said Downer. Back in the United States, Downer authored a report, gave press interviews, talked to people in government, and held workshops with clinicians about her findings.[111] In July of 1990, RHTP invited two pro-choice leaders from England and a prominent French physician who ran a clinic offering RU 486 to the United States for a series of meetings and press briefings, where they shared their experiences with the medication.[112]

In 1992, Bass and Howes founded Reproductive Health Technologies Project in Washington DC as an independent nonprofit, funded mostly by The Tides Foundation and led by reproductive health advocate Kirsten Moore, who served as president and CEO. According to Bass, RHTP acted as a clearinghouse for information on RU 486, "distributing thousands of information kits to organizations, public officials, and the media. We fielded press calls and put journalists in touch with doctors and researchers who could speak authoritatively about the drug. We assisted organizations that were writing resolutions of support, legislators who wanted to introduce resolutions or hold meetings, and academics who were putting together conferences."[113] RHTP served as a forum to discuss concerns among a diverse range of constituencies, including mainstream abortion rights groups, population control groups, and emerging reproductive justice groups formed by women of color.

RHTP recruited a diverse board of advocates to lead the organization. The twenty-three members of the board included the executive director of the National Asian Women's Health Organization, Mary Chung; director of the Native American Cultural Center at North Dakota State Hospital, Mary Louise Defender-Wilson; a National Welfare Rights Union organizer, Cheri Honkala; director of the National Latina Health Organization, Luz Alvarez Martinez; president of the National Black Women's Health Project, Julia R. Scott; and Dr. Helen Rodríguez-Trías, who was president of the American Public Health Association.[114] Marie Bass explained the importance of this diverse group:

> The project's members have learned from each other, the scientist teaching the nonscientist and the nonscientist teaching the scientist. White women learn from Black and Latina women, who explain why they recoil almost instinctively from the introduction of any new, highly touted birth control technology; why they may view it as an attempt to coerce and control rather than liberate them. Middle-class participants learn from poor women about the harsh realities of these women's lives, which overrule the moral or ideological soapboxes that others are privileged enough to speak from.[115]

Martinez, who remembers urging RHTP to expand the board to include more women of color, recalled her excitement about RU 486: "It was something new and I was excited about it because it was another option that women didn't have at that time."[116]

Kimberly Inez McGuire, who was a senior programs and policy associate with RHTP between 2009 and 2011, described how RHTP developed trust among advocates:

> The early work on medication abortion established this integrity and this sense within the community that RHTP could be trusted both to be an honest broker of the science, the facts, the information, but also of bringing people together in a way that allowed them to have their own priorities, their own values…I think about some of those early meetings where it was the first time that you had women-of-color-led reproductive justice organizations alongside researchers, and really treating all the advocates with the respect of giving them all the facts and not just pushing an agenda the way that unfortunately many of those groups have been subjected to, that forceful coalition management, where someone comes to a table and says *this is what we're doing and you better get on board*. RHTP wasn't like that. For RHTP, it was, "we're going to bring this to the table, here's the information, and ultimately you make your own decision." There was a sort of informed consent to coalition building that I think is really rare and is still really rare.[117]

Reproductive health advocate Francine Coeytaux,[118] who was with the Population Council at the time, explained the importance of RHTP:

> The brilliance of RHTP was the model of bringing together a working network of really key individuals in many sectors to discuss new reproductive health technologies. The reason it had so much impact was because of the importance of involving every sector at the table as you're trying to move a new contraceptive idea forward. Somebody who is a legislator and knows how to work the legislation, somebody who is a chemist and knows how to deal with the FDA, somebody who is an MD—all these really top thinkers with a commitment to working together to think through what it would take, what are the obstacles.[119]

This diverse network of people enabled collaboration among various sectors, thereby playing a critical role in eventually achieving FDA approval of RU 486.

RHTP published a widely distributed handbook, titled *The Case for Antiprogestins*, on the science and politics of RU 486, which became a key informational source on the medication.[120] They conducted educational sessions on RU 486 for conferences, workshops, and community meetings for local, regional, and national groups, including major professional associations and outreach to low-income women and women of color. They also provided technical assistance and expertise to national, state, and local policymakers[121] and encouraged medical organizations such as the American Public Health Organization and the American College of Obstetricians and Gynecologists (ACOG) to pass resolutions in support of RU 486, many of which did.[122]

On December 6–7, 1991, the American Society of Law and Medicine convened a landmark conference to assess the medical, ethical, and legal issues surrounding antiprogestins. At the conference, speakers included doctors, attorneys, ethicists, women's health advocates, and others. According to an RHTP report on the 1991 hearing and the conference, "speaker after speaker at both events…argued that antiprogestins are a safe, effective and highly desirable alternative to surgical abortion for the termination of very early pregnancy…and hold tremendous value for the treatment or cure of many other conditions and diseases."[123] Director of the Atlanta Feminist Women's Health Center Janet Callum reported on speaking to French women who had used RU 486: "some women felt that because there was no instrumentation, RU 486 was gentler and less intrusive, and they also appreciated not having to disrobe and lie down before a stranger."[124] At the end of the conference, 137 participants wrote a letter to the president of Hoechst Celanese Ernest Drew, demanding the company market RU 486 in the United States.[125]

Another key advocate for RU 486 was the Feminist Majority Foundation, which launched a campaign for RU 486 in June 1989. Former National Organization for Women (NOW) president Eleanor Smeal and feminist Peg Yorkin, who chaired the FMF board, led the campaign.[126] Yorkin later donated $5 million toward bringing the abortion pill to the country.[127] Smeal said at the time, "We intend to visit the pharmaceutical leaders, the medical health leaders to urge them to rise up against this movement that is denying the best of medical research, and the best that modern medicine can provide for the modern woman."[128] Her plan gained urgency a month later when the Supreme Court ruled in *Webster v. Reproductive Health Services* to expand state powers to restrict privately funded abortion services in state facilities. FMF hired Jennifer Jackman to head the Campaign for RU 486 and Contraceptive Research, which was based in Boston. "The first thing we did was put together a scientific team, and they explained to us exactly how it worked and its safety," said Smeal. "We talked to the most preeminent doctors in the field."[129] Smeal recruited Carl Djerassi, who helped develop the oral contraceptive pill. "I just called him. His wife was a feminist. He then helped me put together a team of scientists. He said he'd serve on it, and he'd help get some other scientists," said Smeal.[130] FMF then sought to educate the public about RU 486 and convince Roussel Uclaf and Hoechst AG that there was widespread support for the medication in the United States. They also sought to neutralize anti-abortion threats to organize economic boycotts of the companies by showing widespread support for RU 486 in the United States. Smeal said most people were supportive of the campaign, but that some abortion providers worried that RU 486 might undermine the clinic system because any doctor could offer it.[131]

FMF ran a direct mail campaign, sending eight million letters to women's rights supporters with information about RU 486 and petitions to Hoechst AG and Roussel Uclaf, which they asked recipients to complete and mail back in. To support the petition, NOW organized a "Freedom Caravan" to collect petition signatures, which traveled to New Jersey, Pennsylvania, Massachusetts, Nevada, Oregon, and other states, collecting signatures along the way.[132] In less than four years, they collected 700,000 petitions. FMF also collected petitions from scientists by mailing and faxing various lists of scientists, Nobel laureates, and faculty, as well as distributing the petitions at conferences.

On July 23, 1990, an FMF delegation met with Roussel Uclaf officials, bringing petitions signed by 115,000 Americans and weighing 800 pounds![133] The delegation included Smeal, Yorkin, NOW president Patricia Ireland, and FMF Director of Policy and Research Jennifer Jackman, as well as prominent scientific and medical leaders, including Djerassi, the Dean of Columbia School of Public Health Dr. Allen Rosenfield, and president of the American Public Health Association Dr. Myron Allukian (see Figure 1.1). When they arrived at the office of Roussel Uclaf's CEO Edouard Sakiz, Smeal was surprised to find out that Sakiz and Djerassi already knew each other. "They were buddies," said Smeal. "I just knew [Djerassi] was one of the best scientists in this field in our country. As things happen worldwide, people who

FIGURE 1.1: FMF delegation visits Roussel Uclaf in Paris, France, in 1991 to deliver thousands of petitions asking the company to release RU 486 to the US market. Those pictured from left to right include Dr. Catherine Euvrard (Roussel Uclaf), Dr. Myron Allukian (President, American Public Health Association), Dr. Judith Resnick, Peg Yorkin (FMF), Patricia Ireland (NOW), Dr. Eduoard Sakiz (Roussel Uclaf), Eleanor Smeal (FMF), Ariel Mouttet (Roussel Uclaf), Allan Rosenfield (Dean, Columbia University Mailman School of Public Health), Dr. Carl Djerrasi (Stanford University), who has been credited with developing the birth control pill, and Dr. Diane Robins (photo credit: Jennifer Jackman).[134]

are doing something in the avant-garde, they know each other. As it turned out, they had worked together on research, so that was helpful."[135]

The first thing that happened was that Sakiz said he thought it was very important that RU 486 obtain FDA approval in the United States because the FDA had a "gold seal of approval," and if the FDA approved a drug, then it would become a drug that would be used widely around the world. Smeal described Sakiz's motivations: "He made it very clear that the reasons he had worked on this so hard was he thought that it would save women's lives throughout the developing world and it would create healthier babies when they did come because the mother herself would be in better condition."[136] To publicize the life-saving benefits of mifepristone, FMF made a bracelet saying how many women die from botched, illegal abortions each year. Jennifer Jackman explained the important role that these meetings played:

> That meeting was really critical because it's how we got to know the senior people at Roussel, especially Dr. Sakiz and his right-hand person, Catherine Euvrard. We got to know them and realized that these are people who support women's reproductive rights. They're in this for the right reason. They were constrained institutionally because they were owned by Hoechst AG, a parent company that was quite conservative, based in Frankfurt. They wanted us to generate pressure on them to counter the anti-abortion pressure. They welcomed a campaign that would demonstrate that there was support for the drug. So we were trying to do that through showing public scientific support.[137]

After meeting with officials at Roussel Uclaf, the delegation flew to Frankfurt, Germany to meet with Hoechst AG officials, shipping the petitions to arrive for the meeting as well.

FMF returned to meet with company executives on February 20, 1991, and again in 1992, delivering an additional 110,000 petitions, including more than three thousand petitions from medical experts. During the 1992 trip, Smeal, Yorkin, and Jackman met with women in the Bundestag, German federal parliament, to discuss the RU 486 campaign (see Figure 1.2). Catherine Euvrard said later that the petitions were "very important" in convincing the companies to find a way for RU 486 to be marketed in the United States. "It was concrete because you have all those petitions. It was fifty/fifty so why choose one over the other. Our position was just to put the drug on the market and to let women decide. It's a personal decision of a woman," said Euvrard later. "Thanks to FMF and other groups, we had proof that such a medicine was necessary and good."[138]

To put peer pressure on Roussel Uclaf, FMF also urged scientific and medical associations to pass resolutions supporting RU 486 research and condemning the import alert. On June 27, 1990, the American Medical Association policy committee voted unanimously to support the testing of RU 486. Eight months later, the American Association for Advancement of Science followed suit. Advocates eventually secured

FIGURE 1.2: During the 1992 trip to Frankfurt, Germany to meet with Hoechst, Smeal, Yorkin, and Jackman (on the right) meet with German Medical Women's Association Vice President Gertrude Zickgras, Medical Women's International Association General Secretary Carolyn Motzel, and State of Hessen Minister of Health Iris Blaul to discuss the RU 486 campaign (photo credit: Jennifer Jackman).

RU 486 endorsements from almost every scientific and medical organization in the country.[139] FMF also had a campaign to collect petitions from individual scientists. Jackman explained, "the whole idea behind the scientific outreach was to put pressure on Roussel Uclaf from the community that mattered to them, those they would see as their peers, because Roussel really was a first-rate kind of pharmaceutical company that valued scientific research."[140]

FMF organized direct actions as well, such as attending stockholder meetings and holding demonstrations at public events. In April of 1992, FMF announced a "Web of Influence" campaign, publicizing the names of companies doing business with Roussel Uclaf and Hoechst, and urging people to contact these companies to tell them to ask Roussel Uclaf and Hoechst to make RU 486 available in the United States. In April 1992, FMF held an RU 486 picket at Trevira Twosome race in New York City, sponsored by Hoechst Celanese and Nike (see Figure 1.3). At the time, Hoechst Celanese was the 100 percent-owned subsidiary of Hoechst AG and Nike used Hoechst-produced fibers in its sports attire. RU 486 was also a major focus of massive abortion rights rallies in Washington, DC, in April 1989 and April 1992. FMF and NOW pledged to boycott the pharmaceutical companies if they did not bring the medication to the United States.

At the state government level, FMF worked to persuade legislators to pass resolutions in favor of making RU 486 available in the United States. New Hampshire passed a resolution in 1991, followed by California, Maine, and Hawaii. Lawmakers in at least

FIGURE 1.3: As a part of the Web of Influence Campaign to bring RU 486 to the United States, FMF held a demonstration in April 1992 at the Trevira Twosome Race in New York City, which was sponsored by Hoechst Celanese and Nike. Protesters held signs saying, "Fight Breast Cancer" and "Say No to Brain Tumors, Say Yes to RU 486," referring to research suggesting other uses for RU 486 (photo credit: Jennifer Jackman).

eight other states introduced resolutions to support RU 486. Local lawmakers also acted. New York City Mayor David Dinkins organized thirty mayors to urge the Bush administration to reverse its opposition to RU 486 and support testing of RU 486 in the United States.[141] New York City Comptroller Elizabeth Holtzman threatened to have the city's hospital system stop buying products from companies affiliated with Roussel Uclaf and Hoechst AG.

Another organization—Abortion Rights Mobilization (ARM), formed by the founding chair of NARAL Lawrence Lader—also helped raise public awareness of RU 486. Lader published two books—*RU 486: The Pill That Could End the Abortion Wars and Why American Women Don't Have It* (1991) and *A Private Matter: RU486 and the Abortion Crisis* (1995). In his 1991 book, Lader characterized RU 486 as revolutionary, with the potential to give a woman "full control over her abortion in the surroundings of her choice," allowing women to obtain abortions in their doctor's office rather than an abortion clinic and avoid the "physical invasion of the body" required by procedural abortion.[142] Lader argued that fundamentalist opposition to abortion was rooted in men's anger at "the women's movement and the sexual revolution, which have tested and eroded male dominance." He explained:

> Their recourse is to keep women cloistered at home as the bedrock of family values. The most obvious restriction on women is to force them to bear a child against their will. The war on abortion and birth control thus protects and reinforces the sentence to bear children. By contrast, RU 486 guarantees women freedom of choice through a private, simple, and almost painless abortion—no punishment for women, no control for men.[143]

Lader tirelessly promoted the books, traveling around the country giving talks and regularly speaking with media outlets about RU 486.

Lader was very effective at increasing public awareness about RU 486. "Larry was one of a kind. He was a character," said Smeal. "He felt that we had to get a lot of press to win this one. He would always come up with ideas, and we frequently would be responsive to it."[144] Lader heard about a law empowering the US government to take a patent for an essential drug that was being withheld from the US market. He had the idea to use this law to pressure Roussel Uclaf and Hoechst AG to allow RU 486 into the United States. "That was Larry's idea, and he took it to Ron Wyden," said Smeal. At that time, Ron Wyden was a young member of the House of Representatives from Oregon. "Wyden took us all seriously and had hearings. Those hearings were very important because Eduard Sakiz at Roussel Uclaf could use them in his bargaining with Hoechst AG. In other words, 'you guys are going to lose this patent because the United States isn't going to take this.' They thought that the Congress was going to act. That was important."[145]

Rep. Wyden held congressional hearings in 1990, 1991, and 1992 on the Bush administration's import alert on RU 486 before the Small Business Subcommittee on

Regulation, Business Opportunities, and Energy.[146] On November 19, 1990, the first hearing examined the import ban's effect on medical research. Scientists testified about how the import alert interfered with research into potential uses of RU 486 to treat illnesses, including Cushing syndrome, breast cancer, and meningioma. Wyden accused the FDA of "arbitrary, political, and unscientific RU 486 policies."[147] At the end of the hearing, Wyden introduced a bill to remove the import ban, which died in committee.[148] The media covered the hearings extensively. Wyden then held another hearing in December of 1991, where leading European researchers, clinicians, and public policy experts testified about the European experience with RU 486. American scientists, pharmaceutical industry representatives, and political activists testified about factors preventing RU 486 from coming to the United States. Eleanor Smeal testified that the import alert harmed the reputation of the United States: "If we permit these forces to stop the pursuit of knowledge, the United States will not be a first-rate country in terms of health care, scientific research, or human rights."[149] At the 1992 hearing, a brain tumor patient, actress Cybill Shephard, and several pro-choice groups testified. Wyden expressed frustration that Roussel Uclaf had decided to go forward with breast cancer trials in Canada, but refused to do so in the United States.[150] The committee heard testimony from a man with recurrent meningioma, who recounted his difficulties with obtaining RU 486 from Roussel Uclaf to treat his condition. While Roussel Uclaf told him he could arrange a compassionate use exemption from the import alert through the FDA, the FDA told him he could not receive the exemption without a written guarantee of supply from the company, which the company would not provide without FDA approval.[151] The hearings repeatedly exposed that the FDA had acted politically rather than based on scientific evidence in imposing the import alert. In 1991, Wyden and Rep. Henry Waxman (D-CA) introduced the "RU 486 Regulatory Fairness Act" to reverse the import alert. The bill had sixty-eight other supporters in Congress, but never passed.[152]

To generate more publicity and awareness about abortion pills, Lader directly challenged the import ban in 1992 by arranging for a pregnant American woman named Leona Benten to travel to London to obtain RU 486, then travel back to the United States and carry the medication through customs. ARM had alerted customs officials and the press in advance, so when customs officials confiscated the pills, ARM began a press conference announcing their plan to file a lawsuit challenging the confiscation and the import ban (see some of the press coverage in Figure 1.4). Lader, who had written a biography of Margaret Sanger in 1955, was inspired by Sanger's use of this strategy in the 1936 case, *United States v. One Package of Japanese Pessaries*. Sanger arranged to have a Japanese doctor mail contraceptives to her clinic in New York to challenge the law. Customs seized the package and Sanger sued. She won the case.[153] Lader explained his hope: "We were looking for a strategy that would challenge President Bush and the Hoechst company directly, a way to dramatize the absurdity of their positions and bring the importance of RU 486 to the country and the media in vivid and simple terms."[154]

FIGURE 1.4: A July 1, 1992 press conference held by Lenore Benten and Lawrence Lader at John F. Kennedy airport was widely covered in the press (photo credit: Carrie N. Baker).

The Benten case generated extensive publicity and highlighted how the FDA's import ban was based on politics rather than science and harmed women. A federal district court judge ruled in Benten's favor, stating it was likely that "the decision to ban the drug was not from any bona fide concern for the safety of users of the drug, but on political considerations having no place in FDA decisions on health and safety."[155] The case was eventually overturned on appeal,[156] but achieved Lader's goal of raising awareness about RU 486, exposing the government's biased actions and the harmful impact they had on women. "The case had been a legal gamble from the start, of course, but it had turned out far more successfully than anyone expected," Lader said afterwards. "Leona personally had lost, but the movement had made a striking advance in bringing the issue of RU 486 to national attention and shaking up the government's rigidity in the process."[157]

A second ARM strategy focused on developing an RU 486 clone to break Roussel Uclaf's monopoly and put pressure on the company to either market RU 486 in the United States or turn over its patent to a US-based company. Lader hoped to test the clone under New York's "mini-FDA" law allowing research on new medications. Lader found a Chinese doctor to provide copies of their abortion pill as well as to share the results of their clinical tests of the medication. ARM then raised money, found scientists, and set up a lab in Westchester, New York, to produce their own abortion pill.

On January 1, 1993, Lader held a press conference urging Health Secretary Donna Shalala to "contract with a drug company in this country or elsewhere to manufacture and distribute RU 486 to American women at cost."[158] Then on February 17, 1993, Lader announced ARM would begin testing Chinese abortion pills in the United States. In late March 1993, the ARM lab had produced 50 grams of RU 486—enough to supply abortions to about one hundred women. Lader explained, "testing this small a number would essentially be symbolic, but it would prove to the country that RU 486 could be made here, and a lot more of the drug would be available shortly thereafter."[159] ARM then obtained FDA authorization to test their own pills under the Population Council's IND approval. At a press conference on April 1, 1993, Lader showed the pills ARM had developed to reporters, stating, "Our purpose is to pressure Roussel Uclaf. We are trying to get them into immediate and decisive action."[160]

Both ARM and FMF worked to educate the public about possible other uses of the medication, including treatment for Cushing syndrome, brain tumors (meningioma), breast cancer, endometriosis, fibroids, and postpartum depression. Some hoped the medication could reduce the need for Caesarean births by helping to dilate the cervix. Baulieu even argued that RU 486 could be developed as a once-a-month contraceptive, which would block implantation. "The whole concept of abortion must change," said Baulieu, noting that pregnancy does not commence until a fertilized egg is implanted in the uterine wall. "If it works, it will be the end of contraceptives and the end of abortion," said gynecologist Raymond Faraggi. "No more daily pills, no more IUDs. You take a pill on the twenty-fifth to twenty-eighth day of your menstrual cycle regularly, every month. It means the end of abortion, anyway, and an end to all our problems."[161] Baulieu, who continued to promote RU 486 throughout the 1980s despite hate mail and threats, published a book in 1990 in which he optimistically argued, "paradoxically, the 'abortion pill' might even help eliminate abortion as an issue."[162]

Between the late 1980s and early 1990s, over three hundred newspapers across the United States editorialized on RU 486, with 95 percent supporting research, even including newspapers in conservative areas of the country. On December 11, 1990, the *Herald-Press* in Huntington, Indiana wrote in support of research on RU 486: "blocking medical progress is where the sensible public should draw the line…the best solution is to restore sanity to the abortion debate, and that can only mean respecting the honorable American institution of personal choice." An editorial in the newspaper *Mail* in Charleston, West Virginia, said, "The right-to-life movement is jeopardizing its claim to compassion for all, born and unborn, in its unreasoning opposition to the so-called abortion pill, RU 486. By refusing to allow research on the drug for uses other than abortion, the pro-lifers risk looking like new-Luddites who refuse to acknowledge the benefits of technological progress." The St. Petersburg *Times* editorialized on November 21, 1990, "Approval of RU 486 is not tantamount to endorsement of abortion. Indeed, there are surely thousands of American who are opposed to abortion, but who would use the drug for its other valuable functions."[163] Much coverage framed RU 486 as a breakthrough that could completely change abortion. For example, *Time* magazine ran a cover story on mifepristone in June 1993 with the headline, "The Pill That Changes Everything"[164] (see Figure 1.5). This *Time* cover indicated the high hopes that people had for what mifepristone could do for women.

FIGURE 1.5: *Time* magazine cover in June 1993 (courtesy of *Time*).

Abortion rights supporters in Congress tried to pressure the Bush administration to lift the import ban and approve the medication. Rep. Pat Schroeder (D-CO) and Senator Paul Wellstone (D-MN) introduced legislation to remove the Bush administration's import alert. In addition to holding hearings on the import alert, Rep. Wyden sent a letter to Roussel Uclaf urging them to market RU 486 in the United States and notifying them of three small pharmaceutical companies interested in marketing RU 486—Gynex, Cabot Medical Corporation, and Adeza Biomedical Corporation.[165] But Roussel Uclaf said they would only license the drug to a major pharmaceutical company. The company's reluctance led reproductive rights advocates to develop legal strategies attempting to compel the company to make the drug available. University of Southern California law professor Erwin Chemerinsky argued withholding the medication violated California's constitutional right to privacy. ARM suggested the federal government might have the right to seize patent rights and Rep. Jerry Nadler (D-NY) investigated the possibility of new legislation to remove the patent.[166]

The 1992 elections turned the political tides in favor of RU 486. In the fall of 1991, President George Bush nominated Clarence Thomas to the Supreme Court. During the confirmation process, law professor Anita Hill notified the FBI that Thomas had sexually harassed her in the early 1980s, while she worked for the Office of Civil Rights in the Department of Education, and then later at the Equal Employment Opportunity Commission. Chair of the Senate Judiciary Committee Joseph Biden called a public hearing on the matter, where the ten white members of the Committee questioned Hill and Thomas, treating Hill terribly and then confirming Thomas's nomination. This spectacle led to tremendous anger among women and mobilized them to run for office and vote in record numbers. In the 1992 elections, Americans elected pro-choice Democrat Bill Clinton as president of the United States and elected a record number of women and pro-choice members of Congress. The change created a more favorable political climate for RU 486, but advocates still had a long road to travel before achieving FDA approval of mifepristone.

FDA APPROVAL OF MIFEPRISTONE

In the November 2022 Alliance for Hippocratic Medicine lawsuit challenging the FDA approval of mifepristone, anti-abortion doctors alleged that the Clinton administration's FDA "fast tracked" the approval of mifepristone.[167] Abortion opponents had argued for years that the approval process had been "politicized science" and that the Clinton administration had manipulated the approval of mifepristone and endangered women's health.[168] In fact, it took the entire two terms of Clinton's presidency for the FDA to approve mifepristone.

During the 1992 campaign, Clinton pledged his support for bringing RU 486 to the United States. After the election, FMF sent letters to Roussel Uclaf and Hoechst

AG informing them that the political climate was much more favorable for RU 486. Feminist organizations, who had strongly supported Clinton's campaign, raised the issue of RU 486 in early meetings with the president and his advisors. Within days of his inauguration and on the twentieth anniversary of *Roe v. Wade* on January 22, 1993, President Clinton directed the Secretary of Health and Human Services Donna Shalala to take steps to rescind the FDA import alert on RU 486 and to promote the "testing, licensing, and manufacturing" of RU 486 in the United States.[169] In response, Shalala published a notice in the *Federal Register* directing the FDA "to initiate an immediate and thorough review of the health and safety implications of the potential import of RU 486 for personal use." Then Shalala urged on the negotiations between the FDA and Roussel Uclaf. Eleanor Smeal declared that the Clinton administration actions were "the end of an era of medical McCarthyism" in which Republican ideology "interfered with the conduct of scientific research and medicine."[170] Despite Clinton's actions, it would take another *eight years* before the medication would receive FDA approval.

In December of 1992, after the election but before the inauguration of Clinton, FDA Commissioner David Kessler wrote to Roussel Uclaf encouraging the company to submit an application to license RU 486 in the United States.[171] On February 24, 1993, Kessler met with Sakiz to discuss how to bring RU 486 to the United States by licensing the medication to another entity, such as a US-based pharmaceutical firm, a research center, or a university. Under pressure from all sides, Roussel Uclaf decided they would not market the medication themselves, but would negotiate giving the patent to market RU 486 in the United States to the Population Council. Catherine Euvrard explained why they chose the Population Council:

> The idea was to give away the compound, but not to give to an organization which was not reliable. We preferred not to give to somebody who was just interested in making money. We knew the Population Council was not interested in making money, but was interested in doing what was good for women. The Population Council had doctors and knowledge, competence and experience to test new drugs, to do clinical trials, to register with the FDA. The Population Council was a very reliable partner.[172]

The Population Council worked primarily in the global South, but reproductive health advocate Francine Coeytaux and others convinced the organization to work on FDA approval for RU 486. "We had to convince the board of directors of the Population Council that it was okay for them to spend money and time on bringing [RU 486] to the US because the mission of the Population Council was only to work for developing countries," said Coeytaux, who worked for the Population Council and was involved with RHTP. According to Coeytaux, "The board of trustees said, 'Our mission is to work in developing countries. Why should we invest in the US?' We were able to make the case that if we are going to work in developing countries, we cannot go around advocating for a method that has not been approved by the US FDA. We have too many historical examples of that not working out. So that's how we convinced the board of directors of the Population Council to do the work that allowed us to get to the FDA."[173]

The Population Council agreed to run clinical trials on RU 486, to apply for FDA approval, and to find companies to manufacture and distribute the medication in the United States. The Population Council's director of reproductive health Dr. Beverly Winikoff gave George Zeidenstein a lot of credit for this move: "The Population Council put itself on the line. We had a very brave CEO, George Zeidenstein, who was willing to bring this up to the board and advocate for being the agency that would take it on for the US. He saw the importance of it and he was a person who stood up for what he thought was right. He's an unsung hero," said Winikoff.[174] Roussel Uclaf and the Population Council began negotiations on the details to transfer the patent for the US market.

On April 20, 1993, Dr. Kessler and Dr. Sakiz publicly announced that Roussel Uclaf had made a verbal agreement with the Population Council of New York to supply two thousand pills for testing and all of its research on the pill's development.[175] To put pressure on Roussel Uclaf to move quickly with US clinical trials, Larry Lader and Eleanor Smeal announced a strategy to remove Roussel Uclaf's patent on RU 486, using an existing law that allows Congress to remove patents on products not being marketed in the United States. Lader also announced that the RU 486 compound had been replicated by scientists in New York state. Then at a press conference sponsored by Physicians for RU 486, Rep. Ron Wyden promised to hold a Congressional hearing on removing the RU 486 patent from Roussel Uclaf if there was no agreement to commence US trials in three months. In June 1993, when the anti-abortion group Operation Rescue organized a demonstration at the French embassy, FMF organized a counter-protest that outnumbered RU 486 opponents by five to one. Meanwhile, the Institute of Medicine suggested an expedited new drug application (NDA) be submitted to the FDA for the use of RU 486 as a method of early abortion and urged the FDA to consider the French research. The FDA agreed to consider this research, but insisted on testing in the United States as well.

In the meantime, FMF urged Hoechst AG and Roussel Uclaf to allow a US distributor to sell RU 486 until an American manufacturer was established and gained FDA approval. Smeal sent a letter to Hoechst AG CEO Wolfgang Hilger urging the company to permit the sale of RU 486 to the United States during the interim period. She also sent another installment of 100,000 RU 486 petitions.[176] When negotiations between Roussel Uclaf and the Population Council stalled in October of 1993, FMF conducted a "No More Delays" petition campaign to urge Hoechst AG to make RU 486 available for testing in the United States immediately. On the twentieth anniversary of *Roe v. Wade* in January of 1994, FMF shipped another fifty thousand petitions to Hoechst

AG. Meanwhile, in February 1994, British doctors began offering abortion pills to US women who could travel to Britain.[177]

When no agreement between Roussel Uclaf and the Population Council had been reached for over a year, Shalala set a deadline of May 15, 1994. Rep. Wyden scheduled a hearing on RU 486 for May 16. On that day, Roussel Uclaf announced they would transfer the patent rights for medical uses of RU 486 in the Unites States to the nonprofit Population Council, for free. The same day at congressional hearings on the transfer of RU 486's patent rights to the Population Council, a Roussel Uclaf representative testified about the importance of the Clinton administration's efforts to their decision: "It was only when President Clinton changed the government policy and specifically asked Roussel to make the procedure available, here, that our client, out of respect for the President of the United States, agreed to make every effort to comply with his request."[178] In a private letter written to Eleanor Smeal two weeks later, Dr. Sakiz attributed this success to the persistence of the women's movement. "It is mainly your own determination and that of all the Feminist Majority Foundation's members and other pro-choice supporters that largely contributed to this successful issue," wrote Sakiz, who by the time of the transfer had stepped down as CEO of Roussel Uclaf but still served as chair of the Board of Supervisors.[179] Smeal credited Sakiz: "He knew it would save countless lives of women by reducing maternal mortality rates. If it was okayed scientifically by the FDA, which has high standards, then people would realize it was a safe medicine and it would be distributed around the world. He was trying to get an important medical development to people in poverty who didn't live in conditions that a surgical abortion requires—with sterilized equipment and clean water. A pill would be safer and easier to administer."[180] After the transfer, since this drug would no longer be licensed or developed in the United States by Roussel Uclaf, people no longer called it RU 486, but instead referred to the medication by its scientific name, mifepristone.

Building on this progress, advocates kept up the pressure on Congress. In the fall of 1995, RHTP conducted a briefing on medical abortion for legislative aides of Congressmembers who supported abortion rights. Advocates also kept pressure up on medical organizations to pass resolutions supporting the FDA approval of mifepristone. In November of 1995, the family planning section of the American Public Health Association passed a resolution supporting the expansion of options for early abortion.

In response to the announced transfer of patent rights, and after years of threatening to boycott, abortion opponents launched a boycott against Roussel Uclaf and Hoechst. Catherine Euvrard at Roussel Uclaf said she did not believe the boycott would work because "American doctors prescribe drugs according to criteria which are rational, and not emotional. I don't believe for one minute that American doctors' professionalism would allow them not to prescribe a drug that they know will help a sick patient."[181] A Hoechst Celanese spokesperson questioned the efficacy of a boycott strategy when she said, "We're an industrial company, so we do not sell consumer products. I don't know how a consumer would tell."[182] Anti-abortion groups nonetheless threatened to pressure doctors not to prescribe Hoechst-made medications.

Once they had the patent rights, the Population Council turned to conducting clinical trials and finding a US manufacturer. Lawrence Lader of ARM offered to work with the Population Council to produce and test abortion pills, but the Council declined the offer. "Larry Lader was an impatient guy. He was like the schill in front of the carnival, getting people riled up," said Beverly Winikoff. "The way he was managing was to make it a public issue. The way the Pop Council was doing it was to make it quiet and gentlemanly."[183] The Population Council's clinical trials were funded by George Soros's Open Society Institute, the Kaiser Family Foundation, and the Buffett Foundation, as well as the Council's own resources. The Buffett Foundation made at least $2 million in interest-free loans to the Population Council used to conduct the clinical trials.[184] The Council immediately began trials of the drug with two thousand women at seventeen sites in fifteen states, using the same protocol approved in France except that they tested the medication through sixty-three days rather than just forty-nine days, which was the timeframe used in France.[185] One of the sites was the Brookline, Massachusetts, Planned Parenthood clinic. In November, after the clinic made a public announcement that it would be dispensing mifepristone, protesters began demonstrating outside the clinic. The next month is when John Salvi shot and killed Shannon Lowney. After the murder, the clinic stopped dispensing mifepristone.[186]

Meanwhile, advocates turned to another medication that could end a pregnancy: methotrexate. In July of 1995, RHTP convened a meeting in Washington, DC for family planning and reproductive rights advocates to meet with scientists and doctors working on methotrexate. The meeting included people from the National Institutes of Health, FDA, Contraceptive Research and Development (CONRAD) Program, and private industry.[187] The following month, on August 31, 1995, Dr. Richard U. Hausknecht published a study in *The New England Journal of Medicine* showing that the cancer drug methotrexate combined with misoprostol was a highly effective and safe method of abortion. Out of 178 women, 171 had a successful abortion after one dose of methotrexate and one dose of misoprostol—a 96 percent success rate. There were no serious side effects or complications for anyone.[188] A wave of headlines and editorials expressed hope that this combination of inexpensive medications would solve the abortion issue and enable women to avoid anti-abortion activists' harassment outside of abortion clinics, which had been virulent in the early 1990s. *The Washington Post* editorial board argued, "intimidation loses its power when abortion drugs can be prescribed in any doctor's office and taken in the privacy of any home. These truly private actions afford no opportunity for the kinds of pressure, harassment and in some cases violence now used to deter women from entering abortion clinics and doctors from working in them."[189] *The New York Times* editorial board announced, "in one swift technological leap, women may be able to bypass the jeering pickets and potential violence that make visits to abortion clinics such trying and dangerous experiences."[190] *The Wall Street Journal* reported that Delta Science Research Foundation was trying to raise $6 million to finance a large-scale clinical trial.[191] Another study in early September showed similar effective results.[192] In March of 1996, researchers at the University of California, San Francisco announced that they would be testing methotrexate as an abortifacient.[193] Methotrexate eventually became a common treatment for ectopic pregnancies, but was not used more widely for abortion. An early researcher on methotrexate and mifepristone, Dr. Steve Eisinger at University of Rochester, later explained: "Methotrexate is a cancer drug with some potential dangerous side effects and it doesn't work as well as mifepristone."[194] Nevertheless, in the mid-1990s, the methotrexate studies put pressure on the Population Council to move quickly with their mifepristone trials.

On March 18, 1996, the Population Council submitted an NDA to the FDA for mifepristone combined with misoprostol as a method for early abortion based on data from 2,500 French women and the promise they would submit data from 2,100 American women. By this time, there was research showing that a lower dose of mifepristone was effective through sixty-three days of pregnancy, but the Population Council did not submit this research so as not to delay the approval process further.[195] Advocates knew that clinical practice would follow the evidence so that physicians could still prescribe the medication beyond forty-nine days of pregnancy.[196] On July 19, 1996, the FDA Advisory Committee on Reproductive Health Drugs held public hearings on mifepristone safety and efficacy at which more than thirty people testified, two-thirds strongly in favor of making mifepristone available in the United States.[197] The FDA took unusual security precautions for the all-day meeting, stationing uniformed police officers at the entrances and requiring attendees to pass through metal detectors. The FDA assembled people at a Washington, DC hotel and transported them in vans to the hearing site.[198] Cynthia Pearson at the National Women's Health Network remembered an anti-abortion member of the committee who objected to approving the medication. Referring to the committee's task of weighing patient risks and benefits, the anti-abortion committee member said, "there is certainly no benefit to her baby." Pearson also remembered that one woman who supported abortion rights was taken off the committee.[199]

Nevertheless, on July 19, 1996, the Committee recommended the FDA approve mifepristone and misoprostol for abortions up to seven weeks gestation, but recommended close medical supervision of mifepristone administration. Then on September 18, 1996, the FDA issued an "approvable letter" for mifepristone for early abortion, stating the combination of mifepristone and misoprostol was safe and effective when used under close medical supervision, but noted that additional information was needed on the manufacturing process and labeling before a final decision would be made.

Larry Lader became impatient to make mifepristone available to women right away, so he devised a scheme: apply to conduct a clinical trial to test the mifepristone he had made inside the country. This plan got around the Bush administration's import ban still in place. Columbia University physician and researcher Carolyn Westhoff met with Larry Lader and other researchers about his plan. "The studies were solely an excuse to be able to distribute mife," said Westhoff. "But there's so much more we can learn. Let's make them real studies," Westhoff told Lader, which they did. "We got an investigation new drug approval from the FDA to do studies of this new molecule." This research provided the first evidence to support a lower dosage of mifepristone that became the modified treatment protocol.[200] Researchers also tested whether the medications were still effective if taken closer together in time. Dr. Eric Schaff conducted research showing that the medications were just as effective when taken twenty-four hours apart as when taken forty-eight hours apart. Then Dr. Mitchell Creinin conducted research showing that an even shorter window of time between taking mifepristone and misoprostol was effective in early pregnancy if the misoprostol was taken vaginally. Dr. Creinin explained: "We did pilot studies looking at a six to eight-hour window. Can we do it in one day? It worked fine. Then I said, can we go further? Let's test the drugs at the same time and then allow people to make a free choice of when they want to have their abortion. Do you want to have it two hours from the time I see you in the office? Do you want to have it tomorrow? Do you want to have it in a couple of days when the weekend comes?"[201] As compared to oral or buccal administration of mifepristone, vaginal use also had fewer side effects such as nausea and vomiting. Taken buccally, the medications are most effective if taken twenty-four hours apart.[202]

Meanwhile, with the support of ARM, researchers at the University of Rochester obtained FDA approval in July 1996 to test mifepristone on two thousand women. "It just kept dragging on the Pop Council side. So we felt that if we could test thousands of women, that would show it was safe and effective. That would create a wave of momentum that would be hard to stop at that point," said Dr. David Horn of Columbia University, who worked with Lader.[203] Dr. Eric Schaff at the University of Rochester ran the trials. Lader hoped to support the Population Council's work, and speed it up.[204] In July 1997, ARM announced they had received funding from the John Merck Foundation to expand the testing to ten thousand women. The research was conducted on women in New York, Nebraska, Vermont, Montana, California, and Washington. Although the Population Council held the US patent rights to RU 486, the FDA permitted others to copy the patented drugs for research use so long as they were not sold commercially.[205] ARM supplied researchers at the University of Rochester with mifepristone. "We got from Larry all the mifepristone we could possibly use," said Dr. Steven Eisinger, one of the researchers leading the study along with Dr. Eric Schaff. "It came in bulk form—pounds and pounds of it. It was a powder. We had the Pharmacy Department at the University of Rochester package it in capsules. They made sure the dosage was correct and tested it for safety and purity."[206] The researchers tested a lower 200-milligram dosage of mifepristone, which had fewer side effects, and allowed patients to take misoprostol vaginally at home, requiring only two doctor's visits. The research, published in 1999 and shared with the FDA, showed that mifepristone and misoprostol administered in this fashion were safe and effective.[207]

In addition to obtaining FDA approval, the Population Council had to find a drug company willing to manufacture and market the drug in the United States. Large drug companies were wary of product liability lawsuits after the A.H. Robins Company had to pay millions of dollars in compensation and punitive damages to women who were harmed by the Dalkon Shield, an intrauterine contraceptive device (IUD) that caused pelvic infection, infertility, unintended pregnancy, and death in the 1970s and early 1980s.[208] US pharmaceutical drugs may have also been unable to obtain liability insurance because of large damage awards to women claiming injury from contraceptive drugs.[209] The bottom line—uncertainty about making a profit—dissuaded many large, for-profit drug companies from taking on RU 486. Big drug companies were also the target of threatened boycotts by anti-abortion groups and pressure from conservative investment funds. As a result, companies such as Teva, Merck, Abbott Laboratories, Johnson & Johnson, and Upjohn declined to pursue the medication.[210] "Pharmaceutical companies abhor controversy unless they stand to make a great deal of money for their trouble," said Marie Bass of RHTP. "The profit potential for RU 486 was nowhere near enough to make up for the headache a company would face. Major American companies wanted nothing to do with it."[211]

In 1995, the Population Council entered into a contract with Gedeon Richter of Hungary to manufacture mifepristone. They then sought another company to market the medication in the United States. Of five companies submitting proposals to market mifepristone, the Population Council selected a company named Advances in Health Technology (AHT), headed by Joseph Pike, a lawyer with whom they had previously worked on an IUD. On March 31, 1995, the Population Council transferred the exclusive legal right to organize the manufacture and distribution of mifepristone in the United States to AHT.[212] Pike created Danco Laboratories to receive raw mifepristone from the manufacturer and then package, market, and distribute the pills. AHT sublicensed mifepristone to NeoGen Pharmaceuticals, also owned and controlled by Pike, to test and market mifepristone for uses other than abortion. Danco received a $14 million loan from the Packard Foundation in 1996 to bring mifepristone to market in the United States.[213] Pike also raised money from private investors, guaranteeing them anonymity. He created a series of limited partnerships and companies in the Cayman Islands, and raised $13 million from over four dozen investors, including from private equity investors Greg Hawkins and Brad Daniel.[214] But then one of his investors sued him for breach of contract and fraud, alleging Pike had previously been disbarred in North Carolina for falsely inflating the cost of a piece of property to two investors. The Population Council then sued Pike for fraud.[215] In a settlement, Pike sold all his interests in Danco to Advances for Choice. Dutch attorney Jack Van Hulst became the president and chief executive of Advances for Choice.[216]

Meanwhile, Gedeon Richter backed out of its contract to manufacture mifepristone in February 1997, further delaying the introduction of the drug. Finding a new manufacturer was difficult because the anti-abortion movement continued to threaten boycotts. NRLC began a boycott of Hoechst's antihistamine Allegra in April 1997, after Roussel Uclaf and Hoechst agreed to grant the rights to mifepristone to Sakiz, announcing the boycott in full-page advertisements in *USA Today* and other publications.[217] As a single-product company, Danco was immune to anti-abortion boycotts. Anti-abortion extremists also threatened to bomb manufacturers and distributors of mifepristone.[218] In June 1998, Danco announced they had found a manufacturer willing to make the drug. Nevertheless, fearing anti-abortion violence, the FDA and the Population Council made the unprecedented decision to keep the manufacturer's name secret.[219] The manufacturer was later revealed to be Shanghai Hua Lian Pharmaceutical Co. Ltd., which was owned by the Chinese government. Despite the risks, researchers continued to study mifepristone and published their results. In April 1998, *The New England Journal of Medicine* publish a study showing that mifepristone in combination with misoprostol terminated 92 percent of pregnancies when taken in the first forty-nine days of pregnancy.[220]

Opposition to FDA approval of mifepristone was strong. In 1998 and 1999, Rep. Tom Coburn (R-Okla.) led the charge to stop FDA approval of mifepristone, along with two other Republicans, Reps. Chris Smith of New Jersey and Dave Weldon of Florida. Conservative staffers formed the "Values Action Team" to coordinate efforts to stop the approval.[221] Coburn introduced an appropriations bill amendment to block the approval of the drug by the FDA. FDA lawyers expressed concerns that the bill would prevent the approval of medications such as methotrexate that could be used to terminate pregnancy but also used to treat other conditions. After long debates, the House voted to adopt the amendment in 1998 by a vote of 223 to 202, and again voted for it in 1999 by a vote of 217 to 214, but the amendment died in a Senate committee.[222] When Kessler left the FDA in 1998, conservative members of Congress grilled Clinton's nominee to head the FDA, Dr. Jane Henney, about mifepristone.

After research showed that mifepristone was effective in treating brain tumors and providing palliative care for several forms of cancer, including breast and ovarian cancer, the FDA agreed to allow use of the drug under a highly restrictive and hard-to-access "compassionate use program," where the FDA allowed patients to use medication for conditions for which it had not yet been approved. Roussel Uclaf and later Sakiz's company Exelgyn provided mifepristone to US patients under this program, but in late 1998, Exelgyn decided they could no longer do this. After the Population Council and Danco Group declined to take on the compassionate use program, the FDA authorized FMF to assume sole responsibility for administering the mifepristone compassionate use program for seriously ill patients in the United States in January of 1999.[223] Smeal explained how FMF ended up with that program: "They needed a compassion use distributor, but nobody would do it. Catherine Euvrard and Jennifer Jackman came up with the idea for the Feminist Majority to do it. They first came to me and I said, 'we're not doctors!' But before I knew it we were retaining a doctor."[224] FMF hired Dr. Beth Jordan to administer the compassionate use program. But few doctors and patients knew about this option and accessing the medication under this program was very cumbersome. Physicians intending to administer mifepristone for any use other than early abortion had to obtain an IND permit from the FDA, which they granted only when patients had exhausted other treatment options and suffered from serious diseases for which mifepristone showed some research promise as a treatment. The physicians then had to apply to FMF for supplies of mifepristone for each patient. FMF distributed mifepristone at cost to the patients' physicians.

In the first two years, FMF provided mifepristone to seventy-one patients—fifty-three women and eighteen men—for treatment of meningioma, leiomyosarcoma, breast cancer, and Cushing syndrome.[225] FMF president Eleanor Smeal explained why the organization did this: "We thought that if people could see it was used for other illnesses, they would start understanding that you can't politicize the drug. Mifepristone had more restrictions than some of the opioids that were really dangerous, which was wrong. This pill can treat other diseases, most of which do not only affect women. We need breakthroughs in the treatment of cancer. This is an antiprogestin. And some cancer cells are dependent on progesterone for growth. For us not to recognize that and not to encourage research, that's the politicization."[226] FMF later sponsored clinical trials on use of mifepristone to treat ovarian cancer, with good results, but they couldn't afford to do the second round of trials and had to abandon the program.[227]

In February of 2000, the FDA issued a second "approvable" letter, but told the Population Council that they would impose several extraordinary restrictions on mifepristone, including requiring physicians to be listed on a national registry, requiring the use of ultrasounds to date pregnancies, and limiting prescription rights to licensed physicians or doctors already performing aspiration abortion or those with hospital admitting privileges.[228] Many people believed that the FDA imposed these restrictions not because of concerns about the safety of mifepristone, but because of the politically volatile context and fear of violence. ACOG opposed these restrictions as unnecessarily burdensome on patients and physicians.[229] The Population Council also fought the restrictions.[230] In June of 2000, FMF launched an emergency campaign to urge the FDA to reject these unnecessary restrictions.[231] Another obstacle to FDA approval was opposition by the manufacturer of misoprostol, Searle. Fearing controversy, the company lobbied hard to keep misoprostol out of a medical abortion regimen at least until its patent ran out in July 2000.[232] Then in August, as FDA approval was imminent, Searle issued a statement indicating that its gastric ulcer treatment was contraindicated for use in pregnant women.[233]

After a long fight by anti-abortion activists to block the drug from the US market, the Clinton administration's FDA finally approved mifepristone for use within the United

States on September 28, 2000—just before the 2000 presidential election. At the time, the FDA refused to reveal the names of the manufacturer or the FDA employees involved in approving the drug, citing fear of anti-abortion violence. The threats were so serious the agency had to increase security at its offices.[234] Danco had an unlisted telephone number and revealed only that their office was located in midtown Manhattan. At the time, *The Washington Post* described the company as "one of the most enigmatic companies in the pharmaceutical industry."[235] The company's CEO was Roy Karnovsky, a former Merck & Co marketing executive, and Dr. Richard Hausknecht was the part-time medical director. Hausknecht was an associate professor of obstetrics and gynecology at Mount Sinai School of Medicine in New York, the medical director for Planned Parenthood of New York City, and served on an advisory board for Planned Parenthood. Danco's director of public affairs was Heather M. O'Neill, who previously worked at the Population Council. *The Washington Post* described the company as mission driven and dedicated to making mifepristone available to American women.[236]

When the FDA approved mifepristone, they placed the medication under a regulatory restriction called subpart H. Under this restriction, the FDA prohibited retail pharmacies from stocking and distributing mifepristone, instead requiring mifepristone to be dispensed in an office, clinic, or hospital by a physician registered with the drug manufacturer. The physician had to be capable of assessing the duration of pregnancy and to diagnose ectopic pregnancies. The FDA required patient access to a physician who was capable of administering a blood transfusion or doing a surgical abortion due to the rare possibility of adverse reactions such as excessive bleeding or incomplete abortion. Contrary to the scientific evidence demonstrating the safety of mifepristone, the FDA required a black box warning on the package insert—the strongest warning that the FDA requires—notifying consumers that medical studies indicated that the drug carried a significant risk of serious or even life-threatening adverse effects. The FDA approved use of mifepristone for only the first seven weeks (or forty-nine days) after a patient's last menstrual period, required patients to sign a patient agreement form confirming that they had received counseling on the risks associated with the medication, and required three office visits by the patient. The FDA required secure manufacturing, receiving, and holding areas for the drug, and secure shipping procedures, including tamper-proof seals, controlled returns procedures, a tracking system that could trace individual packages to a patient while maintaining patient confidentiality, and the use of authorized distributors with the necessary expertise to handle distribution requirements.[237] The FDA's medication abortion protocol required a 600-milligram dose of mifepristone dispensed to patients in clinic, then a 400-microgram oral dose of misoprostol administered in clinic forty-eight hours later, and finally, a follow-up in-clinic appointment to confirm the pregnancy had successfully ended.[238]

The FDA approved mifepristone under subpart two of subsection H so they could place restrictions on the medication and require post-marketing surveillance to establish that the safety results shown in clinical trials occurred in the much wider population. Abortion rights supporters opposed these restrictions, and were frustrated that the FDA insisted on them, but they were also eager to get the FDA to approve mifepristone before Republican George W. Bush became president in January of 2001.[239] Ironically, abortion opponents would later claim the FDA used subpart H to speed up approval of the drug and that therefore the approval was invalid. They also argued that the Clinton administration fast-tracked approval for mifepristone, causing the FDA to ignore mifepristone's risks to women—arguments that would form the basis of the legal case by the Alliance for Hippocratic Medicine, attempting to remove mifepristone from the market after the Supreme Court overturned constitutional abortion rights in 2022.[240] In fact, the process took many years, and the drug received considerably more scrutiny than was typical.

The tense political climate at the time the drug was approved has led many to believe that the FDA decision to place mifepristone under severe restrictions was the result of political pressure and anti-abortion threats of violence, rather than science.[241] "It was to pacify the right-to-life movement in our country," said Eleanor Smeal.[242] Beverly Winikoff said FDA staff members were "frozen with fear." She said the FDA typically had detailed meeting minutes with participants' names listed, but that they did not do this for mifepristone for fear the names of staff members working on the application would be revealed and they would be endangered.[243] Winikoff described the precautions taken by the FDA to protect people from anti-abortion violence during an FDA advisory board hearing on mifepristone in 1998: "We weren't allowed to know where it would be. We were assigned to go to a gathering place, and then we were loaded into buses and then they took us there. It was all secret because they thought somebody would throw a bomb in it. It was unbelievable how they were just so scared. Everyone was scared."[244] Cynthia Pearson of the National Women's Health Network agreed: "The FDA's visceral fear of violence on that day was emblematic of their fear of all kinds of attacks. They had a specific fear around the day that they were going to be meeting publicly to discuss it, but they also feared that they would be attacked by Congress and take a lot of criticism for approving the abortion pill." Asked whether she thought that was why the FDA put mifepristone under so many restrictions, Pearson responded, "I know it is," citing conversations she later had with Dr. Philip Corfman, the Executive Secretary of the Fertility and Internal Health Advisory Drugs Committee inside the FDA.[245] Pearson credited Corfman with guiding mifepristone "through a complex and politically charged approval process."[246]

But Kirsten Moore, who was at RHTP at the time and later worked to loosen FDA restrictions, said the FDA restrictions on mifepristone had more to do with the conservative and bureaucratic nature of the FDA. "Everybody assumes there was political pressure. I don't think that's the case here. They are bureaucrats. They get very conservative and cautious. They aren't regular abortion providers. This is an unknown world for them. They're a little freaked out by it, and they're like, 'Oh, we have to put as many belts and suspenders around this as we can because it's abortion.' It's not a part of mainstream health care. People don't have experience doing it. They imagine the worst and that's what they then regulate against."[247] Amy Allina, who was at the National Women's Health Network at the time the FDA approved mifepristone, explained it this way: "The entire process of bringing mifepristone to the United States was politically constrained. There was no piece of it that happened without a high level of awareness that it was politically fraught. It was the agency trying to stay out of the political line of fire." Allina said the FDA was as cautious as possible while "still getting to the outcome of approving a drug that clearly had a track record that merited approval." She noted, however, the outcome "reflects a failure on the part of our movement that we made them feel like it was safer to go in that direction than to do what the data showed would have been correct."[248] Allina also said that the restrictive design of the clinical trials gave the FDA an excuse to approve the drug for use in the same way it had been provided in a clinical trial, even though that's not how drug approval normally works. "Normally they do a clinical trial in very specific conditions, and then the drug is approved and it's out there, and it's up to clinicians to provide it safely," said Allina. "The FDA doesn't regulate the practice of medicine. But in this case, they put all of these belts and suspenders around it to try to make sure that there was very little deviation."[249]

In addition to the FDA restrictions, access was limited by the high price of mifepristone. Roussel Uclaf gave the patent to the Population Council because they wanted a nonprofit to distribute the medication at a cheap price so that it would be accessible to poor women but Danco charged a high price for the medication—initially over $100 a pill. Smeal said she believed the Population Council gave the mifepristone patent to a private company because they wanted a company with experience in making and distributing medications, but they couldn't find a nonprofit that had this capacity. "They felt that you needed somebody with experience of the private corporations and that's why I think they did it. But the price was kept high, and that was a very big disappointment to Sakiz," said Smeal.[250]

In addition to approving mifepristone, the Clinton administration finally rescinded the import alert on mifepristone in the fall of 2000. In November of that year, the first shipments of mifepristone arrived in the United States from China and Danco began selling the medication. The Population Council subsequently transferred ownership of the Mifeprex NDA to Danco. Led by FMF, ARM, and RHTP, women's health advocates had finally achieved their long-fought-for goal of FDA approval of mifepristone. Advocates had worked hard to raise public awareness of abortion pills (see Figure 1.6), to mobilize people to demand access to this important new medication, and to pressure drug manufacturers and the government to bring the medication to the American market.

Scholars have argued that the greater numbers of women in Congress and the executive branch after 1992 put mifepristone on the public agenda and drove approval of

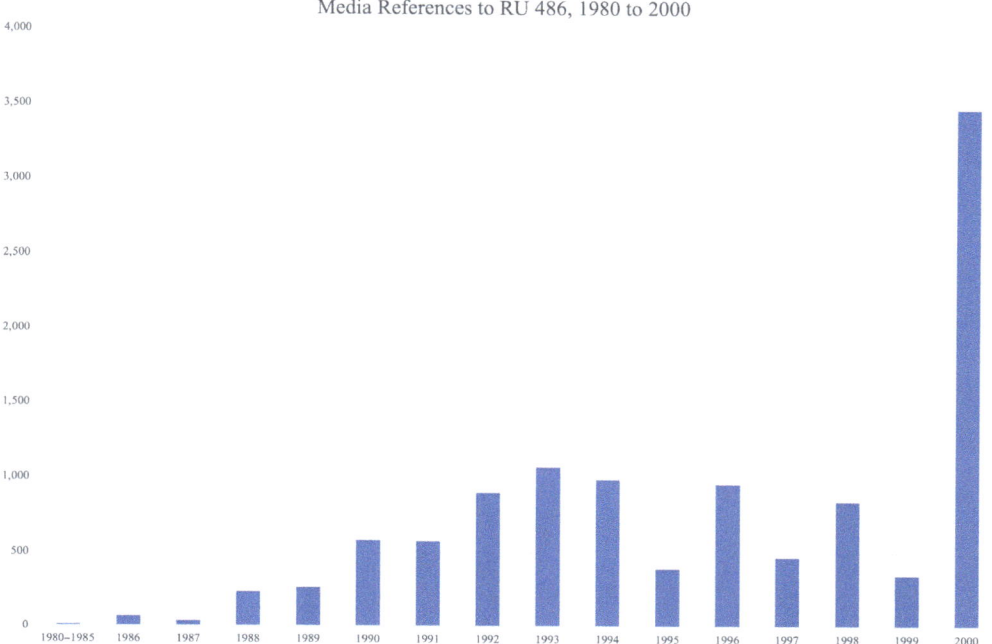

FIGURE 1.6: Media references to RU 486 spiked in 2000. Based on Access World News database.

the drug. The 1991 Anita Hill and Clarence Thomas hearings mobilized women to run for office and vote in higher numbers than ever, pushing women's representation in Congress to over 15 percent, a critical mass capable of rallying support from the party's leaders and moving issues onto the policy agenda. Female leaders in Congress, such as Rep. Pat Schroeder, played an important role in advancing FDA approval of mifepristone. By contrast, all of the leading opponents of FDA approval of mifepristone in Congress were Republican men. Women's groups also played a key role in the election of Bill Clinton, which spurred him to appoint women to high-level office, such as Donna Shalala, who advanced the FDA's approval of mifepristone.[251]

By the time the FDA approved mifepristone, many other countries in Europe had already done so. In early 1997, Hoechst AG bought the remaining Roussel Uclaf stock, then on April 8 announced the end of its manufacture and sale of Mifegyne, which became its brand name for RU 486, and its transfer of worldwide patent rights for RU 486 to Dr. Sakiz, without remuneration. Sakiz, who had retired from Roussel Uclaf in 1993, formed a new company, Exelgyn, to develop and distribute RU 486 globally. By 1999, governments had approved mifepristone in Austria, Belgium, Denmark, Finland, Germany, Greece, Luxembourg, the Netherlands, Spain, and Switzerland. Over the following decade, Exelgyn obtained approval for mifepristone in twenty-eight other countries. In 2003, Dr. Beverly Winikoff formed an organization named Gynuity Health Projects to work on increasing the availability of reproductive medications on the global market. In 2004, the World Health Organization approved mifepristone with misoprostol. By 2020, more than 90 countries had approved mifepristone. Many countries made the medication much more accessible than the United States. For example, since 2017 Canada has permitted any physician or nurse practitioner to prescribe mifepristone and any pharmacist to dispense it.[252]

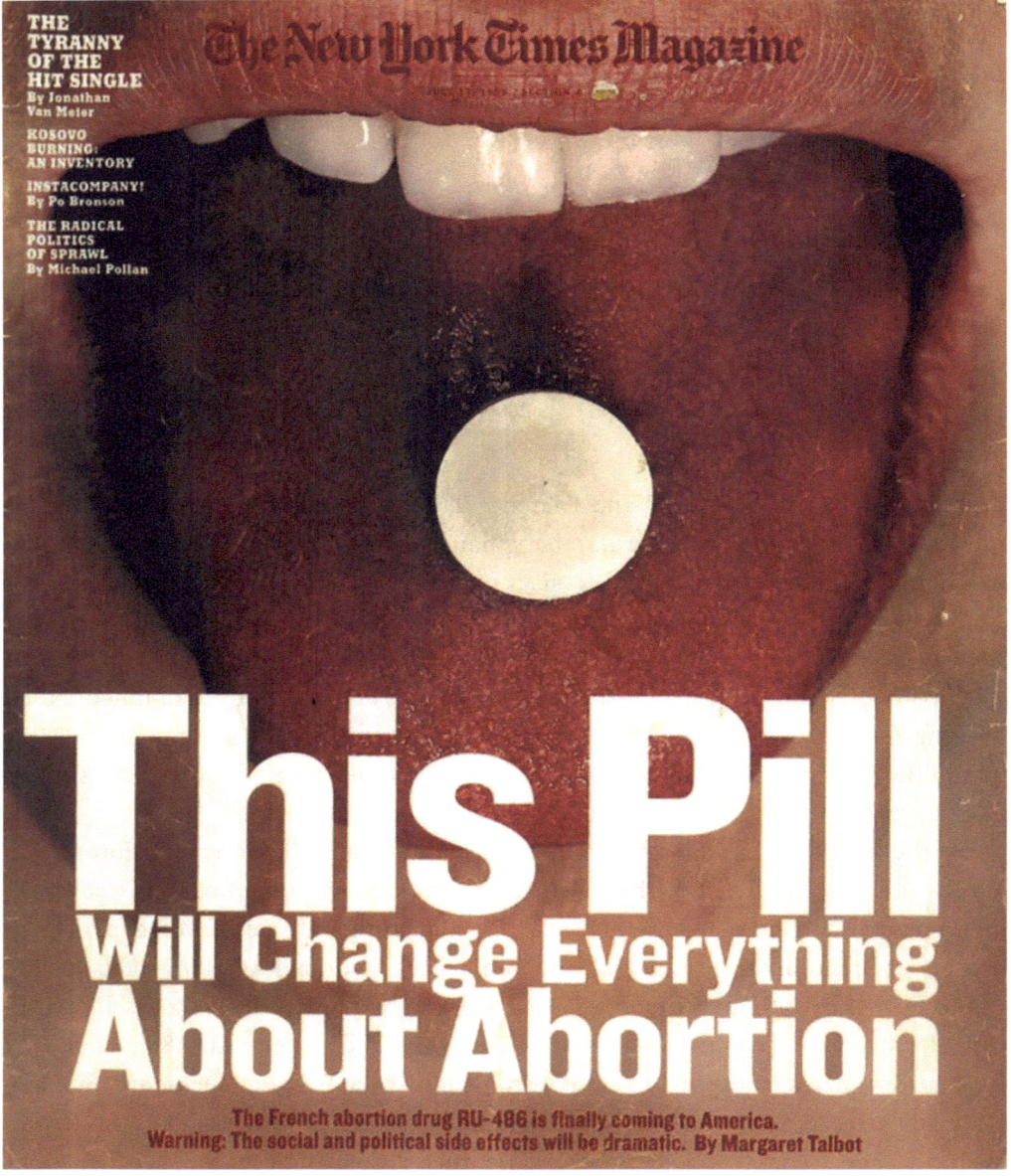

FIGURE 1.7: In anticipation of FDA approval of mifepristone, *The New York Times Magazine* published a cover story in July of 1999 with the headline, "This Pill Will Change Everything About Abortion."

Back in the United States, the pro-choice medical and political communities hoped mifepristone would address the chronic shortage of abortion providers in many places.[253] Because medication abortion did not require surgical skills, they hoped that primary care doctors would offer medication abortion integrated into their office practices so access would increase and abortion opponents would not be able to target and protest this service.[254] In his 1991 book, Lader wrote: "The introduction of RU 486 into the United States could help solve this problem [of provider shortages]. If doctors could give the pill in the privacy of their office, without the glare of publicity, abortion would become as routine as the administration of an antibiotic."[255] In his 1995 book he predicted, "If enough doctors administered the abortion pills from their offices, the extremists would have trouble identifying them, invading the premises, or harassing them with picket lines."[256]

Advocates also pointed out how medication abortion had several advantages over procedural abortion. No instruments enter the uterus, so there is no possibility of perforation of the uterus and little risk of infection. Also, there are no anesthesia-related complications because anesthesia is not used for medication abortion as it sometimes is for suction abortion. Medication abortion was safer than procedural abortion, and much safer than childbirth.[257] Finally, mifepristone enabled women to obtain abortions earlier in pregnancy. Physicians often waited until after eight weeks to perform procedural abortions because before that time the embryo is so small that aspiration abortion could fail or be incomplete.[258] With FDA approval, advocates hoped abortion pills would create greater access to early abortion in the United States.

In 1993, *Time* magazine had proclaimed on its cover that RU 486 was "The Pill That Changes Everything." Six years later, *The New York Times Magazine* cover still promised a revolution, declaring, "This Pill Will Change Everything About Abortion"[259] (see Figure 1.7). Hopes were high, but would the pill live up to these hopes? Reproductive health advocates had their work cut out for them to make it happen.

CHAPTER 2

"Thankful for Crumbs": The Fight to Expand Abortion Pill Access, 2000–2019

In the early days, we imagined that medication abortion was going to go into primary care. It was going to be family physicians and nurse practitioners who would provide this care, not abortion clinics.

Tracy A. Weitz, Director for the Susan Thompson Buffett
Foundation and co-founder and Director of the
Advancing New Standards in Reproductive Health

Abortion pill advocates had achieved a significant victory when the FDA approved mifepristone for use in the United States in September 2000, but getting the pills out to the women who needed them would prove to be an even more difficult task. Not only did advocates for mifepristone have to deal with the onerous restrictions placed on the medication by the FDA, but they had to negotiate with a conservative and costly medical system. Despite mainstream medicine having largely abandoned abortion care, which was offered mainly at specialized clinics, advocates hoped that a wider range of clinicians would offer medication abortion to their patients. Advocates organized efforts directed toward obstetrical and gynecological doctors, primary care providers, and advanced practice clinicians, but multiple barriers—including FDA restrictions on the medication, abortion stigma, and fear of anti-abortion harassment and violence—discouraged widespread availability of medication abortion for many years. Most medication abortions came to be offered in the same places as procedural abortions—in dedicated abortion clinics from clinicians who were already providing procedural abortion. As a result, these medications did not in fact significantly increase access to abortion, at least initially.[1] A year after the FDA approved mifepristone, the Kaiser Family Foundation reported that only 6 percent of gynecologists and 1 percent of general practice physicians reported that they had provided their patients with mifepristone.[2] A decade later, only 1 percent of medication abortions were done at private physicians' offices; the rest were done at abortion clinics.[3] Meanwhile, Republican states passed an increasing number of abortion restrictions, making abortion health care even more inaccessible and spurring activists to begin organizing to support women who self-induced their own abortions with medications. This chapter traces how and why mifepristone access remained limited after the FDA approved the drug, and how advocates fought to increase access, including persuading the FDA to eventually lift some of its restrictions on mifepristone.

In the early 2000s, public health advocates worked hard to encourage a wide range of clinicians to prescribe abortion pills, including not only doctors already offering procedural abortion, but also gynecologists, family medicine doctors, and advanced practice clinicians. The National Abortion Federation (NAF) and Planned Parenthood, funded by private foundations, rolled out trainings for use of abortion pills and publicized their availability.[4] In 2001, the Center for Reproductive Health Research and Policy at the University of California, San Francisco published a handbook with guidelines for how to provide medical abortion.[5] "We tried to push the least interventionist approach to the provision of that care," said Dr. Tracy Weitz, a co-author of the handbook. For example, the handbook said ultrasounds were not necessary. The handbook was distributed to all members of the American College of Obstetricians and Gynecologists.[6] However by 2000, ultrasounds were commonly used for procedural abortions, so many providers used them for medication abortion as well. Ultrasounds enabled providers to date pregnancies to ensure patients were within the FDA-approved gestational limit for taking mifepristone, but they were used for bureaucratic reasons as well. "Ultrasound had become standard practice in abortion clinics generally, not for safety reasons, but for scheduling reasons—to know exactly how far along somebody is so you can schedule people much faster and easier," said Weitz. "This is a way a clinic can manage its patient population and not necessarily a clinically significant tool."[7] The perception that ultrasounds were necessary for medication abortion contributed to some primary care clinics declining to provide medication abortion because they did not have ultrasound machines, which cost tens of thousands of dollars.

Abortion pill advocates also tried to encourage family care physicians to offer medication abortion. Even after the FDA approved medication abortion, very few fellowship programs offered medication abortion training for family medicine doctors. Dr. Eric Schaff had one at University of Rochester School of Medicine and so did Dr. Marji Gold at Montefiore Medical Center of the University Hospital for Albert Einstein College of Medicine in the Bronx. In 2004, Gold and others created RHEDI (Reproductive Health Education in Family Medicine) to encourage the formation of programs to train family medicine residents in reproductive health, with an emphasis on abortion. "The theory of change was that institutionalized abortion training for family medicine in residency programs would lead to advocacy inside institutions," said Weitz. "Then those professional advocates could change what is considered the standard of care or the standard for the scope of practice. Then they will articulate abortion as part of family practice and that will change malpractice carriers [to being willing to cover it]."[8] Between 2006 and 2020, RHEDI faculty trained over two thousand residents in both medication abortion and procedural abortion. Of those, 24 percent provided abortion after residency, as compared to only 3 percent of comparable family physicians without this training.[9]

But even if a family medicine doctor could get trained, they often faced barriers to offering this care. Dr. Emily Godfrey, who trained with Dr. Schaff between 2000 and 2002, explained: "The FDA requirements made it so difficult for primary care to offer medication abortion because you had to dispense it in your clinic. Your primary care clinic had to be a pharmacy. There was no way around not telling your administration that you're going to be dispensing mifepristone from your clinic. That really put the kibosh on it." When Godfrey went to practice at the University of Illinois in Chicago, she had to fight hard to be able to offer medication abortion. "It took meetings with the pharmacy, and it took all sorts of time to make it happen. It was just so hard. We've always been stretched. The fact that we can't write a prescription for it the way we do with every other medication is a huge impediment in primary care."[10] When Godfrey tried to help others offer this care, she faced more barriers. "There were so many bureaucratic barriers. I tried to help other family medicine clinics when I was in Chicago between 2003 and 2010. Chicago is a progressive town. Family docs wanted to offer this. I tried to help them, but sooner or later somebody up the line was somehow a religiously affiliated hospital or program. You find out that there's some agreement that occurred in 1973 after *Roe*, and somebody signed something saying this hospital will never do abortions."[11] Weitz explained, "there was never any real momentum to change family medicine to incorporate abortion."[12] Columbia University physician and researcher Carolyn Westhoff attributed these barriers to the corporatization of medical practice: "When I started in medical practice 70 percent of doctors were self-employed, and 30 percent of doctors worked for some entity where they got a salary like me working for Columbia. But now those numbers have flipped and probably changes more every day. In those larger entities, there's going to be somebody who objects to abortion. All kind of layers of administration have to agree with what I'm doing."[13]

Another group, the Abortion Access Project (AAP) run by Susan Yanow, worked in the early 2000s to recruit clinicians to offer medication abortion, particularly mid-level healthcare providers who were not physicians but who were qualified to perform medical activities typically performed by a physician (later called advanced practice providers). AAP identified states that allowed advanced practice clinicians to prescribe medications, and then hired people to recruit providers to offer abortion pills. AAP eventually had projects in seventeen states.[14] AAP hired reproductive health advocate Elisa Wells[15] to do this work in Alaska, where she tried to recruit people to prescribe abortion pills. "It was so hard. I think I got one, or maybe two. Most of them were in practice settings that wouldn't allow them to do it," said Wells. Some were at federally qualified health centers restricted from offering abortion care by the Hyde Amendment. Others were at religious organizations that blocked them from doing it. Even Planned Parenthood wouldn't do it initially, said Wells. "It was just really shocking how hard it was to get people to see the potential of these pills."[16] Planned Parenthood eventually added medication abortion when they opened a clinic in Fairbanks.

These efforts to expand access to medication abortion at a broad range of providers were not successful. "By the time mifepristone got approved in the US, the complete consolidation of abortion into clinics had happened, making it almost impossible for it to be offered in any other place," explained Weitz. "Planned Parenthood took advantage of medication abortion and had a massive expansion of its abortion services into their family planning clinics that had never done abortions. But that was the only place where there was any diffusion of medication abortion into non-abortion clinic settings."[17] Even doctors working at abortion clinics were resistant to offering medication abortion. Weitz explained: "Abortion providers didn't like medication abortion. They were like, 'I can do an abortion procedure in a couple of minutes. Why in the world would I do something that drags on for several days?'" Columbia University physician Carolyn Westhoff, who described mifepristone as a "disruptive technology," explained:

> All the various abortion clinics and other abortion providers had a whole workflow set up. Their business models were set up for doing procedural abortions. From the clinician point of view, there's really nothing to gain from doing medication abortion. You've got your schedule. You see all your cases. You go home at the end of the day. Everybody's taken care. You know you're gonna get paid. Mifepristone didn't have a billing code for a long time. I almost got in trouble for billing fraud because you couldn't figure out how to bill mifepristone because it didn't have its own code.[18]

Westhoff also said that doctors didn't want to stock an expensive medication in their office without knowing when they would get paid back. Procedural abortion gave physicians more control than medication abortion.

Research at the time showed that many clinicians had misconceptions about abortion pills—that they were complicated to prescribe, required extensive training and sophisticated backup services, or that hemorrhage was a common risk, which it is not. Others said there was no demand, although research showed that, given a choice, more than half of women chose medication over procedural abortion.[19] Clinicians worried that medication was less reliable or acceptable to patients. Meanwhile, professional organizations in non-reproductive health specialties did not provide guidance about how to use this new technology.[20] In 2003, Coeytaux, Moore, and Lillian Gelberg published an article in *Perspectives on Sexual and Reproductive Health* explaining the dilemma: "patients deserve to receive abortion care from their own provider, and medical abortion makes this feasible. However, neither US women nor their providers seem to have grasped this possibility. Clients assume that their providers 'do not do abortions' and therefore do not ask them for this method. As a result, providers are not experiencing a demand for the service."[21] Coeytaux, Moore, and Gelberg made recommendations for how to convince new medical providers to offer medication abortion, including getting information to generalists, improving access to training for primary care providers, and increasing demand. Otherwise, they warned, "we will have squandered the opportunity this new technology offers us to increase access to safe abortion for women everywhere."[22]

Researchers and advocates later argued that FDA restrictions on mifepristone "set the tone for widespread misperceptions about the complexity and safety of medication abortion."[23] The FDA imposed burdensome requirements to register with the drug manufacturer and dispense the medications themselves, which many were not willing to undertake. The FDA requirement that patients make multiple clinic visits increased the cost and burdens of providing medication abortion as well. Some insurance companies denied medical liability coverage to non-specialists, or charged cost-prohibitive rates for this coverage.[24] Many providers feared being labeled abortion providers and becoming subject to protests and violence.[25]

Despite this situation, many reproductive health advocates did not object to the FDA's tight restrictions on the medication. Francine Coeytaux, who worked at the Population Council at the time, explained: We said, "thank you very much FDA," when they gave us this horrible, horrible ruling. It's partly because everybody had already been through the wringer. We were thankful for crumbs. And then, over time, we forgot that we were given crumbs. We forgot that it was politically motivated. We just all adapted to trying to take advantage of what we were given.[26] Winikoff, however, remembers it differently. She said they started immediately on research to support loosening restrictions on mifepristone, acknowledging that the research often took years to complete so the process was slow. "We were always working on peeling off the restrictions. Like peeling a banana. One thing, then another thing."[27] Winikoff left the Population Council in 2003 to form Gynuity Health Projects. "The person who assumed the presidency of the Pop Council was scared of the work we were doing and didn't want us to do it," said Winikoff.[28]

Opinion research from the early 2000s revealed strong public support for abortion pills, bolstered by the fact that the medication was administered early in pregnancy. But research also showed that opposition to the medication was related to fear that the drug would "allow women to make hasty decisions about abortion without consulting family and friends." Researchers at the time suggested that "pro-choice advocates should emphasize that RU 486 is prescribed after consultation with a doctor."[29] This perspective, along with the election of anti-abortion conservative George W. Bush, may have fueled reproductive health advocates' reluctance to challenge the in-person distribution requirement for mifepristone in the 2000s. Bush appointed a strong abortion opponent, former Wisconsin Governor Tommy G. Thomson, to replace Donna Shalala as Secretary of Health and Human Services. Thomson promised to order a review of the FDA's approval of mifepristone.[30] He also announced that the Hyde Amendment restricting Medicaid funding for abortion applied to medication abortion and that state abortion restrictions would apply to medication abortion, including waiting periods, parental involvement laws, physician-only laws, and targeted regulation of abortion clinics, known as TRAP laws, which imposed expensive modifications to buildings and the purchase of expensive and unnecessary medical equipment.[31] These laws, combined with burdensome FDA restrictions on mifepristone, meant that few doctors who were not already offering abortion services could do so.

The application of the Hyde Amendment to medication abortion meant that Indigenous women were not able to access abortion pills through the Indian Health Service (IHS). The Hyde amendment did cover abortion for rape and incest, but the medications were not made available at IHS. In a survey conducted by the Native American Women's Health Education Resource Center (NAWHERC) in 2002, only 5 percent of the IHS Service Units contacted performed abortion procedures at their facilities and none of them had Mifeprex readily available for patient use.[32] The Hyde Amendment also blocked access to abortion pills for women serving in the US military and those working for the federal government.

Some conservative states passed laws specifically restricting the use of medication abortion. Michigan legislators, for example, passed a law prohibiting state-mandated abortion literature from including information about any procedure that uses a drug not specifically approved for use in an abortion. The FDA had approved misoprostol, the second drug used in medication abortions, as an ulcer drug and not as an abortifacient, so the law made medical abortion with misoprostol illegal.[33] The Center for Reproductive Rights (CRR) challenged the law and the state eventually settled the case, allowing providers to create their own abortion literature if there was no state-approved literature.[34] Abortion advocates focused most of their efforts on blocking or challenging new laws restricting medication abortion access, but California passed a law to encourage further research into mifepristone as a treatment for purposes other than abortion.[35] Meanwhile, activists pushed for increasing access on college campuses. FMF organized a campaign called "Prescribe Choice" to increase abortion access on campus.[36] In May of 2001, the National Abortion Federation launched a $2 million public education campaign on mifepristone, publishing ads in national magazines, including *Self* and *People*. The ads offered information on mifepristone as well as directed readers to a toll-free hotline and website.[37] Despite all of these efforts, the FDA restrictions on mifepristone meant that few doctors provided medication abortion, which remained largely limited to medical providers at abortion clinics, thereby not significantly increasing the number of places where women could access abortion.

Doctors' resistance to offering medication abortion increased when, in the early 2000s, several cases of the extraordinarily rare but universally fatal clostridium sordellii infection occurred in patients taking mifepristone and vaginal misoprostol. In 2003, the FDA launched an inquiry into the possible role of mifepristone in the death of a California woman, Holly Peterson. Concerned about how the FDA might react, the National Women's Health Network and the Public Citizen Health Research Group wrote to the FDA in early 2004, reminding the agency of the strong safety record of mifepristone.[38] In 2005, the FDA issued a public health warning about mifepristone/misoprostol-induced abortion and its association with C. sordellii-related deaths. In May of 2006, the CDC, FDA, and the National Institute of Allergy and Infectious Diseases held a joint scientific gathering on the deaths of four women after taking abortion medications. In response, Gynuity, Ipas, NAF, NWHN, and RHTP pressed the agency to fully investigate the cases.[39] Amy Allina, who was a staff member at NWHN at the time, explained: "NWHN used its FDA policy and public health expertise to hold agencies accountable for treating mifepristone fairly, with rigorous regulation and without subjecting it to extra scrutiny or unnecessary restrictions driven by abortion politics."[40] Mifepristone likely did not cause the clostridium sordellii infections, but these fatalities led to a shift away from vaginal administration of misoprostol to oral administration, despite increased gastrointestinal side effects.[41]

In the face of these headwinds, the use of medication for abortion as a percentage of all abortions increased slowly but steadily in the first seven years after the FDA approved mifepristone, from 1 percent in 2000 to 13 percent in 2007, according to the Centers for Disease Control data collection from thirty-three states.[42] Compared to countries in Europe, however, the United States lagged significantly behind adoption of medication abortion. In 2007, the percentage of all abortions done with medications was over 70 percent in Finland, 68 percent in Scotland, 58 percent in Switzerland, 50 percent in France, and 35 percent in England and Wales.[43]

Whereas in the early 2000s, few people knew about the abortion pills, by the 2010s, many people knew about them and wanted to use them. Michelle Cohen, who worked at abortion clinics in Mississippi and Texas between 2013 and 2018, spoke about what she perceived to be the reasons people sought out abortion pills: "I think a lot of it was their way of reconciling their guilt, their conscience, their fear, and the bullying from the antis, that it wasn't so much of an abortion if they took the pills versus getting a surgical abortion. In conversations I had with patients, their whole thing was, 'I just can't bring myself to have an abortion. It's really not an abortion to me if I take this pill.'"[44] Ironically, anti-abortion propaganda conflating emergency contraception and abortion pills may have contributed to this attitude. "A lot of people were confused because to the antis everything was abortion," said Cohen.[45]

Medication abortion access, however, varied by state. Cohen said that it was easier to get an appointment for medication abortion than surgical abortion in Mississippi, but not in Texas, where the law required four appointments with the same doctor for medication abortion, which was often difficult to schedule. "Where the pill was supposed to be an easier, more convenient option, anti-abortion policymakers in Texas made getting abortion pills treacherous and so stressful," said Cohen.[46] Economics also impacted decisions to use abortion pills, but in varying ways, according to Cohen:

> Here in Mississippi, abortion pills were still more expensive than surgical, but it was more convenient for providers. It was less time consuming to administer abortion pills than it was to do the surgical procedure, so you could service more patients with the pill than you can with surgical procedures. I love the reproductive rights movement, but we need to be real. We need to be honest about what was going on in the world. Capitalism is its own little monster, and so I think that may have been a force for some folks, the pressure to do the pill rather than surgical. I heard that was what was going down in some places. There were people who called me and told me that they were pressured, or they felt pressured, to take the pill route versus the surgical. They wanted the surgical, but they felt like it was being pushed on them to do the pills.[47]

Cohen's comments demonstrate how abortion pill access varied by state and across time, as did women's motivations for using them, and how different factors—including state law, clinic conditions, and economics—pressured women either to use abortion pills or not use them.

FDA RISK EVALUATION AND MITIGATION STRATEGY (REMS) AND MIFEPRISTONE RESEARCH

In September 2007, Congress passed the Food and Drug Administration Amendments Act of 2007, expanding the authority of the FDA to review and regulate medications and medical devices. Among other things, the Act created a new drug safety program called REMS, which allows the FDA to closely monitor medications considered to have serious safety concerns, in order to help ensure the benefits of the medication outweigh its risks.[48] A REMS requires four elements. First, a medication guide or patient package insert to promote safe and effective use. Second, a communication plan for healthcare providers, known as "Dear Healthcare Professional" letters with additional information about the REMS, and other educational materials directed toward the healthcare provider. Third, "elements to assure safe use" or ETASU, which might include provider or pharmacy certifications requirements, dispensing or administration information, patient monitoring, and/or patient enrollment into registries. Finally, the REMS requires an implementation system, which includes how ETASU will be enacted, along with requirements for monitoring and evaluating ETASU implementation by healthcare providers, pharmacists, and others. In June 2011, the FDA established a REMS program for mifepristone, incorporating the restrictions placed on the medication in 2000.[49]

Despite the REMS, medical research continued to show that mifepristone was safe and effective. Many researchers focused on new approaches to increase access to mifepristone for abortion, hoping their results could improve treatment. At the time the FDA approved mifepristone in 2000, research already showed that a lower dose of mifepristone was just as effective with fewer side effects, so many providers offered the lower dosage off label,[50] findings confirmed by later research.[51] Danco charged $270 for the three-tablet 600-milligram mifepristone dose, so lowering the dose to a 200-milligram dose made the medication much more affordable. Research also showed mifepristone was effective through sixty-three days of pregnancy, so some clinicians began offering medication abortion beyond the FDA's recommended forty-nine-day limit.[52] Subsequent research showed abortion pills were effective even later in pregnancy—through seventy days gestation[53] and eventually seventy-seven days.[54] The World Health Organization now says these medications can be used throughout pregnancy at different dosage levels.[55]

From the outset, most clinicians followed the science rather than the outdated FDA label in treating their patients.[56] By 2009, the off-label use of a 200-milligram dose of mifepristone and an 800-microgram dose of misoprostol through sixty-three days was routine in Great Britain, Sweden, and the United States, and endorsed in the guidelines of ACOG and NAF, as well as the Royal College of Obstetricians and Gynecologists and the World Health Organization.[57] FDA labels often lag behind the science because of the high cost of label changes for pharmaceutical companies. As a result, off-label use of medications—allowing physicians to use their professional judgment in treating patients—is a common practice in the United States.[58]

Research showed that misoprostol taken one day after mifepristone was just as effective as when the medications were taken two or three days apart.[59] Clinicians initially administered both medications in person, so a shorter window between administration of mifepristone and misoprostol could expand the number of days of the week clinicians could provide medication abortion to include Thursdays and Fridays. Research also showed that women could safely self-administer misoprostol at home, which not only reduced the need for a second in-clinic appointment but could reduce the cost of medication abortion.[60] This also gave women more flexibility for scheduling an abortion and allowed them to take the medication in a location where they were prepared for the cramping and bleeding, rather than experiencing these on their way home from the doctor's office.[61] These findings were consistent with research from around the world showing women could successfully use abortion medications at home on their own.[62]

Other research showed that misoprostol taken vaginally or buccally (absorbed in the mouth between the cheek and gum) had fewer side effects, such as nausea and vomiting, than if a patient swallowed the medication, because it allowed for a sustained level of misoprostol in the blood rather than the quick peak that rapidly metabolized by swallowing the medication.[63] Research from abroad showed that doses of 50 milligrams of mifepristone and 200 micrograms of misoprostol were effective in pregnancies of less than thirty-five days, with less vaginal bleeding and fewer side effects.[64]

Research on using telemedicine to prescribe abortion pills showed it could be done in a manner that was highly acceptable to patients and providers.[65] Other studies showed that a wider range of medical providers than just doctors could safely offer medication abortion[66] and that pharmacies could safely dispense mifepristone.[67] Advocates would eventually use this research to ask the FDA to modify the REMS to increase access to medication abortion.

Mifepristone became known as an abortion drug, but studies suggested other possible uses, including as a treatment for fibroid tumors—non-cancerous growths of the uterus that often appear during childbearing years.[68] This common condition, which afflicts millions of women in the United States, causes heavy periods, severe pain, and difficulty conceiving. In the early 2000s, researchers at the University of Rochester conducted studies on the use of mifepristone to treat fibroids, using mifepristone they had obtained from Larry Lader of ARM[69] and later directly from Danco.[70] Between 2003 and 2011, Dr. Eric Schaff, Dr. Steven Eisinger, Dr. Kevin Fiscella, and other researchers at the University of Rochester published six peer-reviewed articles showing mifepristone was very effective for treating fibroids. The research was supported by grants from the National Institutes of Health. Eisinger described what he observed when he first gave mifepristone to women with fibroids: "Right away, it was obvious. It was a great success. The fibroids shrunk. The bleeding stopped. Patients' quality of life improved dramatically. They felt better, had more energy, more color in their cheeks. They would go about life with a lot more enthusiasm. The scores on quality of life were so dramatically different that we actually considered the possibility that mifepristone was a mood enhancer." Before treatment, many of the patients were anemic due to heavy bleeding from fibroids. "Their blood counts went up dramatically," reported Dr. Eisinger, who said as little as 2 milligrams of mifepristone daily was effective for reducing fibroids.[71] According to Dr. Eisinger, fibroids have progesterone receptors that may contribute to their growth. Mifepristone can block these receptors, which may be why the medication shrinks the fibroids. At the time, the only treatment for fibroids was surgery, including hysterectomies.

Despite promising results, the researchers were not able to obtain funding to continue the research. "Under normal circumstances, if you've got these kind of results from a trial like this, you would do a phase three trial, and it would be funded by a pharmaceutical company," said Fiscella.[72] Eisinger said Danco was interested and supportive of the research: "Danco asked us what it would cost to do the 'big' study that would allow FDA approval of mife for fibroids. After much number-crunching we told them $28 million. They offered us $300,000! It was all they had."[73] Fiscella said, "I think it's likely that they were not able to raise the capital."[74] Anti-abortion politics as well as violence and boycott threats may have discouraged any other pharmaceutical company from co-sponsoring the trials, said Fiscella. "I suspect the stigma of mifepristone probably made it a challenge to partner with other pharmaceuticals. Often times you do that, co-sponsor this. This wouldn't have been a lot of money for some of these giant pharmaceuticals. There was nothing else on the market. It was an important niche. If it wasn't mifepristone, I think it would have been a slam dunk."[75] Without funding, they had to drop the research. "We wanted to sanitize the reputation of mifepristone," Eisinger later said. "We wanted to make it harder for the anti-abortionists to demand banning the drug on the grounds that it was dangerous or something like that. If we could find a useful non-abortion application, that would be helpful."[76] No one in the United States subsequently pursued research on mifepristone for the treatment of fibroids, but researchers in other countries did, including India, China, Italy, Japan, and Nigeria.[77]

The REMS meant that women could not access mifepristone for off-label use to treat fibroids either. Dr. Fiscella said women in the study begged him to continue the treatment. "I had so many emails from the women in the study, who said, 'How can I get this medication after the trial?' Over and over again, we had to say, 'We're sorry. The drug is highly restricted to pregnancy termination. It's not available in the United States.' That's all we could say," said Fiscella. "The women were very disappointed."[78] According to Dr. Fiscella, the research was strong enough to support prescribing the medication off label to treat fibroids, but that was not possible because the FDA blocked pharmacies from dispensing mifepristone—including compounding pharmacies that could make pills in the appropriate dosage to treat fibroids. The medication only came in 200-milligram capsules, but the fibroids dosage was 5 milligrams. "If mifepristone were prescribed like any other medication, if it didn't have all of these REMS restrictions, compounding pharmacies would have been happy to put it into powder and create capsules for 5-milligram doses and give them to patients under a doctor's order. That would have made a lot of women happy."[79]

Some research has also suggested that mifepristone could be helpful for treating endometriosis, where tissue that normally lines the inside of the uterus—called the endometrium—grows outside the uterus.[80] Endometriosis afflicts an estimated 10 percent of reproductive-age women. Common treatments include laparoscopic surgery—involving the cutting and removing of endometrial tissue or destroying it with a laser beam or electric current—and hysterectomies. Mifepristone could have been a non-surgical alternative for treating endometriosis with the potential to reduce unnecessary hysterectomies. But the FDA REMS restrictions limited research and use of the medication to treat endometriosis. Other research indicated that mifepristone could be effective in treating depression, including postpartum depression, which affects one in nine new mothers each year,[81] and treating Gulf War illness,[82] which increases risk of heart disease, stroke, and type 2 diabetes.[83] Some evidence also indicated mifepristone could be an effective form of contraception and was an emergency contraceptive.[84] Yet, despite mifepristone's promise to provide women with health-enhancing treatments, the FDA restrictions stymied the development of the medication for these uses. "Most new applications of existing drugs are discovered and even developed by physicians using drugs off-label, but that path is not easily accessible because of the REMS," said Francine Coeytaux.[85]

Physicians at Stanford Medical School, however, were able to conduct research on use of mifepristone to treat Cushing syndrome. Cushing syndrome is when a benign tumor causes the pituitary gland to make too much of a hormone (called adrenocorticotropic hormone or ACTH) that stimulates the production and release of cortisol from the adrenal glands. The adrenal glands help control heart rate, blood pressure, and other important body functions. Excess cortisol causes problems with the body's hormone balance and leads to high blood sugar in patients with Cushing syndrome. As a hormone receptor blocker, mifepristone blocks the absorption of cortisol to restore hormonal balance. In 2012, the FDA approved mifepristone for adult patients with Cushing syndrome who have type 2 diabetes or glucose intolerance and have failed surgery or are not candidates for surgery. The Silicon Valley-based drug company Corcept Therapeutics began marketing mifepristone as the medication Korlym to control high blood sugar in patients with Cushing syndrome.[86] In 2018, they were charging $550 for one 300-milligram tablet of mifepristone.[87] Korlym was not subject to a REMS or in-person distribution, despite the fact that it was taken daily in higher doses than the single 200-milligram dose of Mifeprex. As Policy Advocacy Director at the National Women's Health Network Sarah Christopherson later noted, "the risk to making mifepristone widely available for abortion has nothing to do with health and everything to do with politics."[88]

SELF-INDUCED ABORTION?

The election of Barack Obama in 2008, and the surge of the rightwing Tea Party movement, led to a wave of abortion restrictions in conservative states. In 2011, in the run up to the 2012 presidential elections, conservative states passed a record number of abortion restrictions: ninety-two new restrictions on access to abortion services in twenty-four states, shattering the previous record of thirty-four restrictions set in 2005.[89] These restrictions included abortion bans, waiting periods, ultrasound requirements, insurance coverage bans, targeted regulations of abortion providers, and prohibitions on telemedicine abortion. Although early gestation bans were unenforceable under *Roe v. Wade*, high numbers of abortion restrictions continued to pass in subsequent years (see Figure 2.1).

In light of these growing restrictions, reproductive health advocates began to research and organize around "self-induced abortion."[90] They initially focused on the use of misoprostol alone for abortion. The use of prostaglandins for inducing abortion was discovered in the 1960s by Dr. Marc Bydgeman at the Karolinska Institutet in the Netherlands. Misoprostol for abortion was first widely used in the late 1980s by women in Brazil, where abortion was severely restricted. In 1986, Brazil approved Cytotec—the brand name for misoprostol—for treatment of ulcers. When women discovered that misoprostol caused abortion, they requested it from pharmacies for this purpose. Gynecologists and obstetricians supported this use because of the reduction of morbidity and mortality due to illegal and unsafe abortion, often done by the introduction of caustic substances into the uterus or use of knitting needles

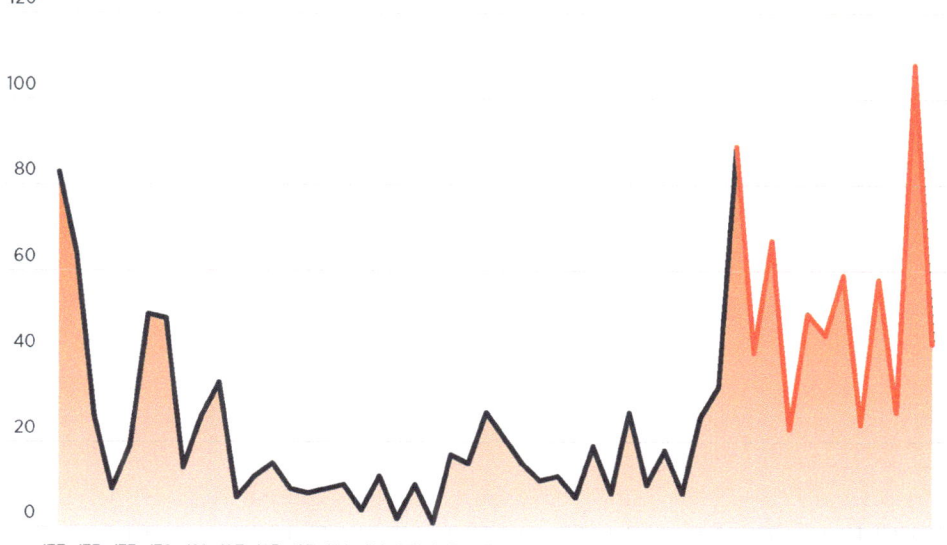

FIGURE 2.1: US states passed an accelerating number of abortion restrictions after the election of President Barack Obama in 2008 (courtesy of Guttmacher).[230]

to dislodge a pregnancy. In response, and under pressure from the Catholic church, the Brazilian government began to restrict Cytotec in the early 1990s.[91] Nevertheless, knowledge about misoprostol spread across Latin America and around the globe.[92] In November of 1990, women's rights activists from across Latin America met in Argentina to share the knowledge about misoprostol for medical abortions. Delegates from the United States attended.[93] Shortly after, reports circulated of self-induced abortion with misoprostol in immigrant communities in the United States, including a cross-sectional study published in 2000 of 610 women from the Dominican Republic in New York City showing that 37 percent (225) admitted familiarity with the use of misoprostol as an abortifacient and 5 percent (29) reported personal use of misoprostol.[94] By 1999, misoprostol was available in over sixty countries worldwide for as little as thirty-five cents per 200-microgram tablet.[95]

Reproductive health advocate Susan Yanow at the Abortion Access Project (later named Provide) read this research and also heard about people using misoprostol to self-induce abortion in the United States. "I knew that people were getting pills in bodegas in East Boston. I was curious about it. I wanted to learn more, so we had several meetings," said Yanow, who was also involved with the international organization Women on Waves. Founded by a Dutch physician named Rebecca Gomperts, Women on Waves provided abortion pills to women living in countries where abortion was illegal by sailing to the international waters near these nations and transporting women out to the ships.[96] The Abortion Access Project convened a Misoprostol Alone Working Group between 2004 and 2010, which included Ibis Reproductive Health, Gynuity Health Projects, National Latina Institute for Reproductive Health, and later, the Center for Reproductive Rights. The Working Group sparked several research projects, developed talking points, and began to raise awareness about self-induced abortion in the United States. The Working Group also discussed whether it was ethical to recommend self-induced abortion with misoprostol given it was not considered the "gold standard"—that is, clinic-based medical care with mifepristone and misoprostol.[97] Ibis Reproductive Health and the Office of Population Health at Princeton University developed a website, www.medicationabortion.com, in the early 2000s, providing information on three early abortion regimens, including misoprostol alone, in multiple languages. People from 208 countries used the website, but over one-third of visitors to the website in 2009 were from the United States and Mexico. Google search trends also revealed an increasing number of searches for "Cytotec," the brand name for misoprostol, from people in the United States over this period.[98] Meanwhile, research on misoprostol alone showed high levels of effectiveness. In 2007, a systematic review of published research found that the efficacy of misoprostol alone ranged from 84 to 96 percent.[99]

In several states, police and prosecutors charged women with crimes for using medications to self-induce abortions. In 2004, South Carolina authorities arrested a twenty-two-year-old undocumented migrant farmworker, Gabriella Flores, for taking misoprostol sent to her by her sister in Mexico to end a sixteen-week pregnancy. At the time, misoprostol was widely available from pharmacies in Latin America.[100] Prosecutors initially charged her with murder. Flores spent four months in jail before the charges against her were reduced to violating a ban on "illegal abortions."[101] Then in early 2007, authorities in Massachusetts arrested a teenaged immigrant woman, Amber Abreu, for using misoprostol she had obtained from her sister in the Dominican Republic. Abreu was indicted for procuring a miscarriage.[102]

In response to these cases, the organization Provide commissioned the CRR to conduct legal research on laws in Illinois, New York, South Carolina, and Texas that could be used against people who self-induce an abortion. CRR identified a wide range of state and federal, civil and criminal laws that could be used to target women self-inducing abortion. In response, Gynuity and the RHTP co-hosted a meeting in New York City in August 2009 to examine the legal issues related to women's use of misoprostol outside of the formal medical system.[103] The meeting convened twenty-three medical providers, lawyers, women's health advocates, researchers, and policymakers. The meeting generated creative strategies to reduce the possibility of criminal prosecution of women who self-induce an abortion, including educating the legal and medical communities, the media, and women themselves, as well as legislative and policy advocacy.[104] In addition to educating people about the use of misoprostol, Winikoff said she hoped the discussion of using misoprostol alone for abortion would put pressure on Danco to reduce the price of mifepristone: "if people know there's a competing thing, even if it's not quite as good, at some price point, you begin to lose people."[105] A 2010 study revealed that between 6 and 12 percent of pregnant women surveyed in clinic waiting rooms in Boston, San Francisco, New York, and a city in Texas had tried to self-induce abortion, with higher rates in cities along the United States–Mexico border.[106]

Between 2009 and 2011 with grant funding, Yanow conducted trainings on misoprostol in the Rio Grande Valley of Texas. She created a manual about how people were safely using misoprostol for self-induced abortion. She trained over seventy people, from young clinic defense activists to people from abortion funds, and then she trained another forty community health workers (promotoras). She also conducted research on follow-up care for people self-inducing abortions.[107] In the following years, Yanow worked to educate the reproductive health and rights communities about self-induced abortion, presenting at professional conferences, such as the NAF annual meeting, as well as training a wide range of groups about self-induced abortion, including the National Network of Abortion Funds. "My goal was to bring our movement to the recognition that what we then called self-induced abortion was potentially a revolutionary method of ensuring reproductive justice," said Yanow.[108] Research published in 2010 based on surveys of 9,493 patients at 95 facilities reported that 1.2 percent of women obtaining abortion reported having ever used misoprostol on their own to "bring back" their period or end a pregnancy and 1.4 percent reported using other substances, such as vitamin C or herbs.[109] Reports of criminalization also indicated the growing prevalence of self-induced abortion. In 2012, a Pennsylvania mother Jennifer Whalen was criminally prosecuted for ordering abortion pills online for her 16-year-old daughter, who used them in the early weeks of unplanned pregnancy. She could not afford to take her daughter to the nearest clinic, seventy-five miles away. Whalen was sentenced to nine to eighteen months in jail.[110]

Despite the risk of criminalization, increasing abortion restrictions generated further organizing on self-induced abortion. In June of 2013, Texas Republicans introduced a bill that would have shut down most of the abortion clinics in the state. Rep. Wendy Davis staged a thirteen-hour filibuster to block the bill from passage. During her filibuster, President Barack Obama tweeted his support, intensifying interest and support. A live stream of the filibuster on YouTube attracted more than 150,000 viewers.[111] A similar bill later passed, leading to the closure of more than half the clinics in the state.

At the time, immigrant women were obtaining misoprostol within their communities, said Diana Lugo-Martinez, who was Senior Director of Community Engagement Programs at the National Latina Institute for Reproductive Justice between 2013 and 2017. Undocumented women in the Rio Grande Valley who could not afford abortion health care in the United States and could not travel across the border to obtain abortion pills in Mexico because of their immigration status were able to buy misoprostol in community flea markets. Lugo-Martinez explained:

> It was a matter of on some levels access and on some levels, community practice. We had a tradition of community healing cultures. There might not necessarily be a culture of accessing care from doctors. For example, part of my family is from Puerto Rico and given the devastating impact of sterilization and experimentation on our communities, folks did not trust doctors. So you find other avenues of care. In the Dominican Republic, they had the community health care worker model that comes from the developing world because folks could not make it to the one town that has the hospital.[112]

In the news coverage about the Texas legislation, *The New York Times* quoted a community educator at the National Latina Institute for Reproductive Health saying, "The only option left for many women will be to go get those pills at a flea market. Some of them will end up in the E.R."[113] Diana Lugo-Martinez, who was at the National Latina Institute of Reproductive Health at the time, believed this led to Immigration and Customs Enforcement (ICE) raids on the community. "When you shine a spotlight on a particular community, a particular access point for that community, so that more people are aware, there's a detrimental impact on our most marginalized communities," said Lugo-Martinez.[114]

The new Texas law led Susan Yanow and Marlene Gerber Fried to convene a secretive meeting in Texas in October 2013 to discuss the future of abortion access. Sponsored by the Civil Liberties and Public Policy Program at Hampshire College, the meeting was organized to offer support to people on the front lines in Texas. It included providers, activists, and people from abortion funds from Texas and South Dakota, where advocates were also facing draconian restrictions. "We felt like we needed to have a conversation that was inside the family about what things people can do, what people need support for, what people were prepared to do, and what were the limits of the law," said Fried. "It was a moment where medical abortion was not well accepted and certainly not self-managed medical abortion. I think it shifted people's thinking about what was possible. I feel like we were softening the ground within a movement where you would have thought this ground would already be softened, but it wasn't yet."[115]

Two months later, on December 4, 2013, advocates with backgrounds in the global women's health movement organized a meeting in Washington, DC, to share what they knew about the self-use of pills to safely end an unwanted pregnancy. The organizers of the meeting were Francine Coeytaux, who was at the Public Health Institute; Leila Hessini of the global reproductive health organization Ipas; and Amy Allina and Kate Ryan of NWHN. The meeting brought together twenty-nine advocates, researchers, and community-based activists from ten US states and the Netherlands to the offices of the Association of Reproductive Health Professionals for a "strategic conversation about how to ensure that women in the US have the information, resources, and support they need to use abortion pills safely."[116]

At the meeting, advocates discussed the history of self-induced abortion, lessons from other countries, and organizing around misoprostol in the United States. They discussed the research on self-induction in the United States,[117] gaps in research, and areas for future research. Participants brainstormed about what to call self-induced abortion so as to be informative but not stigmatizing, and debated whether misoprostol alone was substandard care compared to the mifepristone/misoprostol regimen.[118] They then discussed internet sources for misoprostol, including Women on Web—a website selling abortion pills to women in 102 countries where safe abortion services were not available. Despite not serving the United States, the website had recently experienced a dramatic increase in searches and questions from people in the United States. Wells presented the findings from "Surfing for Abortion," a report on research about the availability of abortion pills on the internet. The report recommended improving access to online information about misoprostol as a harm reduction strategy. Harm reduction strategies work to lessen the negative consequences associated with criminalized behaviors, such as needle and syringe programs for drug users or condoms for sex workers. In the context of abortion, this would include identifying reliable sources for misoprostol and informing people about the legal implications of self-inducing abortion in the United States.[119] Lynn Paltrow of National Advocates for Pregnant Women presented information on arrests of women self-inducing abortions.

Participants then shared ideas for future action. They discussed how to publicize information on self-induced abortion without causing a crackdown on availability of medications or prosecution of women who use abortion pills. They brainstormed about advance prescriptions for misoprostol and adding the medication to collaborative practice agreements with pharmacies. They discussed using a train-the-trainer model to educate people about self-induced abortion and organizing a "red tent network" for women to support each other through the process. On the legal front, they proposed developing a network of attorneys to represent women arrested for self-inducing abortion and a legal defense fund to defend them. They also discussed the need for educating healthcare providers on what self-induction looks like and how to provide follow-up care.[120] Many of these ideas would become a reality in subsequent years.

The next year, Coeytaux and Wells intensified their efforts to find ways to increase access to abortion pills. Wells said she was inspired to do this work when she read a study published by Coeytaux and others at the Public Health Institute and Ipas on community-based organizations sharing misoprostol information in two countries with restrictive abortion laws, Kenya and Tanzania. Twenty-eight community groups were given small grants to disseminate information on the correct use of misoprostol for both postpartum hemorrhaging and abortion, and they were connected to pharmacies selling misoprostol. The groups developed numerous creative strategies to reach diverse audiences and ensure access to misoprostol pills. The groups attributed their success to having addressed the use of misoprostol for both indications and to using a harm reduction approach to frame their advocacy. The study concluded that "even where abortion is legally restricted and socially stigmatized, community-based organizations can publicly and openly share information about misoprostol and refer it to women by using innovative and effective strategies, without political backlash," and that communities were eager for this information.[121]

After reading this study, Wells called up Coeytaux and said to her, "This is the most exciting thing I've seen in years. Why can't we do something like this in the US?!"[122] That led to the formation of Plan C. A student working with them, Victoria Nichols, came up with the name Plan C. Whereas Plan B *prevented* pregnancy, mifepristone and misoprostol were something you could take when Plan B didn't work. "We purposely chose a name that didn't automatically equate with abortion to leave open the possibility of menstrual regulation and period pills," said Wells.[123] Plan C would work to raise awareness about abortion pills, recruit more US providers to offer medication abortion, and inform people about affordable access to abortion pills from abroad. The organization would come to play an important role in increasing access to abortion pills through telemedicine and online suppliers as states tightened restrictions on medical providers in the United States, especially after the Supreme Court reversed constitutional abortion rights in June of 2022.

In their work to increase access to abortion pills, Coeytaux and Wells drew upon experience they shared in their years-long campaign to increase awareness and acceptance of emergency contraception, create a dedicated emergency contraception product (later called Plan B), and win FDA over-the-counter approval for it. In advocating for abortion pills, they would draw on successful strategies they had used in the emergency contraception campaign, including a major, ongoing media campaign to raise public awareness, working directly with healthcare providers to educate and reassure them, developing public- and private-sector collaborations, obtaining funding to achieve their goals, conducting a large-scale demonstration project, obtaining ACOG support and FDA approval, and making access easier through advance prescription as well as phone and pharmacy prescription. In these ways, advocates successfully moved emergency contraception "from secret to shelf."[124] A report by Coeytaux and two other advocates explained their strategy:

> The overarching reason for the success to date is that activists began with what was intrinsically a very good idea and then were able to collaborate on multiple fronts to overcome blockages and carry the idea to fruition. To bring the method to market required activists to set the snowball rolling and keep it rolling forward. It took a combination of women's advocates, providers, entrepreneurs, legal and regulatory fighters and the foundation world, working together from all different angles and willing to take risks.[125]

They highlighted an important lesson learned: "We learned that our fears—fears of opposition and backlash—may have held back advances unnecessarily. Many of the activists were nervous or afraid of what the anti-choice movement would do and some admit having let fear influence their willingness to move forward." They summed it up: "Be Bold. Give women the information and let them decide."[126] The FDA eventually moved emergency contraception over the counter. Coeytaux and Wells used this extremely successful blueprint in their fight to increase abortion pill access.

Coeytaux and Wells were further inspired to work on increasing access to abortion pills when they were in Ethiopia in 2014, conducting research on treating postnatal hemorrhage with misoprostol. They knew that pharmacies sold abortion pills, so they tried to buy some. Wells explained what happened next:

> We sent our female colleague in and said, "See if you can get abortion pills." She came out five or ten minutes later and she had a pack. They cost six or seven dollars. Well, we were standing there together just in awe. The pharmacists gave her a few instructions about how to use it, which was good, and then we saw it was a DKT[127] brand so we knew it was a good product. We were standing there on the street of this little city, saying, "How is it that in this resource-poor country that is really stretched for health care and resources, that this product could be available, whereas in our country it's not available in this way?" It was basically over

the counter, or a little bit behind the counter because they had to talk to the pharmacist to get it. That was really the genesis of the idea to move forward and to do more.[128]

In the United States at the time, abortion pills were available only from certified doctors, who usually charged between $500 and $700 for them and required multiple in-person appointments. "The discrepancy between what I knew was possible and what was happening here in the US motivated me to found Plan C," said Coeytaux.[129] "Everywhere else you can get these mailed to you. Why can't we?"[130] The first dedicated product containing both mifepristone and misoprostol pills called Medabon had launched in Nepal in 2007 and was registered in forty countries by 2016, but a dedicated product was not available in the United States.[131]

In 2015, Coeytaux, along with Leila Hessini of Ipas and Amy Allina of NWHN, published a paper calling for "bold action to meet women's needs: putting abortion pills in U.S. women's hands."[132] They made two proposals: first, eliminate the FDA's medically unsupported restrictions on access to mifepristone and, second, promote the off-label use of misoprostol alone. Coeytaux and her colleagues asked, "Why are we not telling women about this safe and effective method?" They argued:

> We realize just how audacious our proposal is. However, women are paying the price for our current timidity. We believe it is time to use this potentially game-changing technology to facilitate women's agency and autonomy, reduce barriers to care, and improve health outcomes. And maybe, just maybe, by putting these pills in women's hands, we can help to reframe the way people think about abortion—toward a process managed by and controlled by women.[133]

But many women's health advocates resisted these proposals. Some argued misoprostol alone lowered the standard of care. Coeytaux, Hessini, and Alina countered by noting the insurmountable barriers to accessing mifepristone experienced by many US women. To those concerned about health risks of misoprostol alone, they noted the likelihood of being harmed by misoprostol was very low and easily mitigated. They acknowledged some legal risk, especially in restrictive states, but noted that off-label use was both legal and common in the United States, making a parallel to off-label use of birth control pills as emergency contraception before the FDA approved Plan B. Through Plan C, Coeytaux hoped to help the United States catch up with the rest of the world:

> Because of these REMS, we were left behind the rest of the world. We continued to think that it was okay and we didn't double check. That's what the idea for Plan C was: to bring back the evidence to the US and force all of us in the US to recognize that we had put our blinders on and we moved forward. We did the best we could with the blinders that we had. Then it was time to take off the blinders.[134]

But Coeytaux faced an uphill battle convincing people in the reproductive rights movement to take these bold steps. When she met with a coalition of state-based law centers, the reactions were mixed. "Within our group of state-based law centers, there was a span of opinions, from really risk-averse people, to the people who were saying, 'Great, let's make this happen,'" said Jenifer McKenna, the executive director of the Alliance: State Advocates for Women's Rights & Gender Equality. "There were people who were worried that Francine was putting too much information on the website, that she was putting the people involved at risk. People who were more attached to institutional and clinical expertise were concerned that the legal landscape was too uncertain."[135]

In mid-2015, the RHTP commissioned Coeytaux and Wells to write a research-based white paper on how to apply the lessons learned from emergency contraception to "create new paths to abortion care."[136] Released in July 2016, the white paper focused on "self-induced abortion" using misoprostol alone, which they described as a "powerful tool for expanding access to abortion care options." Drawing on harm-reduction models and self-help frameworks, Coeytaux and Wells suggested misoprostol for early abortion "may be the new 'best kept secret'" and called this method a "potentially game-changing technology for women's health."[137] The RHTP white paper, called "The Tale of Two Methods," compared emergency contraception to misoprostol, describing the key similarities and differences. Coeytaux and Wells noted that the medications were similar in that they were both easy to use, prescribed off label, and required medical providers to "let go of control of the product." Off-label use, which posed liability concerns, required educating clinicians about how to prescribe the medications off label. They were both viewed as a second-tier choice—neither had pharmaceutical company interest and both were seen as associated with sexual irresponsibility and stigma. The white paper also explained the key differences between emergency contraception and misoprostol for abortion. The different challenges were legal restrictions on abortion and the complexity of the regimens and need for follow-up care. Other differences provided new opportunities, including new communication platforms (e.g. the internet and social media); new dispensing options, including online websites that sell pills and telehealth services; women already leading the way on misoprostol use for abortion; and new allies, including the robust reproductive justice movement.

In conclusion, Coeytaux and Wells made several recommendations. First, they recommended supporting women's self-care with misoprostol by raising awareness about the option through public education campaigns, providing access to reliable and legitimate medical and legal information about misoprostol, and facilitating self-access to the medication by sharing information about sources of supply, identifying and verifying online services that ship misoprostol to the United States, and establishing alternative supply mechanisms such as pill banks. Their second recommendation was to facilitate access to misoprostol through the medical community, including advance prescription, pharmacy access, and telemedicine. Finally, they recommended pursuing the development of a dedicated product packaged for abortion use.[138] In their conclusion, Coeytaux and Wells summed up their approach:

> We believe achieving meaningful access to medication abortion will necessitate a radically different approach, one that acknowledges that given adequate information and access to a product, women can use the method safely and effectively without intervention from a healthcare provider. In this approach, providers and advocates must see themselves as supporters of women rather than providers of services. Although this paradigm shift to give women the means to care for their own reproductive health will likely unsettle some providers and regulators, it has already been proven feasible by women around the world.[139]

These recommendations went too far for many reproductive healthcare providers and advocates, but became the blueprint for Plan C's approach to mifepristone and misoprostol.

As the reality of self-induced abortion became clearer, many advocates had increasing concerns about the legal implications. In 2015, the Center on Reproductive Rights and Justice at Berkeley Law School sponsored the formation of the Self-Induced Abortion (SIA) Legal Team, a consortium of organizations with the goal of "using law and policy tools to ensure people throughout the U.S. can end their own pregnancies outside of the formal healthcare system with dignity, safe from the threat of arrest for themselves or anyone who assists them."[140] The SIA Legal Team advocated for expanding access to reliable information about abortion medications, halting the criminalization of people self-inducing abortions, improving self-help or community-based access to abortion medications, and building legal support for people self-inducing abortions.

The same year, two reproductive justice activists, Pamela Merritt and Erin Matson, formed Reproaction, a "left-flank culture change organization" working to increase access to abortion and advance reproductive justice through "strategic communications, opposition research and community organizing," including non-violent direct action.[141] "We knew then, in 2015, that medication abortion was going to be key," said Merritt, "that it was a liberating reality that Europe had been experiencing for many, many years, and that Americans should have access to. The anti-abortion movement was terrified because you can't stop medication abortion. The entire region of South America and Central America proved that medication abortion is wonderful and as liberating, in my view, as the vote. It takes the power away from the healthcare industry, away from providers, and away from legislators, and puts it in the hands of the pregnant person. It is a liberation tool."[142] Reproaction worked to educate the public as well as legislators, policymakers, activists, and progressive people about self-managed abortion with pills and the World Health Organization protocol for abortion pills. Susan Yanow trained Reproaction staff to share information about self-induced abortion, and the organization shared this information at community meetings and house parties in Missouri, Illinois, Arkansas, and elsewhere. Merritt explained:

> We had organizers on the ground who would contact an individual who had a network of friends. They would organize the food and beverages and open up their home. I did one training in a Union office. I did one in a sex-positive coffee shop. The only thing we were making sure was that the people who were coming to the house party were properly vetted so that we could ensure safety. We were well trained in how to talk about self-managed abortion with pills as information sharing rather than advice.[143]

In this way, Reproaction prepared for the impending fall of *Roe v. Wade*. Merritt later joined Medical Students for Reproductive Choice, which worked to train medical students in abortion in over thirty countries, including countries where abortion was illegal.

In 2015, RHTP brought together several organizations to discuss self-induced abortion, including the SIA Legal Team, the National Institute for Reproductive Health, Vision First, Reproaction, and Physicians for Reproductive Health. Coeytaux and Wells presented a paper on strategies used to increase access to emergency contraceptive pills and how these strategies could be used to expand access to misoprostol.[144] At the meeting, they decided to recruit a broader, more diverse range of organizations to participate in the conversations. Amy Allina, who coordinated the meetings, explained:

> Our instinct, which has since been proven correct, was that people who face the greatest barriers to care are going to be among the most likely to self-manage. We know now that people self-manage both as a proactive choice, because it's what they want, and because they face barriers to care. But still those communities where the barriers are greatest have a higher prevalence of self-managing. But then the other reason was that we knew the big risk with self-managed abortion was criminalization and we knew who was most likely to be criminalized. One of the things that made people hesitate to talk about self-managed abortion—to shine a light on it as a path to ending pregnancy—was a fear of increasing the risk of criminalization. None of those organizations wanted to be out there doing that without having visible vocal leadership from communities that are at greatest risk for criminalization across the board for any pregnancy outcome.[145]

Therefore, they reached out to organizations representing women of color, immigrant women, and low-income and poor women, and recruited several organizations to participate, including the National Latina Institute for Reproductive Health, Advocates for Youth, the National Network of Abortion Funds, the National Asian Pacific American Women's Forum, and the independent abortion provider Whole Woman's Health. This group later became the "Generative Learning Community" (GLC) for "self-managed abortion," as they decided to call it. Many thought the label "self-induced" was too medical, while "self-managed" had a sense of personal empowerment.[146] This group focused on, as Allina described, "working to shift the public conversation and the public narrative about self-managed abortion, instead of talking about it as a dangerous way to end a pregnancy and as a negative outcome of restrictions on clinical care, to having people understand it as an act of defiance and something that can be perfectly safe, effective, and supported as something that can be done in community."[147]

The risk of criminalization, however, loomed. In May 2016, a 40-year-old web developer named Ursula Wing launched a website selling abortion pills. Years before, Wing had purchased abortion pills online from abroad and used them herself. In 2012, after she wrote about her experience on her blog, *Macrobiotic Stoner*, she received responses from many women requesting information about how she did it, which inspired Wing to start her business. She ordered the medications from India and created a web page called "My Secret Bodega," where she sold mifepristone and misoprostol for $85 with expedited shipping, billing her customers for jewelry. She mailed inexpensive jewelry in a shipping envelope with a packet of pills taped behind a hidden panel. The return address read "Fatima's Bead Basket." In 2017, when Plan C evaluated eleven websites selling abortion pills, Wing's website performed the best. When Plan C published their results, Wing's weekly orders spiked from just a few to sixty a week. During two years in business, Wing served thousands of customers across the country.[148]

But then in February 2018, a Wisconsin man named Jeffrey Smith was arrested for allegedly giving his pregnant partner mifepristone he had purchased from Wing. The FDA learned about Wing and began an investigation. In June 2018, the FBI showed up with a search warrant at Wing's apartment. She was accused of supplying abortion-inducing pills without a prescription to customers in the United States. Wing was unrepentant: "I want some copycats," said Wing in an April 2019 *Mother Jones* article. "There's not enough people doing this."[149] Wing eventually pled guilty to conspiracy to defraud various US governmental agencies. In July 2020, a Wisconsin federal judge sentenced her to a two-year term of probation and a fine of $10,000. She also had to forfeit $61,753, which was the cost of the pills she sold.[150] Wing's case, however, did not discourage other people from establishing similar abortion pill businesses in subsequent years as increasingly burdensome legal restrictions on abortion drove many people to seek alternative avenues to obtain abortion pills outside of the formal medical system.

CAMPAIGN TO REMOVE FDA RESTRICTIONS

While some advocates worked to develop support for self-managed abortion, other advocates worked to lift FDA restrictions on mifepristone in response to anti-abortion efforts to use the FDA restrictions to limit access to abortion pills. Research had shown that a lower, 200-milligram dosage of mifepristone was just as effective as the higher 600-milligram dose, and it had fewer side effects,[151] so clinicians used the lower dose off label. Updating FDA labels can take a long time and cost drug makers many millions of dollars, so off-label use of drugs is common and accepted.[152] Abortion opponents, however, called for state laws prohibiting off-label use of mifepristone by penalizing physicians who did not follow the FDA label, hoping to discourage the use of medication abortion.[153] Ohio, for example, passed a law in 2010 requiring abortion providers to use the FDA dosage level for medication abortion, which resulted in the need for more medical interventions to complete abortions, more side effects, higher costs for abortion, and an 80 percent decline in medication abortion in Ohio between 2010 and 2014.[154] Research revealed the Ohio law was associated with reduced access among women who were younger, Black, less educated, and in lower socioeconomic groups.[155] This situation led advocates to press for revisions to the FDA label for mifepristone.

In 2015, Winikoff convened the Coalition to Improve Access to Mifepristone in the United States, which held regular meetings of reproductive health researchers, providers, and advocates in New York City to discuss mifepristone access. This group included Planned Parenthood, NAF, NARAL, and others. Concerned about conservative attacks on medical providers who offered 200-milligram doses of mifepristone off label, they urged the drug manufacturer Danco to petition the FDA to modify the Mifeprex label. Danco said they didn't have the funds to file a supplemental NDA to make the change, which could cost millions. In response, reproductive health advocates agreed to help Danco raise foundation money to support making the application. At Coalition meetings, Coeytaux tried to persuade the Coalition to require Danco to push for the full elimination of the REMS rather than just a modification of the label, but the Coalition members supported Danco's plan to request more limited changes. Francine Coeytaux explained:

> It suited everybody. The Coalition members didn't have problems with the REMS. They didn't have a problem with the restrictions. They were the people who already had a great agreement with Danco. They loved the special relationship they had with the FDA. The need to change the REMS was not recognized. They were happy with leaving the REMS in place and just asking for modifications. It was shocking, but not totally surprising. But it was maddening and disappointing. I felt like when I looked around the room, everybody else was very much defending the fact that we still needed the REMS, and feeling like we should be thankful for what we had.[156]

Dr. Beverly Winikoff, on the other hand, defended an incremental approach:

> We were always incremental in our approach because IRBs [Institutional Review Boards that approve research projects] wouldn't even touch it if you got too far out ahead of practice. You have to do it incrementally for two reasons. One, it's wise not to change a lot of things all at the same time because if things go bad, then you don't know which to attribute it to. But also,

the more different things you do, the more somebody is gonna find something bad about it. So one by one by one is a little bit easier, but it takes more time.[157]

Winikoff also said that Danco did not want to ask the FDA to remove the REMS. "I think the REMS may have had some commercial advantage for Danco. And without Danco being on board, we couldn't do it," said Winikoff.[158] Kirsten Moore of the EMAA (Expanding Medication Abortion Access) Project also believed Danco did not want the REMS removed, which she attributed to concern about market competition. She argued that the burdensome REMS restrictions discouraged other companies from developing a generic medication that would compete with Danco's brand name medication.[159] Not until 2019 did the FDA approve a generic mifepristone, marketed by the company GenBioPro, founded by abortion pill advocates. Dr. Carolyn Westhoff agreed: "Danco silently dragged their feet on the REMS issue because it would have paved the way for GenBioPro to bring their generic to the market."[160] Cynthia Pearson of NWHN suggested that the Obama administration's refusal to make Plan B emergency contraception fully over the counter may have made people believe the FDA would be unlikely to remove the REMS on mifepristone. "There was some realism to the desire to scale back our ask because we can't win the whole thing," said Pearson, noting that Obama had bargained away abortion funding for Washington, DC, during budget negotiations with Republican leader John Boehner.[161] Dr. Carolyn Westhoff agreed that the Obama administration was not hospitable to advances in reproductive health: "Obama was not very good on reproductive health in general. He had some deeply conservative views on reproductive issues. He wanted to see things restricted. That's how he came across, because at every single opportunity, he traded away reproductive rights."[162]

Contrary to the claims of many activists, however, a medical consultant with Danco, Dr. Mitchell Creinin, argued that Danco *did* want to remove the REMS. "Danco fought hard to remove the REMS multiple times, but the FDA made it really clear throughout the whole process the REMS was not going away," said Creinin.[163] He attributed the FDA's refusal to remove the REMS to the political pressure they were under. Creinin explained:

> The FDA is a government agency and answers to Congress. As an agency, they have to say, "What are we gonna do in a balance here to make ourselves functional?" Do they want to create something where they are spending so much time and effort dealing with the repercussions of a decision? Or do they want to have the time and effort to approve other drugs? Taking away the REMS would mean constant inquiry from all the Republicans in Congress. You know the amount of work and effort it's going to take for them to constantly deal with this battle? Danco is not a bad player. Danco fought tooth and nail to get rid of the REMS. The FDA is not a bad player because the FDA is trying to say, "Look, we have all this business

to do." If we've gotta deal with all of these Congressional inquiries and all these other problems that are gonna arise from this, what's the best balance here? It doesn't mean that they're doing wrong by people. They're just trying to find a middle ground so that everything can move forward.¹⁶⁴

Creinin argued the FDA worked hard to increase access to mifepristone despite extreme political constraints.

In May of 2015, Danco submitted a supplemental NDA to the FDA to obtain approval to alter the Mifeprex indication, dosing regimen, and labeling to reflect an updated, evidence-based prescription regimen. Danco proposed decreasing the mifepristone dosage to 200 milligrams, increasing the gestational age limit up to which the medication could be taken to sixty-three days, eliminating the requirement that the dose of misoprostol be administered in a medical facility, removing the requirement of an in-person follow-up appointment, and expanding who could prescribe mifepristone beyond physicians. But they did not challenge several restrictions that were part of the REMS, including the provider certification requirement and the in-person distribution requirement for mifepristone.¹⁶⁵

Nevertheless, individual members of the Coalition pushed for full removal of the REMS. In November 2015, twelve leading researchers and four organizations—including the National Public Health Association, NAF, Ibis, and Gynuity—submitted a letter to the FDA asking the agency to change the label in three respects: 1) the location where the patient should take mifepristone should not be restricted; 2) an in-person visit should not be mandated for follow-up assessment; and 3) any licensed healthcare provider—not just physicians—should be able to prescribe the drug. They also asked for the elimination or substantial modification of the REMS, including the in-person distribution requirement, the provider certification requirement, and the patient agreement form. Finally, they asked for an extension of the gestational age limit for medical abortion to seventy days. ACOG submitted a separate letter making the same request. Then in February 2015, thirty policy, advocacy, social science, research, and academic organizations submitted a letter to the FDA asking them to lift the REMS.¹⁶⁶ Winikoff, Westhoff, and other researchers also decided to publish a special issue of the journal *Contraception* with the latest research to support removal of the REMS, which they did in the fall of 2015.¹⁶⁷

In March 2016, during the last year of the Obama administration, the FDA issued a new REMS for mifepristone and updated the mifepristone label, modifying the dosage protocol to 200 milligrams of mifepristone followed twenty-four to forty-eight hours later with an 800-microgram dose of misoprostol taken buccally. The FDA extended the recommended duration for use of the medications to ten weeks (seventy days after the last menstrual period). The FDA also eliminated the requirement that the dose of misoprostol be administered in a medical facility and allowed a remote follow-up visit, reducing the required number of visits from three to one. The FDA replaced the term "physician" with "healthcare provider," opening the door for nurses, nurse midwives, and physician's assistants to dispense the medication. Finally, the FDA eliminated the requirement that prescribers report all nonfatal serious adverse events.[168] Kirsten Moore gave the FDA credit for many of these changes: "Danco has said it fought the REMS, but people from the FDA said Danco was dragging its feet in the whole process and it was the FDA that took the initiative of changing the label. Danco sent in data to go through nine weeks, and FDA said, actually, we're going to go through ten weeks. It was the FDA that said, we're going to change 'doctor' to 'licensed healthcare provider,' and we're going to remove from the label the requirement that patients take the drug in clinic."[169] The FDA, however, refused to eliminate the patient agreement form that FDA experts had determined was duplicative of standard informed consent practices and recommended removing, but the FDA commissioner at the time, Robert Califf, overruled the recommendation. "For the commissioner to be involved in the granular details of a REMS, even down to the inclusion of an agreement form, and for the head of CDER [Center for Drug Evaluation and Research—the entity within FDA that traditionally has the final say] to openly acknowledge it, was a shocking break from the norm—and almost certainly represents the tip of the iceberg of political interference," said advocates at NWHN.[170]

Also in 2016, the FDA granted a research exception to the REMS for Gynuity Health Projects to study telemedicine abortion. The study, called TelAbortion, began in four states: New York, Hawaii, Oregon, and Maine. TelAbortion involved all the same steps and procedures as an in-person medical abortion, but the patient did not have to travel to an abortion clinic. Under this study, the FDA allowed clinicians participating in the study to provide medication abortion care by videoconference and mail without an in-person visit to the abortion provider. In order to receive care, the patient had to be in one of the study states during the videoconference, and had to have a mailing address in that state so the provider could mail the medications. The patient had screening tests as needed with nearby healthcare providers, then a videoconference with the abortion provider. If the patient was eligible for medication abortion, the provider then sent mifepristone and misoprostol with instructions by mail. Follow-up was done remotely by phone with local or home tests. Preliminary results of the study, published in September of 2019, showed that the direct-to-patient telemedicine abortion service was safe, effective, efficient, and satisfactory.[171] The TelAbortion study eventually expanded to nine more states, including Washington, New Mexico, Colorado, Georgia, Iowa, Minnesota, Illinois, Maryland, and Montana. Many physicians, however, were resistant to telemedicine abortion. "Such a big idea is so scary," said Dr. Carolyn Westhoff. "I think it took many of us a whole lot of experience to start feeling comfortable with telemedicine abortion. This was something that was so new. So we were all too conservative in the beginning. One of the first little steps was saying, 'we can be flexible about when you take the misoprostol. You can take the miso at home. You know you don't need to come for so many visits.' Gradually, gradually we demedicalized it."[172]

While the FDA changes in the mifepristone label opened the door to less burdensome restrictions, the agency left the REMS in place, including the provider certification and in-person distribution requirements. Despite the ongoing FDA restrictions on mifepristone, the use of medication abortion increased steadily over time. The Guttmacher Institute reported that 17 percent of all recorded abortions in 2008 were done with medications, 24 percent in 2011, 31 percent in 2014, and 39 percent in 2017 (60 percent of abortions performed within up to ten weeks gestation). By 2020, the percentage of medication abortions overall had risen to 53 percent of all recorded abortions (see Figure 2.2).[173]

In the summer of 2016, the Supreme Court released a five to three decision strengthening abortion rights. In *Whole Woman's Health v. Hellerstedt*, the Court considered two provisions of a Texas law, one requiring that physicians who performed abortions have admitting privileges at a nearby hospital, and another requiring abortion clinics in the state to have facilities comparable to an ambulatory surgical center. A majority of the Court ruled that these requirements placed a substantial obstacle in the path of women

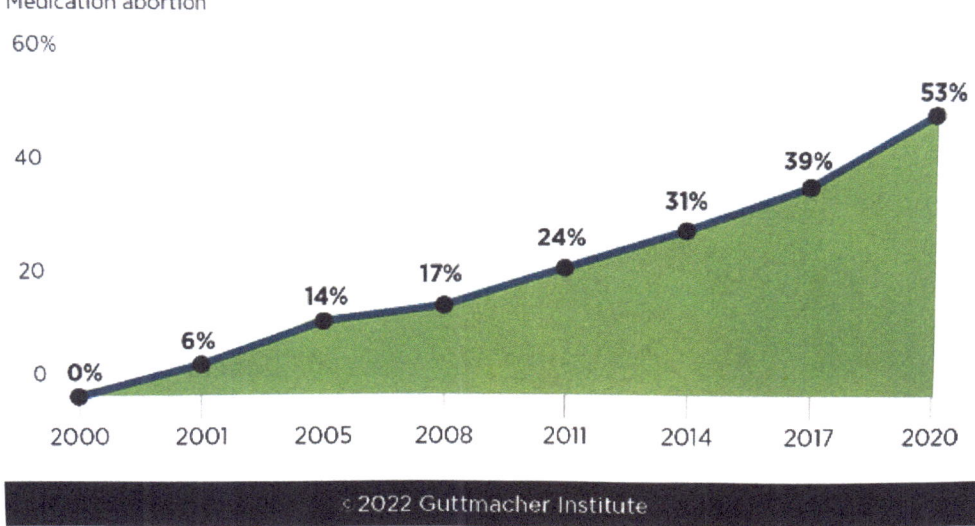

FIGURE 2.2: The percentage of medication abortions of all abortions in the United States between 2000 and 2020 (courtesy of Guttmacher).[231]

seeking an abortion, constituting an undue burden on abortion access, and therefore violated the Constitution. The majority ruled that courts must "consider the burdens a law imposes on abortion access together with the benefits those laws confer," and that courts retained "an independent constitutional duty to review factual findings where constitutional rights are at stake." They ruled that an uncritical deference to legislative factual findings was inappropriate. This decision created a strong new rule to challenge state laws restricting abortion based on dubious claims that the restrictions protected women's health. Abortion rights supporters planned to use this decision to challenge the increasing number of state restrictions on abortion, from mandatory waiting periods to ultrasound requirements and other measures that burdened abortion access with no clear medical benefit and, in some cases, medical detriments.

Things were looking up for abortion rights advocates, but then a seismic political shift changed their fortunes: the election of Donald Trump for president. During his campaign, Trump had pledged to nominate anti-abortion people to the Supreme Court, and sure enough, over his four years in office, Trump appointed three people who held strong anti-abortion views—Neil Gorsuch, Brett Kavanaugh, and Amy Coney Barrett—shifting the balance of power on the Court from a five to four pro-choice majority to a six to three anti-abortion supermajority. The need for abortion pills became more urgent than ever.

POLITICAL SHIFTS AND MOVEMENT MOBILIZATION

The same month the *Hellerstedt* decision came down, Plan C launched a new website sharing information about self-managed abortion, including how people were obtaining abortion pills online. Researchers at Plan C began testing websites selling abortion pills to evaluate the reliability of their services. They then teamed up with Gynuity Health Projects to expand the research. They submitted the pills they purchased to lab testing to measure the amount and quality of the medications. In 2017, Plan C and Gynuity Health published a study of eighteen online abortion pill vendors. The study concluded that ordering abortion pills online was simple, affordable, and safe. The cost of the pills, including shipping, averaged about $235 for an "abortion kit" containing both mifepristone and misoprostol. Buying misoprostol (Cytotec) alone was less expensive. The websites allowed standard mechanisms for payment, including credit cards, money wires via Western Union, and bank transfers from platforms such as Transferwise, Bitcoin, or PayPal. All of the mifepristone pills ordered contained the expected amount of mifepristone and all of the misoprostol pills contained misoprostol.[174] Plan C shared the results of this research as a "Report Card" on their website, providing detailed information about product costs, ship times, and service reliability. Plan C continued to test new online sellers of abortion pills and then update the information on their website, helping people to find reliable sources for abortion pills.

As Plan C began receiving media attention, mainstream reproductive health organizations distanced themselves from the organization, believing what Plan C was doing was illegal. Plan C's fiscal sponsor, Oakland-based Public Health Institute, dropped them so they had to find a new fiscal sponsor, which became NWHN.[175] Foundations, too, refused to fund them and even the Generative Learning Community refused to include them.[176]

Two days before the 2016 presidential election, Plan C co-directors Elisa Wells and Francine Coeytaux laid out their vision in an article, "Mail-Order Abortion: The Future is NOW," published on the reproductive rights news website Rewire News. They pointed out how women in dozens of countries around the world were using services such as Women on Web, Women Help Women, and safe2choose for online consultations and express delivery of highly effective and safe early abortion pills directly to their homes, all without a physical exam. But none of these organizations offered services in the United States because they feared the virulent US anti-abortion movement might shut them down. "What is needed is for the medical field to fully relinquish control of the method, thereby empowering women to manage their own care should they choose to do so," said Wells and Coeytaux. They explained how they were working to inform women about this option and identify individual providers who would "champion women's self-use of abortion pills and be willing to pilot approaches that put the pills more directly into women's hands."[177]

In addition to supporting self-managed abortion, reproductive health advocates continued to press the FDA to remove the REMS restrictions by challenging the FDA restrictions in court, lobbying the FDA to remove the restrictions, and reinterpreting the REMS restrictions to allow the mailing of abortion pills. In 2017, the Reproductive Freedom Project of the American Civil Liberties Union (ACLU) sued the FDA in the case of *Chelius v. Azar*, seeking the removal of the REMS restrictions on mifepristone. In the complaint, brought on behalf of providers and patients in Hawaii, the ACLU argued that the REMS violated women's rights to liberty, privacy, and equal protection as guaranteed by the Constitution by imposing significant burdens on abortion access without proof of a valid medical justification.[178]

Reproductive rights advocates also pressured the FDA directly to release mifepristone from the REMS classification, arguing that the restrictions were medically unnecessary.[179] In January 2018, the American Medical Association—on a motion from the Medical Student Section—passed a resolution urging the FDA to remove the mifepristone REMS.[180] Kirsten Moore founded the EMAA Project, which worked to inform the FDA about the latest medical and scientific evidence relating to mifepristone and the REMS.[181] In March 2018 in response to a Congressional inquiry, the Government Accountability Office (GAO) issued a report on the FDA's Mifeprex labeling changes and ongoing monitoring efforts. The GAO found that the FDA followed its standard review process, based its approval on peer-reviewed published research, and determined the rates of adverse events were acceptably low.[182] In June of 2018, research showed mifepristone could effectively be used for miscarriage management.[183] The same month, the executive board of ACOG issued a position statement urging the FDA to remove its restrictions on mifepristone.[184] In August of 2018, the American Academy of Family Physicians adopted a resolution stating that the REMS classification on mifepristone was not based on scientific evidence, and limited access to abortion care and the best evidence-based medical management of miscarriage.[185] Despite the onslaught of pressure, the FDA did not lift the REMS or change the mifepristone label.

Meanwhile, Coeytaux and Wells moved ahead with actions to expand access to medication abortion through telemedicine. In early 2018, they published an article in the *Stanford Social Innovation Review* with Dr. Sophia Yen titled "Reproductive Health Care by Mail." The article called for telemedicine abortion.[186] "Web-based, medically supported models of medication distribution by mail are demonstrating a new means of service delivery for reproductive health care that greatly increases access and puts convenience, confidentiality, and control in users' hands."[187] To realize their vision, Plan C had for several years been trying to recruit an organization based outside of the country to offer telemedicine abortion to people inside the United States. They spoke with several organizations without success. "I had been begging every year. Please, please, please," said Coeytaux. "Nobody wanted to touch the US. They gave two reasons. One, they focused on countries where abortion was illegal. And secondly, they said, 'You take care of your own—you're the richest country in the world. And, well, we know how much money the antis have. We don't want them coming after us.'"[188] After hearing about "The Tale of Two Methods" report, a man at one of the organizations agreed to start serving the United States, said Coeytaux. Plan C raised $50,000 to support the organization, but they later backed down and returned the money. Eventually the Dutch physician and activist Rebecca Gomperts agreed to serve the United States. Coeytaux explained, "She said, okay, this has gotten ridiculous. I can do it. I'm not US-based. I'm based in the Netherlands. I'm going to do it, and then she started Aid Access."

For decades, Gomperts had offered medication abortion services to women living in countries where abortion was illegal or inaccessible. In 1999, she founded Women on Waves then, in 2006, she founded Women on Web, offering medication abortion services via the internet and shipping pills through the mail. Women on Web, however, did not serve people in the United States because abortion was a constitutionally protected right. But in 2018 when Women on Web began receiving a voluminous number of inquiries from people in the United States who could not access abortion because of legal restrictions and high costs, Gomperts considered serving the United States. "Gomperts saw the real obstacle course that people in the United States were having to go through to access abortion," said Dr. Abigail R.A. Aiken, who conducted research on Aid Access. "She could see it was legal in name, but it was not legal in practice."[189] With Plan C's support, Gomperts formed Aid Access to provide low-cost abortion pills to people in the United States. Aid Access required an online consultation to determine eligibility for using abortion pills and provided information about how to use them. Dr. Gomperts then sent prescriptions to a pharmacist in India, who shipped the medications directly to US residents. Patients received the medications in two to three weeks. Dr. Gomperts charged a sliding scale fee up to $105.[190] Between 2018 and 2020, Aid Access received 57,506 requests from people in the United States seeking abortion pills.[191]

Plan C supported Gomperts in several ways. Initially, they helped her find grants and pro bono legal assistance. "We tested her service from a user perspective and provided feedback to make it more appropriate for a US audience," said Wells.[192] Plan C shared information about Aid Access on their website and helped with their media visibility. In 2020, they found providers to take referrals from Aid Access in states where telemedicine abortion was legal. They also strategized with Gomperts as new issues arose, such as offering advance provision pills so people could have them on hand in case they needed them. While Plan C supported Aid Access, they remained fiscally independent from them. Coeytaux explained: "We were really careful from the get-go that she do it completely alone. We never gave her any funding, and in fact, whenever I would go and meet her, I never even paid for lunch for her, or she never bought me lunch. I mean we were so careful not to have any money exchange between us, so we could say, and honestly mean, that we are totally separate entities. Yes, we partner. But that's it."[193]

Research conducted with Aid Access patients revealed highly positive experiences with the service and very low rates of complications. Between March 2018 and March 2019, Aid Access mailed abortion medications to 4,584 people. Of the 2,797 people who used the medications and responded to a follow-up survey, 96.4 percent reported successfully ending their pregnancy without further intervention and only 1 percent reported any treatment for a serious adverse event, a rate only slightly higher than in clinical settings. No deaths were reported to the service by family, friends, the authorities, or the media. Respondents reported positively about their experiences of using abortion medication through Aid Access: 98.4 percent were satisfied with their abortion experience; 95.5 percent said using Aid Access was the right choice; 98.1 percent felt they had enough information on how to use the medications; and 93.4 percent felt they had enough information on what to expect from the process.[194] "This study is the first evidence from the US context that self-managed medication abortion provided using this online telemedicine model is safe, effective and acceptable to users," said the study's lead author, Dr. Abigail R. A. Aiken, associate professor at the University of Texas at Austin's LBJ School of Public Affairs.[195]

One area of concern had been that medication abortion outside of the formal US healthcare system might delay a diagnosis of an ectopic pregnancy—a dangerous condition where a fertilized egg implants and grows outside of the uterus. But Aiken found the opposite: people were diagnosed with ectopic pregnancies right away during the initial screening of patients, which often happened more quickly than clinic-based care because patients could get telemedicine appointments right away rather than having to wait for an in-clinic appointment. The research also showed that patients' self-reporting of their last menstrual period was an accurate method for determining gestation duration in early pregnancy, meaning ultrasounds were not necessary. Finally, the research provided evidence that medication abortion after ten weeks is effective and safe, although slightly less so than before ten weeks. Of the patients taking abortion pills before ten weeks of pregnancy, 97 percent successfully ended their pregnancies. The success rate for people taking the pills after ten weeks was 92 percent. While only 0.08 percent of patients with pregnancies up to ten weeks had complications, 2.3 percent after ten weeks did. "It's of course higher, but it's not alarmingly high," said Aiken, noting that the World Health Organization had approved the use of abortion pills through twelve weeks of pregnancy. "I think self-managed telemedicine abortion will become seen as more legitimate and more of a real part of good quality, safe, effective care as we see more of these results and see more about how it's operating and working," she said. "I think it's a very legitimate option and so important because of its affordability."[196]

In February 2017, the international organization Women Help Women formed a US project, "Self-Managed Abortion. Safe and Supported" (SASS), to provide information and support on using abortion pills to end an unwanted pregnancy without a clinician. In January 2018, SASS launched a website located on servers overseas with abortion information and an encrypted portal through which people could access counselors based overseas. Through this secure portal, people could ask questions about how to get and use abortion pills.[197] Whereas Plan C took a very public approach of creating a website where they shared information about how people were obtaining and using mifepristone and misoprostol, SASS was more secretive and spread information using a "train-the-trainer" model, where they would train others on how people were using abortion pills, and then encourage the people they trained to train others. They hoped that in this way, they could build community-based networks of people knowledgeable about abortion pills.[198]

Around this time, NWHN came out in support of self-managed abortion. According to Sarah Christopherson, NWHN went through a months-long education and persuasion process with their board. In the spring of 2017, NWHN published an article in the newsletter to their membership stating their support for self-managed abortion: "We believe that women and people who can become pregnant should have access to safe, affordable abortion care with the assistance of a medical provider if and when they so choose. Without exception. Women should not have to see a doctor or 'get permission' from the medical community before ending their pregnancy with an FDA-approved medication."[199] In this article, they stressed that "medication abortion without the involvement of a provider is not a failure of the system; rather, it is one option that women ought to be able to choose." They argued, "we must trust people to make the decisions that are right for them."[200]

Surveys of US women visiting abortion clinics in 2017 showed that 1.4 percent reported ever having attempted to self-manage an abortion. Based on this, researchers estimated that 7 percent of women in the United States would attempt to self-manage an abortion at some point in their lives. They found that non-Hispanic Black and Hispanic women were more likely than non-Hispanic White women to have attempted self-managed abortion, as were women living in poverty.[201] Another study of people searching for abortion care on Google in 2017–2018 found that 28 percent reported attempting self-managed abortion, with 18 percent reporting use of mifepristone and/or misoprostol.[202]

As abortion access tightened, advocates at some abortion funds across the country began providing misoprostol to people who could not travel to obtain care. They obtained the medication from abroad at a cost of $55 for a bottle of one hundred tablets, and worked with local doulas to support people using misoprostol for abortion. "It was very widespread, well before *Roe* fell," said one advocate, who began mailing misoprostol pills to people in 2019. "In our little area, I knew of three different doulas who were doing it. Then we started doing it. I figured if there were three in my little metropolitan area that there must be several in every metropolitan area. I assumed there were thousands of networks all around the country."[203] In 2019, researchers published a systematic review of studies on misoprostol alone for first-trimester medical abortion, revealing high rates of efficacy.[204]

Some advocates, however, were concerned that if people obtained abortion medications outside of the formal medical system, they may be subject to investigations and possibly criminal prosecution. While the FDA considered it "illegal" for overseas pharmacies to ship medications into the United States, this practice was common and the FDA had a policy of non-enforcement about importation of up to a ninety-day supply of medicines for limited use.[205] While only one state—Nevada—had an explicit criminal prohibition against individuals self-managing abortion, thirty-eight states had feticide laws that equated causing the loss of a fetus with murder, although most explicitly excluded pregnant people from criminal penalties.[206] Nevertheless, some anti-abortion prosecutors across the country had investigated and criminally charged people for self-managing abortion.

Prosecutors used a range of laws against pregnant women, including laws against feticide, child neglect, practicing medicine without a license, and possession of a dangerous substance. As an increasing number of people began self-managing their abortions, advocates became concerned about the legal risks, particularly for women of color and others living in communities subject to increased surveillance and criminalization. In 2018, If/When/How created the Repro Legal Helpline—a free, confidential helpline for callers to get legal information or advice about self-managed abortion. The helpline assisted people concerned about being criminalized for ending, or attempting to end, a pregnancy to learn more about their rights, submit questions by phone or through encrypted communication, and get connected with an attorney in their state if needed. In March of 2019, the SIA Legal Team at Berkeley merged with If/When/How to become If/When/How: Lawyering for Reproductive Justice, which ran the Repro Legal Helpline. "With added legal and policy expertise, we'll draw on our roots in the movement and connections across communities to educate, train, organize, and mobilize a network of legal professionals who can bring their skills and privilege to bear on reproductive oppression in myriad ways," said Mariko Miki, the organization's deputy director.[207] In 2019, If/When/How published a study reporting twenty-one adults were criminalized for self-managed abortion with medications since 2000.[208]

Advocates also created medical support services for people self-managing abortion. Two primary care physicians in New York, including Dr. Linda Prine, formed the Miscarriage and Abortion Hotline in 2019. The M+A Hotline, as it was called, started with eleven volunteer clinicians, who answered texts and calls from people with questions about abortion pills and miscarriage. To ensure confidentiality, the M+A Hotline used an encrypted platform and did not ask people for any identifying information. Callers asked questions about how to take the pills, their symptoms, whether the process worked, and contraception options going forward.[209]

Meanwhile, Plan C focused on developing telemedicine abortion by promoting research on the "test-free" telemedicine model of providing abortion pills to patients. They first approached researchers at Advancing New Strategies in Reproductive Health (ANSIRH) at the University of California, San Francisco to do a study in California, but the FDA refused to approve their study. So Plan C took the idea to Washington state. They approached Dr. Deborah Oyer at Cedar River Clinics in the Seattle area with the idea of offering an asynchronous telehealth abortion service based on data showing that blood testing and ultrasound tests were not needed to safely offer medication abortion. Oyer ended up providing telemedicine consultations by videoconference, not asynchronously, and giving patients the option of receiving the medications by mail or by picking them up from the clinic, including at a remote site in Yakima. Lawyers at NAF discouraged Oyer from mailing the medications. They wanted everyone to stay within the strictest definition of the REMS—interpreting the word "dispensing" in the REMS to mean in-person dispensing—because lawyers had filed a lawsuit in Maryland asking a federal court to order the FDA to allow mailing abortion pills during the pandemic and they didn't want to put that case in jeopardy. "I knew I was pushing the bounds by mailing the meds, but one could argue that if the meds were sent by and from the clinic that they were 'dispensed' by the clinic," said Oyer.[210] Plan C supported this interpretation of the REMS.

Plan C raised money to hire Dr. Emily Godfrey at University of Washington to conduct research on the new telemedicine delivery approach. Dr. Godfrey found that telehealth abortion improved access to reproductive health services, especially for people living long distances from specialized family planning clinics.[211] Dr. Godfrey and colleagues also conducted research on family physicians providing telemedicine abortion in New York, New Jersey, and Washington state, who used asynchronous online consultations and medications mailed directly to patients. The research found that this model was successful.[212] Meanwhile, people flocked to the Plan C website, which received around fifty thousand hits per month in 2019 from all over the United States, with over half of those visitors seeking out the Report Card.[213]

Plan C was further inspired by new research demonstrating the safety and efficacy of self-managed abortion in India. In late 2017, researchers at the International Institute for Population Sciences in Mumbai, the Population Council in New Delhi, and the New York-based Guttmacher Institute published the first national study of the incidence of abortion and unintended pregnancy in India.[214] They estimated 15.6 million abortions were performed in the country in 2015 and concluded that "close to three in four abortions are achieved using MMA [medical methods of abortion] drugs from chemists and informal vendors, rather than from health facilities. MMA is safe and effective when used in accordance with World Health Organization guidelines."[215] This research demonstrated the widespread and safe use of abortion medications outside of the formal medical system.

In August of 2019, more studies confirmed the safety of using telehealth for medication abortion. Based on data from five states where participants had a videoconference with a clinician and pre-treatment laboratory tests and ultrasound, the TelAbortion study found that direct-to-patient telemedicine abortion service was safe, effective, efficient, and satisfactory, with 93 percent of patients having complete abortions without a procedure, and only two hospitalizations out of 248 patients. All patients who completed questionnaires were satisfied with the service. Researchers concluded, "the model has the potential to increase abortion access by enhancing the reach of providers and by offering people a new option for obtaining care conveniently and privately."[216] Meanwhile, ANSIRH at University of California, San Francisco advanced an aggressive research agenda to support increasing access to medication abortion and eventually removing all FDA restrictions on mifepristone. For example, one ANSIRH researcher completed a study about the barriers to medication abortion experienced by public university students in California, which supported the passage of a law in 2019 requiring public universities to offer abortion pills.[217]

Advocates also pushed for a generic mifepristone to help lower prices and increase access. Danco's patent expired in 2004, but no one stepped forward to create a generic until years later. Around 2012, several mission-driven pharmaceutical professionals formed the company GenBioPro with the goal of bringing a generic mifepristone to the market. Before coming to market, GenBioPro advocated for reduced dosage requirements, fewer required patient visits, and other improvements to access.[218] With the support of the Packard Foundation, GenBioPro pursued the approval of a generic with the FDA. The head of the FDA at the time, Dr. Scott Gottlieb, was focused on increasing the number of generic medications on the market in order to encourage competition, especially for drugs in the REMS program.[219] On April 11, 2019, the FDA approved GenBioPro's generic mifepristone.[220] Coeytaux said the generic made a huge difference:

> The minute GenBioPro was in the act, all sorts of things started happening. Danco reduced its price because there was competition. All the stuff that we did with the providers during COVID—we couldn't have done it with Danco. Danco wasn't interested at all in anything innovative because they were happily doing their thing and already had their people on board. So having competition in the market was critical.[221]

FDA approval of the generic set price competition in motion: GenBioPro set their price lower than Danco, which then dropped their price. Lower prices and more options increased access to mifepristone for clinicians and patients across the country. The generic also established competition for new services from the drug sponsors, such as mail order at scale, but it also extinguished the rationale for Danco to pursue the miscarriage indication since most pharmacies could swap out brand-named mifepristone for the generic, regardless of what the prescription was written for.[222] Dr. Mitchell Creinin, however, believed that the drop in price had only a "marginal benefit" for patients because clinics did not drop their prices for medication abortion.[223]

But anti-abortion advocates pushed back against increasing access. In March of 2019, the Trump administration's FDA issued a warning letter to Dr. Gomperts, demanding that she stop "causing the introduction of a misbranded and unapproved new drug into interstate commerce."[224] The FDA threatened to seize the drugs. Gomperts explained what she did next: "I stayed in my bed for three days, researching and reading everything that existed on the FDA regulations, calling all the people I could call in the US. I came to the conclusion that it's okay, I can do this."[225] Then she fought back. In September 2019, Gomperts sued the FDA, alleging they had seized between three and ten doses of abortion drugs she had prescribed through Aid Access since March and that the government had blocked Aid Access from receiving payments from some patients.[226] The lawsuit was eventually dismissed, but Gomperts continued to mail the medication and did not experience any more interference.

Anti-abortion states also tried to block the increasing access by fighting for restrictions at the state level, including passing laws banning mailing of abortion pills, requiring ultrasounds which limited telemedicine access, and requiring that physicians alone may prescribe mifepristone. For three weeks in June of 2019, the Missouri health department required doctors prescribing abortion pills to conduct an extra medically unnecessary pelvic exam on their patients before the state-mandated waiting period so that patients had to have two pelvic exams to receive the pills—one when they initially saw the doctor and a second when patients came back for the pills. In other words, doctors were forced by the state to insert their fingers into patients' vaginas while pressing their abdomens to feel their reproductive organs, for no medical reason. One doctor described the requirement as "state sanctioned, essentially, sexual assault."[227] After three weeks, doctors at the one remaining abortion clinic in Missouri, a Planned Parenthood clinic in Kansas City, refused to comply with the order, and the state health department backed down, rescinding the requirement.[228] During that time period, over one hundred women experienced invasive, medically unnecessary, and unwanted vaginal probes, by order of the state. In response, Planned Parenthood created a new clinic across the river in Illinois so as not to be subject to the Missouri Department of Health.[229] Meanwhile, states increasingly passed abortion bans, hoping to tee up a case for the Supreme Court to finally overturn *Roe v. Wade*. These developments spurred Plan C to push harder to make abortion pills available by telemedicine and mail. The declaration of a pandemic in March 2020 created new opportunities to make this vision a reality.

CHAPTER 3

"Greased the Wheels": COVID-19 Pandemic and the Rise of Telemedicine Abortion

The COVID-19 pandemic led to a fundamental shift that eventually would greatly increase access to abortion pills: the advent of telemedicine abortion, where doctors consult remotely with patients and mail abortion pills to them. This shift was particularly significant because it undermined a central strategy of the anti-abortion movement: to limit abortion to a dwindling number of brick-and-mortar clinics and then target patients and healthcare providers entering these clinics with harassment and violence. As Republican lawmakers passed increasingly burdensome laws and drove clinics out of business, this strategy made abortion increasingly inaccessible, especially for people living far from cities where abortion clinics were generally located. Telemedicine abortion offered a convenient, private, and more affordable way to access abortion care, no matter where people lived, for the first time in American history. Through litigation and grassroots advocacy, reproductive health advocates demanded that the FDA remove its burdensome and medically unnecessary in-person distribution requirement for mifepristone. Their success led to the creation of many virtual abortion clinics. While some mainstream abortion clinics resisted the rise of telemedicine abortion, fearing it might undermine their business model, many abortion doctors and other clinicians welcomed the increased convenience for patients. But advocates saw the writing on the wall: *Roe*'s days were numbered. Alternative supply systems would be necessary to ensure ongoing access to abortion pills post *Roe*. So activists organized for that looming reality by setting up a web of organizations to support people self-managing abortion. These efforts experienced some resistance from within the abortion rights movement, from some clinic-based abortion providers who did not believe women were capable of using abortion pills on their own, but also from some reproductive justice activists fearful of the legal risks for people self-managing abortions. This chapter traces these important developments and divisions during the first year of the pandemic.

Shortly after the World Health Organization declared COVID-19 a pandemic in early March 2020, several states such as Texas declared that abortion was not essential health care and therefore had to be delayed in order to conserve personal protective equipment (PPE), such as masks and gloves. Reproductive health advocates responded by asserting that abortion was time-sensitive, necessary medical care. But they also used the pandemic as an opportunity to promote telemedicine abortion. They argued that telemedicine abortion could minimize exposure to COVID-19 without using PPE. Medical researcher and doctor Daniel Grossman of ANSIRH at University of California, San Francisco said at the time, "During the pandemic, it would be possible to provide medication abortion through eleven weeks of pregnancy without an in-person visit and by mailing pills to a patient. This would reduce the patient and clinician's risk of acquiring the virus and not a single piece of PPE would be used."[1]

In 2020, demand for telemedicine services in the United States soared. Abortion health care was no exception. But the FDA restrictions under REMS for mifepristone were widely interpreted to block telemedicine abortion. The Trump administration suspended in-person dispensing requirements for all medications under REMS except for one—mifepristone—disallowing telemedicine abortion while allowing telemedicine access to medications far less safe than mifepristone, including for opioid drugs like fentanyl and OxyContin.[2] Building on evidence of telemedicine abortion's safety, researchers and clinicians published a new protocol for medication abortion that did not require an in-person meeting between patients and clinicians. In early 2020, Elizabeth Raymond from Gynuity and nine doctors and public health experts published a "no-test" medication abortion protocol.[3] This protocol challenged the standard medical protocol requiring two tests to determine eligibility for a medication abortion. The first test was an ultrasound, to ensure the pregnancy was within the FDA's gestational limit of seventy days and was not ectopic. The second was a blood test to determine whether the patient had a Rh-negative blood type—in which case they may receive counseling and/or anti-D immunoglobulin treatment. These tests, which were not required in other countries, had to be done in person, thereby precluding fully remote telemedicine abortion. Research in the early 2000s indicated that these tests were medically unnecessary, but they became the standard of care. Dr. Emily Godfrey believed this was done at least in part to prevent family care physicians from offering medication abortion and thereby taking business away from obstetricians, gynecologists, and abortion clinics. "OB/GYNs [obstetricians and gynecologists] can be very unfriendly to family physicians and very territorial. They're not always welcoming of the family docs. But it's very regional," said Godfrey. For the same reason, family care providers sometimes had a hard time finding an obstetrician or gynecologist to agree to provide back-up care in case their patients needed a procedural abortion, which discouraged them from offering medication abortion.[4]

Based on extensive medical research, Raymond and her colleagues concluded that ultrasound and blood tests were usually unnecessary for safe and effective abortion because women could reliably report their last periods for dating pregnancy, and abortion in early pregnancy does not create an immune response. The study cited research conducted in the United States, Mexico, and Moldova where medical professionals provided medication abortion to 406 patients without a screening ultrasound or pelvic examination.[5] No serious adverse events resulted from the omission of these tests, and participants were highly satisfied. They noted that international organizations for the past fifteen years had safely provided abortion pills by mail to tens of thousands of patients screened only by a brief medical review and that in many European countries medical standards do not recommend Rh testing for abortion or miscarriage in early pregnancy. In addition to the preliminary tests, standard medical protocol required a follow-up appointment to confirm the absence of a continuing pregnancy. The no-test protocol recommended a planned follow-up contact conducted by videoconference, telephone, patient portal, email, or text, along with urine pregnancy tests that the patient purchased online or from a local pharmacy and performed at home. The new protocol allowed for clinicians to safely administer medication abortion to their patients without any preliminary tests or in-person encounters.

One of the study's co-authors, Dr. Jamila Perritt, reported that her patients had responded very positively to the new protocol. "Folks love it. They opt for it. Especially [women] who are confident about when their periods are," said Dr. Perritt. "Sixty-two percent of folks who have abortions already have children. Many already know their blood type. They can tell you. People are really good at self-screening. If we actually trust people, as providers we can stand with them in partnership. This is a really good way to take care of our community."[6] Dr. Perritt was hopeful the no-test protocol would increase access. "This is a move toward a broader goal," Dr. Perritt said. "This medication is safe. People know how to take it on their own. We should trust people to care for themselves in the way that they see best. And the evidence supports it. My hope is that this no-test protocol is an early step to broadening access."[7]

Dr. Perritt predicted that the elimination of unnecessary medical tests would likely decrease the cost of abortion health care and increase access because ultrasound machines can cost providers $30,000—at the low end. If states mandated ultrasounds or standard medical protocols recommended them, doctors could not provide abortion care without making this sizable investment, said Dr. Perritt. Similarly, standard Rh testing increases the cost of abortion—since, in order to be able to perform the testing, providers have to be part of a system of regulation and inspection by health departments, which could be burdensome for a private practice. "Because of the way that medication abortion is restricted, part of the cost of medication abortion includes mandated ultrasounds, blood work, and follow-up appointments," said Dr. Perritt. "If based on [the no-test] protocol, we are able to show that this medication is safe and effective and works really well, then the hope will be that the cost will go down."[8] The publication of the no-test medication abortion protocol by Raymond and her coauthors in April of 2020 was "hugely important" in getting people to accept the no-test model, said Wells.[9]

Around this time, several organizations made statements affirming a no-test protocol. On March 30, 2020, the American College of Obstetricians and Gynecologists issued guidance stating that clinicians could perform an assessment, counseling, and consent for medication abortion by video or telephone and that an ultrasound and Rh testing were not necessary in most cases.[10] Similarly, the Reproductive Health Access Project, which trains and supports clinicians to make abortion, contraception, and miscarriage care more widely accessible, issued a "no-touch" medication abortion protocol that did not require in-person visits and tests. Cynthia Pearson, executive director of the National Women's Health Network, publicly noted that the FDA REMS restriction on mifepristone did not explicitly require providers to perform ultrasounds. "I believe that the assumption that an ultrasound was required was a result of community standards, under which most clinicians used ultrasound to date pregnancies," said Pearson.[11]

Advocates argued the REMS restriction especially harmed marginalized women. "Policies need to work for all women, including women who have trouble getting time off work, who have trouble traveling, who have limits on their financial situations," said Cynthia Pearson. "To help those that need it most, the REMS restriction needs to be gone."[12] Pearson also expressed concern that the REMS restriction might discourage some doctors from providing medication abortion because they don't want to be on a registry that could be made public, making them and their families the target of anti-abortion harassment and violence at clinics and even at their homes. "Abortion providers are singled out for public attacks, including violent attacks. It's common sense that that would stand in the way of at least some providers who might otherwise be willing to write prescriptions for mifepristone."[13] While the list of mifepristone providers was supposed to be confidential, some providers feared that anti-abortion politicians would try to obtain the lists of providers from drug manufacturers and make their names public. Finally, Pearson said that the REMS stigmatized medication abortion, and contributed to the misperception that medication abortion was dangerous. "The fact that the FDA has kept medication abortion in a restricted access program for twenty years contributes to that false sense of abortion as being dangerous," said Pearson.[14] "The REMS restriction has been wrong for twenty years," said Pearson. "It is extra wrong now."

On March 30, 2020, a coalition of twenty-one state attorneys general led by California Attorney General Xavier Becerra sent an forceful letter to the US Department of Health and Human Services and the FDA, urging the Trump administration to waive or utilize its discretion on enforcement of its REMS designation.[15]

"As communities across the nation shelter in place to help prevent the spread of COVID-19, we must ensure that women can continue to safely access essential health services including safe and legal abortion," said Attorney General Becerra. Another signatory of the letter, New York Attorney General Leticia James, spoke up, calling on the FDA to lift the REMS restrictions on mifepristone. "As the coronavirus spreads across the country and residents are asked to stay at home, the federal government should be doing everything in its power to ensure women can maintain control of their reproductive choices," James said in a press release. "Control over one's reproductive freedom should not be limited to those able to leave their homes as we battle the coronavirus. Our coalition [of attorneys general] is calling on the federal government to make mifepristone more easily accessible so that no woman is forced to risk her health while exercising her constitutional right to an abortion."[16] The American College of Obstetricians and Gynecologists, the American Medical Association, and the American Association of Family Physicians all supported removal of the REMS on medication abortion for the duration of the pandemic.

Reproductive health advocates also pressed the Trump administration to lift the FDA's in-person distribution requirement for mifepristone. On April 6, 2020, NWHN sent a letter on behalf of eighty women's health organizations to FDA Commissioner Stephen Hahn demanding that the FDA remove the REMS restriction on mifepristone.[17] Then on April 27, Cynthia Pearson of NWHN teamed up with former FDA Assistant Commissioner for Women's Health Susan Wood in an opinion piece published in *The Hill* entitled "The U.K Allows Home Use of the Abortion Pill—the U.S. Should Do the Same." Noting that at the end of March, the United Kingdom authorized physicians to provide medication abortion through telemedicine for the duration of the coronavirus crisis, they argued that in light of the pandemic, the FDA "should allow pregnant people to get the pill where they take the pill—at home—and not require them to make an unnecessary and risky visit to a clinic."[18] NWHN created a social media campaign called "Get the Pill Where You Take It—At Home!" with the hashtag #FreeTheAbortionPill, a video, a petition, and digital billboards in New York state. On their website, NWHN shared data on the safety of abortion pills, noting they were six times safer than Viagra—yet the FDA allowed men to receive this medication by mail. Dr. Jamila Perritt of Physicians for Reproductive Health spoke out about the safety of abortion pills. "There are more complications and deaths associated with Tylenol than mifepristone," said Dr. Perritt. "If we are looking at it truly based on safety, then the argument doesn't hold water."[19] Cynthia Pearson said that the moment was right for the campaign. "We might not have even tried without the pandemic. But it was just the moment. Things were really different. We realized, we could do things now that we couldn't have done two or four months ago."[20]

Members of Congress put pressure on the FDA as well. On April 14, 2020, Senators Patty Murray (D-Wash.), Elizabeth Warren (D-Mass.), and Tammy Baldwin (D-Wisc.) sent a letter asking the FDA to lift the restriction during the pandemic.[21] In June, a group of 109 lawmakers, led by Reps. Diana DeGette (D-Colo.), Barbara Lee (D-Calif.), Ayanna Pressley (D-Mass.), and Jan Schakowsky (D-Ill.) sent a letter urging the FDA to permanently ease the dispensing restrictions on mifepristone. "The REMS in its current form creates an illogical situation in which a patient can meet with her doctor by telehealth from the safety of her home, take the pills at home, safely have her abortion at home, and follow up with her doctor after the abortion by telehealth again, but must first travel in the midst of a global pandemic just to pick up the pills from a registered facility or provider," the lawmakers wrote to FDA Commissioner Stephen Hahn. "For many patients, this requirement can mean taking public transportation, riding in someone else's car, or traveling hundreds of miles away from home to another county or state—significantly increasing their risk of exposure to the virus. It also means that some providers and clinic staff are forced to have unnecessary in-person interactions that increase their own exposure risks."[22] NWHN's Sarah Christopherson drafted the letter and lobbied members of Congress to sign it. NWHN also collected over twelve thousand signatures on a petition demanding that the FDA allow people to receive abortion pills through the mail. In September, NWHN staff delivered the petition signatures via a twenty-foot banner that they held up in front of the FDA headquarters (see Figure 3.1). The FDA did not respond.[23]

FIGURE 3.1: Sarah Christopherson, NWHN Policy Advocacy Director; Gabriela Salas, Policy Fellow; and Julia Kagan, Interim Communications Associate, holding a banner with the names of people signing the petition, in front of the FDA offices in Washington DC (courtesy of NWHN).

Meanwhile, Plan C began recruiting medical providers across the nation, beginning in March of 2020, asking them to step up and consider providing telemedicine abortion to patients during the pandemic. Hundreds responded to the call. Plan C talked to 120 people to get the first nine providers who offered telemedicine abortion.[24] Plan C then worked with researchers at the University of Washington School of Medicine to examine these remote abortion service operations in four settings: family planning clinics, online medical services, independent primary care practices, and multispecialty health systems. Clinicians used both synchronous methods, taking 10–30 minutes of clinician time, and asynchronous methods, taking 2–5 minutes of clinician time.[25] Based on this research, Plan C and University of Washington created the Access Delivered Provider Toolkit with step-by-step instructions on how to set up telehealth services for medication abortion.[26] Primary care providers, however, sometimes faced barriers to obtaining insurance. Some insurance companies would only cover obstetricians or gynecologists providing this care, or they required a special policy for covering abortion care, which could be expensive, despite the fact that medication abortion was so safe.[27]

In May 2020, ACOG filed a lawsuit challenging the FDA restriction. Represented by the ACLU's Reproductive Freedom Project and joined by the Council of University Chairs of Obstetrics and Gynecology, the New York Academy of Family Physicians, and SisterSong Women of Color Reproductive Justice Collective, ACOG asked a federal district court in Maryland to order the FDA to lift the REMS restriction on mifepristone during the COVID-19 epidemic. The plaintiffs argued that the in-person distribution requirement subjected patients to unnecessary risks of contracting COVID-19 as a condition of receiving the medication. "Our request in this case is simple: the federal government should permit patients seeking safe and effective reproductive health care, which includes care for miscarriage and termination of pregnancy, the same ability to access care and protect themselves from exposure as patients in other contexts are afforded," said ACOG president Dr. Eva Chalas. "Lifting the barriers to mifepristone will allow women, including those from underserved communities that are disproportionately affected by both COVID-19 and the ongoing maternal health crisis, the ability to obtain necessary and essential evidence-based care without having to risk potential life-threatening exposure."[28] SisterSong's executive director, Monica Simpson, said, "It is unconscionable that the FDA is subjecting women of color, who are disproportionately represented among patients seeking abortion and miscarriage care, to life-threatening viral risks as a condition of obtaining these urgent reproductive health services. Because of longstanding disparities in access to and quality of health care and other manifestations of structural racism, Black and Brown people are more likely to have preexisting health conditions that increase the likelihood of severe illness and death from COVID-19."[29]

Rather than trying to change the FDA REMS, some advocates used an alternative approach: reinterpret the REMS as not requiring in-person distribution of mifepristone.

The general consensus was that the REMS required medical providers to meet with their patients twice, once to dispense the abortion pills to them in person, and a second follow-up appointment to confirm the successful termination of the pregnancy. But some medical providers and advocates began challenging this interpretation. Plan C argued that the REMS did not require clinicians to hand the mifepristone to patients in person. The language of the FDA REMS said that pills must be "dispensed in a clinic" but did not explicitly say that the medication must be handed to the patient in person. Elisa Wells told *The New York Times*, "Most U.S. providers have taken the REMS to mean that mifepristone cannot be mailed. We disagree. We think providers have clear latitude to 'dispense' the drug from their offices and then ship it to patients, and we're hearing from more and more of our colleagues who see it the same way."[30] By early 2020, Plan C was working with clinicians across the country to help them register with the manufacturers of mifepristone so they could provide telemedicine abortion and mail pills to patients. Dozens of doctors signed up and some started mailing abortion pills to their patients, despite the REMS.[31]

But the REMS wasn't the only barrier to medication abortion. Nineteen states required the prescribing clinician to be physically present when prescribing the abortion pill, fifteen states required ultrasounds, and thirty-two states only allowed physicians to prescribe mifepristone. These requirements were not medically warranted but served as a mechanism to decrease access to abortion by limiting the number of clinicians able to offer the service and driving up the cost of abortion.[32]

At the time, advocates were very concerned about a Supreme Court case challenging *Roe v. Wade*. The case, *June Medical Services v. Russo*, involved a fifteen-week abortion ban in Louisiana, which was identical to a Texas law the Court had struck down in the 2016 case of *Whole Woman's Health v. Hellerstedt*. With Brett Kavanaugh now on the Court, advocates worried that the Court would overturn constitutional abortion rights and uphold the abortion ban. But on June 29, 2020, Chief Justice Roberts joined Justices Breyer, Ginsburg, Sotomayor, and Kagan in striking down the Louisiana law, although Roberts wrote a concurring opinion inviting another challenge to *Roe*. Thomas, Alito, Kavanaugh, and Gorsuch dissented.

Just weeks later, on July 13, 2020, a Maryland federal court issued an eighty-page decision temporarily suspending enforcement of the FDA requirement that patients make in-person visits to medical providers to get abortion pills. In *ACOG et al. v. FDA*, US District Court Judge Theodore Chuang ruled the FDA requirement of in-person visits during the pandemic imposed a "substantial obstacle" to abortion health care that was likely to be unconstitutional. Judge Chuang's order, which he declared would remain in place until at least thirty days after the end of the federal government's declared public health emergency, allowed patients to receive mifepristone from their doctors through the mail.[33] "Today's decision means that the Trump administration can no longer force patients to incur unnecessary COVID-19 risks as the price of getting abortion care," said ACLU Reproductive Freedom Project staff attorney Julia Kaye, who represented the plaintiffs in the case. "We look forward to a day when federal reproductive healthcare policy is grounded in science, not animus, and this medically baseless requirement is lifted once and for all."[34]

The Trump administration immediately appealed Judge Chuang's ruling to the Supreme Court, attempting to obtain a stay of the lower court's injunction. The Supreme Court denied the request in October 2020, but after the Fourth Circuit upheld Judge Chuang's ruling in November, the Trump administration appealed that ruling to the Supreme Court again.[35] In the meantime, healthcare providers began mailing abortion pills to their patients.

VIRTUAL ABORTION CLINICS

In the months following Judge Chuang's ruling, telemedicine abortion startups opened up across the country, including Just the Pill in Minnesota (Figure 3.2) and Choix in California. New online abortion clinics offered medication abortion for significantly less money than brick-and-mortar clinics, making abortion more affordable, which was especially important for young and low-income women without health insurance.

These virtual clinics screened patients remotely using the no-test, no-touch medical protocol, then mailed abortion pills to eligible patients at home. The nonprofit Just the Pill opened for business on October 12, 2020, offering telemedicine abortion care

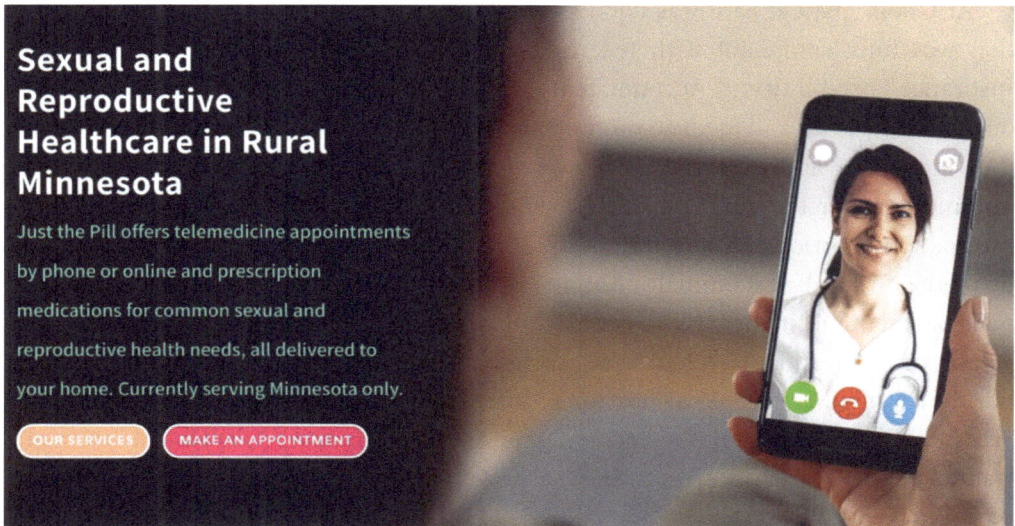

FIGURE 3.2: The website of telemedicine abortion provider Just the Pill opened in Minnesota in October 2020, after Judge Chuang's ruling allowing mailing of abortion pills (courtesy of Just the Pill).

to people in Minnesota.[36] Choix opened on October 28, 2020, offering abortion care to people in California.[37]

At Just the Pill, patients filled out an online form and then had a follow-up phone call with a patient educator and a doctor, who then mailed the pills to eligible patients. There were follow-up phone calls at seven days and four weeks. Just the Pill did not take insurance, but had a sliding scale fee structure up to $350. A Minnesota abortion fund, Our Justice, supported patients who couldn't pay the full fee. According to Medical Director Dr. Julie Amaon, Just the Pill formed to serve people in rural Minnesota who lived far from the state's five abortion clinics, which were concentrated in urban areas. After seeing her first thirty patients, Dr. Amaon reported that most of her patients lived more than one hundred miles from the nearest clinic. Dr. Amaon explained:

> Ninety-seven percent of counties in Minnesota do not have an abortion provider. In our research, people are having to sometimes drive three or four hours for services. That's tough when you have kids at home and you're trying to look for childcare. This is a very safe early option—that you can have a telemedicine appointment with a doctor in the comfort of your home and you get something mailed to your home. You don't have to leave the house. Women know how to take care of their bodies. This is just inducing a miscarriage. This is very safe. People have been doing this for centuries on their own. To have that ability to be able to take care of yourself at home, I think that's just an amazing service. And it should continue to be an option for women.[38]

Just the Pill offered translation services and soon expanded their services into Montana, where they were also licensed to practice and allowed telemedicine abortion.

At Choix, patient care was conducted asynchronously through encrypted texting that was fully compliant with federal privacy standards established by the Health Insurance Portability and Accountability Act (HIPAA) (see Figure 3.3). Patients filled out an online form and medical professionals consulted with them by text or telephone, then mailed the abortion pills. There were follow-up check-ins seventy-two hours and one month after the abortion. Choix charged $199 (compared to $500 for in-clinic medication abortion in California at the time). They did not take insurance, but they worked with the digital mutual-aid abortion fund Reprocare, which supported a sliding scale payment mechanism right on the Choix website. The co-founders of Choix, Cindy Adam and Lauren Dubey, had both worked as clinicians in a primary care practice, but they wanted to be able to provide a different type of care. "We wanted to expand access to folks who have limited access," said Adam, who was CEO at Choix. "We really wanted to help revolutionize abortion care. We are both really passionate about sexual reproductive health care."

Dubey, who was the chief nursing officer at Choix, hoped that services like Choix and Just the Pill would normalize abortion care. "Abortion is a totally normal part of

FIGURE 3.3: An image from the Choix website. The copy reads, "Online access to safe & affordable sexual & reproductive healthcare, including abortion care. Your body. Your health. Your time" (courtesy of Choix).

your reproductive health care. Having a pregnancy that you no longer want to continue is for some people a very huge grave decision and for other people it's not a big deal. People coming to our platform can come with pride or with shame—whatever their own feelings are, we will treat everybody with dignity and respect. We want people to feel like we're their partners in their reproductive future. We're not here to judge them."[39] Telemedicine made abortion accessible for people in rural areas, but it also made abortion access faster and more convenient for people living in urban areas. "In rural parts of California and urban parts of California, the desire is there," said Dubey, "whether it's an access issue or whether it's because the appointments are all booked up in urban areas."[40]

Clinic-based medication abortion care was often time-consuming and costly, said the medical director at Choix, Dr. Aisha Wagner, who noted that clinics were crowded, appointments could take several hours, providers often insisted on an in-person follow-up appointment, and many clinics required ultrasounds and blood tests, which were no longer the standard of care and made abortion care more expensive. "Some people may not have the time and money to go to a clinic and pay the higher cost associated with a medicalized abortion and take the hours of time," said Dr. Wagner. "You need to find childcare, you need to take time off of work."[41] Telemedicine care, on the other hand, could be scheduled quickly and happen wherever patients are, on their phone or computer. And virtual abortion clinics could provide eligible patients care right away, even in early pregnancy, unlike traditional abortion clinics, noted Dr. Wagner. "You usually can't proceed until there's a pregnancy seen on ultrasound. If you're only four weeks pregnant, you're not going to see anything on the ultrasound and therefore you're going to be turned away. For our platform, if you realize your period is two days late, you take a pregnancy test, and your pregnancy test is positive, you can zoom online right away and we can get this taken care of," said Dr. Wagner.[42] Online abortion care also allowed people seeking abortion care to avoid protesters at clinics and maintain more privacy than in-clinic care at traditional abortion clinics. "Even though you know you're going somewhere that's supportive, you're still meeting a lot of people, you're telling your story to a lot of people," said Dr. Wagner. "Even if you're not required to, I think people feel obligated to explain why they're there. It's just emotionally easier to do this at home on your own time."[43]

Reprocare worked with Choix to support their sliding scale fee structure and also offered peer-based support for people during a medication abortion.[44] "The potential for democratizing abortion access through these platforms is promising," said Morgan Love, a Reprocare co-founder and software engineer. "But it is imperative that this not become an 'elite' option, available only for those who can afford to pay out of pocket or have a strong personal network of support from which to draw. Reprocare offers a robust financial support platform designed to shift how abortion funding is achieved and perceived."[45] Reprocare co-founder Phoebe Abramowitz explained: "We were really excited to learn about the prospect of having medication abortion be accessible via the telehealth platforms. But we knew that for it to be truly accessible, it would need to be financially accessible."[46] Reprocare also offered peer-based support for people during a medication abortion through a confidential "healthline." "We provide emotional support and medical information for people planning abortion with pills at home," said Love. "We support the abortion-at-home model and make sure that folks who are having an abortion have peer-based support. We offer culturally congruent care because folks have the right to be supported by people who have a lived experience that resembles theirs," said Love.[47] Reprocare supported all callers, without asking for personally identifiable health information.

After Judge Chuang's ruling, several TelAbortion sites, including carafem and Maine Family Planning, began offering telemedicine abortion care without requiring ultrasounds. The FDA's COVID-19 guidance for testing relating to REMS drugs provided some flexibility in whether clinicians had to do ultrasounds for medication abortion. The guidance stated that healthcare providers should "use their best medical judgment in weighing the benefits and risks of continuing treatment in the absence of laboratory testing and imaging studies."[48]

Carafem, a nonprofit that offered in-person abortion care in several states since 2015, participated in the TelAbortion study from the outset, but expanded telemedicine care significantly during the pandemic after Judge Chuang's ruling. By November of 2020, they were offering telemedicine abortion care to approximately fifty clients a week in Georgia, Illinois, Maryland, Washington, DC, and Virginia combined. Melissa Grant, chief operating officer of FemHealth USA, which owned carafem, said that carafem "seeks to normalize, 'de-medicalize,' and remove the social stigma from the provision of birth control and early abortion care."[49] Carafem offered video visits for medication abortion, which lasted about thirty minutes. Then they provided a secure text messaging platform with a virtual assistant, named Cara, who connected patients with staff if needed twenty-four hours a day, seven days a week. Carafem charged between $325 and $375, depending on the medication selected, and included a follow-up check-in within forty-eight hours and confirmation of a negative pregnancy test at thirty days. Unlike many other telemedicine abortion providers, carafem took insurance, including Medicaid in Illinois and Maryland. Some brick-and-mortar clinics also began offering curbside pick-up of abortion medications after a telehealth consultation.[50]

A key development facilitating access to telemedicine abortion was the decision in the fall of 2020 by the online pharmacy Honeybee Health to dispense abortion pills. Coeytaux and Wells had been working to find a pharmacy to mail abortion pills. "We approached reproductive health delivery services early on and asked them to add abortion pills, but they couldn't get their boards to do it," said Wells. "They thought it was too big a risk and that they would lose business, which I think was totally wrong. Fear and the stigma influenced their decision." Then Judge Chuang ruled that providers could contract with mail order pharmacies to dispense mifepristone.[51] "I heard it on a briefing call by the ACLU and immediately followed up with them to hear more of the details, letting them know that we were already in touch with a pharmacy that wanted to do this—Honeybee," said Wells. "They got it set up about three weeks later!"[52] Honeybee Health, which Jessica Nouhavandi and Peter Wang had launched in California in 2018, sold generic abortion pills at steep discounts without billing insurance.[53] In fall of 2020, they began filling abortion pill prescriptions from certified clinicians in Washington, New York, and New Jersey, and quickly expanded to other states. Honeybee was able to offer low prices because they bought medications directly from FDA-approved, wholesale distributors and cut out intermediaries, such as insurance companies and pharmacy benefit managers. As a result, they could sell generic medications for up to 80 percent less than what traditional pharmacies charged—often less than copays or coinsurance. The option to use Honeybee Health to dispense mifepristone and misoprostol made it easier for healthcare providers to offer medication abortion services because they did not have to stock and dispense the drugs themselves. After screening patients for eligibility, clinicians could just send prescriptions directly to Honeybee, where trained pharmacists would process and ship the medication to the patients directly.

Advocates hoped mail order pharmacies paired with the no-test protocol would increase the likelihood that more family medicine providers who did not own expensive ultrasound machines and did not want to stock and dispense mifepristone themselves would now provide medication abortion services. "The exciting thing is that we're moving towards this twenty-first century model of abortion care where abortion pills can be obtained through a pharmacy like almost every other medication that people get from a doctor, and it can be done without an in-person visit," said Plan C co-CEO Elisa Wells. "This type of access is inevitable. It is the future of abortion here in the United States," she added optimistically.[54] However, while the Honeybee Health board and current investors were very supportive, Nouhavandi said that many people, including those who say they support women's health, were "skittish" about helping startups that work on abortion.[55] Dr. Nouhavandi also spoke out about the importance of increasing access to abortion pills:

> This is a momentous achievement for Americans, particularly for women of color and others who historically faced barriers to reproductive health care that are made even worse by COVID-19. As a pharmacy, we believe everyone has the right to choose whether or not an abortion is right for them. We're deeply honored to be part of the pioneering group of medical professionals who are bringing increased access to safe abortion pills across the country.

Dr. Nouhavandi saw Judge Chuang's ruling as a window of opportunity to prove the viability of a new model of abortion health care: "Abortion pills are extremely safe, effective, and widely used in other countries without the kind of political scrutiny we see in America. We hope that by shipping abortion pills now during COVID-19, we increase access for the years to come."[56] Shortly after, American Mail Order Pharmacy, based in Michigan, began mailing abortion pills to patients who obtained prescriptions via telehealth or in clinic.[57]

ORGANIZING TO SUPPORT INCREASED ACCESS TO ABORTION PILLS OUTSIDE OF THE MEDICAL SYSTEM

The future of *Roe v. Wade* became increasingly precarious when Supreme Court Justice Ruth Bader Ginsburg died on September 18, 2020, just forty-six days before the 2020 presidential election. Donald Trump nominated Amy Coney Barrett nine days later. Despite having refused to hold hearings on President Barack Obama's nomination of Merrick Garland ten months before the election because it was "too close to the election," the Republican-led Senate quickly confirmed Coney Barrett on October 26, 2020, just eight days before the presidential election. She was sworn in on the same day. Conservatives now had a 6–3 supermajority on the Supreme Court, setting the stage for the overturn of *Roe v. Wade.*

Anticipating this development, Plan C rolled out a new website at plancpills.org in November of 2020. The website had comprehensive information about how people in the United States were obtaining abortion pills by mail. The website included a *Plan C Guide to Pills*, searchable by state, with information about telemedicine services available in each state. They listed Aid Access, Just the Pill, and Choix, and added new services as they started up. Aid Access served people in all fifty states, offering online consultations and shipping of abortion pills for a sliding scale fee up to $95. In some states, including New York, New Jersey, Washington, Nevada, Idaho, and Alaska, Aid Access had contracted with US-based clinicians so patients could receive their medications directly from clinicians or from Honeybee Health in just a few days. For people living in other states, Aid Access sent their prescriptions to a pharmacist in India, who shipped the pills to them within two to three weeks.

Plan C also listed websites selling abortion pills, which did not require a prescription or any screening process. Researchers at Plan C ordered pills from these websites, documenting the process, and then tested the medications in a lab to determine whether they were the correct medication and dosage. They never found any fake abortion pills. On their website, they listed the best companies and shared information about cost, payment options, and shipping time. A third option described on the Plan C website was to use mail forwarding to obtain abortion pills from a US-based telemedicine provider, which for people in states without telemedicine providers was quicker than using Aid Access. Plan C described how people were renting an address through mail forwarding services such as iPostal1.com or Anytime Mailbox in a state allowing telemedicine abortion, then doing an online consultation with a telemedicine provider in that state and listing the mail forwarding service address as the shipping address. On the website they explained, "If asked, they confirm they are in that state at the time of the consultation (since the providers are only allowed to serve people in those states)…When the mail forwarding service tells them that a package has arrived at their 'address,' they ask for it to be forwarded to them at their home address."[58] Others used "general delivery" at a US Post Office on the state border to reduce the distance they had to travel. "General delivery" meant that mail was sent to a person at a specific US post office and the person receiving the mail would go there in person to pick it up with an ID that matched the name on the package. There was no need to set up a post office box and no charge for this service.[59] In addition to information about how people were obtaining abortion pills, the Plan C website shared information about medical, emotional, financial, and legal support services, including the M+A Hotline, Reprocare's Healthline, abortion fund information, and If/When/How's Repro Legal

Helpline. The Plan C website also had information for medical professionals about how to become medication abortion providers.[60]

Advocates were optimistic that telemedicine abortion could revolutionize abortion health care by significantly expanding abortion access in the United States. "We've been fighting for a long time to say abortion should remain legal," said Grant of carafem in November of 2020. "But it's equally important in the places where it's legal to make sure it's accessible. Because if you can't get to the care, whether it's legal or not doesn't really matter. So if you're in a small town, and don't have a car, and don't have a job, and are stuck without anyone that's going to be supportive of your decision, then you effectively still have no choice even though it is legal in your state."[61] Advocates hoped the pandemic had opened a door that would be hard to close back up. Once people realized how safe, easy, and accessible medication abortion could be, they were unlikely to go quietly back to the old days of cumbersome, over-medicalized, time-consuming, and expensive abortion health care.

SUPREME COURT STOPS TELEMEDICINE ABORTION

But the counterforces were powerful. In September 2020, nearly a hundred Republicans from both chambers of Congress urged the FDA to take the drug off the market entirely.[62] Despite losing the 2020 election, Donald Trump's administration persisted in a second Supreme Court appeal of the Maryland court ruling allowing telemedicine abortion. On January 12, 2021, just days before the inauguration of Joseph Biden, the six conservative members of the Supreme Court—three of whom were appointed by Trump—granted the Trump administration request to reinstate the FDA rule requiring patients seeking medication abortion to make an in-person visit to their healthcare provider, despite research showing this served no medical purpose.[63]

Justices Sotomayor, Kagan, and Breyer dissented from the Court's majority. Sotomayor joined Justice Kagan in a scathing dissent, castigating the majority for callously forcing patients to expose themselves and others to the deadly COVID-19 virus for no medical benefit. Citing Justice Ruth Bader Ginsburg, Justice Sotomayor wrote:

> Maintaining the FDA's in-person requirements for mifepristone during the pandemic not only treats abortion exceptionally, it imposes an unnecessary, irrational, and unjustifiable undue burden on women seeking to exercise their right to choose. One can only hope that the Government will reconsider and exhibit greater care and empathy for women seeking some measure of control over their health and reproductive lives in these unsettling times… "[Women's] ability to realize their full potential…is intimately connected to their ability to control their reproductive lives."[64]

Sotomayor and Kagan argued that requiring in-person visits to doctors placed an undue burden on abortion access: "Due to particularly severe health risks, vastly limited clinic options, and the 10-week window for obtaining a medication abortion, the FDA's requirement that women obtain mifepristone in person during the COVID-19 pandemic places an unnecessary and undue burden on their right to abortion." They emphasized that many medical offices had closed or dramatically reduced their open hours during the pandemic. They argued that this policy particularly endangered minority and low-income populations, who are "more likely to live in intergenerational housing, so patients risk infecting not just themselves, but also elderly parents and grandparents," making the in-person medical visit a significant deterrent for women seeking medication abortion. Sotomayor also noted the district court's finding that the in-person visit requirement could cause women to miss the ten-week window for a medication abortion. Sotomayor condemned the majority's response that women can just get a surgical abortion as "callous," describing in detail this "far more invasive" procedure:

> Medication abortion involves taking two pills and is the equivalent of an early miscarriage. When a woman undergoes surgical abortion, she requires local anesthesia and sometimes sedation, her cervix is stretched with dilating rods, a tube is inserted through her cervix into her uterus, and, depending on the particular procedure, various medical tools are used to remove fetal tissue from her uterus. On top of this, surgical abortions carry all the same (and likely greater) risks of exposure to COVID-19 as do medication abortion's in-person requirements.[65]

Sotomayor concluded, "Together, patients' health vulnerabilities, public transportation risks, susceptible older family members at home, and clinic closures and reduced services pose substantial, sometimes insurmountable, obstacles for women seeking medication abortions during the COVID-19 pandemic."

After the decision was released, medical providers and advocates expressed outrage. "It is disgraceful and frankly frightening that instead of listening to expert medical and scientific consensus about the safety of medication abortion and the risks imposed by these unwarranted restrictions, the Supreme Court chose to listen to politicians with an anti-science, anti-abortion agenda," said Dr. Jason Matuszak, president of New York State Academy of Family Physicians. "It's past time for the FDA to eliminate these baseless restrictions—not only during the pandemic, but for good."[66] The ACOG president Dr. Eva Chalas agreed: "Despite the administration's claims, the facts in this case remain clear: Mifepristone is a safe, effective medication for termination of pregnancy, and its use should not expose patients or clinicians to added risk of COVID-19 infection."[67] ACLU Reproductive Freedom Project staff attorney Julia Kaye, who represented the plaintiffs, also condemned the decision:

The Court's ruling rejects science, compassion, and decades of legal precedent in service of the Trump administration's anti-abortion agenda. It is mind-boggling that the Trump administration's top priority on its way out the door is to needlessly endanger even *more* people during this dark pandemic winter—and chilling that the Supreme Court allowed it. The Biden–Harris administration must right this wrong on day one and hold firm to its commitment to support both evidence-based regulations and reproductive freedom.[68]

Advocates emphasized the particularly negative impacts on low-income women and women of color, who were more vulnerable to COVID-19. Monica Simpson, executive director of SisterSong Women of Color Reproductive Justice Collective, noted, "With today's ruling, the Supreme Court told people of color that unnecessary risk of exposure to a virus that is disproportionately killing our communities is a fair price to pay for access to abortion. Black, Brown, and Indigenous folks should not have to endure yet another form of state violence while we are fighting for our lives in this pandemic."[69] Sung Yeon Choimorrow, executive director of National Asian Pacific Women's Forum, agreed: "Asian American and Pacific Islander women and other women of color are disproportionately harmed by restrictions on abortion, just as we have disproportionately suffered the health and economic effects of COVID-19."[70] Advocates called on the Biden administration to act immediately to lift the in-person distribution requirement for mifepristone.

As a result of the Supreme Court's January 12 decision, many virtual clinics stopped mailing abortion pills, while others, such as Abortion on Demand, delayed launching. Some found other ways to get abortion pills to their patients like Just the Pill, which started using a Class B RV as a mobile clinic to deliver pills to their patients.[71] Others, however, insisted the REMS did not disallow mailing of abortion pills. In fact, two new virtual abortion clinics launched in early 2021. Hey Jane, which raised more than $3 million in venture capital funding,[72] launched in Washington and New York in January of 2021. Forward Midwifery launched in California in February of 2021.[73] These providers offered services asynchronously by online form, increasing convenience and access to more people.

The Gynuity Health Project's TelAbortion study, which provided medication abortion via the mail as part of a research exception to the FDA restriction, was able to continue, but patients were again subject to the FDA requirement that they obtain ultrasounds beforehand, which meant they had to make an in-person visit to a medical clinic. "The ruling means additional hurdles and barriers to accessing medical abortion and it means putting people's health in jeopardy during a pandemic," said Tara Shochet, co-director of the TelAbortion Project.[74] Advocates at Plan C, however, persisted in their belief that the REMS did not require clinicians to hand the abortion pill to patients in person but required only that the clinician "distribute" the medication to their patients, which Plan C said they could do by mail. Most advocates and doctors, however, believed that an in-person visit was required.

Despite the Trump administration's opposition to abortion and the erection of heightened barriers to reproductive health care and abortion at the state and federal levels, the number of abortions in the United States increased by 8 percent during Trump's presidency—from 862,320 in 2017 to 930,160 in 2020, according to a Guttmacher report. Overall, fewer people became pregnant, but among those who did, a larger proportion chose to have an abortion. About one in five pregnancies in 2020 ended in abortion.[75] Guttmacher suggested several factors may have contributed to this increase, including more unintended pregnancies due to the Trump administration's policy of dramatically slashing Title X family planning services and access to contraception. Other possible factors included expanded access to Medicaid coverage of abortion health care in blue states and impacts of the COVID-19 pandemic. This research revealed a dramatic reversal of a thirty-year trend of declining numbers of abortion, "underscoring that the need for abortion care in the United States is growing just as the U.S. Supreme Court appears likely to overturn or gut *Roe v. Wade*," said the Guttmacher report. "Rather than focusing on reducing abortion, policies should instead center the needs of people and protect their right to bodily autonomy."[76]

According to the Guttmacher report, the number of abortions increased in all four regions of the country between 2017 and 2020. The rise was largest in the West (12 percent increase) and Midwest (10 percent increase); abortions increased 8 percent in the South and 2 percent in the Northeast. But there was significant variation across and within states. In some states—including Illinois, Mississippi, and Oklahoma—there were substantial increases in the number of abortions. In others—such as Missouri, Oregon, and South Dakota—there were substantially fewer abortions in 2020 compared with 2017. Expanded Medicaid coverage of abortion health care likely contributed to more abortions in some states, including a 25 percent increase in Illinois and a 16 percent increase in Maine, which also required private health insurance plans to cover abortion health care for the first time. The increased number of abortions in Illinois was also due to people coming from nearby states that imposed new restrictions, such as Missouri, where the number of abortions decreased from 4,710 in 2017 to 170 in 2020. Illinois actually increased the number of clinics from twenty-five in 2017 to thirty in 2020. Overall, the number of abortion facilities in the United States increased from 774 in 2017 to 790 in 2021, but with significant geographic variation.[77]

COVID-19 had varying impacts on abortion numbers across states. In hard-hit New York, where at least 10 percent of clinics paused or stopped providing abortion care early in the pandemic, the number of abortions dropped 6 percent between 2019 and 2020. Meanwhile, the number of abortions dropped in states like Texas and Alabama, which imposed COVID-19 restrictions on abortion health care, falsely deemed "nonessential," but the number of abortions in surrounding states increased, likely due to women traveling from restrictive states to find abortion health care. The Guttmacher report noted other factors that likely contributed to state variation and overall increase in the number of abortions, including increased fundraising by local and national abortion funds so they could help more people pay for their abortions, increased abortion restrictions and bans (twenty-five states enacted 168 laws between 2017 and 2020, some of which were blocked by courts), and seventy-five new provisions to protect abortion rights (repealing restrictions, expanding insurance coverage, and allowing more qualified clinicians such as nurse practitioners, physician assistants, or certified nurse midwives to provide at least some abortion care). "The Supreme Court is poised to overturn *Roe v. Wade* at a time when need for abortion care has been increasing," concluded the report. "This means the impact of the ruling could be even more devastating than predicted by prior analyses, particularly for people across the country who already struggle to access abortion care."[78]

In December of 2020, the Generative Learning Community (GLC) for self-managed abortion expanded, opening membership to more organizations. GLC grew to over seventy organizations and held meetings every other month as a "gathering space" for "shared learning and problem solving" on self-managed abortion. GLC also engaged in "culture change work" to normalize self-managed abortion.[79] GLC had two goals: "to give every person the option to end a pregnancy safely and with support, within the formal healthcare system, or outside it" and to "ensure no one risks punishment or imprisonment for their reproductive choices or for supporting a person who is self-managing the end of a pregnancy."[80] Their purpose was to normalize self-managed abortion by promoting a "positive narrative, and avoiding harmful messages, about self-managed abortion."[81] They focused on "developing tools and actions for use in communications" and committed to "do nothing that puts pregnant people, or those who support them, at increased risk of investigation, prosecution, and punishment for their reproductive choices." This limited approach later led to a break with Plan C because of their work to make pills available to people in states with abortion bans, which inevitably created some legal risks.[82]

The GLC focused primarily on normalizing abortion pills inside the reproductive health movement. "The medical community could get overly controlling about mifepristone," explained Kirsten Moore. "What the GLC did was hold a mirror up to the medical professionals and say, 'you know you're overthinking this, you're over-traumatizing this.' They consistently normalized the idea that patients can manage their abortions on their own," said Moore, noting that GLC held a full-day workshop on self-managed abortion at a NAF meeting in early 2022. "It's about getting the movement itself to move into the twenty-first century."[83]

THE PENDULUM SWINGS: BIDEN ADMINISTRATION EXPANDS ABORTION PILL ACCESS

Immediately after the 2020 election of Joseph Biden, reproductive rights advocates asked the new administration to review the FDA's abortion pill restrictions. "These restrictions place more of a burden than a benefit on providers and their patients," said Kirsten Moore, referring to the FDA standard for imposing the REMS restriction. "Based on opinion research we conducted last year, people like the idea that women have access to an option for ending an early pregnancy," said Moore. "And they like the idea that it's an FDA-approved drug that's been around for twenty years. We think it's time to revisit these restrictions and move forward."[84]

Even before the election, medical professionals and activists were calling on Biden to reverse the Trump policy and end the FDA restriction on the abortion pill altogether. A coalition of more than ninety women's rights organizations released a "Blueprint for Sexual and Reproductive Health, Rights and Justice" that made two demands with regard to mifepristone. The first was that President Biden issue an executive order on his first day in office directing the Secretary of Health and Human Services to lift the in-person distribution requirement for mifepristone during the pandemic. The second demand was that within ninety days of assuming office, the president direct the FDA to review the mifepristone REMS to determine whether it should be modified or removed to "best reflect scientific evidence and real-world use."[85] On January 27, 2021, Guttmacher Institute's president and CEO Herminia Palacio and Dr. Daniel Grossman of ANSIRH wrote an op-ed in *The Washington Post* urging Biden to remove the in-person distribution requirement. "Facts matter, and the facts couldn't be clearer," they wrote. "In this moment, when the country is looking to the administration to heed public health experts, it must suspend this requirement for the duration of the public health emergency and direct the FDA to ensure its medication abortion policies are aligned with the scientific evidence."[86] At a more personal level, Sarah Christopherson of NWHN found people to speak directly with President Biden about mifepristone. "I spent some time organizing high-net-worth major donors. I had some leftover contacts and some leftover favors to call in from people I knew would be receptive and get it, and be good spokeswomen for it," said Christopherson.[87]

On February 9, 2021, eleven female Democratic members of the House Committee on Oversight and Reform wrote a letter to the Acting Commissioner of the FDA Janet Woodcock[88] urging her to lift the in-person abortion pill distribution requirement. In the letter, they emphasized the FDA's illogical policy on mifepristone: "Of the more than 20,000 drugs regulated by FDA, mifepristone is the only drug that FDA requires patients to obtain in person at a hospital, clinic, or medical office, but it does not restrict the ability of patients to self-administer—unsupervised—at home or at a location of their choosing." They described a strong safety record of mifepristone, and the risks imposed on patients by the in-person distribution requirement. They concluded, "In light of the clear danger that the reinstated requirement poses to people seeking comprehensive reproductive health care at the height of the coronavirus pandemic, we urge you to immediately eliminate the medically unnecessary in-person dispensing requirement for mifepristone."[89]

On March 18, fifty-five reproductive health, rights, and justice groups sent a letter to President Biden urging his administration to lift FDA restrictions on mifepristone. The letter emphasized the burden of the FDA restrictions on marginalized communities:

> Consistent with your important commitment to follow the science in responding to COVID-19, as well as your critical promise to tackle issues of systemic equity across the government, it is imperative that your administration prioritize safe access to medication abortion. Burdensome restrictions on medication abortion, which are not based in medical evidence, deepen the health inequities already experienced by those who are struggling to make ends meet, particularly people of color, who comprise a majority of medication abortion patients and are now being hit hardest by the COVID-19 pandemic.[90]

Along with the letter, they delivered a petition with over 200,000 signatures of supporters.

On April 12, 2021, under the leadership of Dr. Janet Woodcock, the FDA finally lifted the in-person distribution requirement for the duration of the COVID-19 public health emergency, allowing clinicians to resume telemedicine abortion services.[91] In a letter to ACOG and the Society for Maternal-Fetal Medicine, Dr. Woodcock wrote that the FDA would waive the requirement that clinicians dispense mifepristone to their patients in a clinic or hospital setting. The letter said research studies on telemedicine abortion "do not appear to show increases in serious safety concerns occurring with medical abortion as a result of modifying the in-person dispensing requirement during the COVID-19 pandemic."[92] ACOG issued a statement praising the new guidelines: "We are pleased to see mifepristone regulated on the basis of the scientific evidence during the pandemic, rather than political bias against comprehensive reproductive health care, and we look forward to working with policy makers to ensure this principle governs post-pandemic care."[93] Advocates celebrated the decision for following the science. "We know from twenty years of research that medication abortion is extremely safe—even safer than some over-the-counter medications. It's past time to permanently lift the restrictions and make medication abortion more accessible for those who need it," said Dr. Grossman of ANSIRH. Online pharmacies resumed distribution of mifepristone by mail. Sarah Christopherson said all the strategies contributed toward their success: "I don't think any one strategy would have been sufficient on its own. I think it took all of them. It took the medical studies, proving how safe it was. It took EMAA working the inside angle with the FDA staff. It took us and others working the political angle with the incoming Biden administration. It took public outrage. It took all of it."[94]

After their success with lifting the in-person distribution requirement for mifepristone for the duration of the pandemic, reproductive health advocates immediately pressed the FDA to permanently drop the restriction. "We must now fight to make this change permanent, and to lift all medically unnecessary restrictions on medication abortion during the pandemic and beyond," said Cynthia A. Pearson, NWHN executive director.[95] Advocates emphasized that the FDA action was not enough because many states still had laws prohibiting telemedicine abortion or requiring ultrasounds that had the same effect. "This is great that the FDA used science to reduce this barrier, but it's clearly not enough," said Plan C's Elisa Wells. "We have a huge equity issue in our country for access to abortion because of the state-based laws. We know that the people who are the hardest hit by abortion restrictions are people who are already marginalized either by their skin color or their socio-economic status or, in some cases, their gender identity."[96] At the time, a new ban on telemedicine abortions in Ohio had just been blocked by a state court, but other states were considering similar bans, including Indiana, Arkansas, Iowa, Alabama, Texas, Oklahoma, Wyoming, and West Virginia.

Wells predicted that increasing access would create change across the country. "With the FDA ruling and with the types of services that are going to pop up, it's really going to raise awareness in this country that we have this option of abortion pills, which a lot of people don't even know about, and of the fact that you can get them in this very simple, very private, and very safe and effective way," said Wells. "Once that genie is out of the bottle, it's not going back in. It's going to be available in more liberal states. As it becomes more normalized and more mainstream, then people who live in the more restrictive states will have more ammunition to demand access to it in their states as well. That's always been our strategy to start with the low-hanging fruit—the liberal states—demonstrate the model, and then generate demand for it in the states that are more restrictive."[97]

On May 7, the Biden administration announced that the FDA would undertake a full review of the in-person distribution requirement for mifepristone and consider permanently removing it. The announcement came as part of a joint legal filing in the ACLU lawsuit *Chelius v. Becerra*, challenging the REMS restrictions.[98] As a result of FDA actions, more virtual telemedicine abortion clinics opened (see Figure 3.4). Abortion on Demand launched in twenty states and Washington, DC, in April of 2021, conducting appointments by videoconference, using express shipping for next-day arrival, and charging $239. They checked in by text after the patient had taken the pills and offered support from a doctor twenty-four hours a day, seven days a week.[99] Pills by Post, launched in Colorado, Illinois, and Minnesota in the fall of 2021, offered telemedicine abortion by phone consultation for a sliding scale fee of $150.[100] Hey Jane offered telemedicine abortion in Washington and New York for $249 using the Spruce

FIGURE 3.4: Logos from some of the telemedicine abortion providers in 2020 and 2021 (design by Roxy Szal).

app, a HIPAA-compliant texting app, but allowed patients to request a videoconference or telephone call any time.[101] Forward Midwifery offered telemedicine abortion in California by telephone for a sliding scale $150 fee.[102]

More brick-and-mortar reproductive health clinics began offering telemedicine abortion as well, often charging more than virtual clinics but sometimes less than in-clinic medication abortion. Unlike many virtual clinics, brick-and-mortar practices usually accepted insurance. A nurse practitioner, Robin Tucker, at the Bethesda-based Metro Area Advanced Practice Healthcare began offering telemedicine abortion in the fall of 2021, serving people in Virginia, Maryland, and Maine for a sliding scale fee of $150.[103] A reproductive healthcare provider in Seattle, Dr. Deb Oyer, was an early adopter of this approach when she began offering telemedicine abortion via videoconferencing in April of 2020 as part of her reproductive healthcare practice. She accepted health insurance and charged $600 for cash pay patients, which included a follow-up if they needed a procedural completion.[104]

Family medicine doctors also began offering telemedicine abortion as part of their general practice or on the side. Dr. Michele Gomez, a family medicine doctor working for Family Care Associates in Burlingame, California, began offering telemedicine abortion by videoconference to her patients shortly after the pandemic started. She charged a self-pay price of $280 but also accepted insurance.[105] Dr. Alison Case based in Indiana and working at a federally qualified health center began offering telemedicine abortion part time in the fall of 2021 through Whole Woman's Health to people in New Mexico for $400. Half of her patients came from Texas.[106]

Research on telemedicine abortion during the pandemic confirmed that many patients preferred telemedicine to in-clinic abortions. Telemedicine patients reported that they liked to choose their consultation location and reported feeling more relaxed during the consultation, whereas women with in-clinic appointments reported their consultations as "lengthy, chaotic and lacking comfort."[107] One telemedicine patient explained, "I like the flexibility of doing things virtually, so I was able to just do it while I was at work. I didn't have to take time off because I [have to be at work during] the time that clinics are open." Telemedicine patients reported that they appreciated that there was no one else around or that their friends could be with them. On the other hand, an in-clinic patient reported, "While at the clinic, it felt like cattle herding, go in, get it done, go out, and go to the next room." In-clinic patients also reported discomfort having to pass protesters at the clinic. Researchers concluded that telemedicine consultations allowed patients to "feel like their encounter was more controlled and relaxed."[108]

To help medical providers wanting to offer telemedicine abortion, Plan C worked closely with them through the process of registering with the drug manufacturers Danco or GenBioPro, developing their telemedicine platforms, and signing up with Honeybee Health, American Mail Order Service, and later a third dispensary, Manifest Pharmacy. These new telehealth abortion providers made medication abortion more convenient, affordable, and accessible for many people, especially low-income people and those living in rural areas. Some traditional abortion providers, however, did not welcome telemedicine abortion. "Clinics that have been providing in-clinic care all these years are feeling threatened by alternative modes of care," said Emily Godfrey, a primary care provider who conducted research on telemedicine abortion.[109]

To encourage broader access to medication abortion, the New York City-based family medicine doctor Joan Fleischman issued a call to action to primary care providers to integrate early abortion services into their practices. Around sixty clinicians expressed their support. Dr. Michele Gomez and Dr. Erica Bliss from Seattle, Washington, joined Dr. Fleischman to form an organization called the MYA Network to train and support primary care physicians and other medical providers to offer medication abortion. "Early abortion can be part of a regular primary care practice, so the patient doesn't have to be referred anywhere else," explained Gomez. "Because it's medically simple, you don't need to have a high volume to be good at it. Early abortion is not medically complicated and can be safely provided by any primary care clinician with the right training. Telemedicine abortion is particularly easy. Family medicine doctors, primary care internal medicine doctors, and advanced practice clinicians like nurse practitioners and physician assistants are perfectly capable of providing early abortions."[110] The MYA Network created a website listing primary care providers offering medication abortion by state so patients could find them. By early 2022, they listed clinicians in seven states.

According to ANSIRH, the number of providers of medication abortion and telehealth abortion increased significantly between 2020 and 2022. The number of facilities offering medication abortion increased from 733 in 2020 to 773 in 2021 to 789 in 2022. The proportion of those facilities that provided telehealth with the option to have abortion pills mailed to pregnant people increased from 52 (7 percent) facilities in 11 states in 2020 to 91 (12 percent) facilities in 25 states in 2021 to 243 (31 percent) facilities in 27 states in 2022. The number of virtual clinics increased as well. In 2021, 32 virtual clinics were providing care via telehealth in 22 states and DC (4 percent of 773 facilities offering medication abortion). By 2022, 69 virtual clinics provided this care in 23 states and DC (9 percent of 789 facilities offering medication abortion).[111]

As legislators and courts erected higher and more daunting barriers to delay and obstruct access to abortion health care, public health experts began arguing for creative new ways to ensure that people who want or need to end unwanted pregnancies could get abortion pills quickly and use them safely. One strategy was advance provision of abortion pills—to have them on hand prophylactically. In December of 2021, Katherine Ehrenreich, Antonia Biggs, and Daniel Grossman at ANSIRH published an editorial in a leading public health journal, arguing for advance provision of abortion pills as an option and explaining how it could work in practice. They recommended that clinicians who prescribed abortion pills in advance should provide patients with information about how to take the pills and offer support and follow-up care if patients later chose to use them.

Ehrenreich, Biggs, and Grossman argued that this model could significantly shorten the time between the decision to end a pregnancy and having an abortion, and short circuit the medically unnecessary obstacle course that existed in many states for people trying to access medication abortion.[112] "Patients often face unnecessary delays in accessing abortion care—from state-mandated waiting periods to delays due to overcrowded clinics. If patients have pills on hand in advance, those delays are eliminated," said Grossman. "Before emergency contraception (aka the morning-after pill) became available over the counter, clinicians often gave it to patients in advance to have on hand when they needed it. Given the restrictions on abortion, we should think about this strategy for abortion pills."[113] They noted that mifepristone had a shelf life of about five years, and misoprostol had a shelf life of about two years when stored in a dry, dark place. "There are some challenges with advance provision, including the cost of the pills and state legislation that may limit this model," said Grossman. "But I hope clinicians will consider this option given the crisis in abortion access we are currently facing."[114]

Research showed many women wanted to have abortion pills on hand in case they had an unintentional pregnancy. In one national survey, 44 percent of respondents said they would be interested in advance provision of abortion pills. Those who faced barriers to reproductive health care were more likely to want pills in advance.[115] "While a future landscape of medication abortion may include telemedicine and mail-order pharmacy dispensing, advance provision may be a preferable option for those who would continue to face barriers to care," wrote Ehrenreich, Biggs, and Grossman.[116]

As the FDA considered whether to permanently remove the in-person distribution requirement, Plan C and telehealth providers made significant progress in developing systems to get pills in people's hands as easily as possible, preparing the way for what would come as the Supreme Court readied itself to overturn constitutional abortion rights.

CHAPTER 4

"Trying to Shake Abortion Pills Free from the Gatekeepers": Eroding Abortion Rights and Expanding Self-Managed Abortion

FDA restrictions on mifepristone and the medical profession's tight control of abortion pills combined with the anti-abortion movement's success in closing down clinics to leave many women without access to medication abortion. An increasing number turned to self-managed abortion. With a supermajority of anti-abortion judges on the Supreme Court and the overturn of *Roe v. Wade* looming, activists worked to increase access to telemedicine, but they also doubled down on finding creative ways to help people access abortion pills outside of the medical system. Despite the legal risks, US advocates worked with women in other countries to develop alternative supply networks for abortion pills that would play a critical role post-*Roe*. But not everyone agreed with this approach, leading to divisions in the movement. This chapter describes the growing legal restrictions on abortion in 2021, advocates' work to increase access to abortion pills both inside and outside of the medical system, conflicts among abortion advocates about self-managed abortion, and concerns about legal risks.

TEXAS BANS ABORTION: S.B. 8 SPURS SELF-MANAGED ABORTION

In the first four months of 2021, anti-abortion lawmakers introduced 536 abortion restrictions in forty-six states, including 146 abortion bans, according to a report released by the Guttmacher Institute. They enacted sixty-one restrictions in thirteen states, including eight "trigger" bans that would go into effect when the Supreme Court overturned *Roe v. Wade*.[1] As abortion in the formal medical system became less accessible and more expensive, people increasingly turned to alternative sources such as Aid Access to obtain abortion pills.

Online demand for abortion pills had surged when the pandemic hit in early 2020, especially in states that closed abortion clinics such as Texas, where requests for abortion pills made to Aid Access increased by 94 percent.[2] Another surge began on May 17, 2021, when the US Supreme Court announced they would hear a case involving a Mississippi abortion ban. Online searches for terms related to abortion pills such as "misoprostol" and "medical abortion" exploded by more than 5,000 percent in the twenty-four hours after the Court's announcement. "We see a definite spike in visitors to our website when there is news about abortion bans," said Elisa Wells after the announcement. "People are looking for ways to access abortion pills. The need for abortion is never going to go away. When you cut off mainstream supply of it through clinical means, people will look for other ways to access the service."[3]

A similar surge happened on May 19 when the Texas governor signed legislation, called Senate Bill 8 or S.B. 8, banning abortion at six weeks, enforceable by private civil suits.[4] Six weeks is only a week or two after most women first miss a period after becoming pregnant. S.B. 8 allowed anyone to sue another person for assisting someone to have an abortion after six weeks of pregnancy and rewards them with $10,000 and attorney fees if they succeed—creating a bounty-hunting scheme that encouraged the general public to bring costly and harassing lawsuits against anyone who they believed had violated the ban. The law authorized lawsuits against health center staff, abortion funds providing financial assistance, anyone who drives a friend to obtain an abortion or otherwise provides help, and even a member of the clergy who counsels an abortion patient. The law also allowed anyone to file a lawsuit, including a parent, an abusive partner, or even a stranger. By delegating authority to enforce the law to private individuals, Texas hoped to evade judicial review because abortion rights were protected by the 14th Amendment, which applied to state action but not private action. The Guttmacher Institute estimated that the law would increase the average distance traveled one way to obtain abortion care twenty times, from twelve miles to 248 miles. They predicted the law would be particularly harmful to women of color in Texas, where 19 percent of Black women and 20 percent of Latinx women lived in poverty.[5] Reproductive rights advocates challenged the constitutionality of S.B. 8 in federal court, but lower courts ruled against the challengers, who appealed to the US Supreme Court. These developments spurred Plan C activists into high gear (see Figure 4.1).

In the days leading up to the ban's effective date on September 1st, Plan C joined up with Progress Texas to drive a mobile billboard truck around West Texas for three days to educate people about how they could access abortion pills online (see Figure 4.2). "As Texas increases restrictions on abortion care, we're here to let folks know that abortion pills by mail are a safe and effective alternative," said Francine Coeytaux, co-director of Plan C. Advocates drove a truck with illuminated billboards around the Texas towns of Lubbock, Amarillo, Midland, and Odessa. The billboards read, "Missed period? There's a pill for that. PlanCPills.org. #TXDeservesBetter." The back of the truck read "Plan

FIGURE 4.1: Plan C strategy meeting in 2021 (photo credit: Tracy Droz Tragos).

FIGURE 4.2: Plan C's illuminated mobile billboard truck driving a Texas highway to inform the public about how to get abortion pills (photo credit: Plan C).

C. Convenience. Confidentiality. Control. PlanCPills.org." They drove to universities, past City Hall, around the medical district, and in the evenings by bars and restaurants.[6] "We went on an abortion road trip to let people know that you don't need to go on a road trip anymore to get an abortion. You can get an abortion by mail basically anywhere in the United States, including in Texas," said Elisa Wells. "The reception was fantastic."[7] Plan C advocates posted stickers in bathrooms saying, "Want to be unpregnant?" with a QR code for their website (see Figure 4.3).

Throughout the campaign, Plan C shared activist art on Instagram and hosted a lively dialogue in the comments (see Figures 4.4 and 4.5). At one point, Instagram suspended Plan C's account for violating community guidelines by sharing information about abortion. Undaunted, supporters flocked to other platforms like TikTok and Twitter to raise their voices and amplify Plan C information and art. Instagram later reinstated Plan C's account after *Jezebel* published an article condemning the suspension. The campaign sought to reach students in particular. The truck visited Texas Tech University in Lubbock and West Texas A&M near Amarillo, talking to students and handing out flyers. Many students had never heard of online access to abortion pills and expressed interest and gratitude to Plan C advocates for the information. "We want to make sure that people know that you don't have to drive twelve hours for an abortion," said Wells. "You don't have to take time off from work and get childcare and pay hundreds or thousands of dollars in order to get an abortion. You can get an abortion by mail. It's the twenty-first century. Between safe and effective pills by which people can

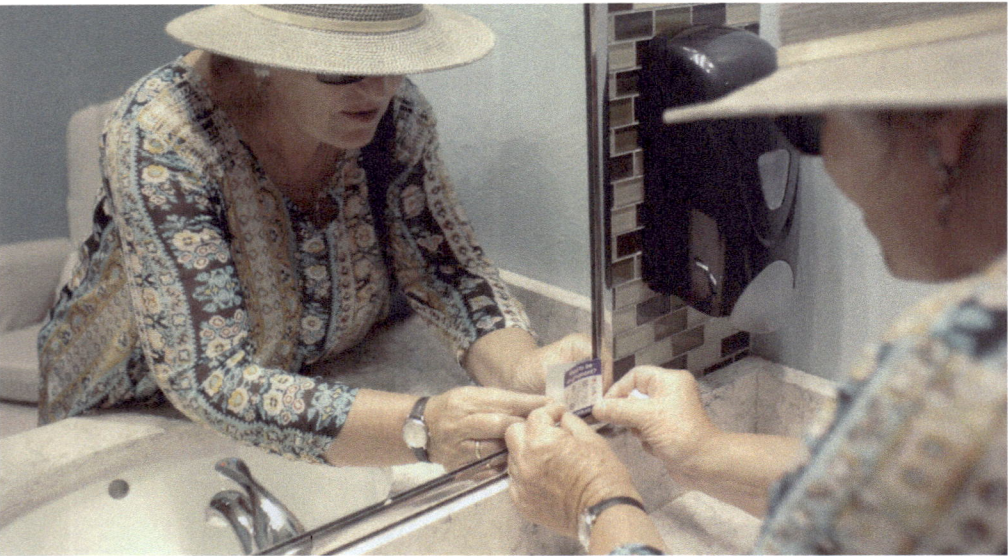

FIGURE 4.3: Francine Coeytaux placing a Plan C sticker on a bathroom mirror in Texas in 2021. The sticker reads, "Want to be unpregnant?" with a QR code to the Plan C website (photo credit: Tracy Droz Tragos).

FIGURE 4.4: Plan C shared this image as part of a social media campaign to inform Texans about how to obtain abortion pills after S.B. 8 went into effect in September 2021 (designed by @yessiichula).

easily self-manage an abortion and the modern miracle of the internet and the global economy, we have access."[8]

The United States Supreme Court allowed S.B. 8 to go into effect on September 1, 2021,[9] leading to the shut-down of abortion services after six weeks across Texas. Anti-abortion groups set up online forms enlisting people to sue and encouraging anyone to submit "anonymous tips" on doctors, clinics, and others who violated the law. The anti-abortion group Texas Right to Life created a website, ProLifeWhistleblower.com, which was quickly flooded with fake reports from abortion rights supporters. In the first week after S.B. 8 went into effect, Plan C saw traffic on its website spike 2,357 percent—with 30 percent of those new visits coming from Texas.[10] While 2,220 Texans had visited the Plan C website in April 2021, 34,996 Texans visited the website in September.[11]

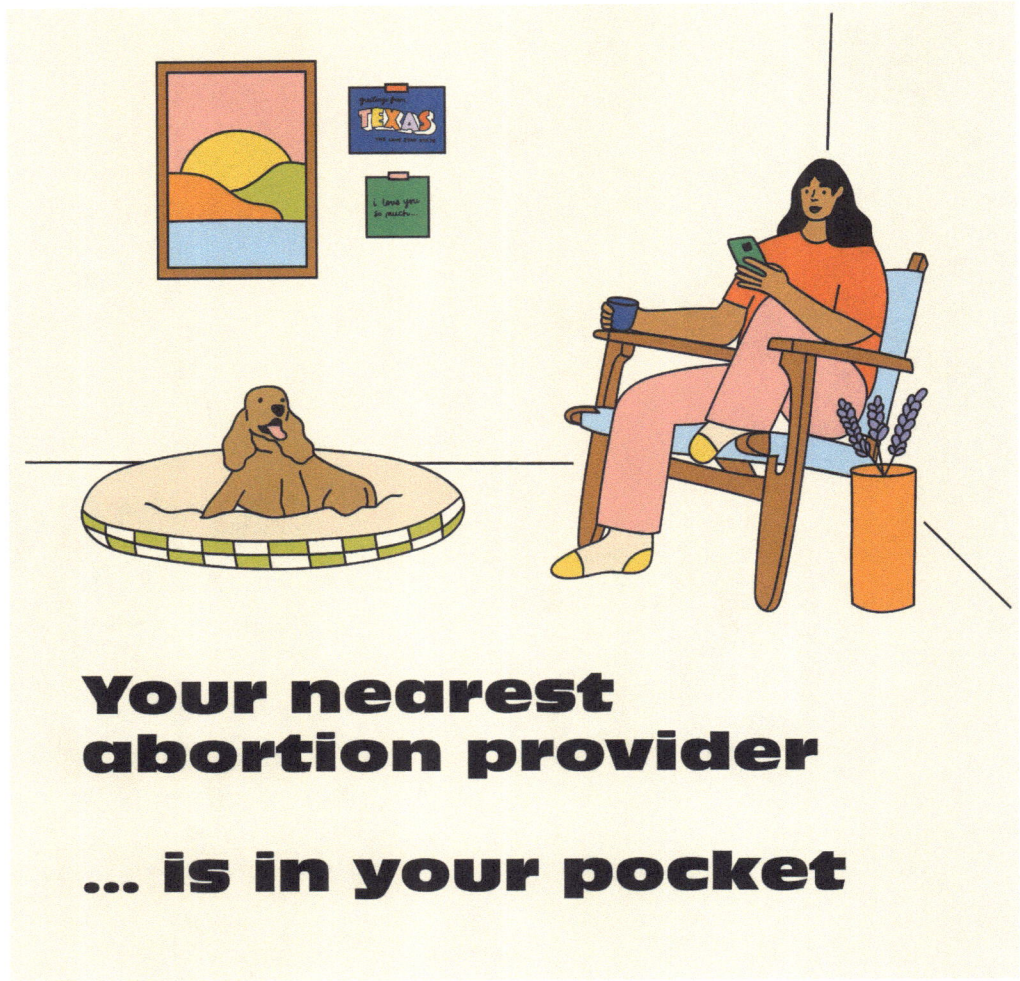

Figure 4.5: Plan C shared this image as part of a social media campaign to inform Texans about how to obtain abortion pills after S.B. 8 went into effect in September 2021 (designed by @rhiannamariechan).

The enactment of S.B. 8 drove people to Aid Access. The average daily requests for abortion pills from Texas to Aid Access increased almost twelve-fold—from 10.8 to 137.7 per day. In the following three months, requests remained higher than before, at 29.5 per month or 174 percent higher than before S.B. 8 went into effect.[12] In a study of the Aid Access website traffic, Abigail Aiken of University of Texas at Austin explained: "The bottom line here is that this study provides us with pretty strong evidence that Senate Bill 8 was directly related to an increase in the need for self-managed abortion in Texas. Senate Bill 8 remains the strictest gestational limit on abortion anywhere in the United States. We know that there has been a decrease in the number of abortions within Texas clinics. A direct result of that has been that more people have been looking into the option of an abortion outside of the formal healthcare setting."[13]

The number of abortions in Texas clinics dropped by over half between September of 2020 and 2021—from 4,511 to 2,164, but Aid Access received 1,831 requests for abortion pills from Texas in September 2021 alone. Aid Access requests in September equaled 78 percent of that month's drop in the number of abortions due to S.B. 8. "We can see here that self-managed abortion is filling a gap that has been left by the impacts of Senate Bill 8 on access to in-clinic care," said Aiken.[14] Even before the law went into effect, providers saw an uptick in abortion pill orders when in late March 2021 the Texas House passed S.B. 8. Requests made to Aid Access increased not only in Texas but in other states as well.[15] "It's a smaller uptick than in Texas but follows a pretty similar pattern," said Aiken. "We wondered if all this attention on S.B. 8 may have drawn the attention of people in other states to self-managed abortion and Aid Access. Even without a law as extreme as S.B. 8, abortion is extremely hard to access in many other U.S. states."[16]

In Mississippi, where there was only one abortion clinic left, many women were already obtaining abortion pills outside of the formal medical system by 2021, according to Michelle Cohen, executive director of Sisters Helping Every Woman Rise and Organize (SHERo) in Mississippi. "People were probably using Aid Access because it was everywhere. But there were other ways that they were getting the pills as well, such as going to Mexico and getting the pills themselves. A lot of activists were preparing for this."[17] Mississippi, like Texas, was one of the states where abortion became largely unavailable even before the Supreme Court overturned *Roe v. Wade*, so people there were early adopters of strategies that later became widespread.

Aiken said increased awareness of abortion pills may have led to more people choosing to self-manage their abortions even when they had access to clinic-based care for reasons of affordability, privacy, and convenience. "Self-managed abortion is the backup, second-string option for many, but for some people, it may be a preference. We know that from prior research," said Aiken. "It may be something they've been unaware of previously, so knowing about it might mean that more people for whom it is a preference might choose it."[18]

Texas's newly enacted abortion ban was blocked by a federal court on October 6, then reinstated on October 8 by the Fifth Circuit Court of Appeals. Meanwhile, the Texas Governor Greg Abbott signed a new law, Senate Bill 4 or S.B. 4, making it a felony for doctors to mail abortion pills to patients. Violating the law was punishable by up to two years in jail and a fine of $10,000. The law applied only to doctors and explicitly exempted pregnant people from criminal penalties for ordering pills online. In addition to banning doctors from mailing abortion pills, S.B. 4 also prohibited doctors from prescribing abortion pills after seven weeks of pregnancy—three weeks before the FDA limit of ten weeks.[19] At the time, Wells said the laws would not affect the flow of abortions pills into the state:

> The antis are trying anything and everything they can to stop access to the medications. The good news for our model is that it's not really going to have any effect on the supply

sources that we point people to, like Aid Access and online pharmacies mailing pills to people in Texas because those are all operating outside of these regulated structures. They probably don't have people sitting in Texas who are doing the mailing, but they are probably mailing from other states or mailing from post office boxes or fake return addresses or hidden return addresses.[20]

Anticipating the overturning of *Roe v. Wade*, Texas politicians in June adopted a "trigger ban" that would immediately outlaw abortion in Texas if the Supreme Court overturned *Roe v. Wade*.

The increase in telemedicine and self-managed abortion in 2021 provided new opportunities for researchers to study abortion pills—research that would play an important role in determining the future of abortion pills in a post-*Roe* America.

NEW RESEARCH SUPPORTS THE SAFETY OF TELEMEDICINE AND SELF-MANAGED ABORTION

As the Supreme Court appeared poised to overturn *Roe v. Wade* and states passed abortion restrictions in unprecedented numbers, many people feared a return to the pre-*Roe* nightmare, when women suffered severe health consequences and even death from illegal abortions. Aiken said her research gave her hope that this would not happen. "I think we're talking about a very different overall picture because of the accessibility of abortion pills and because of the model of care that Aid Access provides," said Aiken. "In the pre-*Roe* period, hospital wards were full of people suffering terrible infections because of the effects of unsafe abortion. Self-managed medication abortion is a lot safer. And, thankfully, people are reporting it as something that is acceptable to them as an experience, which is also very important." Aiken said what happened in Texas showed what could happen in other states in the future. "We definitely have a window on what the rest of the country may look like, especially in states where there are already trigger laws in place where abortion will be banned immediately or severely restricted if *Roe* is overturned. People still need to find ways of accessing the care they need. It's reassuring to think that we have a safe, effective, and acceptable way for people to go ahead and access that care and preserve their reproductive autonomy."[21]

A study released in May 2021 explained why people turned to Aid Access. "Even though we still have the right to abortion in this country, so many people struggle to actually exercise that right and access abortion," said the study's lead author, Dr. Aiken.[22] The study revealed that the rate of requests increased steadily between 2018 and 2020. "As more people are finding out about it, we are seeing the rate of requests going up. As legislators make in-clinic abortion harder and harder to get, people are having to look for viable alternatives," said Aiken.[23] The research found that states with the most policy restrictions on in-clinic abortion had the highest rates of requests to Aid Access, such as Louisiana, Mississippi, Wyoming, and Alabama. The lowest rates of self-managed abortions were in Vermont, Connecticut, Oregon, and California, but requests to Aid Access came from all fifty states. Dr. Aiken attributed this to the burdens inherent in medicalized abortion care: "Even if you live in a state where you don't have to jump through a lot of state-mandated hoops to get an abortion, you still have to take time away from your job, or away from your family, or away from your other responsibilities."[24]

The most common reasons people used the Aid Access services were the inability to afford in-clinic care (73.5 percent), a desire for privacy (49.3 percent), and clinic distance (40.4 percent). Other reasons given were the inability to take time away from work or school to go to a clinic (37.6 percent), greater comfort self-managing their abortion at home (28.2 percent), and greater convenience of self-managed abortion (27 percent). About a quarter of respondents said they were self-managing their abortion because they didn't want to deal with protesters outside of clinics.[25] "Cost and poverty are motivators when it comes to self-managed abortion," said Aiken. "The more people who live in poverty in an area, the higher the rate of requests." A 10 percent increase in the population living below the federal poverty level was significantly associated with a 20 percent increase in requests. States with restrictions on insurance and Medicaid abortion coverage tended to have higher baseline request rates. Traveling long distances to clinics was particularly hard on those in poverty. Counties with high levels of poverty located far from abortion clinics had the highest rates of Aid Access requests. An increase of forty-seven miles in distance to the nearest clinic was associated with a 41 percent increase in requests. However, in places where individuals could not afford the cost of an in-clinic abortion, a shorter distance to a clinic was not associated with improved access.

Dr. Aiken's research highlighted the inequities people experienced. "We already know that access to reproductive health care, including abortion, depends on where you live and how much money you make," said Aiken, "but with our recent evidence showing strong associations between the distance to the nearest abortion clinic or living below the federal poverty level with higher rates of requests for abortion pills online, we can see that state bans are being layered upon structural inequities to restrict abortion access in our communities."[26] Aiken summed up her research: "people are resilient and resourceful. They are going to find other ways. People have always found ways to get the abortion care they need."[27] She also concluded that Aid Access provided quality services. Based on interviews with over eighty people who had used Aid Access services, Aiken concluded, "it's a well-run service. It's trustworthy. It's run by people who actually care about the folks that they are trying to serve. It's also affordable—entirely non-profit."[28]

Research on telemedicine abortion within the formal medical system also showed patients were having positive experiences. Expanding telemedicine abortion services due to COVID-19 not only increased access to abortion health care for people living in states allowing the service, but also created new opportunities for research on the practice both in the United States and abroad, which provided scientific evidence later relied on by the FDA in its consideration of whether to lift the in-person dispensing requirement.

Unlike the piecemeal implementation of telemedicine abortion during COVID in the United States, the United Kingdom implemented a nationwide telemedicine abortion policy early in the pandemic. The Royal College of Obstetricians and Gynaecologists published new guidelines for medication abortion: consultations were encouraged to take place by telephone or video call, and an in-person visit and ultrasound scans were required only if indicated. By the end of March 2020, the British government had issued emergency legal orders allowing no-test medication abortion where abortion providers could treat their patients via telemedicine and mail abortion pills to their patients to take at home.

This shift in policy allowed researchers for the first time to assess a real-world no-test telemedicine abortion care model in a national population. Researchers compared patients receiving the traditional in-patient model of care, with in-clinic ultrasounds, to a telemedicine-hybrid model where patients are screened for eligibility for telemedicine abortion care without an ultrasound but by patients reporting their symptoms. Based on a sample size of 52,142 people, researchers found that the no-test telemedicine abortion model was just as safe and effective as the traditional in-person medication abortion model. Patients actually preferred this option to the in-person model. The study found that patients reliably reported their last menstrual period, with only 0.04 percent estimated to be over ten weeks gestation at the time of the abortion. Overall effectiveness was higher with telemedicine than in-person care (99.2 percent vs. 98.1 percent) and in-clinic and telemedicine abortion were equally safe, with very low rates of serious adverse events (0.02 percent vs. 0.04 percent). There were no cases of significant infection requiring hospital admission, major surgery, or death.[29]

"We have now robust evidence that providing early medication abortion using a model that has no clinical tests and is done by telemedicine is just as safe and effective as a fully in-person model," said Dr. Aiken. "That is particularly significant because we have so many state laws here in the US that are set up to prevent exactly that type of a model from being put into place. This study is showing us that there is really no reason in terms of safety, or effectiveness, or indeed patient acceptability not to go ahead with that kind of model."[30]

In the UK study, telemedicine abortion was in fact superior to in-clinic care in several respects. For example, patients received treatment more quickly. Whereas the wait time for in-clinic medication abortion was 10.7 days, the wait time for patients using the new no-test telemedicine model was only 6.5 days, 4.2 days shorter.[31] "When someone is experiencing a pregnancy that they don't want, the longer they are kept waiting to end that pregnancy, the more likely they are to experience anxiety, stress, and negative emotions," said Aiken. "In terms of good patient care, allowing people to access services when they want to access them is a patient-centered thing to do."[32] As a result, patients are able to receive care earlier in their pregnancy—with duration of the pregnancy at the time of the abortion significantly reduced with the telemedicine model of care. Only 25 percent of in-clinic medication abortion occurred at or before six weeks, whereas 40 percent of telemedicine abortions did. Earlier treatment decreased patients' experiences of nausea or other negative symptoms of early pregnancy.[33]

Telemedicine abortion was also less expensive, said Aiken. "If we require patients to come to a clinic, maybe on more than one occasion, if we are asking them for a waiting period or to come for an ultrasound and then come back for a clinical test and come back for the abortion pills—that adds up. The more you can establish the medication abortion procedure through telemedicine and in somebody's home, the more costs you can avoid to both the patient and the healthcare system."[34] She noted affordability was particularly important in the United States because, unlike the UK, the United States does not have universal health care and many patients pay for abortion out of pocket. Furthermore, Medicaid does not cover abortion, and many states block private insurance plans from covering it. Finally, anti-abortion laws were leading to the closure of many clinics so patients often had to travel long distances to reach in-person care, which increased not only the cost but also the likelihood of exposure to COVID-19.

Aiken conducted additional research on whether the telemedicine-hybrid model of care decreased the number of patients seeking medication abortion outside the formal healthcare setting. In January 2021, Aiken and colleagues published research showing that demand for medication abortion from abroad—through the online telemedicine service Women on Web during COVID-19—decreased significantly in Great Britain, which she attributed to the implementation of a fully remote no-test telemedicine abortion service. In other countries, such as Northern Ireland and Portugal, where abortion services were provided mainly in person in hospitals, or abortion was unavailable and international travel was prohibited during lockdown, demand for telemedicine abortion from Women on Web went up significantly.[35]

Aiken concluded that the evidence for the safety and efficacy of telemedicine abortion was compelling. "We have the outcomes of over fifty thousand medication abortions before and after the service change. It's a really big sample size and that helps us to be confident in our estimates. The bigger the sample size, the sharper the estimates of safety and effectiveness," said Aiken. "We also were able to account for 85 percent of all the abortions that took place during our study period. So we feel pretty good about applying the results of that study to the population because we have such a large and widespread sample."[36]

Research on telemedicine abortion in the United States showed levels of safety and efficacy similar to the UK study. Gynuity published a study in March of 2021 showing that the TelAbortion services with ultrasounds were just as safe and effective as in-clinic medication abortion.[37] In August of 2021, the first-ever study on the safety and effectiveness of new online clinics offering telemedicine abortion without ultrasounds was published. The research tracked the efficacy and safety of fully remote, asynchronous medication abortion care provided by the virtual clinic Choix to 141 patients between October 2020 and January 2021. Among the 110 patients reporting outcomes, 95 percent had a complete abortion without intervention, 5 percent required medical care to complete the abortion, and no patients reported any major adverse events. The study concluded that this "efficacy rate is similar to in-person provision, suggesting that abortion provided via telehealth is feasible and safe."[38] The study's lead author Ushma Upadhyay, an ANSIRH researcher and associate professor at University of California, San Francisco, stated, "This study shows that abortion can be as simple and private and autonomous as having a telehealth consultation with a clinician and having medications mailed directly to you at your home or your friend's home."[39] Upadhyay hoped her research would encourage more providers to offer telemedicine abortion: "This research means providers can assess whether a patient is eligible just by a simple conversation with her about her medical history. That opens the door for so many additional clinicians that can offer this service, campus student health centers, rural nurses and doctors, family practice physicians. This study is one step towards making medication abortion more normalized and integrated into primary health care."[40] Upadhyay hoped her research would convince the FDA to remove their in-person distribution requirement for mifepristone.

Other researchers spoke out about the importance of telemedicine abortion as well. In July of 2021, the journal *Contraception* published a special issue on the mifepristone REMS.[41] Articles included in the issue described the REMS as "needless and unlawful barriers to care," noting the disproportionate burdens of the REMS on vulnerable populations and several advocated for removing the in-person dispensing requirement.[42] Advocates submitted this new research to the FDA as it considered whether to permanently remove the REMS on mifepristone.[43]

FDA LOOSENS REMS RESTRICTIONS ON MIFEPRISTONE

In light of the research showing the safety of abortion pills and telemedicine abortion as well as the growing restrictions on abortion access in many states, members of the US House of Representatives took action to support medication abortion. On August 17, 2021, Reps. Carolyn Maloney (D-NY), Diana DeGette (D-Colo.), Barbara Lee (D-Calif.), and Ayanna Pressley (D-Mass.) jointly announced a resolution to support "equitable, science-based" policies governing access to the abortion pill. "Patients should be able to receive medication abortion in the way that makes most sense for them, from the provider of their choosing, whether that is at a health center, their local pharmacy, or delivered to their home," the resolution stated.[44]

The resolution had seventy-five original sponsors and soon gained another ten. "Mifepristone is extremely safe—the FDA's own data confirms this," said Maloney, who was chairwoman of the Committee on Oversight and Reform. "It's time that we trust the science and ensure access to safe, legal abortion, particularly for communities where abortion care has been historically pushed out of reach."[45] The resolution was endorsed by more than forty medical, reproductive rights, reproductive justice, and legal advocacy organizations, including ACOG, Physicians for Reproductive Health, and NWHN. Nevertheless, anti-abortion states continued to pass further restrictions on the medication, often falsely claiming the laws would protect women's health. Around this time, Dr. Daniel Grossman and other researchers published a study showing that medication abortion care with mifepristone dispensed by pharmacists was effective, with a low prevalence of complications, and patients were satisfied with pharmacists dispensing the medication.[46]

Even as state restrictions on abortion were tightening, the FDA moved in the other direction, to a degree. On December 16, 2021, the FDA partially lifted the REMS restriction by removing the longstanding rule that healthcare providers must dispense mifepristone to patients in person. Advocates applauded this change. "The FDA's decision to permanently remove the in-person pill pick-up requirement is a major step forward that will enable many more patients to get this safe and time-sensitive medication as soon as they are ready, without travel-related expenses and delay," said Georgeanne Usova, senior legislative counsel at the ACLU. "From the person living in a rural community hundreds of miles from the nearest clinic to the patient who wants to access this essential care in the privacy and comfort of their home, the FDA's decision will come as a tremendous relief for countless abortion and miscarriage patients."[47]

Kristin Moore of EMAA also applauded the decision. "Today, after reviewing years of evidence on the safety and effectiveness of medication abortion care, the FDA removed some outdated barriers. The in-person dispensing requirements on medication abortion care have proven to be unnecessary during the pandemic, and the FDA did the right thing today by lifting them. Certified prescribers no longer have to be both doctor and pharmacist—meaning they can just write a prescription and have that prescription filled by a pharmacy."[48]

Politicians spoke out in support of the FDA change. "For too long, patients have had to jump through burdensome hoops just to get medication abortion that we know is safe and effective," said Senator Patty Murray from the state of Washington. "For some women, that's meant finding time off from work or finding childcare to travel long distances to a clinic, and being harassed as they enter the provider's facility—all to take a pill that is safe to take at home. That's why I'm so relieved that today the experts at the FDA are lifting some of these restrictions and making it easier for patients to get and take medication abortion."[49]

Despite lifting the in-person distribution requirement, the FDA kept mifepristone within its highly restrictive REMS drug safety program. Under the REMS restrictions, healthcare providers still had to register with the drug manufacturer to become certified to prescribe mifepristone. Advocates condemned the restriction as unnecessary and contrary to medical science. "The FDA's failure to remove all of the restrictions on mifepristone ignores the science and smacks of political interference," said Elisa Wells."[50] Kristin Moore agreed that the FDA should remove the REMS: "More change is needed. With access to abortion hanging by a thread nationwide, the FDA must permanently lift all the restrictions on medication abortion care so people can get the care they need in the way that makes sense for them, including by going to their own healthcare professional."[51]

Advocates pointed out the negative impact the remaining restrictions would have on marginalized people. Destiny Lopez, co-president of All* Above All, said:

> While the action today will go a long way for people seeking care, other barriers remain and must be lifted once and for all. At a time when abortion care is under attack like never before, especially for folks working to make ends meet, we can't afford partial solutions. The FDA must permanently lift all restrictions on medication abortion and states with politically motivated bans on medication abortion, particularly via telehealth, must reverse these policies so people can get care in a way that makes sense for them.[52]

Francine Coeytaux argued that the prescriber certification requirement had been a significant barrier to increasing the number of clinicians who could offer medication abortion, noting that many providers could not become certified because they worked within institutions that would not allow them to apply.

FDA made another change in the REMS, however, that would reduce the burden on clinicians who prescribe mifepristone: they announced they would for the first time allow brick-and-mortar pharmacies to dispense the medication. Advocates hoped this would mean more medical providers would be willing to apply for certification and prescribe abortion pills in the future. Some envisioned a larger impact. In their 2021 book *Controlling Women*, Kathryn Kolbert and Julie F. Kay dreamed about the potential impact of pharmacy distribution of mifepristone: "CVS has over 1,100 MinuteClinics that already offer contraceptives, pregnancy and STI testing, and primary care to patients in over thirty-three states. Imagine the possibilities."[53]

But the FDA still blocked the abortion pill from being available in pharmacies in the same way that any other drug was, instead requiring pharmacies to register with the drug manufacturer and become certified in order to dispense mifepristone. Dr. Daniel Grossman of ANSIRH said, "The FDA has not yet issued guidance about what this certification process will entail. But why is it necessary? Viagra is riskier, yet pharmacies aren't certified to dispense that."⁵⁴ Coeytaux pointedly condemned the pharmacy certification requirement in stronger terms:

> It's purely political. These pills should not only be in pharmacies, they should be available over-the-counter. But instead, years later, we're still in a place where people think of this as a drug that is so dangerous it has to be in a black box. We're supposed to be happy. I don't feel like we should accept these crumbs anymore. We're supposed to celebrate the crumbs, when in fact, it's egregious. The FDA is supposed to be ruling based on data and evidence, not politics.⁵⁵

The FDA began a year-long negotiation process with the drug manufacturers Danco and GenBioPro about how the pharmacy certification process would work.

Other bureaucratic barriers also slowed access to telemedicine abortion. While the FDA allowed telemedicine, they maintained the requirement that clinicians obtain a patient agreement form, which for large online medical systems could be difficult, said Dr. Godfrey. "We haven't been able to launch telemedicine for a number of reasons. One reason is the patient agreement form. It's very difficult to do electronically in big health systems that have contracts with medical records providers that are in place for decades. They're not nimble. They can't just contract with DocuSign," said Godfrey. "You have to remember these huge medical systems are run by lawyers and there's just no flexibility in the system."⁵⁶

Nevertheless, the partial removal of the FDA REMS restriction opened the doors to expanded telemedicine abortion access in many states. By March 2022, twenty-four states and the District of Columbia had telemedicine abortion access (see Figure 4.6). Telemedicine abortion providers could continue to provide the service in states where it was allowed.

But even with the more relaxed FDA rule, many people still faced state-level barriers to accessing medication abortion. At the time, nineteen states still required the prescribing clinician to be physically present when prescribing the abortion pill, thereby blocking telemedicine for abortion. "Eliminating the in-person dispensing requirement may reduce the distances patients will have to travel—but they will still need to be in a state that allows telemedicine medication abortion to have the pills mailed to them," said Grossman.⁵⁷ Three states banned mailing abortion pills to patients outright, and mailing bans in another three states were blocked by courts.⁵⁸ But even in states banning the mailing of abortion pills, people could still obtain them from Aid Access and from online distributors based outside the country.

The FDA decision to allow telemedicine abortion spurred anti-abortion lawmakers to introduce new restrictions on medication abortion. In the first three months of 2022, lawmakers introduced eight measures that would ban medication abortion outright, nine measures that would prohibit the mailing of abortion pills, eleven measures

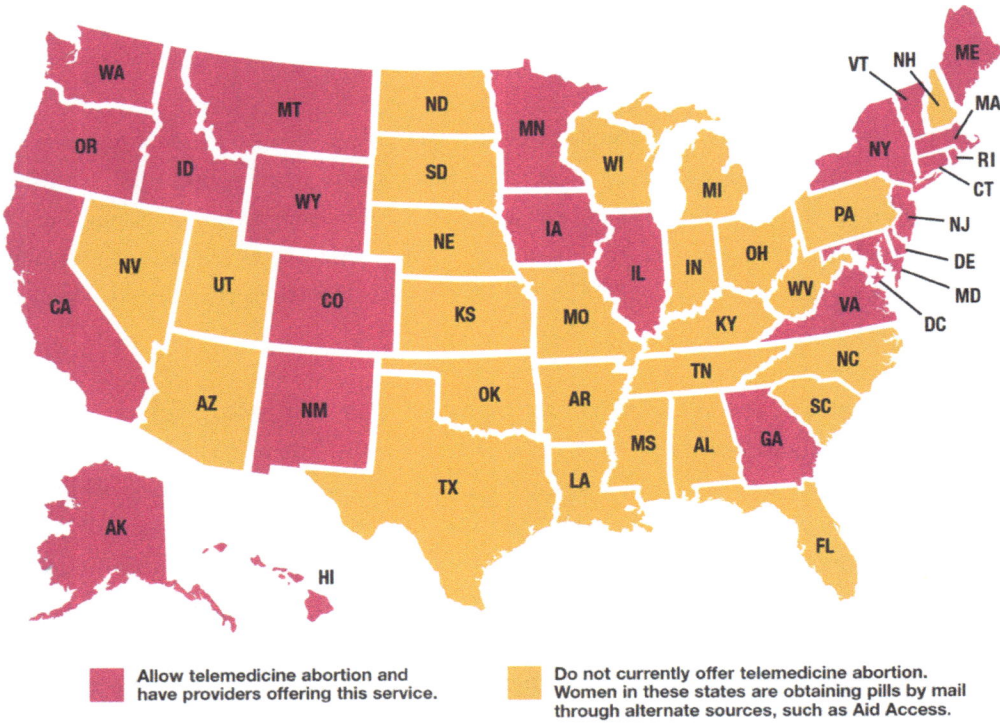

FIGURE 4.6: States with telemedicine abortion access in March 2022 (courtesy of Guttmacher).

that would restrict the administration of abortion pills to physicians, and five measures that would limit the provision of abortion pills to a specific point in pregnancy.[59] Reproductive rights lawyers, including the ACLU, argued that these laws were preempted by the December 2021 FDA decision and would later file lawsuits challenging measures that conflicted with the FDA rules.[60] In the face of growing restrictions, advocates continued to expand avenues for accessing abortion pills outside of the formal medical system and develop resources to support people self-managing their abortions, but not without resistance.

SPREADING THE WORD ABOUT ABORTION PILLS

In response to conservative states passing abortion bans and the impending Supreme Court ruling in the Mississippi abortion ban case, Plan C began a nationwide publicity campaign to get the word out about abortion pills. In April of 2022, Plan C teamed with reproductive health, rights, and justice advocates in New York City to plaster the subway system with information about how to find abortion pills and access free legal advice about using them. From Queens to the Bronx, in Brooklyn and Manhattan—including Times Square—over 250 posters shared abortion pill information in English and Spanish with the millions of people passing through subway stations and riding

Chapter 4: Eroding Abortion Rights and Self-Managed Abortion • 137

FIGURE 4.7: Plan C and If/When/How advertise abortion pill information in the Nassau Ave subway station in New York City (courtesy of Plan C).

the trains each day (see Figure 4.7).[61] "As politicians and courts continue their assault on abortion access, we are spreading the word that these medically safe and effective pills are available by mail in all fifty states," said Elisa Wells. "Everyone deserves access to this modern medical technology, and we provide the information that people need to take back control of their reproductive autonomy."[62]

At each location there were two posters—one with information about how to access abortion pills through Plan C's online Guide to Abortion Pills, and another poster with information on how to access free legal help via the Repro Legal Helpline. "As more and more states are enacting restrictions on access to abortion care, which should be basic, accessible medical care, we want people to know that there are alternative routes of access to these pills in all fifty states," said Wells. "A lot of people don't even know about abortion pills, let alone that they can be available very conveniently and quickly through an online consultation that may or may not involve a video visit, and with the pills mailed directly to your home."[63] She explained:

> Even in a state that has mainstream telehealth medication abortion services, there might be some people who prefer to obtain pills from alternate sources—maybe they're undocumented, maybe they don't want any record of this on their credit card or they don't want parents knowing about it for whatever reason. There might be people who just prefer to keep it more private and self-managed. So we want them to know about this.[64]

Plan C also began a program to train people as "ambassadors" to distribute information in their communities about abortion pills and Plan C's guide to pills.

The rise in self-managed abortion was reflected in an increased number of calls to the Miscarriage and Abortion (M+A) Hotline. In January 2021, the M+A Hotline answered 109 calls and twenty-three text messages. In January 2022, they answered 149 calls and 426 text messages. By March of 2022, M+A Hotline had over forty volunteers, including physicians, nurses, and midwives, who came from across the country. "People are doing this safely, but we're just here to provide reassurance that they're doing what they need to do. And that it's a safe process that they can take care of at home," explained the M+A medical director April Lockley in March of 2022. "Unfortunately, people in more restrictive states, people that are poor, people of color, they have an even more difficult time accessing abortion services, especially since it's more stigmatized in certain areas. And so the anonymity of being able to ask their questions through a hotline, and a resource that we provide without having to provide their name or talk face to face with anyone is a good resource for many people in the community."[65]

Groups promoting self-managed abortion experienced resistance to their work, including censorship on social media. When Reproaction posted graphics with medically accurate information about abortion pills in the fall of 2021, Facebook removed these posts. "Facebook said that we had violated their community guidelines," said Kara Mailman, Reproaction's senior research analyst. "They didn't explain how or what guideline we had specifically violated and we have not been given recourse for appeal."[66] A month after removing Reproaction's graphics, Facebook was still blocking the organization from purchasing ads to share crucial information about medication abortion with patients in need. "Facebook is letting anti-abortion organizations take out abortion pill reversal ads, while suppressing our fact-based posts about abortion pills," said Mailman. "This ongoing bias shows that Facebook doesn't have an interest in fairly moderating according to their own community guidelines."[67]

SASS also experienced censure of their social media posts. Meta removed two posts, one on Facebook and one on Instagram.[68] In both cases, SASS appealed the removal of the posts and both were put back up. "What really stood out for me was the innocent nature of the posts—just the graphic saying you can have an abortion at home," said SASS's media team coordinator Peggy Cooke. "I don't understand why Facebook reacts so quickly to things like that but then so slowly or not at all to actual horrible things that people say to each other."[69] Cooke explained how the posts' removal interfered with SASS's mission to get accurate information about abortion pills to people. "We are a volunteer team. It costs time and energy to appeal it, and check to see if it got put back up. If one person or twenty people see that post, that makes a difference," said Cooke.[70]

The Center for Countering Digital Hate and Reproaction both called on Facebook to stop spreading abortion pill misinformation and blocking medically accurate information about medication abortion. The Center for Countering Digital Hate started a petition urging the tech giants to enforce their policies against ads with misleading health claims, to refuse ads from organizations that repeatedly violate their rules, and to contribute their revenues from "abortion pill reversal" ads to reproductive health charities. They also called on social media platforms to ensure that users known to have been exposed to misinformation received accurate information.[71] Reproaction also had a petition telling "Facebook and Instagram that censoring vital, fact-based medical information about abortion pills is unacceptable" and encouraged people to contact Meta to complain.[72] "Allowing the promotion of unscientific anti-abortion propaganda while removing information about a safe, common medical procedure is wrong," said Mailman.[73]

Advocates for self-managed abortion also experienced resistance from medical professionals and even some reproductive rights advocates who were uncomfortable with Plan C's increasingly visible advocacy of Aid Access and self-managed abortion. Francine Coeytaux explained:

> We were trying to shake abortion pills free from the gatekeepers—the medical gatekeepers and the legal gatekeepers and the activist gatekeepers of safe abortion, who have, to their credit, made abortion safe in our country, but are watching their agency, their locus of control, their power dissipate because they are no longer needed. Abortion pills are so safe they should be over the counter. If you take that statement to its logical conclusion, over the counter means you don't need a gatekeeper that gives you a prescription. You don't need a gatekeeper that asks you a whole bunch of questions before granting access to the pill. Our premise with Plan C from the get-go was that these pills are so safe and effective, they should be over the counter. If you go with that premise, we need to just get out of the way.[74]

Advocates split on how to react to the six-week abortion ban in Texas. While reproductive rights groups like Planned Parenthood and National Network of Abortion Funds insisted the movement should invest in creating ways for people to travel out of Texas to get abortions, Plan C advocated for sharing information about how people can obtain abortion pills from Aid Access, from websites selling pills and from telemedicine providers in the United States using mail forwarding. Some medical providers and advocates expressed concern about the safety of abortion pills outside of the formal medical system, while reproductive justice advocates expressed concern about potential criminalization of people using abortion pills outside of the formal medical system.

LEGAL RISKS OF SELF-MANAGED ABORTION

Advocates generally agreed that the risks for self-managing early abortion were low, but that women of color and low-income women faced higher risks. In fact, only one state at the time explicitly prohibited self-managed abortion—Nevada—and only after twenty-four weeks. Dr. Beverly Winikoff, president of Gynuity Health Project, said she did not know of any successful prosecutions of women who self-managed an abortion using pills in early pregnancy. Elisa Wells said she knew of twenty-one prosecutions of people for self-managing abortion later in pregnancy out of the tens of thousands of people who have successfully self-managed their abortions in the previous twenty years. "When you do the math—dividing twenty-one prosecutions by the tens of thousands of people who have managed their own abortions—you can see that the risk is actually very, very small," said Wells.[75] "If you order a drug by mail and take it early, in the first trimester, and nobody finds a fetus somewhere, you are much less likely to get in trouble than if you do it in the second trimester," said Winikoff.[76]

By misapplying and misusing laws, however, some district attorneys were finding ways to prosecute people who self-managed their abortions. One of the earliest prosecutions on record for self-managing abortion with abortion pills occurred in Massachusetts in 2007, and there were two cases in New York in 2011—all under criminal abortion laws that were later overturned.[77] Abortion pill advocates advised people who self-managed their abortions about steps they could take to reduce their chance of legal problems. They told them that in the very rare case that they had to seek medical help, they did not need to say that they used abortion pills. The symptoms of abortion with pills were very similar to a natural miscarriage. At the time, there was not yet a reliable and accessible test to tell the difference[78] and the treatment was the same for both conditions. If they used abortion pills as directed by the World Health Organization (under the tongue or in the cheek), there was no residue that might be observed by medical professionals (vaginal use of the abortion pill may leave an observable residue). The few cases in which women were criminally prosecuted for self-managing their abortions usually involved a situation where the woman told a doctor or nurse that she had used abortion pills, cases in later pregnancy where there was some sort of physical evidence, and/or when someone who knew the woman reported her.

By the middle of 2021, states were adopting a record-breaking number of abortion restrictions, the Supreme Court had allowed a six-week abortion ban to go into effect in Texas, and the court had agreed to hear a case involving a fifteen-week abortion ban in Mississippi. The Guttmacher Institute reported that lawmakers across forty-seven states had introduced 561 provisions restricting abortion since January of that year, including 165 abortion bans. A staggering eighty-three of those restrictions were enacted across sixteen states, including ten bans.[79] Seeing the writing on the wall, Plan C worked to expand options for people to obtain abortion pills by mail. While importing drugs into the United States for personal use was generally illegal, the FDA made some exceptions, including in situations when "the drug is for use for a serious condition for which effective treatment is not available in the United States."[80] In fact, the FDA had a policy of non-enforcement toward importation of medicines for personal use up to ninety days. Elisa Wells explained how Aid Access protected itself from prosecution: "Aid Access is set up to comply with all the requirements in the places that they operate: Dr. Gomperts is licensed as a physician, so providing care legally. She writes a prescription for the patient, who then submits it to the pharmacy. The pharmacy is licensed to fill the prescription. And, because the doctor and pharmacy are both offshore, they feel protected from prosecution in the states that don't allow telemedicine abortion."[81]

While legal consequences for self-managing abortion were rare, dozens of women had been investigated and sometimes prosecuted for ending a pregnancy.[82] For example, in 2011, prosecutors in Idaho charged an unemployed mother of three, Jennie McCormick, with unlawful abortion after she used abortion pills purchased online to end a late second trimester pregnancy. A judge later dismissed the charges as unconstitutional, and a federal appellate agreed.[83] While there have been no successful prosecutions of women who self-managed an abortion using pills in early pregnancy, prosecutors disproportionately targeted low-income women using Medicaid, immigrant women, and women of color with these kinds of charges.[84] There had, however, been the successful prosecution of Ursula Wing in 2020 for distributing abortion pills (see chapter 2).

In June of 2021, If/When/How's executive director Jill Adams reported that by the end of 2020, they were fielding ten times as many inquiries on their Repro Legal Helpline as they were at the start of the year.[85] "Whether someone self-manages an abortion because they were unable to access clinical care, or because it was the care that felt right for them, no one should be punished for ending their own pregnancy, or helping someone else do so," said Rafa Kidvai, If/When/How Legal Defense Fund director. Melissa Torres-Montoya and Sara Ainsworth at If/When/How raised concerns about the criminalization of people self-managing abortion before the American Bar Association and worked for a resolution against the criminalization of self-managed abortion and pregnancy loss, which the American Bar Association finally adopted on February 21, 2021.[86]

To ensure anyone targeted with criminal prosecution received legal representation, If/When/How: Lawyering for Reproductive Justice launched a nationwide Repro Legal Defense Fund in June of 2021—a first-of-its-kind resource to support women and others investigated, arrested, or prosecuted for self-managed abortion. The fund began providing money for bail, legal representation, expert witness fees, or other expenses of litigation. "We've seen political attacks on clinical abortion care ramp up significantly in recent months, making it more critical than ever that we protect and defend people who self-managed abortions," said Kidvai.[87] If/When/How also pledged to educate healthcare providers about the law to discourage reporting of people using abortion pills, noting that leading medical organizations had said that reporting people causes tremendous harm.[88]

Elisa Wells emphasized that people should be able to make their own decisions about legal risk: "Of course, I don't want to in any way trivialize the traumatic impact these unjust prosecutions have had on the women who have been charged. But, people who are seeking abortion pills are looking for a solution, and I would guess that most would consider the benefit of having access to the pills to far outweigh any very small legal risk they might face."[89] Pamela Merritt, co-founder of Reproaction, noted how legal risks were higher for people of color, but there were also risks in not being able to access an abortion: "There are risks on both sides, but I believe that people have to make their own decisions about what is right for them and their families and their circumstances. I think we need to respect the intelligence of pregnant people."[90]

In response to concerns about criminalization of self-managed abortion, advocates also began to educate people about how to maintain their privacy while searching for abortion pills online. The Digital Defense Fund advised people to use virtual private networks like Tor, which blocked trackers and ads and automatically cleared search history. They also advised people to turn off face ID, talk in person or over the phone, delete any period or fertility apps, leave their phones at home when they can, and keep online purchases discreet by using cash or online currency such as Bitcoin (see Figure 4.8).

Fears about criminalization of people self-managing abortion with pills flared when on Thursday, April 7, 2022, Texas police arrested a woman and charged her with murder for allegedly self-inducing an abortion using pills. The woman, twenty-six-year-old Lizelle Herrera who lived near the Texas–Mexico border, was held in Starr County jail

FIGURE 4.8: How to protect your privacy when searching for abortion pills on your phone (courtesy of Digital Defense Fund).

on a $500,000 bond. The murder charge was in direct conflict with the constitutional right to abortion established in *Roe v. Wade* in 1973. Texas did not have a law making self-inducing an abortion a crime and two recent laws restricting abortion in the state—S.B. 8 and S.B. 4—explicitly exempted pregnant women. Despite these explicit exemptions, prosecutors obtained an indictment from a grand jury and the Starr County Sheriff's Office arrested and jailed Herrera "on the charge of murder after [she] did then and there intentionally and knowingly cause the death of an individual by self-induced abortion."[91]

Reproductive justice advocates in the community, led by the Frontera Fund, organized a protest at the Starr County Jail on Saturday morning and urged people to call the jail demanding the release of Herrera. Calls poured in from across the country. By Saturday afternoon, If/When/How's Repro Legal Defense Fund paid Herrera's bail and she was released. Advocates then urged people to call the Starr County District Attorney Gocha Ramirez, demanding that he drop the charges. The next day, Ramirez issued a press release, stating that the arrest was improper and he would file a petition to drop the charges, which he did on April 11. Ramirez reportedly apologized to Herrera in a text sent to her lawyer, Calixtro Villarreal on Sunday, saying Ramirez should never have been charged.[92] A law professor at University of Texas, Austin, Stephen Vladeck, commented at the time: "There are two possibilities. Either this was a really unforgivable accident or it was a deeply malicious and cynical ploy. I continue to be deeply troubled by the universe in which so many people are willing to brush aside fairly basic propositions about how our legal system is supposed to work."[93]

Herrera's case was part of a longstanding pattern of politically motivated prosecutors stretching the law in order to criminally prosecute pregnant women for the outcomes of their pregnancies, said Lynn Paltrow, executive director of the National Advocates for Pregnant Women, which fights criminalization of pregnant people. "This arrest was inevitable," Paltrow said. "It's been inevitable ever since Texas passed its so-called Prenatal Protection Act, which amended its murder laws to reach the 'unborn.' It's inevitable every time a state passes one of those laws, even when it includes an explicit statement that it may not be used to arrest the pregnant woman herself."[94] The Prenatal Protection Act, enacted in Texas in 2003, created a new crime of feticide by expanding the definition of an "individual" under the criminal homicide law to include a fetus and an embryo. Advocates of the law claimed they wanted to protect pregnant women, and they explicitly exempted prosecution of pregnant women under the statute, but the laws became a way to redefine when life begins. "What we know, whatever their intent, is that laws that equate pregnancy termination with murder, which is what the Texas Prenatal Protection Act is, are used against pregnant women, not for them," said Paltrow.[95]

The Texas law was part of a wave of feticide laws passed in the early 2000s in response to the murder of Laci Peterson, who was eight months pregnant, by her husband Scott

Peterson in 2002. Congress passed the "Unborn Victims of Violence Act," signed by George Bush on April 1, 2004, creating a new federal crime for causing the death or injury to an "unborn child" during the commission of a crime against a pregnant woman. By 2022, thirty-eight states have feticide laws and at least twenty-nine of these laws apply to the earliest stages of pregnancy. Most, but not all, explicitly exempt pregnant women, as the Texas law did, but prosecutors still used these laws against them. "Vigilante prosecutors all across the country have been deliberately misusing existing law to arrest people for their pregnancy outcomes, including abortion," said Paltrow. "Whoever presented Hererra's case to the grand jury absolutely had an obligation to know what the law says. And the law in Texas very, very clearly says on its face it does not permit prosecution of the pregnant person."

Paltrow published extensive research on criminal prosecution of pregnant women across the country and within the state of Texas under feticide laws as well as laws against manslaughter, child endangerment, and distribution of drugs to minors (through the umbilical cord).[96] "Prosecutors who bring cases like this are trying to groom people in the United States to think of those who have abortions as criminals," said Paltrow. "That stigma, eventually, is likely to stick and results in efforts to throw them in jail."[97]

Paltrow lauded local advocates who organized protests shortly after Herrera's arrest. "The immediate response from Frontera Fund and South Texans for Reproductive Justice brought attention to the misuse of this law by the police and prosecutor," said Paltrow. "That misuse of law happens often, but it's only after a public outcry that prosecutors are prevented from abusing their authority to subject people to prosecution for nonexistent crimes."[98] Paltrow also believed that the Herrera case would undermine public health. "Somebody who went for help in a medical setting was turned over to the police. The last thing we should be doing if we want to protect public health is make people afraid to go to their healthcare providers and speak honestly with them."[99]

While the Texas feticide law, as well as S.B. 8 and S.B. 4, explicitly exempted pregnant individuals from prosecution under these laws, advocates worried that could change if the Supreme Court overturned the constitutional right to abortion established almost fifty years ago in *Roe v. Wade*. "I think that has always been a political calculus by the anti-abortion supporters in the Texas Legislature," said Vladeck. "It's a lot easier to build consensus around these measures when the putative offenders—the villains in the story—are not the pregnant individuals, who may in many cases be pregnant for reasons beyond their control, rather than providers. The providers are much better boogeymen for the legislature than the individuals. Indeed, when S.B. 8 was going through the legislature, a sustained effort was made to say 'we are not punishing the pregnant person.'"[100]

But many believed that would change in the absence of *Roe*. The National Association of Criminal Defense Lawyers published a report in August of 2021 calling attention to the dramatically increasing criminalization of reproductive health in recent years.

The report highlighted current criminalization of pregnant women and the threat of increasing criminalization if the Supreme Court overturned abortion rights in *Dobbs v. Jackson Women's Health Organization*. "A close analysis of existing and emerging state law belies the common perception that enforcement will be limited to abortion providers and irrefutably shows that erosion of a precedent that has stood for nearly half a century may well open the floodgates to massive overcriminalization," wrote National Association of Criminal Defense Lawyers executive director Norman Reimer in the report's preface.[101]

On May 5, 2022, someone at the Supreme Court leaked a draft opinion in the Mississippi abortion ban case, sending shock waves across the country. Authored by Samuel Alito, the ninety-eight-page draft opinion, dated February 10, indicated the Court was preparing to fully reverse the half-century-old precedent of constitutional abortion rights established in *Roe v. Wade* (1973) and reaffirmed in *Casey v. Planned Parenthood* (1992). Abortion rights advocates expressed concerns that overturning *Roe* would increase discrepancies in access to abortion health care across the country. "In a post-*Roe* world, we would become a country of haves and have-nots—where some people have access to legal abortion and others do not," said Elisa Wells of Plan C. "In restricted states, abortion would become almost impossible to obtain—except through self-managed options, which would likely put people at legal risk, especially those who are already marginalized due to their skin color, economic status, or gender identity. In states without these restrictions, abortion is likely to continue to be readily available through modern, safe telemedicine and clinic-based services."[102] Shortly after the opinion leaked, traffic on the websites of Plan C and Aid Access surged.[103] In the weeks after the Supreme Court leak, Honeybee Health saw an 80 percent increase in demand for abortion pills.[104]

In response to the leaked opinion, Los Angeles-based filmmaker Jessica Sarah Flaum released her film, *Abortion: Add to Cart*, about self-managed abortion. The film provided a roadmap for how people could have safe abortions post-*Roe*—even in states that ban abortion. "With the recent leak from SCOTUS [Supreme Court of the United States], we decided to release our film publicly to be a resource in preparation for an upcoming post-*Roe* world," said Flaum, who made the film available on YouTube.[105] The film featured two abortion storytellers and interviewed activists from the organizations Plan C and If/When/How.

In June, as the Supreme Court decision came closer, a coalition of over seventy reproductive health, rights, and justice organizations created a new campaign, Abortion on Our Own Terms, to educate the public about the safety and effectiveness of self-managed abortion using medications, supported in part by the Packard Foundation and Hewlett Foundation. On their website, Abortion on Our Own Terms explained what self-managed abortion was, provided educational resources, and gave several ways to get involved and take action, including readymade stickers, GIFs, short informational videos, and infographics for supporters to download and share.[106] "These Supreme Court justices can't put abortion pills back in the bottle," said Erin Matson, co-founder and executive director of Reproaction and a steering committee member of the Abortion on Our Own Terms coalition.[107] The campaign's primary focus was on education and culture change. "Our long-range vision includes abortion pills on the shelf, abortion pills for free on college campuses, abortion pills in vending machines. I hope that we get to a point where people can keep abortion pills in their medicine cabinet in case they need them. We've got to build cultural acceptance and get out the word about how to self-manage abortion with pills because folks are looking for the information and states are failing to allow clinic-based access."[108]

With the Supreme Court decision in *Dobbs* looming, advocates anticipated that people from states banning abortion would flock to states where it was still legal and clinics would be inundated with patients, creating long waits for in-clinic abortion care. To address this anticipated influx of patients, California-based Women's Reproductive Rights Assistance Project (WRRAP) created a new "abortion pills by mail" program to fund telehealth abortion providers in twenty states. They believed that telehealth providers could absorb a lot of the demand and free up brick-and-mortar clinics to focus on providing in-clinic procedures. "WRRAP is expanding access by intentionally choosing friendly states to abortion access," said Sylvia Ghazarian, executive director of WRRAP. "The reality is that SCOTUS will probably severely weaken or overturn *Roe*. Medication abortion will become more critical in the delivery of care to many people unable to access or afford care in a clinic."[109]

By June 2022, WRRAP was working with nine telehealth abortion providers that offered services in twenty states, including Forward Midwifery, Pills by Post, Choix, and carafem. In creating their new abortion pills by mail program, WRRAP worked closely with Plan C. Unlike most abortion funds that required patients to call them directly for assistance, WRRAP funded abortion providers directly, which meant faster, more confidential care. "We wanted to streamline the process. It alleviates a lot of steps and makes it a smoother experience for the patient," said Ghazarian. "Telehealth abortion care is the wave of the future in terms of being able to provide access to the largest number of patients across the US. We want to support these services," said Ghazarian.[110]

Meanwhile, new research added to evidence showing the safety of telemedicine abortion. A study with a sample of over four thousand patients from fourteen clinics—the largest US-based study of the no-test approach to date—showed that medication abortions without an ultrasound or pelvic exam were just as safe as those with them[111] and that medication abortion after ten weeks was safe and effective, although slightly less effective than earlier in pregnancy.[112] The WHO endorsed the use of abortion pills through twelve weeks of pregnancy in 2022.[113] Based on this research, many abortion providers in the United States extended their telemedicine abortion service up to twelve weeks of pregnancy.

While advocates expanded their support for telemedicine abortion and self-managed abortion in response to the impending decision in *Dobbs*, they also pursued a much more ambitious dream: over-the-counter abortion pills. In February 2022, researchers at ANSIRH released a study finding that pregnant women seeking abortion care were overwhelmingly interested in having over-the-counter access to medication abortion.[114] The researchers surveyed 1,687 pregnant people seeking abortion care at seven abortion clinics in six states (Alabama, California, Florida, Illinois, North Dakota, and Texas) between October 2019 and March 2020. They proposed a scenario where people could buy abortion pills legally without a prescription. The pills would come with detailed information about how to take them and a twenty-four-hour telephone number to call with questions. The scenario allowed patients to ask a pharmacist any questions they might have and then go to a clinic afterwards to make sure the abortion was successful. "Our research finds that people are really interested and supportive of an over-the-counter model of abortion care," said lead author of the study Dr. M. Antonia Biggs, associate professor at ANSIRH. "They perceive it to have the advantages of being safe, convenient, affordable, and private."[115]

The survey found that 83 percent of abortion patients were in favor of over-the-counter medication abortion, a significantly larger proportion than the 37 percent reported in a similar 2017 survey.[116] Participants highlighted several advantages of over-the-counter medication abortion, including privacy (69 percent), earlier access to care (69 percent), and convenience (65 percent).[117] "There are many restrictions on abortion in general," said Biggs. "People often live far away from clinics. If you had over-the-counter access without a prescription, you could go to any pharmacy. Most people live near a pharmacy. Many said that they thought it would also be more private and more convenient. They prefer to have an option where they could manage their abortion on their own at home."[118]

Cost was also an important factor for respondents. The average cost of in-clinic medication abortion in the United States was over $500, while the medications themselves cost less than $100. "People are really in need of an affordable option," said Biggs. "It's very likely that over-the-counter medication abortion would be cheaper than an in-person option, particularly if it's covered by insurance. At the very least, it would reduce the cost of travel to clinics that are often many miles away. We found that the people who were most interested were those who had experienced financial barriers accessing care."[119]

Biggs hoped that the FDA would one day approve over-the-counter access to abortion pills, but emphasized that insurance coverage for the medications would be critical. "What will be really important as we move forward is to ensure that people can have affordable access to this option, and that it be covered by insurance—that it doesn't leave people out. Affordability is really critical to increasing access to abortion."[120] Research on demand was a required step in the process of making medication abortion available over the counter. "One of the important pieces of the research is to demonstrate that there is interest," said Biggs, who noted the next step in the research—a label comprehension study—was already underway. Previous research had shown that clinician support for a less medicalized model of medication abortion—without ultrasounds or blood tests—had increased in response to a strong safety record for abortion pills as well as the rise of telemedicine during the COVID-19 pandemic. Biggs and her colleagues at ANSIRH hoped the FDA would one day approve over-the-counter access to abortion pills. "You have to be visionary," said Biggs. "I don't know when it will happen. But we have the research to show that it's safe. The more evidence we have, the more likely it is that we're going to make a change."

Meanwhile, advocates prepared for a post-*Roe* future. After the FDA permanently removed the in-person dispensing requirement in December 2021, telemedicine abortion expanded significantly. As Texans traveled to states with legal abortion, telemedicine abortion played an important role in helping to meet demand, and served as proof of concept for a post-*Roe* future.

CHAPTER 5

"Mail Those Pills No Matter What": The End of *Roe* Spurs Efforts to Expand Abortion Pill Access

If we can't get laws passed, we may need to be proactive anyway, because people desperately need our care. We may just need to mail those pills no matter what. I don't think the optics of doctors going to jail because they are getting medications to people who need and want them will win the Republicans votes. Those of us in the blue states really need to step up and be proactive.

Dr. Linda Prine[1]

On June 24, 2022, a conservative supermajority of the United States Supreme Court issued a sweeping decision erasing a half century of federal protection for abortion rights and opening the door to state restrictions and bans on abortion health care. Some states had "trigger" laws, designed to go into effect immediately. Other states had pre-*Roe* abortion bans that went into effect. Abortion rights advocates filed suits in many states to stop abortion bans and succeeded in obtaining stays on bans in some states. By November 2022, twelve states had banned abortion at fertilization; one had a six-week ban and two more had fifteen-week bans. Another fifteen states had highly restricted access to abortion, including bans on telemedicine abortion. *Dobbs v. Jackson Women's Health Organization* made a bad situation worse. Under *Roe* and *Casey*, abortion had been hard to access for many women, especially those living in rural areas or on reservations, and those relying on federal health insurance programs. The Hyde Amendment blocked coverage for abortion care, with only narrow and rarely used exceptions for cases of rape, incest, and life endangerment. Indian Health Services, for example, rarely provided abortion services, including abortion pills, even for these exceptions.[2] While Indigenous women always had to travel long distances to access medication abortion, the situation became more dire as clinics closed in many states.

With the end of *Roe*, reproductive rights advocates shifted into high gear, developing new strategies and pushing legal boundaries to increase access to abortion pills. Several states passed provider shield laws covering telemedicine abortion services. While some abortion providers began mailing abortion pills to people living in states with bans, others did not agree with this strategy and believed that the legal risks were too high for patients and providers. In states where abortion was still legal but abortion pills were restricted, advocates challenged those restrictions. In states where there were no restrictions, advocates pushed for expanded access, including legislation requiring public universities to offer abortion pills in student health clinics. Advocates also worked at the federal level to expand access, including filing a citizen petition challenging the FDA REMS restrictions on mifepristone. Outside of the medical system, activists developed grassroots community networks offering free abortion pills to people living in states banning abortion. Finally, activists pursued creative strategies to combat abortion pill stigma and ensure ongoing access to abortion pills post-*Dobbs*. This chapter describes these important initiatives in the period right after the Supreme Court overturned constitutional abortion rights.

THE IMMEDIATE AFTERMATH OF *ROE*'S FALL

Within weeks of the Supreme Court's overturning of *Roe v. Wade*, the Biden administration quickly acted to protect abortion access. On July 8, 2022, President Biden issued an executive order on "Protecting Access to Reproductive Healthcare Services," which directed the Secretary of the Department of Health and Human Services (HHS), Xavier Becerra, to submit a report within thirty days identifying potential actions to protect and expand access to abortion, including medication abortion.[3] Reports of pharmacists refusing to fill prescriptions for misoprostol led HHS Secretary Xavier Becerra to issue guidance on July 13 to pharmacies explaining that withholding medications because they might cause miscarriage or abortion violated section 1557 of the Affordable Care Act.[4] Then on August 3, 2022, Biden issued another executive order directing HHS to do more to ensure access to reproductive health services, and misoprostol in particular, because women were being denied this medication for miscarriages.[5]

Overall, the official number of abortions dropped 6 percent in July and August of 2022, with over ten thousand fewer abortions reported in those months.[6] But the rates were vastly different across states. Reported abortion in states with restricted access dropped 32 percent between April and August 2022, while reported abortion in states with protected access increased by 11 percent. Evidence suggested, however, that self-managed abortions soared after *Dobbs*.[7] Before the Supreme Court's abortion decision leaked on May 2, requests for abortion pills to Aid Access averaged around eighty-three a day. After the leak, that number jumped to 137. After the court decision on June 24, the daily average increased to nearly 214. Over July and August, that amounted to

13,268 requests; most were filled. Together these studies indicated that many people living in restrictive states were accessing abortion by traveling to states where abortion was legal, or were self-managing their abortions by ordering abortion pills online.[8]

Despite new abortion restrictions, abortion pill advocates vowed to help people find ways to access medication abortion, both inside and outside of the formal US medical system.[9] "No matter what happens to laws, abortion pills aren't going anywhere—and information about how they work belongs to everyone," said Reproaction's executive director Erin Matson shortly after the fall of *Roe*. Advocates shared resources for finding and safely using abortion pills, including Plan C, SASS, Aid Access, the M+A Hotline, and Repro Legal Helpline. Detailed instructions for how to take abortion pills were available in twenty-seven languages at HowToUseAbortionPill.org. A young venture capitalist from Boston, Nathaniel Horowitz, formed Mayday Health, to share information about how to access abortion pills through Aid Access.[10] "As we continue to navigate the national crisis of abortion bans, more people are seeking to self-manage their abortion with pills," said Kimberly Inez McGuire, executive director of URGE: Unite for Reproductive & Gender Equity. "They know where and how to get the medication, and they're choosing it because it provides control over their reproductive lives."[11]

While the largest increase in requests to Aid Access came from states with restricted access to abortion, every state had increased requests for abortion pills during the post-leak and post-decision periods. In states with total abortion bans, 31.4 percent of respondents cited "current abortion restrictions" as a reason for their request pre-decision, versus 62.4 percent after the decision. In states with no current restrictions, 12.5 percent of respondents cited "possible future legal restrictions" versus 35.5 percent post-decision in states with no current restrictions on abortion.[12] "The increases indicate that while abortion bans create access barriers that lead to more people self-managing their abortions, self-managed abortion is also a method of choice for some," said lead researcher Dr. Abigail R.A. Aiken of the University of Texas at Austin. "The increase in the visibility created by the *Dobbs* decision means that more people are aware of self-managed abortion as an option. However, interest in self-managed abortion is not new. It has existed for centuries, and now self-managed abortion with pills is backed up by studies proving its safety and effectiveness."[13]

In addition to Aid Access, a Mexico City-based telemedicine abortion clinic—Telefem—began serving people from the United States in July 2022. Telefem offered telemedicine abortion services to US residents and then mailed abortion pills to secure pickup locations along the United States–Mexico border for $150.[14] The Mexican Supreme Court had decriminalized abortion in September 2021. Mifepristone and misoprostol were legal in Mexico and doctors were allowed to prescribe them across state lines. Telefem opened its doors to Mexicans in November 2021, but soon people from other countries began contacting them for help. They realized they could serve people from other countries who could travel to Mexico and pick up abortion pills in a safe location near Mexico's borders, such as Guatemala to the south and the United States to the north. Once patients received their package, Telefem providers walked them through the entire process by telemedicine (text, phone call, or videoconference). Telefem recommended that people take the pills in Mexico rather than carrying them back to the United States because of risks of carrying controlled medications across the border. People could be asked to show proof they needed those medications. In case of complications, Telefem referred patients to a network of doctors and clinics along the Mexico border. Telefem director and midwife Paula Rita Rivera described their service: "It's very important to us that people who don't have access or who don't know what to do can find Telefem. We follow a personalized method, giving attention to each woman. We care about the person that is seeking our services."[15]

For women living in states with abortion bans who wanted to receive pills promptly from US-based telemedicine providers, some used mail forwarding, but concern about the legal risks to patients and providers grew post-*Dobbs*. In March of 2023, several telehealth clinicians spoke anonymously to *Ms.* magazine about what they wished their patients knew about mail forwarding. "If patients are doing mail forwarding, or if they're having a friend get the package, it's not really something that we can know about as clinicians, because we really can only be prescribing to the states where we're licensed," said one telehealth clinician.[16] They explained:

> For example, if a clinician serves California, the patient should be in California and receiving mail in California. Now, if it's someone who lives in Texas, and they've set up mail forwarding in California, or a friend is going to take that package in California and then mail it on to them, they could say something like, "I'm traveling to California to pick up this package." That's fine, as long as it's not blatantly obvious that they won't be in the state where they are receiving it.[17]

If a patient told their clinician they were located in a different state during the consultation or that they were using mail forwarding, telehealth clinicians may not feel they could serve them. "We want to help you, but we can't know that you're doing mail forwarding," said one telehealth clinician. Another clinician summed it up concisely: "Don't ask, don't tell." One telemedicine abortion virtual clinic, Abortion on Demand, required a videoconference consultation and checked patients' IP addresses to ensure they were physically located in a state where the clinician was licensed to practice. Most clinicians, however, did not do that. "We shouldn't know if patients are doing mail forwarding, because it tells us that they're not in the state where they say they are and where we are licensed," said another clinician.[18]

Some telehealth clinicians were careful to stay within the most conservative interpretation of the law, but others were less worried about trying to insulate themselves from any potential legal repercussions, especially when women were desperate for medical care in the face of unjust restriction on abortion access. "There's too much time spent worrying about the 'what ifs?' instead of 'what now?'" said one telehealth abortion clinician. "It comes down to risk tolerance. We all have different risk tolerances. The way I look at risk is, 'What's the worst thing that can happen if I get caught, and how likely is it?' Those two things make me do things that a lot of people would be too nervous to do."[19] Clinicians were already allowed to serve their established patients by telemedicine when the patients were traveling in states where the clinician was not licensed, but generally clinicians were only allowed to serve new patients located in states where they were licensed. Some advocates argued that the law of the state where the telehealth provider was located should apply rather than the law of the state where the patient was located. But in the absence of clear law on that point, telehealth clinicians who knowingly served patients located in states where they were not licensed risked losing their medical licenses.

While telehealth and mail forwarding worked for many people, several providers and Plan C reported that some mail forwarding services refused to forward abortion pills. "They open it because they say it's a suspicious package. I think they know exactly what the packages look like, even though they're just a FedEx package," said one clinician. "Then they send an email to the patient and say, 'Per our policy, we can't forward this to you.' They say you can come pick it up in person if you want, but I don't recommend that anyone go in person to do that. These refusals to forward have been very few, but it's still something people should know about."[20] Another clinician said she believed it's "still relatively uncommon" that mail forwarding services are opening people's packages, but wanted patients to know about this possibility. "If we talk to them on the phone, we subtly tell people to use a friend rather than one of the mail forwarding places," said the clinician.[21]

On the legal risks of forwarding abortion pills for a friend, one clinician noted, "I'm not aware of a single case of someone being caught forwarding abortion pills for someone else. We need to lower everyone's fear levels because fear makes things seem abnormal, and they're not."[22] For patients, self-managed abortion was not against the law in most states. Only Nevada explicitly prohibited self-managed abortion. However, reproductive justice advocates worried about increasing criminalization post-*Dobbs* and increasing surveillance by anti-abortion police and prosecutors, especially for communities of color who were already over-surveilled. In 2022, If/When/How published updated research showing that between 2000 and 2020, sixty-one people were investigated and/or prosecuted for self-managed abortion. Of those sixty-one, just over half involved abortion pills. There were no known cases of people investigated or arrested for using abortion pills early in pregnancy. Healthcare providers notified law enforcement in 45 percent of the sixty-one cases and acquaintances in just over a quarter of the cases. Most cases (87 percent) led to arrest and 92 percent proceeded through the criminal court process, with 44 percent pleading guilty and 9 percent resulting in a guilty verdict after a trial. Of the sixty-one cases, 44 percent were non-Hispanic white and 41 percent were minoritized racial and ethnic groups (15 percent were not reported). Over half (56 percent) lived in poverty.[23] A 2023 study on the criminalization of pregnancy by the organization Pregnancy Justice found sixteen cases of criminal prosecution for self-managed abortion between 2006 and 2022.[24]

New York telehealth abortion clinician Linda Prine expressed skepticism about claims that ordering abortion pills by mail was legally risky, noting that the number of people ordering abortion pills online has "gone through the roof since *Roe* fell." Yet she has heard of no one who had been arrested for getting pills in the mail and using them in early pregnancy.[25] In March 2023, an ex-husband sued three Texas women for wrongful death because they helped his ex-wife obtain abortion pills to end her pregnancy.[26] Republicans also introduced bills in several states to criminalize the use or distribution of medications for abortion, but they did not pass.[27]

If/When/How legal support counsel Rebecca Wang admitted that the legal risks for people ordering or forwarding pills were minimal, but varied depending on the particular laws of the states where people were located, whether people were talking to others about the activities they were engaging in, and personal identity factors because people of color tended to be more heavily surveilled by law enforcement. "If people are receiving medications from a valid telemedicine service and a licensed provider within the United States, the likelihood that they're going to face legal risk for receiving those services or those pills is very, very low," said Wang. "If a provider is comfortable with absorbing some legal risk, any patients they see are not going to face legal risk for using those services."[28] In September of 2023, however, *The New York Times* reported that scientists in Poland had developed laboratory tests to detect abortion drugs in people, creating new worries for advocates of self-managed abortion.[29]

In addition to telemedicine abortion, activists also developed new community networks to share abortion pills. Soon after *Dobbs*, activists in the United States connected with global feminists who had for years run accompaniment networks to provide abortion pills and support to people living in countries banning abortion. Ibis Reproductive Health described the accompaniment model as follows:

> Abortion accompaniment is characterized by activist-driven, community-based strategies to facilitate use of de-medicalized approaches to widely available medications. Accompaniment follows a shared understanding of safe abortion as not only evidence-based but also a practice that is caring, autonomous, and free of violence, stigma, and judgement. Feminist accompaniment groups promote horizontal peer-to-peer learning, and take great care to center the needs, desires, and empowerment of the aborting person.[30]

Relying on guidance from the World Health Organization, accompaniment groups trained volunteers to provide medication abortion counseling and guidance as well as emotional and physical support over the phone, through secure digital platforms, or in person. In addition, they provided information about how to access health care, sometimes collaborating with supportive clinicians and they informed people how to avoid legal scrutiny. Research showed that accompaniment is extremely safe and 97 percent effective without surgical intervention through thirteen weeks of pregnancy.[31] Accompaniment groups also supported second-trimester abortions, which research showed were over 76 percent effective during the second trimester of pregnancy and 95 percent effective with additional medical interventions.[32] In 2022, abortion accompaniment groups and networks operated in approximately fifty countries around the world, including the Mobilizing Activists around Medication Abortion (MAMA) Network in Africa and the Red Compañera in Latin America.[33] In Mexico, there were over 350 regional networks, many of which were set up over the previous two decades by Las Libres.[34] According to Ibis Reproductive Health, accompaniment "seeks to affirm abortion as a valid and valued reproductive choice, in which people who have abortions are enabled as the protagonists of their own abortion process."[35]

Even before *Dobbs*, as legal restrictions limited abortion access in the United States, Las Libres began providing support to women in the United States, at first in immigrant communities and then more widely.[36] Las Libres activists organized a series of meetings with activists on both sides of the border. Americans in Mexico as well as volunteers inside the United States formed a US project to support people in the United States with self-managed abortion. Inspired by this work and the global movement for self-managed abortion, activists inside the United States began creating their own organizations to support people with self-managed abortion, such as Red States Access and We Save Us. By April 2023, Red States Access offered free abortion pills to women in over ten states banning or heavily restricting abortion, including Alabama, Arkansas, Florida, Idaho, Louisiana, Missouri, Oklahoma, South Dakota, Utah, and Wisconsin. We Save Us offered free abortion pills to women in Indiana, Ohio, and Kentucky.[37] The organizations also provided doula support for people using abortion pills. The Plan C Guide to Pills indicated the states served by each group. At that time, Aid Access also served people living in states with abortion bans, but they shipped the medications from a pharmacy in India, which could take two to three weeks. To speed delivery of pills to people in states with bans, Francine Coeytaux worked with Aid Access to find distributors within the United States, including harm reduction organizations, so patients could receive their medications within days instead of weeks.[38] At the same time, they developed a plan to allow US-based clinicians in states protecting abortion rights to serve patients in states restricting abortion.

THE PUSH FOR TELEMEDICINE ABORTION PROVIDER SHIELD LAWS

To protect telemedicine abortion clinicians who offered care to patients from out of state, abortion rights advocates pushed for provider shield laws that included telemedicine. While several states passed provider protections, most of these laws did not apply to telemedicine providers. But on July 29, 2022, Massachusetts passed the nation's first provider shield law that covered clinicians sending abortion pills directly to people who were physically located in states with abortion bans.[39] The law had robust protections for healthcare workers who provided abortion services to patients living outside the state—both those who traveled to Massachusetts for care, and those who received care in their home states from Massachusetts providers via telemedicine. The Massachusetts law meant people living in states with abortion bans could receive telemedicine abortion care from US providers and obtain FDA-approved abortion pills promptly by mail, rather than having to order pills from outside of the country.

To shield healthcare workers from criminal investigation and prosecution by police and prosecutors from anti-abortion states, the new law prohibited the extradition of Massachusetts providers who lawfully provided abortion care in Massachusetts to a resident of a different state where the procedure was illegal. The law also prevented Massachusetts law enforcement officers or employees from providing information or assistance to any federal or state law enforcement agency or private citizen in relation to an investigation or inquiry into protected reproductive healthcare services. To protect healthcare workers from civil suits, the law created a new civil remedy for clinicians in Massachusetts to countersue if they were the subject of criminal prosecution or civil lawsuits filed by someone outside of the state, enabling them to recover an amount equal to the damages assessed in these out-of-state lawsuits. The law also protected providers' professional licenses and access to malpractice insurance, even if they faced out-of-state civil lawsuits for providing lawful abortion care in Massachusetts.[40]

These protections meant people living in states with abortion bans or telehealth abortion restrictions could still receive telehealth abortion care from Massachusetts providers. The law also increased abortion access for minors, since Massachusetts did not require parental consent or notification for minors aged sixteen and seventeen. Therefore, teenagers who did not want to involve their parents but who lived in states with parental notification or consent requirements could receive confidential telehealth abortion care without informing their parents.[41] Legal scholars questioned the constitutionality of telemedicine provider shield laws, arguing that they "strike at the heart of basic, fundamental principles of law in our federalist system—interstate comity and cooperation." They also noted that the law did not protect providers if they left the state, or cover patients or those helping them in their home states.[42] By January of 2023, one Massachusetts clinician was offering telemedicine abortion services to people in states with restrictive abortion laws.[43]

After the law was signed, Vice President Kamala Harris traveled to Massachusetts and met with lawmakers and advocates in Boston. At this meeting, Harris described Massachusetts as "a national model for protecting reproductive rights on the state level," and she encouraged the leaders to support state legislators across the country who were fighting for abortion protections.[44] Telemedicine abortion clinicians also celebrated passage of the Massachusetts law. "The Massachusetts shield law is a huge breakthrough for getting pills to women in restricted states," said Dr. Linda Prine, telemedicine abortion advocate and co-founder of the Miscarriage and Abortion Hotline. "Clinicians now have the backing of their state laws, protecting their license and practice, as well as the federal protection of prescribing an FDA-approved medication. We are hopeful that other pro-choice states will soon follow suit."[45]

In early 2023, Dr. Linda Prine, Dr. Maggie Carpenter, and reproductive rights attorney Julie F. Kay formed the Abortion Coalition for Telemedicine Access to advocate for telemedicine provider shield laws to enable licensed providers to serve people anywhere in the United States, so that healthcare providers in blue states could help people in red states obtain abortion medications by telemedicine. Another organization, Healthcare Across Borders, run by Jodi Jacobson, was also working to pass telemedicine provider shield laws.

On January 9, 2023, New York state Senator Shelly B. Mayer (D) introduced a law to protect New York clinicians providing telemedicine abortion services to patients located in states banning or severely restricting medication abortion.[46] The bill passed out of committee on January 17 and was then introduced in the Assembly by member Karina Reyes (D). The law shielded clinicians and pharmacists throughout the state from criminal prosecution, extradition, loss of license or malpractice insurance, and from subpoenas of their medical records for prescribing and sending abortion pills to people who needed them anywhere in the United States.[47] Prine explained how the law would solve a piece of the abortion access problem:

> Before *Roe* fell, 75 percent of people got their abortions under eight weeks. Early abortion is safer, and people want to get their abortion right away. Now, it's really hard in all of these red states. If you can get an abortion at all, it's hard to get it early. This law doesn't help people with fetal anomalies who are thirteen-plus weeks. It doesn't help when people need procedures and can't have them. But this would at least allow people to go back to having a really early abortion in the safety of their own home. It would be a big step towards alleviating the suffering.[48]

Prine organized a campaign urging New Yorkers to contact their state legislators and ask them to protect telemedicine abortion across state lines.[49] Some expressed concerns that states might criminally prosecute people receiving abortion pills, which Prine vigorously disputed:

> There was this narrative that this might be dangerous to people in the South if we started mailing pills there. And we're like, wait a minute. People need their pills. The laws so far are against the providers of pills, not the patients. Patients are getting pills where they can,

but they're getting them later in pregnancy than they should be getting them. Now they will have the option of quickly getting their pills from a licensed clinician. And there'll be FDA-approved pills instead of paying a lot to get them from an overseas pharmacy with no directions on how to take them. This is harm reduction. What we're doing is not adding risk. We are reducing risk.[50]

Nevertheless, Prine admitted there was legal risk for physicians doing this work. At seventy-one, she said, "doctors like me who are at the end of our careers, we should be the ones to step up" to take the chance.[51]

Others expressed concerns that providers offering this care would not be guaranteed protection from criminal and civil lawsuits in red states. Prine countered:

Lawyers are telling us, you're still at risk. Bad things can happen to you. We're like, look, abortion doctors are always at risk. We signed up for that. We know that that's part of doing this work. Maybe this is increasing our level of risk, and maybe it's a different kind of risk, but we're used to being at risk and we're okay with that. So let us decide the risks we want to take. Just give us the best law you can and we'll run with it because people need it. People really, really, really need it. They needed it months ago.[52]

Prine called for creative approaches to increase reproductive healthcare access now. "We learned from the November election that people in our country really want abortion to remain accessible. Yet despite that, the red states remain on the offensive and plan to pass more restrictive laws. Thus, those of us in blue states need to become equally proactive and get positive things done," said Prine, who advocated for even stronger laws:

We should also think about more radical laws we could pass, like making mifepristone over the counter or available via "standing orders" for pharmacists or nurses, or legalizing advanced provision. Blue states should pass laws that challenge the FDA regulations just like red states have done when they make this federally approved medication illegal. Let's make it more accessible. We would actually be following the science to do so.[53]

In addition to New York, the Abortion Coalition for Telemedicine Access pushed for telemedicine abortion provider shield laws in other states, including in Washington state, California, Vermont, Colorado, Maryland, and New Jersey.[54]

On April 27, 2023, the state of Washington enacted a provider shield law protecting medical professionals in the state offering telemedicine abortion to people out of state.[55] Within days, a Washington doctor was offering this service to people in Idaho and Utah,[56] joining a doctor in Massachusetts offering telemedicine abortion to people in other restrictive states under the protection of the Massachusetts telemedicine provider shield law. Then Colorado and Vermont passed telemedicine provider shield laws and clinicians from those states began serving patients in states with abortion bans or restrictions on telemedicine abortion.[57] In June of 2023, New York passed a telemedicine abortion provider shield law and providers immediately started providing services to people living in states banning abortion.[58] In October of 2023, California passed a telemedicine abortion provider shield law.[59]

Telemedicine providers promptly began serving patients in states with bans from states with shield laws. In June 2023, Aid Access set up operations in shield law states in order to avoid shipping from outside of the country and customs delays that would sometimes take up to three weeks.[60] Aid Access offered telehealth abortion for $150 or less to people in all fifty states with delivery in two to five days. In the first month of operation, they mailed abortion pills to 3,500 people in states banning abortion, and to fifteen thousand people total across the country.[61] "It's nice to be playing offense, not defense," said a New York physician working with Aid Access.[62] Aid Access served women who were up to thirteen weeks pregnant and applied the law of the state in which the providers were located. New York, for example, did not have a parental consent law so clinicians there could serve people of any age from any state.[63] A second company, Abuzz Health, also began offering telemedicine abortion for $0 to $150 to people in thirty states with delivery in one to five days. This company also operated from within shield law states. According to Wells, by July of 2023, there were over a dozen clinicians in shield law states offering telemedicine abortion to people in restricted states.[64] Women in Mississippi, for example, were receiving telemedicine abortion care from clinicians in states with provider shield laws, according to Michelle Cohen of SHERo.[65] By October of 2023, Aid Access was serving over 5,500 people a month in banned or restricted states.[66]

Telemedicine providers also provided services along the borders of states with bans. Hey Jane, for example, saw a 164 percent increase in patients, with a 301 percent increase in patients in Illinois, a 231 percent increase in patients in Colorado, and a 178 percent increase in patients in New Mexico—all border states. Hey Jane reported that people were coming to them earlier in pregnancy after *Dobbs*: the average gestational age of their patients went down to around six weeks pregnant at the time of intake.[67] In October of 2023, the Massachusetts Medication Abortion Access Project began offering telemedicine abortion to people in all fifty states.[68] By offering care earlier in pregnancy, virtual clinics relieved pregnant women of the discomforts of ongoing pregnancy symptoms.

These mission-driven clinicians offered telemedicine abortion services for sliding scale fees. In 2023, three clinicians—Christie Pitney, Julie Jenkins, and Ruchi Kaul—formed the Abortion Freedom Fund to support telehealth abortion. Another abortion fund, WRRAP, also supported telehealth. But neither of these funds would support Aid Access clinicians serving people in states with abortion bans. By fall of 2023, approximately three-quarters of Aid Access patients were located in states with bans and approximately a third of those clients needed financial aid, which amounted to $20,000–25,000 a month per clinician, an unsustainable burden.[69]

Another obstacle was that clinicians serving states with bans had to dispense the medications themselves, which meant stocking, packaging, and mailing medications. After California passed its telemedicine provider shield law, advocates hoped Honeybee Health would dispense abortion pills to people in states with bans.[70]

Legal experts predicted anti-abortion states would file legal challenges to these telemedicine provider shield laws. "The interjurisdictional abortion wars are coming," said David Cohen, Greer Donley, and Rachel Rebouché in *The Columbia Law Review*.[71] They argued shield laws were a way for the abortion rights movement to "pivot from defense to offense," and that they helped women for whom travel is not possible. But providers offering abortion services to people in states with bans could be subject to extradition if they were to leave the protective states. These legal risks led some groups to not prioritize these types of shield laws, such as the New York Civil Liberties Union and Planned Parenthood in New York. "You don't want to send providers false assurances that they are totally protected by the law," said Katharine Bodde at New York Civil Liberties Union.[72] On the other hand, Julie Kay of the Abortion Coalition for Telemedicine Access believed the new telemedicine provider shield laws stood on very firm constitutional and legal grounds. "They don't conflict with constitutional law or interstate law. They've been very well researched and carefully crafted by law professors and reproductive rights attorneys and legal counsel of the state governments," said Kay. "The amount of kicking the tires and looking under the hood that went on in New York alone has been significant, and certainly way more than a lot of other legislation that has been passed."[73]

In addition to supporting the passage of shield laws, Abortion Coalition for Telemedicine Access works to implement these laws. "We help medical providers get up and running, such as getting medical malpractice insurance, setting up electronic medical records, and explaining how to ship pills," said Kay. "Telemedicine shield laws are excellent, but there is still some legal risk for providers, so Abortion Coalition for Telemedicine Access advises them on how to minimize that risk," said Kay. Abortion Coalition for Telemedicine Access also worked to decrease stigma. "The stigmatization is magnified because it's abortion, because it's medication abortion, because it's telemedicine, and because it's across state lines," said Kay. "We've gotten a lot of resistance, even from providers and practitioners that support abortion politically but who are not fans of the model of telemedicine abortion. The medical profession tends to be conservative with a small 'c,' but these medications have been proven safe and effective for decades. So part of our work is educating providers and the general public."[74] Kay said they also experience resistance from lawyers in the reproductive rights movement. She explained:

> Lawyers are trained to be super double cautious. Globally, in places where abortion has been banned or severely restricted, you have to work within that context. One year after *Dobbs*, we're still having a really hard time adjusting to that in the United States. It's a luxury that we may have as activists, but certainly people who are seeking abortion services in ban states don't have. Our mission is to provide reproductive health care as a human right. If we're not taking a risk, we are shifting the risk onto the people who are the most vulnerable.[75]

In these and other ways, activists sought to make abortion pills a safe, convenient, and private way to end an early pregnancy.

LITIGATION AND LEGISLATION TO EXPAND ABORTION PILL ACCESS AT THE STATE LEVEL

In addition to pushing for telemedicine provider shield laws, abortion advocates challenged state restrictions on medication abortion. By mid-2022, nineteen states imposed in-person dispensing requirements and many imposed other restrictions that went beyond FDA requirements, such as only allowing physicians to dispense the medication, requiring the patient to consume the medication in the presence of a provider, and requiring multiple in-person visits to obtain the medication. In October 2021, Texas had banned clinicians from prescribing abortion pills after seven weeks of pregnancy—three weeks before the FDA time limit of ten weeks. Legal scholars and advocates questioned the constitutionality of these additional restrictions on abortion pills.[76] In March 2023, Wyoming specifically banned abortion pills—becoming the first state to do so. In late June, a federal court blocked the law before it was supposed to go into effect on July 1.[77] Six states banned mailing abortion pills, but courts blocked the laws in all the states but for Arizona.[78]

University of Pittsburgh law professor Greer Donley argued that state bans of an FDA-approved abortion medication may violate the supremacy clause of the Constitution. The supremacy clause established that federal laws take precedence over state laws that are in conflict and prohibits states from interfering with matters that are exclusively entrusted to the federal government—such as the regulation of medications. "To get an FDA approval for a drug, it can take decades and can cost hundreds of millions of dollars to produce the amount of research and data that's required," said Donley. "That comes with a license to sell the product in fifty states. If states could just ban different types of products that are FDA approved, you can imagine that pharmaceutical companies would be quite upset about that because that is really curtailing their market for their product, which they worked so hard to be able to sell."[79]

Professor Donley cited a 2014 case where the Massachusetts governor issued an emergency order banning the prescribing and dispensing of the FDA-approved opioid Zohydro. The producer of the drug sued in federal court and the court ruled that the emergency order was preempted by federal law under the supremacy clause. The court blocked the order and allowed sale of the drug. The court ruled that allowing the law to stand would "undermine the FDA's ability to make drugs available to promote and protect the public health."[80] Temple University law professor Rachel Rebouché and others argued that banning abortion medications similarly usurped the power of the FDA because it in effect takes mifepristone off the market.[81] Shortly after the Supreme Court overturned *Roe v. Wade*, Attorney General Merrick Garland issued a statement saying that state restrictions on mifepristone were preempted by federal law. "The FDA has approved the use of the medication mifepristone. States may not ban mifepristone based on disagreement with the FDA's expert judgment about its safety and efficacy," said Garland.[82]

GenBioPro challenged state restrictions on mifepristone in October 2020, when the company sued Mississippi in federal court for its restrictions that went beyond the FDA rule, including a law allowing only physicians to dispense the drug and requiring in-person dispensing.[83] After *Dobbs*, they withdrew this case, but filed another in a federal court in West Virginia in January 2023. The second lawsuit argued that the state's abortion ban and specific restrictions on medication abortion violated the supremacy clause and the commerce clause of the Constitution. "Congress subjected [mifepristone] to a substantial and detailed federal regulatory program with which West Virginia law interferes. That state law must give way to the comprehensive federal regime Congress enacted and the Food and Drug Administration implemented," the complaint stated. "West Virginia's ban and restrictions impermissibly restrict patients' access to mifepristone and GenBioPro's opportunity and ability to market, promote, and sell the medication in the State."[84] Representing GenBioPro, Skye Perryman, the president and CEO of Democracy Forward, argued, "Our case makes clear that nothing in the Court's decision last year in *Dobbs* displaced Congress and FDA's role in deciding whether medications are safe and effective and determining which regulations should be imposed on mifepristone. States cannot substitute their medical and scientific judgments for judgments FDA has made, and doing so undermines not only access to medication, but the country's entire drug regulation system."[85] In August of 2023, the federal district court dismissed GenBioPro's challenge to the West Virginia abortion ban, which the company appealed to the Fourth Circuit.[86] The district court, however, also ruled that a law restricting doctors from prescribing mifepristone via telemedicine was "unambiguously preempted" by FDA regulation of mifepristone because Congress had allocated to the FDA alone the right to dictate the manner in which mifepristone may be prescribed. This ruling had the potential to help people in states that still allowed some abortions but blocked telemedicine abortion, such as Arizona, Florida, Georgia,

Iowa, Kansas, Montana, Nebraska, Nevada, North Carolina, Ohio, Pennsylvania, South Carolina, Utah, and Wisconsin.

In another federal case filed in January 2023, a North Carolina doctor named Amy Bryant challenged her state's laws imposing medically unnecessary restrictions on physicians prescribing mifepristone to their patients. North Carolina required doctors to dispense mifepristone in person in a specially certified surgical facility after state-mandated counseling and a mandatory 72-hour delay. "We know from years of research and use that medication abortion is safe and effective," said Dr. Bryant. "There's no medical reason for politicians to interfere or restrict access to it, or for states to force doctors to comply with mandates not supported by medicine or science. These burdensome restrictions on medication abortion force physicians to deal with unnecessary restrictions on patient care and on the healthcare system."[87] Bryant's lawyer Eva Temkin of King & Spalding explained: "Congress has made clear that FDA is tasked with establishing regulatory controls for this drug to ensure safety and patient access in the least burdensome way. State politicians cannot stand in the shoes of the FDA to impose restrictions on medication access that FDA has determined are not appropriate and that upset the careful balance FDA was directed by Congress to strike."[88] Other states had similar restrictions on medication abortion (see Figure 5.1).[89]

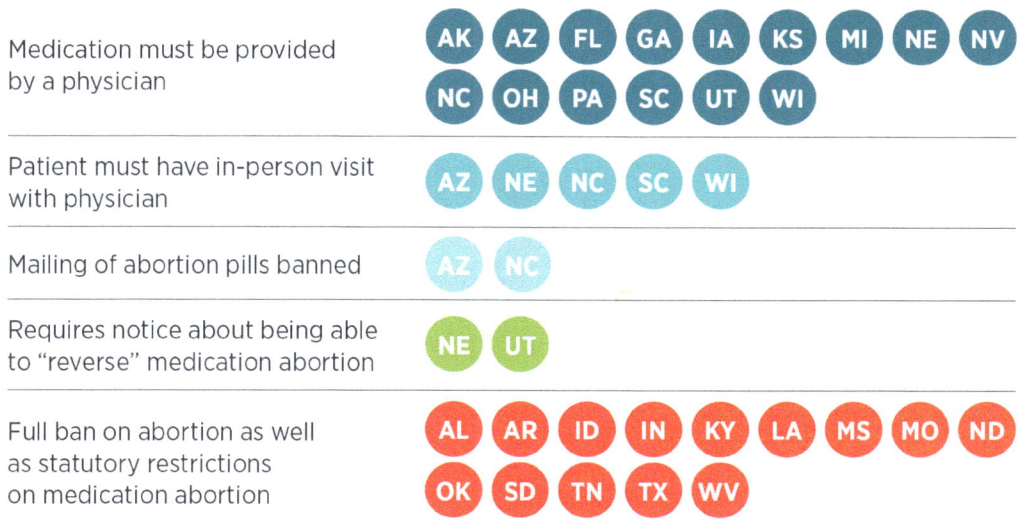

FIGURE 5.1: Contrary to FDA regulation, many states required physicians to dispense mifepristone directly to patients and required patients to have an in-person visit with the physician (courtesy of Guttmacher Institute).

On April 30, 2024, the federal court ruled that some of the state's restrictions placed on dispensing abortion pills that went beyond the controls set by federal regulators were unlawful, including prohibiting healthcare providers other than physicians from prescribing the drug; requiring in-person prescribing, dispensing, and administering; mandating the scheduling of an in-person follow-up appointment; and requiring non-fatal adverse event reporting to the FDA. However, the court ruled that North Carolina could impose requirements that had not been expressly considered and rejected by the FDA or that focused more on the practice of medicine and a patient's informed consent. This included the state's requirements for an in-person advance consultation, use of an ultrasound, an in-person examination, blood type testing, and adverse event reporting to state health authorities.[90] Advocates vowed to keep fighting for FDA preemption of state restrictions.[91]

In addition to challenging laws restricting medication abortion, abortion pill advocates pushed for new state laws to expand medication abortion access. Following California's lead,[92] advocates in Massachusetts pushed for legislation to require university campus health centers to offer medication abortion.[93] For many college students, access to abortion health care was critical for continuing their education, but unnecessary barriers placed heavy burdens on students seeking this care. Although student health insurance plans covered the cost of abortion in Massachusetts, campus health services did not provide this service. This forced students to travel off campus to obtain abortion pills, sometimes requiring them to travel long distances on public transportation because of the limited number of abortion providers in the state, leaving large geographic gaps.

Research on how many students were likely affected by the lack of medication abortion services on campuses and what burdens they experienced showed that between forty and sixty-four public university students in Massachusetts were obtaining medication abortions each month, amounting to 480 to 768 students each year. The study then measured the distance from each of Massachusetts's thirteen four-year public university campuses to the nearest abortion clinic, and calculated the distance and travel times by public transportation between the campuses and nearest clinics. The results were that students had to travel between two and forty-two miles to obtain abortion pills at off-campus clinics. If a student had to use public transportation, this travel could take between eighteen and four hundred minutes one way to reach the closest abortion clinic. As many as 93 percent of students at these universities were more than thirty minutes from the closest abortion facility via public transportation. Students from University of Massachusetts Amherst—the state flagship public university—had to travel twenty-five miles to reach the closest abortion provider, Planned Parenthood of Western Massachusetts in Springfield. If they had to take public transportation, the bus ride was two hours and eighteen minutes one way. To travel to the clinic, obtain the health care they needed, and travel home by bus took almost a full day—time few students had to spare between classes, jobs, and other activities.[94]

Advocates argued that the burdens caused by forcing students off campus to obtain abortion pills fell disproportionately on women of color, lower-income students, and those with other family or work responsibilities that placed demands on their time and finances. These students were less likely to have the resources to travel long distances to obtain the health care they needed. Advocates also argued that increasing access to medication abortion was critical for gender equity as well as racial and economic justice for Massachusetts college students. According to the Guttmacher Institute, almost 40 percent of women seeking abortion health care did so because having a child would interfere with their education. Research showed that access to contraception and abortion improve women's educational attainment. Women who had a child while in college were less likely to graduate than those who did not, and 89 percent of students said that having a child while in school would make it harder to achieve their goals.[95] Advocates argued that students should not have to get on buses and travel long distances to pick up abortion pills from unfamiliar clinicians. Students deserved to have a familiar place to access the abortion health care they needed with nurses and doctors they already knew and who had their medical records. They also warned about making students have to hunt for abortion clinics to get the health care they needed. They noted that on-campus health services varied in the amount of information they provided about how to find abortion health care off campus, often leaving students in the position of having to figure out how to obtain care on their own and putting them at an increased risk of reaching out to one of the many anti-abortion centers masquerading as reproductive health clinics, which targeted college students and could delay or even prevent access to real health care. In July of 2022, shortly after the *Dobbs* decision, the Massachusetts legislature passed a law requiring public colleges in Massachusetts to provide medication abortion services in campus health centers.[96]

Advocates in other states pushed for similar measures. In December of 2022, students from Columbia University's Reproductive Justice Collective, Barnard College, City University of New York (CUNY) and State University of New York (SUNY) rallied at the Women's Health Protective Association Fountain in Riverside Park. Students called on New York state lawmakers to pass a bill to make medication abortion available on all eighty-nine CUNY and SUNY campuses across the city and state. Joined by sponsors of the bill, Assembly members Harvey Epstein and Senator Cordell Cleare, the young demonstrators also called on New York Governor Kathy Hochul to support the bills and incorporate funding for them into her first executive budget. "In this post-*Roe* landscape, it's critical we ensure young people can get on-demand access to medication abortion we need," said Niharika Rao of the Reproductive Justice Collective and a youth abortion activist with Advocates for Youth. "We cannot let extremists politicize abortion care—yet today restrictions exist that are based in politics and not on the science. Medication abortion is common, extremely safe, and just like other services offered in primary care settings."[97]

At the time, health centers at many public university campuses in New York did not offer medication abortion. "Students rely on their health centers for medical care," said Epstein. "Abortion is medical care, yet far too many schools do not provide access to abortion services at their health centers. As we face an increasingly hostile environment for civil rights, in New York we're fighting back to guarantee not only the right to abortion but access to it for a population that has limited time, resources and transportation options."[98] Students faced other obstacles accessing abortion care as well, such as lack of information about how to find abortion providers. "On-campus provision actually makes insurance coverage easier, reduces precious travel time for students, and can help to increase young people's awareness about their options," said Rao.[99] "Far too often, students seeking abortions have to travel off campus and potentially face academic and financial losses—sometimes with the added emotional toll of having to seek care completely on their own," said Sean Miller, Northeast regional director for Young Invincibles, a national nonprofit dedicated to amplifying the voices of young adults.[100] Offering medication abortion on university campuses was also a social justice issue, said Miller, because the lack of abortion access was "disproportionally harming young women from low-income, Black and brown families."[101]

Advocates expressed concern that laws banning abortion in other states would force people to travel to New York to get care, increasing wait time at clinics in the state and putting pressure on local abortion funds and doctors. "New York is a destination state. Our clinics are being overwhelmed. It's becoming harder to get appointments," said one student at the rally. "Additionally, it's becoming harder when the alt-right here in New York, upstate and in the city, have been emboldened and have increased their tactics of harassing and intercepting patients at clinics."[102] The proposed legislation required CUNY and SUNY campuses across the city and state to provide access to medication abortion at student health centers that served over half a million students, 57 percent of whom were women. Schools would also have the option to contract with a third party to provide the services. Schools that demonstrated they could not fulfill the mandate would be required to provide referrals off campus to hospitals or clinics. The legislation also established a "public college and public university student health center abortion by medication fund" jointly overseen by the State Comptroller, health commissioner, and chancellors from SUNY and CUNY. "As New York becomes a destination state for abortion access, we must reduce wait times and funding pressure by making on-campus abortion pills available to students," said Rao.[103] On April 28, 2023, New York enacted a law requiring public universities in the state to offer medication abortion through campus health centers.[104]

While the legislation only applied to public universities, advocates hoped the legislation would influence private colleges and universities to also offer medication abortion in their on-campus health centers. In October of 2022, Barnard College became the first private college in New York to pledge to offer medication abortion at its student health center. "Health care is a human right and an essential aspect of making this principle manifest is ensuring that comprehensive care is available in a direct, unfettered, and accessible way," said Senator Cordell Cleare. "For the hundreds of thousands of college students in New York State, campus health centers are the first, best, and only option for timely medical care and attention. Our legislation is needed because these centers must provide a full scope of services, including medication abortion, which will ensure the health, safety and well-being of students."[105] The New York law passed in May of 2023.[106]

FEDERAL INITIATIVES TO EXPAND ABORTION PILL ACCESS

In addition to state-level initatives, advocates worked at the federal level to increase access to abortion pills. In Congress, Rep. Cori Bush of Missouri introduced the Protecting Access to Medication Abortion Act (H.R. 767), Rep. Kathy Manning of North Carolina introduced a resolution declaring the authority of the FDA to approve drugs for abortion care (H.R. 309), and Rep. Patrick Ryan of New York introduced a measure declaring that state restrictions on dispensing medication abortion were preempted by federal law (H.R. 2573). Across the aisle, anti-abortion legislators pushed restrictions on abortion medications. For example, in September of 2023, Rep. Andy Ogles of Tennessee introduced The Ending Chemical Abortion Pill Act (H.R. 5806). In a deadlocked Congress, none of these measures advanced.

Reproductive health providers and advocates, however, pressed the FDA to expand access to mifepristone by focusing on a non-abortion use for the drug: miscarriage treatment. ACOG, the American Medical Association, and forty-seven other organizations representing reproductive healthcare providers, researchers, and advocates filed a citizen petition, urging the FDA to approve mifepristone for treatment of incomplete miscarriages.[107] In combination with misoprostol, mifepristone was known as the best treatment for miscarriage, but abortion bans created barriers to accessing the medication. "The confusion that the opposition has sown with all their legislation plus the risk of criminalization equals chaos. And that just leads to cruelty. That's what we're seeing. People are being denied care in real time and lives are totally upended," said Kirsten Moore at the EMAA Project, which joined the petition.[108] The FDA had approved mifepristone for pregnancy termination, but did not explicitly label the drug for use in miscarriage care. The citizen petition asked the FDA to modify the drug's label to add an indication for miscarriage treatment and to remove requirements that clinicians and pharmacies be certified to prescribe and dispense the drug, which created barriers to access for miscarriage. Advocates noted that approximately 25 percent of all pregnancies ended in miscarriage.

To treat a miscarriage, some clinicians took a wait-and-see approach, with active monitoring in case symptoms such as infection developed and required intervention.

Other clinicians offered medications to complete the miscarriage or manually emptied the uterus. For patients choosing medication, the well-established standard of care was mifepristone in combination with misoprostol. Clinicians could prescribe mifepristone for miscarriages as an off-label use, but only if they were a certified prescriber because of the FDA's REMS restrictions. Because of this restriction, many clinicians in medical offices and emergency rooms could not prescribe the medication. As a result, the most commonly used medical protocol for miscarriage management was misoprostol alone, but research showed that the combination of mifepristone and misoprostol was faster and more effective for miscarriage care as well as less painful than misoprostol alone.[109] The lack of mifepristone labeling for miscarriage was also making the medication vulnerable to bans in states hostile to abortion. They noted that lawmakers in Alabama and Arizona had introduced legislation to ban mifepristone.[110] "These are wholesale bans on mifepristone for any use and, if enacted, will prevent clinicians from providing the gold standard miscarriage care in their communities of practice, harming public health," said the citizen petition. "Even without a wholesale ban on mifepristone, clinicians in states that ban abortion may be hesitant to prescribe a drug that has only been approved for abortion even for a legal, off-label use, like miscarriage management."[111]

Advocates hoped that adding miscarriage management to the label would legitimate this important use and make it harder for states to ban the drug. "The FDA has the authority delegated by Congress to regulate the safety of drugs and what should be on the market and how it can be on the market. States should not be able to override FDA authority," said Moore.[112] In addition to relabeling mifepristone, the petition asked the FDA to eliminate the requirement of clinician certification to prescribe and dispense mifepristone. "ACOG is encouraging doctors to become certified prescribers if they wanted to do miscarriage treatment, even if they don't want to do abortions. But they'd have to certify and say that they themselves were an abortion doctor, and that is a hurdle," said Moore.[113] Requiring providers to become certified to prescribe mifepristone was not only an administrative burden, but it could open them up to risks of violence and harassment because of the medication's association with abortion. The petition cited research showing that physicians who only planned to prescribe mifepristone for miscarriage care still feared becoming targets of anti-abortion protesters.[114]

The citizen petition also asked for removal of the pharmacy certification requirement, arguing the requirement was unnecessary and created barriers to access, especially for poor and rural women. The petition asked the FDA to remove a requirement that patients receiving mifepristone sign an informed consent form saying they are using the drug for abortion. "Asking a miscarriage patient to attest to having an abortion will confuse patients at best, but due to the prevalence of abortion stigma, it might also add emotional harm to their miscarriage experience," said the citizen petition.[115] Moore emphasized the urgency of these changes so that patients could access the best care possible in a time of crisis. "If you're talking about someone who's seeking treatment for miscarriage, they want to go to their own healthcare provider and get their prescription filled as quickly as possible," said Moore.[116]

On January 5, 2023, the FDA rejected the citizen petition, stating that Danco would have to submit an NDA for the FDA to change the label on the mifepristone and that the request to use enforcement discretion to remove the REMS was not properly the subject of a citizen petition under FDA's regulations.[117] On February 1, 2023, eight US senators sent an open letter to Danco Laboratories, urging them to submit an application to the FDA to add miscarriage management to the medication's label. "Currently, access to abortion has been restricted, or will likely be restricted, in twenty-four states. Not only do these laws take away the reproductive rights of women, but they also endanger the lives of people experiencing early-pregnancy miscarriage," said the senators.[118] Because of legal concerns about mifepristone, they noted, healthcare providers were instead prescribing high doses of misoprostol to ensure effectiveness, resulting in severe cramping, "making it a longer, more dangerous, and psychologically taxing process." "People experiencing miscarriage deserve access to safe and effective treatment, without added and unnecessary pain," said the lawmakers. "Women in need of mifepristone for earlypregnancy miscarriages are experiencing barriers to effective and safe treatment because this drug is commonly used in medical abortions. Updating mifepristone's label will make this drug accessible for miscarriage management without fear of criminal action against healthcare providers."[119] The senators implored Danco to submit a request to the FDA to add miscarriage management as an indication to the mifepristone label.

In the letter, the senators cited research showing that over one million women in America experienced a miscarriage every year—as many as 26 percent of all pregnancies—noting that miscarriage was more common among Black and lowincome women. Research showed the combination of mifepristone and misoprostol significantly improved the management of early pregnancy loss, resulting in fewer complications and reducing the likelihood of patients needing an additional procedure. Yet a 2023 study found that between 2016 and 2020, only 1 percent of over twenty-two thousand patients nationwide who took medication to treat miscarriages received the recommended two-drug protocol. Misoprostol on its own was much less effective than the two-drug combination, requiring follow-up surgery to complete the miscarriage in roughly 25 percent of cases.[120] "Patients experiencing an early miscarriage should have access to the most effective medication available," said Kirsten Moore. "Given the uncertain and hostile legislative climate in some states, it is vitally important to add miscarriage to the mifepristone label."[121]

While the FDA did not act on ACOG's citizen petition nor the senators' letter, they did announce, on January 3, 2023, the new certification process for brick-and-mortar pharmacies to become eligible to sell mifepristone—a process the FDA negotiated with the abortion pill manufacturers Danco and GenBioPro after the agency announced it would make this change in December of 2021. Before that, certified providers had to stock and dispense the pills themselves, or rely on mail order pharmacies that dispensed the medication. With the new certification process, providers could just write a prescription and have it filled by certified brick-and-mortar retail pharmacies, making it more quickly and conveniently available to patients. Reproductive rights advocates celebrated the change, hoping it would expand access to abortion pills.[122] "Today's announcement means that people who live in states that have not banned medication abortion care may soon be able to walk into their neighborhood pharmacy and walk out with their medications in hand," said Kirsten Moore. "By allowing brick-and-mortar pharmacies to dispense medication abortion care, the FDA is treating medication abortion like the safe, effective, time-sensitive care that it is."[123]

But advocates were concerned that the FDA created barriers to mifepristone being available in pharmacies by requiring pharmacies to register with the drug manufacturer in order to dispense the drug, despite the fact that mifepristone was safer than many over-the-counter medications, including Tylenol. "Even as the FDA drops one onerous restriction, it adds another—a certification requirement for pharmacies, which is not supported by medical evidence and could present a large enough hurdle that will dissuade some from dispensing [mifepristone]," said Upadhyay at ANSIRH. "With abortion restricted in large parts of the country, we need our public health policies to follow the science so people can have access to this essential medication."[124]

Advocates expressed concern about whether busy pharmacies would be willing to take on the extra work to become certified to dispense abortion pills. "This is just a bunch of paperwork that doesn't add any value," said Moore. "These certification requirements unfairly limit the pools of prescribers and pharmacies for no good reason." Moore nevertheless hoped pharmacy distribution would mean more medical providers would be willing to become certified and prescribe abortion pills in the future. "We are moving this product from what used to be a very niche category with a very small circle of players into the mainstream," said Moore.[125] Pharmacy access was important to normalizing abortion pills and making them more accessible. "Today, we celebrate this progress and tomorrow, we'll continue to work towards a world with no restrictions on medication abortion care," said Moore.[126] Several retail pharmacy chains, including Walgreens, CVS, and Rite Aid, announced they would seek certification to sell abortion pills in states where legally permissible.

In response, anti-abortion groups organized a national day of protests on February 4 targeting chain pharmacies to discourage them from dispensing mifepristone. The protests were organized by a group calling themselves the Progressive Anti-Abortion Uprising (PAAU). The group claimed to be peaceful and progressive, but its members had repeatedly broken the law to achieve their goal of intimidating, harassing, and blocking women from accessing reproductive health care. PAAU planned protests for February 4 at pharmacies across the country, including in Boston, New York City, Washington, DC, Chicago, Los Angeles, and San Francisco.[127]

The February 4 action was co-sponsored by two other anti-abortion groups: Survivors of the Abortion Holocaust and Live Action, which on January 26 disrupted a Walgreens shareholder meeting in Newport Coast, California. Two anti-abortion extremists broke into the building where the meeting was to take place and hid out in a closet for nine hours waiting to ambush and disrupt the meeting. "These extremists are infamous for stalking physicians, invading clinics, and bullying patients and clinic staff," said duVergne Gaines, director of FMF's National Clinic Access Project. "Groups like PAAU, the Survivors, and Live Action are doing their best to grab headlines and terrorize pharmacies out of providing critical access to the abortion pill, but they must be stopped."[128] According to Gaines, members of PAAU had connections to violent, anti-abortion extremists. PAAU director of activism Lauren Handy, who claimed to be a feminist, was trained by one of the leading extremists in the anti-abortion movement, Jeff White, founder and leader of Survivors of the Abortion Holocaust. White, who had been arrested dozens of times for blockading clinics, disorderly conduct, stalking, and more, served time in federal prison for defrauding numerous state Affordable Care Act programs of over $27 million. Handy studied and worked with White for two years in California, according to Gaines.[129] Handy faced criminal charges in several states, including Michigan, DC, Virginia, and Ohio. Among other convictions, a Michigan jury found Handy guilty of trespassing and resisting police during a protest at an abortion clinic in Flint in 2019.

On January 22, 2023, President Biden issued a presidential memorandum directing the Secretary of HHS, in consultation with the Attorney General and the Secretary of Homeland Security, to consider new guidance to support patients, providers, and pharmacies who wished to legally access, prescribe, or provide mifepristone—no matter where they lived. The president called for new actions to ensure that patients could access reproductive health care and abortion medications free from harassment, threats, or violence.[130] "Americans support abortion, period, and pharmacy access to the abortion pill is long overdue," said Gaines. "Pharmacies need to stand firm against this fringe group, and law enforcement must be vigilant against these extremists to ensure safe access to all pharmacies—and abortion clinics."[131]

On March 2, Walgreens announced that it would not dispense mifepristone in twenty US states, including several where abortion remained legal—like Alaska, Iowa, Kansas, and Montana. Amidst an ever-changing set of laws regarding abortion care, pharmacists said they were struggling to navigate "blatant contradictions between state and federal law that make it very challenging to identify what is legal and what is not legal," according to E. Michael Murphy, a spokesperson for the American Pharmacists Association. "We are very concerned…because we as pharmacists want to ensure the patients have access to the best possible care that's informed by evidence."[132] The announcement was a response to a letter sent to Walgreens in February by nearly two dozen Republican state attorneys general, who threatened legal action if Walgreens dispensed the drugs. The attorneys general sent similar letters to CVS, Albertsons, Rite Aid, Costco, Walmart, and Kroger. After significant backlash, Walgreens walked back its plan not to dispense abortion pills in states where abortion was still legal. In a statement on March 6, the pharmacy chain vowed to offer mifepristone where it was still possible to do so. "We want to be very clear about what our position has always been: Walgreens plans to dispense mifepristone in any jurisdiction where it is legally permissible to do so," Walgreens said in its statement. "Providing legally approved medications to patients is what pharmacies do."[133] Many remained skeptical about whether Walgreens would in fact do so.

In early October 2023, GenBioPro announced on their website the names of eighteen brick-and-mortar pharmacies that were dispensing mifepristone. The pharmacies listed included independent community drugstores, university-affiliated outlets, and compounders located in nine states: Arizona, California, Maryland, New York, Pennsylvania, South Carolina, Washington, Wisconsin, and Texas. There were no chain pharmacies on the list, although CVS and Walgreens assured the public they still planned to dispense the medication.[134] The same month, New York City's public hospitals began offering telemedicine abortion.[135]

EXPANDING ABORTION PILL ACCESS OUTSIDE OF THE MEDICAL SYSTEM AND THE LAW

In addition to groups working to expand *legal* access to abortion, grassroots networks expanded to provide extralegal access to abortion pills for people living in the United States. AccessMA, WeSaveUs, ARTogether, IdahoAccess, and OKAccess formed after *Dobbs* to mail abortion pills for free to people living in states with abortion bans (see Figure 5.2). Red State Access (see Figure 5.3) provided information on how to access abortion pills for free through these community networks.[136]

By July of 2023, twenty-five US-based distributors located across the country were mailing mifepristone and misoprostol to people living in states with bans. Community networks were able to obtain the medications from overseas suppliers, bring them into the country, and then mail them from within the United States so that people received the medications promptly. Depending on their supply and people's preferences, they would mail the pills loose in bubble wrap (for confidentiality purposes) or send them in blister packs. They served people of all ages, at all gestational stages, using different protocols for people in later pregnancy and offering doula support, either in person or virtually. They provided detailed information about how to use the pills by email, with e-learning tools, and ensured that people were within thirty minutes of emergency care in the rare event that they needed it. They urged people to flush any misoprostol they did not use. They were careful to use encrypted apps and aliases. In the first year, these organizations mailed abortion pills to over twenty thousand people. These

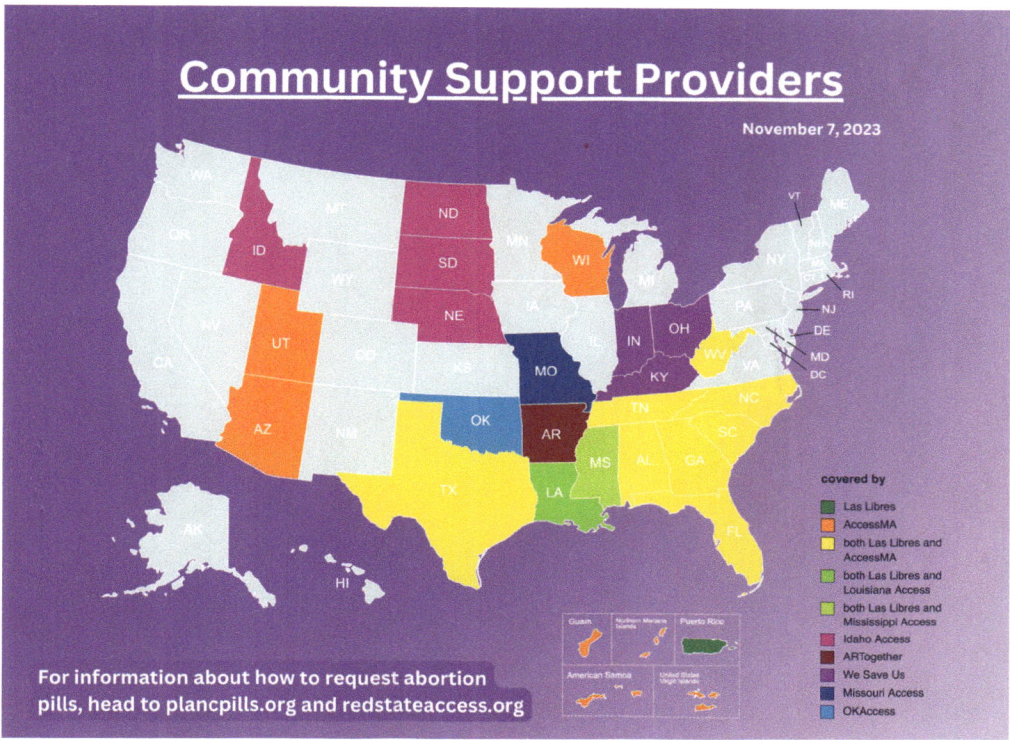

FIGURE 5.2: Red State Access Instagram post indicating what states are served by different US-based networks as of November 7, 2023 (designed by Lara I. for Red State Access.).[195]

organizations received contributions from small donors and large ones, although as they ramped up their work and became higher profile, large donors withdrew from supporting them for fear of legal risks. Advocates in these groups accepted the legal risks of doing this work because they knew that many people could not travel out of state to obtain abortion care, and felt strongly that no one should be forced to give birth against their will. These organizations did not advertise, but spread the word by word of mouth and through Plan C. Some people within the movement were uncomfortable with their operations and spoke out against them. Sometimes their shipments of pills from abroad were confiscated, but most of the time they reached their destinations.[137]

In addition, accompaniment networks in Mexico expanded their work in the United States. Mexico-based networks serving people in the United States included Las Libres,[138] Colectiva Bloodys, Marea Verde, Matamoros Decide, and Red Necesito Abortar. Providing support to thousands of women self-managing their abortions all over the United States, these organizations emphasized "the guiding principles of women's autonomy, horizontality, dignity, and safety."[139] They trained volunteer community-based activists about how to support people using the pills outside of clinical settings and how to handle medical complications remotely. By May of 2023, Las Libres had trained about fifty networks of women in the United States to provide abortion assistance.[140] At

FIGURE 5.3: Red State Access image used on social media (courtesy of Red State Access).[196]

the time, Las Libres in Mexico alone was receiving two hundred to three hundred calls each day from the United States and claimed to have served over twenty thousand people since they began working with people in the United States. "A year ago, there was a lot of fear in the U.S., but now we know there are many abortion networks in the U.S. and that they have been multiplying," said Verónica Cruz Sánchez, director of abortion assistance organization Las Libres.[141] Las Libres helped US-based activists create their own networks in the US. While Mexico-based Las Libres activists used social media to communicate, US-based Las Libres activists concerned about security and criminalization used encrypted apps like Signal, especially after the Nebraska case where prosecutors used Facebook messages to charge a mother and daughter for self-managed abortion. Whereas in Mexico misoprostol was widely available over the counter, that was not the case in the United States so US activists had to help people obtain abortion medications. Accompaniment occurred both virtually and in person. The US-based networks often maintained relationships with physicians in the community who were willing to respond to emergencies, or provide follow-up care, although they did not usually participate directly.[142] By November 2023, Las Libres in the United States reported they had already served approximately ten thousand people.[143]

Red State Access and its partners struggled to maintain funding. They spent about $10 per package, most of which was shipping, but they couldn't accept any individual donations without revealing their personal identity. They also couldn't send money to the mailing volunteers without leaving a trail. They often ran out of money and had to pause services, especially as the donations after *Dobbs* tapered off.[144] For example, on October 10, 2023, AccessMA had depleted funding for its free program in ten states so they were only able to send medications to people who were undocumented, unbanked, advanced gestation, minors, and domestic violence clients. They directed other clients in affected states to two low-cost online vendors on Plan C. According to one researcher, "a significant portion of people reaching out to these networks are in controlling environments, can't leave a financial trail, can't leave the house without the partner/parents noticing etc. There's definitely been an uptick of these cases since the price drop on Plan C. Now, only people in really desperate situations reach out."[145] Despite these setbacks, Red State Access continued to help develop new partners, including Mississippi Access, Louisiana Access, and Texas Red Transfronteriza.[146] Another organization, TSA Health, formed to provide "free religious telehealth abortion care" in New Mexico, with plans to expand to states banning abortion. TSA Health was founded by The Satanic Temple, known for challenging abortion bans based on First Amendment religious arguments.[147]

In addition to community support networks providing free abortion pills to people living in states with bans, dozens of companies offered abortion pills online for as little as $25, with prompt delivery in all fifty states.[148] For example, in July of 2023, a website called MTP Pharmacy delivered abortion pills in three days for $37 to people living in any US state or territory. Another group called Private Emma delivered abortion pills in three to four days for $49. Safeabortiononline.com delivered abortion pills in four days for $50. Plan C, which tested websites selling abortion pills, including conducting product testing of the medications, listed the top twenty-five online suppliers in order of cost on their website, regularly updating the list with the latest prices, which led to price competition. "They're all looking at our list and they're saying, 'How can I get a higher ranking above this other one,'" said Wells. "So they set their price just a little bit below and then the next one contacts us and says, 'Okay, well, I want to be a little bit below that price.' It got really outrageous at one point, where one of them went down to like $25."[149] None of these suppliers required a prescription and many provided abortion pills in advance so people could have them on hand in case they experienced an unintended pregnancy. "We welcome these price reductions by the online retailers because we know the base cost of the product is quite low" said Wells, who estimated that the pills cost the suppliers about $2 to $3. Online sellers charged hundreds of dollars before *Dobbs*. "We recognize the price gouging that was going on previously, so we're glad that competition in the marketplace is resulting in more affordable products for people who need them."[150] According to Wells, several of the companies were longstanding pharmacies that offered many medications, whereas others were newly formed, independent, mission-driven companies created by reproductive health advocates wanting to ensure access to abortion pills, such as Private Emma, An Idle Timer, Medside 24, and ybycmeds. Wells noted the competition was fierce among these companies, so much so that she had to send out a code of conduct companies had to comply with in order to be listed.[151]

While most websites did not do any sort of medical screening of customers for eligibility to use the medications, one claimed to: Private Emma. Private Emma began selling abortion pills in the United States in November 2022. A representative of the company claimed they were a charitable organization that had for years provided "sanitary products" to women in Africa. They claimed to have a medical director who screened each customer to ensure they were eligible to use abortion pills. By July of 2023, Private Emma had mailed mife/miso combi packs to close to eight thousand people in the United States. The company had two warehouses inside the United States so they were able to mail medications promptly to their customers. Their medications came from India and were brought into the country by mail or courier. They initially charged $105 for the mife/miso combi pack, but they were eventually able to drop their prices to $49 as they increased their efficiency and volume over time. They were able to get the medication for between $2 and $3, plus shipping from India of about $1 per package. Priority mail cost $10, and they had costs of rent on the warehouses, payments to couriers, and employee costs (they had five employees). In their first nine months of operations, they had five thousand combi packs confiscated during shipment. An employee of Private Emma described the risks they faced doing this work: "People are putting their livelihoods on the line because people could go to prison for doing something like this. We've got people involved in India, in Africa, and in the States. Everyone is risking something to be involved in this organization to be able to make it more affordable and make it more accessible."[152]

The work of organizations providing information about and access to abortion pills had an increasingly significant impact as more states restricted access to abortion in the medical system. Between April of 2022 and April of 2023, the Plan C website had 2.4 million visits, over three times as many as the previous year, when they had 719,000 visitors. The day after the *Dobbs* decision alone had 559,000 visits. By May of 2023, Plan C had seven to eight thousand visitors to their website each day. Legislation introduced in Texas to suppress abortion pill information specifically mentioned Plan C.[153] Aid Access, listed on Plan C's website, served over 300,000 people between 2021 and 2023.[154] Many other people were ordering pills through websites.[155] The SASS website received around thirteen thousand visits each month, and the organization conducted an increasing number of abortion pill trainings. In 2022, SASS train-the-trainer sessions reached at least 983 people across the United States, including in states with abortion bans and severe restrictions on access. SASS worked with Advocates for Youth to reach at least an additional 132 people, most of whom were located in Texas, where abortion was completely banned with very limited exceptions. They also had a dedicated social media team that spread information about abortion pills on the internet.[156] According to Ariella Messing, executive director of the Online Abortion Resource Squad, posts on their abortion subreddit increased to more than 1,300 posts a day by May of 2023.[157]

On the other hand, people in organizations inside states with abortion bans had to be careful about how they shared information. "I cannot say anything dealing with how to get the abortion pills," said Michelle Cohen of SHERo Mississippi. "It's unfortunate that I cannot post Plan C information, but I definitely personally support Plan C and their mission." Instead, Cohen posted links to other organizations with general information about abortion pills. "I post on all of our social media handles the people who are trusted folks that you can go to for information, but it can't be just information about where to get pills. That's how I can save myself. I have to be real clear not to post any images of the pills because the anti-abortion lawmakers can come at me and say, 'Oh, you're advertising where people can get pills.' There's a fine line that I have to walk here in Mississippi when it comes to even discussing abortion pills."[158] Reproaction co-founder Pamela Merritt spoke about the importance of sharing information about abortion pills, particularly in communities where people need it most:

> I think more people know about pills now than they did before *Dobbs*, but it's whether the right people know about pills—the people who need them as opposed to people who would like them. I don't feel that in North St. Louis city folks know about being able to access medication abortion at online pharmacies or any of that. So how are activists reaching those people? I would say the best way to reach them is through information sharing in an intimate

setting, where people can ask questions and be respected and feel comfortable receiving and sharing the information. I know there are organizers who are doing that. It's just a little tricky finding people in states with abortion bans to go out and do that.[159]

Merritt said that while information sharing is protected by the First Amendment, she knew there were legal risks. "The reality is that the Attorney General in the State of Missouri is absolutely unhinged, and is somebody who wants to throw people in jail. By the time you litigate the First Amendment protection, you've been through hell."[160] Merritt however said she was willing to take those risks. "I've structured my life so that I can take risks that other people don't. You know a lot of the folks who are best suited to go into certain communities are also folks who are incredibly vulnerable to that kind of prosecution. That said, there are activists on the ground who are doing it."[161] Merritt also said people were likely getting abortion pills through the street economy. "One of the things I learned from volunteering for five years in North St. Louis is that the street economy is real and people get everything that they need through a completely separate economic system. That includes diapers, formula, and probably misoprostol."[162]

Merritt, however, expressed frustration with activists who talked about abortion pills as if they would solve the problem of abortion access. "This is not the cure to all that ails us," said Merritt, who explained that many people don't live in circumstances where they can self-manage an abortion:

> The reality on the ground is that self-managed abortion with pills from an online pharmacy is probably the best thing for somebody at Washington University in St. Louis who misses a period. Awesome, fantastic. But for the sisters who are on the North Side or in Bootheel, we are at the exact same crux that we were on abortion access without Medicaid abortion coverage. Access was good for them but not for me. It bothers me when people are like, "Oh, it's gonna be great! It's just this wonderful thing." And I'm just like, you obviously have never lived in a house with three other families in a one-bedroom, one-bathroom situation while you're self-managing your abortion after thirteen weeks because you weren't sure how pregnant you were because you didn't go to the doctor, and then somebody calls the police because they were just tired of you being on the sofa. There's not a lot of privacy when you're poor. It frustrates me. But I think that when I first began work on self-managed abortion with pills versus now, there's more of an acknowledgment that it is not going to make everything okay.[163]

Merritt said she knew many young people who did not have a permanent place to live and did not have a reliable and confidential address to receive abortion pills by mail.

In October 2023, the Society for Family Planning reported that abortion actually increased the year after *Dobbs* by 2,200 abortions. While abortions plummeted in states banning abortion, they increased dramatically in states where abortion was still legal.[164] These numbers did not include abortions accessed outside of the formal medical system, which were likely happening in great numbers. Other research showed that telehealth abortion in particular made timely abortion care possible, especially for younger people, those experiencing food insecurity, rural residents, and those living far from an abortion facility.[165] American women discovered, as women knew across the globe in countries where abortion was illegal, that they could not wait for permission to have abortions, but they were also not going back to the days of dangerous, coat-hanger abortions. The internet and abortion pills had created a new reality. "A lot of us local people, local activists, organizers, and local groups were not waiting around for a national plan or a national strategy," said Michelle Cohen of SHERo in Mississippi. "There were a lot of us who had been doing this work, and so there were plans in place and folks helping their communities because the government does not give a damn about us and the legal system does not give a damn about us."[166]

REFRAMING ABORTION PILLS AND EARLY ABORTION

Anti-abortion advocates had had tremendous success in stigmatizing abortion and framing abortion pills as dangerous and hard to use. In response, abortion advocates developed creative strategies to counter anti-abortion rhetoric and images saturating the internet and political discussions portraying embryos in early pregnancy as fully formed miniature human beings. New abortion restrictions passed by legislatures across the country referred to embryos as "babies" and claimed there was a "fetal heartbeat" at six weeks of pregnancy. In response, the MYA Network developed the Issue of Tissue Project, which showed what tissue removed during early abortions looked like.[167] "There's a lot of *mis*information out there and many people have come to believe it," said MYA Network co-founder Dr. Michele Gomez, a family care physician in Burlingame, California. "There's also accurate information out there but mostly in the form of highly magnified embryos at these early stages. People have a right to know and understand that they are magnified."[168]

Advocates argued that before nine weeks of pregnancy, when 80 percent of abortions take place, the embryo was not visible with the naked eye in the pregnancy tissue removed during an abortion. There was no "heartbeat" at six weeks of pregnancy, only the electrical activity of cells before an actual heart is formed, said Gomez. "The anti-choice movement has been showing inaccurate and graphic pictures for a long time, and these images shock us so they tend to stick with us," said Gomez. "Without factual images to counter the inaccurate images, many people just accept the only things they've ever seen, which is completely understandable. Seeing actual images of early pregnancy tissue, as seen with the naked eye, can help people replace the graphic and inaccurate images they may have come to accept as true."[169]

MYA Network's Issue of Tissue Project shared accurate images of early pregnancy tissue. After manual aspiration abortions, they rinsed the blood from the tissue removed from the uterus and photographed it for pregnancies of five weeks through nine weeks. After an egg joins with a sperm at fertilization, it's called a zygote. After five days of development, it's called a blastocyst. The blastocyst embeds in the uterine wall and becomes an embryo at around ten to twelve days after fertilization. At around the tenth week of pregnancy it becomes a fetus.

In the MYA Network pregnancy tissue photos, the embryos were too small to see with the naked eye. At five weeks of pregnancy, the tissue is about one-quarter-of-an-inch wide. At six weeks of pregnancy, the tissue is a little over half-an-inch. At seven weeks of pregnancy, the tissue is one-inch wide. At eight weeks of pregnancy, the tissue is two-and-a-half inches wide. At nine weeks of pregnancy, the tissue is about three-inches wide, while the fetus is 7/8 of an inch (see Figure 5.4). Gomez said the MYA Network's decision to share these images grew from their own experiences as clinicians. "Many of us in the MYA Network provide in-office abortions by manual uterine aspiration, which is a simple, non-surgical procedure that takes five to ten minutes to complete and can be done with only ibuprofen for pain control," she said. "We've often had the experience of a patient asking to see the pregnancy tissue after the procedure, and then being very surprised by what they see."[170]

They argued that seeing the tissue resulting from pregnancy termination could dispel the myths surrounding abortion, help clear up confusion and misunderstandings resulting from anti-abortion misrepresentations, and combat abortion stigma and shame. "In my experience, pregnant people and their partners have felt some relief when they see the tissue, because it doesn't look like what they've seen in anti-choice imagery," Gomez continued. "We in the MYA Network discussed this, and decided that as clinicians we wanted our patients to have more information, so they could be better informed."[171]

On their website, the MYA Network shared recordings of patients speaking about their surprise and relief after viewing their own pregnancy tissue after an abortion.

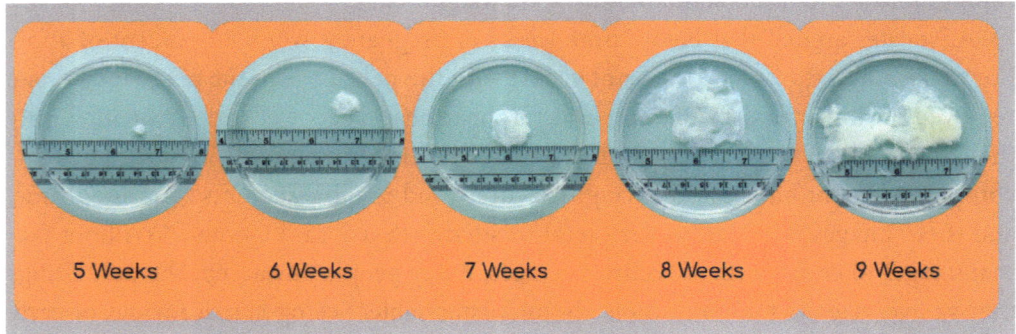

FIGURE 5.4: These photos show pregnancy tissue extracted at five to nine weeks of pregnancy, rinsed of blood and menstrual lining. The images show the tissue in a petri dish next to a ruler to indicate its size. The tiny embryo is embedded in the tissue (courtesy of MYA Network).

One woman explained, "It wasn't what I expected at all. It was so small…and seemed a lot less scary." Others spoke about how seeing their pregnancy tissue relieved feelings of guilt. "It just looked like mucus, it was just a little thing…nothing that made us feel guilty," said another patient after viewing her pregnancy tissue.[172] After the MYA Network published the images, TikTok influencers used them to raise awareness about early abortion and point out the absurdity of this early pregnancy tissue having more rights than the actual person who is pregnant.[173] "A lot of people are comforted by seeing these images—they're just so different from what they'd previously seen," said Gomez. "People need and deserve facts, love, and compassion to make decisions about their own bodies and their own lives."[174] Advocates as far back as 1995 had argued for showing women abortion tissue to demystify abortion and relieve anxiety and fear.[175]

Other reproductive health clinicians developed a different, innovative strategy to expand access: "missed period pills." For patients who had missed a period and did not want to be pregnant, clinicians began prescribing "missed period pills" or "late period pills" without prior pregnancy confirmation. The pills were the same regimen for medication abortion—200 milligrams of mifepristone and 800 micrograms of misoprostol. Misoprostol could also be used alone to restore menstruation. "If people want their periods to return and do not want to be pregnant, these medicines provide a benefit for them, regardless of their pregnancy status," said Dr. Teresa DePiñeres, a physician who advocated for missed period pills and worked with the organization Period Pills. "Offering more options for fertility control is a good thing," said DePiñeres.[176]

Advocates said some people preferred not to know if they were pregnant and others simply wanted to avoid waiting to confirm a pregnancy or schedule an abortion. The pills could be taken even if menstruation was just a few days late. Period pills could relieve the anxiety of waiting for a period to come, and the stress of taking a pregnancy test when a person didn't want to be pregnant. Gynuity research showed period pills provided psychological and emotional benefits, especially in social contexts where abortion-related stigma exists.[177] "There's not a right or wrong way. It's just another option for getting the care we need, and to practice bodily autonomy," said DePiñeres. "Most studies show that when people have options, they feel more satisfied with the care they receive."[178] DePiñeres noted that people often chose to take medicines that they may not need in order to prevent an unwanted condition, such as emergency contraception after unprotected sex or anti-malarial pills if they travel to a country with malaria cases. These medications had the psychological benefit of reducing stress and anxiety about an unwanted condition.

Research indicated strong interest in missed period pills. A 2020 study of 678 people in two states found that 70 percent of those who did not want to be pregnant said they would prefer period pills instead of a test to confirm pregnancy. "If such a service were available, demand could be substantial," they concluded.[179] The researchers noted missed period pills could alleviate the impact of restrictive social norms and abortion-related stigma, which is associated with "increased anxiety, stress, depression, social isolation, negative self-evaluation and somatic symptoms."[180] By fall of 2022, period pills were available via telemedicine in six states—California, Colorado, Massachusetts, New Mexico, Oregon, and Washington—and in the District of Columbia as part of a pilot study run by the University of California, San Francisco. The National Working Group on Period Pills advocated for making period pills more accessible in the United States. Formed in 2019, the group had twenty-one members by 2022, including medical clinicians, lawyers, reproductive justice leaders, and researchers. The working group also had fourteen organizational members, including five universities.[181]

Researchers at the University of California, San Francisco, began a clinical trial on missed period pills to evaluate women's experiences of using misoprostol alone to bring back a missed period. In the trial, participants took misoprostol after missing a period but without knowing whether they were pregnant. The study's goal was to assess "the feasibility and acceptability of this traditional concept of menstrual regulation."[182] Advocates hoped period pills could help avert the negative consequences of new abortion bans, in effect in over a dozen states across the country. "In the United States, we are going to see increased maternal mortality because there are going to be more unwanted pregnancies under conditions that are not safe," said DePiñeres. "More people are going to need abortions in places where they don't have that option. This is a way to potentially mitigate or circumvent some of that."[183]

Abortion pill advocates pursued other forms of research to increase abortion pill access. Aid Access founder, Dr. Rebecca Gomperts, began testing mifepristone for contraception, with the goal of making a weekly 50-milligram dose of mifepristone available over the counter on pharmacy shelves within ten years. In May 2022, the Moldovan Department of Health gave approval for the clinical trial of mifepristone for contraception. More than fourteen medical centers, including seven hospitals, committed to participate in the study. Researchers began enrolling patients in Moldova in August 2023 and then expanded the study to the Netherlands, working with Leiden University Medical Centre. Researchers planned to include 949 women who would use mifepristone weekly for a year. Gomperts hoped that easy access to mifepristone as birth control would then make it available for abortion if necessary. Approval of mifepristone for contraception would also make it available as a morning-after pill, for use within 120 hours after unprotected intercourse. "It would allow us to move flexibly between the medicine's different indications as weekly contraceptive, as an on-demand method used before or after sexual intercourse or as an early medical abortion method, depending on our life circumstances," said Gomperts.[184]

In order to understand how to increase access, advocates also studied attitudes toward abortion pills in particular communities. In May of 2023, researchers at the National Asian Pacific American Women's Forum and Ibis Reproductive Health published a study about barriers to medication abortion for people within

Asian American, Native Hawaiian, and Pacific Islander communities. The study was funded by the Society of Family Planning. Barriers included community stigma toward abortion, sexual, and reproductive health care, a lack of family support, and the unavailability of language support for limited-English or non-English-speaking patients at abortion clinics.[185] To address the digital divide, a new organization, Reproductive Health Initiative for Telehealth Equity & Solutions, formed in 2022 to better understand and remedy unequal access to the internet and telehealth-capable devices, as well as digital literacy.[186]

Other activists worked to destigmatize abortion by challenging myths about abortion being difficult or traumatic. When activist and artist Jex Blackmore appeared on Fox News Detroit on January 23, 2022, with reporter Charlie Langton and anti-choice advocate Rebecca Kiessling, they held up a mifepristone abortion pill and swallowed it with a sip of water, saying "I want to show you how easy and safe it is by taking it myself." Blackmore's Fox appearance went viral on social media, angering critics on both ends of the political spectrum. Blackmore's action was a part of a guerrilla campaign for mail-order abortion pills launched on January 22, the anniversary of *Roe v. Wade*, by a group of Detroit activists affiliated with the group Shout Your Abortion. The campaign included pasting more than one hundred posters on buildings and walls across the city with the message, "ABORTION PILLS FOREVER," along with the website address, "shareabortionpill.info," where people could find information about how to order abortion pills by mail.[187] Within the reproductive health community, the GLC continued their work to normalize self-managed abortion by attending and presenting at conferences of organizations such as the National Abortion Federation, the Society for Family Planning, the Abortion Care Network, Creating Change, Essence Fest, and the State Innovation Exchange.[188]

Public awareness of abortion pills and self-managed abortion was increased with the release of a documentary called *Plan C* by filmmaker Tracy Droz Tragos. Tragos began working on a film about the work of the organization Plan C in 2019, but after *Dobbs* she rushed to finish so she could premiere the film at Sundance Film Festival in Park City, Utah in January 2023. "Once *Roe* fell, there was an urgency to get the film done and get it out there," said Tragos. "The work of these intrepid activists must be known."[189] The film featured Francine Coeytaux as well as several telemedicine providers such as Dr. Julie Amaon of Just the Pill, Dr. Razel Ramen of Pills by Post, and midwife Christie Pitney of Forward Midwifery. The film also featured the work of Dr. Rebecca Gomperts of Aid Access. "We have so much more access to abortion pills today than we did in 2014," said Coeytaux at the premier. "We can truly say to anybody no matter what state you live in, you can get abortion pills mailed to you. It's still not over the counter. It's still not in pharmacies. It's still not $5. There's a lot of work to be done, but we're a hell of a lot closer. Many people now know there are pills for abortion and that they are safe and effective. We've made a huge amount of progress so far."[190]

In addition to Plan C advocates and clinicians, the film featured advocates from several other organizations supporting people using abortion pills, including Dr. Linda Prine of the Miscarriage and Abortion Hotline, and lawyer Farah Diaz-Tello of the Repro Legal Helpline. The film also included several interviews with people whose identities were protected, including two people who ordered pills in states with abortion bans and someone from a US-based harm reduction organization that mailed pills to people in states with bans. "The film did a brilliant job of telling the stories of people who need abortions and the efforts of activists and providers trying to meet that need," said Elisa Wells. "The film shows the harm that abortion restrictions are causing people and the possibility of a different solution that hasn't been well known in the past, which is telehealth and abortion pills."[191]

While the world was focused on the Supreme Court's dismantling of constitutional abortion rights, these activists had been working hard behind the scenes to prepare for a post-*Roe* future by empowering people to access abortion pills no matter where they lived or what they could pay. "The film tells stories of new models of care, and new and alternate routes of access," said Amy Merrill, Plan C co-founder and digital director. "We hope the film raises widespread awareness about this very real option and generates new hope, creativity, and momentum."[192] The film made clear the United States was increasingly divided between abortion haves and have-nots, where people in blue states had increasing options to obtain private, convenient, and affordable telehealth abortion, while people in red states faced increasing barriers and legal risks to obtaining this care. To address these disparities, a tight network of committed reproductive health advocates and a growing network of organizations were fighting to create access for people no matter where they lived. "What we want people to know with this film is that abortion pills are available in all fifty states by mail," said Elisa Wells. "We know that part of the narrative is that you can travel to a different state to get care, but you don't need to do that. You can get access to these safe and effective pills by mail in all fifty states. We now need to work on policy to ensure that there's no risk of criminalization."[193]

At its Sundance premiere, *Plan C* elicited three standing ovations from audience members, with people laughing and cheering but also squirming uncomfortably in their seats as they contemplated the struggles people were encountering trying to access abortion pills post-*Roe*. "We hope the film reminds people that they don't have to accept reality as it is now," said Merrill. "Together we can stand up to bullying, use the digital tools in our pockets to spread information, and build new systems that center the individual, their decisions, and their rights."[194]

Abortion pills were becoming an increasingly accessible, safe, and effective alternative to clinic-based care, which was becoming inaccessible because of abortion bans. In response, the anti-abortion movement increasingly focused on trying to restrict access to abortion pills.

CHAPTER 6

"Putting the Genie Back in the Bottle": Post-*Dobbs* Attempts to Block Mifepristone

By April of 2023, thirteen states had banned most abortions. Georgia and Florida banned abortions at six weeks of pregnancy. Another eight states had bans blocked by courts.[1] A study released in April of 2023 revealed that in the first six months after the *Dobbs* decision in June 2022, there were about thirty-two thousand fewer recorded clinical abortions than expected in the United States, an average of about five thousand fewer legal abortions each month than in the months before the ruling—a drop of about 6 percent. In April and May, there were an average of about eighty-two thousand abortions each month. From July through December, that fell to an average of seventy-seven thousand clinical abortions per month. In the thirteen states with bans, clinic-based abortions fell more than 95 percent, while the average number of clinical abortions in other states increased slightly on average. But abortions surged in some states, such as Minnesota and Kansas, to which people traveled to have legal abortions. The study did not measure the number of self-managed abortions, so the actual number was likely much higher than the reported number.[2] In this increasingly fraught political landscape, where fewer women had access and women without access were seeking to self-manage abortions, pills became the frontline of the battle for abortion access.

In April 2023, the conservative Heritage Foundation published the ninth edition of its strategy blueprint, *Mandate for Leadership: The Conservative Promise*, where they laid out their strategy on abortion pills, including to reverse FDA approval of mifepristone, end the mailing of abortion pills by reviving the long-dormant 1873 Comstock anti-obscenity law, limit use of abortion pills to seven weeks gestation, block telemedicine abortion, pressure the FDA to conduct inspections of Danco and GenBioPro as well as facilities manufacturing pills, and impose burdensome reporting requirements on clinicians prescribing mifepristone.[3] Anti-abortion groups hoped to take advantage of the many federal judges appointed by the Trump administration, from the Supreme Court down to district trial courts. These judges emboldened organizations such as the conservative legal group Alliance Defending Freedom (ADF), which worked to make abortion illegal nationwide and to roll back health care advances like medication abortion. Anti-abortion groups, including an expansive network of "crisis pregnancy centers" (CPCs), attempted to interfere with access to medication abortion by spreading disinformation about abortion pills. Finally, anti-abortion prosecutors charged women for obtaining and using abortion pills. This chapter chronicles these efforts, and how abortion rights advocates responded.

Across the country, anti-abortion states made clear their plan to criminally prosecute women using abortion pills and those helping them. In August 2022, shortly after the Supreme Court released the *Dobbs* decision, Nebraska prosecutors brought felony charges against a forty-one-year-old mother and her seventeen-year-old daughter for illegally performing an abortion after the mother bought abortion pills and her daughter used them to end a pregnancy. Nebraska law enforcement officials subpoenaed Facebook to turn over messages between the mother and daughter discussing abortion pills, and Facebook complied.[4]

Then in January 2023, the attorney general of Alabama, Steve Marshal, announced that women who used abortion pills were exempt from the state's feticide law, but could be prosecuted under other state laws. "The Human Life Protection Act targets abortion providers, exempting women 'upon whom an abortion is performed or attempted to be performed' from liability under the law," said Marshall, but "it does not provide an across-the-board exemption from all criminal laws, including the chemical-endangerment law." Alabama's chemical-endangerment law criminalized anyone who "knowingly, recklessly or intentionally causes or permits a child to be exposed to, to ingest or inhale, or to have contact with a controlled substance, chemical substance, or drug paraphernalia."[5]

These two stories raised concerns that anti-abortion prosecutors would escalate criminal prosecutions against people using abortion pills post-*Dobbs*. While only one state—Nevada—explicitly banned self-managed abortion after 24 weeks when the Supreme Court overturned *Roe*, legislators threatened to pass more bans, but no additional states did that in the two years after *Dobbs*. Members of the Texas Right to Life expressed frustration that the Texas legislature failed to enact new laws encouraging criminal prosecutions. "While leftist groups traffic abortion pills over our southern border or ship them to college dorm rooms, politicians failed to address this scourge," said Texas Right to Life in a May 29, 2023 email to supporters.[6] In May of 2024, Louisiana legislators introduced legislation to place mifepristone and misoprostol on the list of controlled substances in the state, but they exempted pregnant women who possess these medications for their own consumption and allowed people who have a "valid prescription" to obtain them from pharmacies. There were no exceptions for people supporting a pregnant woman.[7] Nevertheless, abortion advocates expressed concerns that prosecutors would increasingly bring criminal charges against people for self-managing their abortions, and would disproportionately target low-income women and women of color.[8]

Despite the legal risks of self-managing abortion, research showed that many women were willing to use abortion pills, especially those experiencing clinic access barriers. In a study of 19,830 patients attending forty-nine abortion clinics in twenty-nine states, one in eight considered self-managing before attending the clinic, and of these, one in three attempted to do so. Women without access to clinics and those who preferred at-home care were more likely to consider self-managed abortion.[9]

The criminalization of self-managed abortion was part of a wider anti-abortion campaign to stigmatize abortion pills and discourage people from using them. The campaign spread disinformation about the safety of abortion pills, advocated dangerous "abortion pill reversal" theories through CPCs pretending to be abortion clinics, and brought a legal challenge to the FDA's approval of mifepristone. By moving abortion out of brick-and-mortar clinics, abortion pills posed a deep threat to the anti-abortion movement's central strategy of physically interfering with access to abortion. Just as abortion pills were finally becoming more accessible after years of tight restrictions by the FDA, the anti-abortion movement poured tremendous resources into trying to block women's access to abortion pills.

ABORTION PILL DISINFORMATION

To interfere with abortion pills access, the anti-abortion movement developed a coordinated campaign to spread misleading and false information about the safety and efficacy of medication abortion. In February of 2022, the right-wing Family Research Council (FRC) published a report titled "The Next Abortion Battleground: Chemical Abortion".[10] Founded in 1983 as a division of James Dobson's religious right organization Focus on the Family, the FRC was one of the far right's most powerful advocacy groups, fighting against abortion, stem-cell research, and LGBTQ equality, and promoting "the Judeo-Christian worldview as the basis for a just, free and stable society."[11] The FRC's "chemical abortion" report used inflammatory and misleading language. For example, they used the phrase "chemical abortion" to make abortion pills sound dangerous. Throughout the report, they referred to embryos and fetuses as babies, and they described misoprostol as a drug that "'yanks' the baby out" of the womb. They referred to medication abortion as a "violent regimen." The report repeatedly referred to the "abortion industry"—an attempt to make doctors and other clinicians providing abortion health care sound nefarious and exploitative.

The FRC report inaccurately claimed that abortion pills posed "profound dangers" to women, citing the rarest and most severe drug reactions from the mifepristone medication guide, and framing them as common. FRC claimed that abortion caused depression and that medication abortion was "uniquely traumatic" to women, more so than aspiration abortion—a claim repeatedly disputed by major medical organizations, including the American Psychological Association.[12] FRC inaccurately claimed that mifepristone was "subject to the FDA's drug safety program—Risk Evaluation and Mitigation Strategy (REMS)—because it carries such life-threatening risks."[13]

At the end of their report, FRC called on the FDA to strengthen restrictions on the abortion pill, prohibit telemedicine abortion, and require doctors to conduct unnecessary physical examinations of patients receiving the abortion pill. These barriers would have significantly decreased access to medication abortion and increased the costs. FRC also called for the criminal prosecution of Rebecca Gomperts of Aid Access, cracking down on online pharmacies that sold abortion pills, and shutting down Gynuity Health Projects' TelAbortion study.

The FRC talking points proliferated across the anti-abortion movement, appearing in the materials of anti-abortion CPCs and legal pleadings challenging the FDA's 2000 approval of mifepristone. FRC's panicked rhetoric revealed abortion opponents' fear of the power and control that abortion pills could give to women. An affordable, widely accessible abortion pill that women could obtain through the mail and take in the privacy of their own homes would not only greatly increase access, but would also allow women to avoid anti-abortion protesters at clinics.

Taking a bizarre turn in November 2022, Students for Life circulated a petition claiming that abortion pills caused pollution and supporting legislation to require people using abortion pills to collect the products of their abortions and submit them to their medical providers for disposal.[14] Then in April of 2023, Students for Life submitted a citizen petition asking the FDA to prohibit access to mifepristone until the agency studied whether trace amounts of the pill in wastewater posed any risk to "endangered or threatened species or designated critical habitats."[15] They claimed the FDA approval of mifepristone violated the Endangered Species Act, and they threatened to sue the FDA if the agency did not respond within 180 days.

By 2023, anti-abortion groups were operating over 2,500 CPCs around the United States.[16] CPCs were designed to discourage pregnant women from having abortions by claiming to offer unbiased counseling about abortion. In fact, they spread scientifically inaccurate information and used scare tactics. They often attempted to appear like medical clinics, even though few were, and they used non-diagnostic ultrasounds to falsely signal medical legitimacy, while collecting people's personal and health information, with no privacy protections.[17]

A primary strategy used by CPCs to stigmatize abortion pills was to promote "abortion pill reversal"—the idea that giving pregnant women high doses of progesterone would counteract the effects of mifepristone and stop an abortion. ACOG described "abortion pill reversal" as "unproven and unethical" and "dangerous to women's health."[18] Clinical trials of the abortion pill reversal procedure ended after participants experienced dangerous hemorrhages requiring hospitalization.[19] "Claims regarding abortion 'reversal' treatment are not based on science and do not meet clinical standards," declared ACOG.[20]

In the fall of 2021, Reproaction and the Center for Countering Digital Hate raised an alarm about social media companies circulating anti-abortion groups' "abortion pill reversal" claims, while at the same time blocking factual information about abortion pills from reproductive health groups. The Center for Countering Digital Hate published a report titled "Endangering Women for Profit," which reported that Facebook and Google accepted between $115,400 and $140,667 for ninety-two ads promoting "abortion pill reversal" between January 2020 and May of 2021. Almost all of these ads—98 percent—promoted websites that claimed abortion reversal was "effective." These anti-abortion ads received up to 18.4 million views, including 709,870 impressions from minors between the ages of thirteen and seventeen. By targeting minors, these ads violated Facebook's policy against advertisements to minors that promoted unsafe services or that "exploit, mislead, or exert undue pressure on the age group targeted."[21] Co-founder of Reproaction Pamela Merritt described "abortion pill reversal" as part of the long history of white supremacist medical experimentation on Black and Latinx people. "The abortion pill reversal tactic is another attack on the profession of medicine. It's a continuation of the careless disregard for the health of people in marginalized communities. It's like experimentation. They know that it's not been vetted, but they're willing to experiment with people's health and their future fertility."[22]

CPCs promoted "abortion pill reversal" online and at their brick-and-mortar locations as well. To lure in unsuspecting people, CPCs mimicked reproductive health clinics, often intentionally locating these centers next to abortion clinics and using names like "Center for Pregnancy Choices" and "Your Options Medical." Despite appearances, these organizations—often run by white evangelicals—used medically inaccurate information and coercive tactics to obstruct women's access to abortion, contraception, and even prenatal care. A study of over six hundred CPC websites in nine states revealed that one-third of CPCs promoted "abortion pill reversal."[23] Almost two-thirds made patently false or biased medical claims, including that abortion caused breast cancer and infertility—which ACOG states is untrue.[24] Many told women that abortion causes depression, a claim debunked by the American Psychological Association. Many inflated miscarriage rates to encourage women to delay care until it was too late to use abortion pills or access abortion legally. Such delay tactics were dangerous, especially for women with ectopic pregnancies and those who planned to continue their pregnancies and needed prompt prenatal care.[25]

A range of advocates worked to expose these anti-abortion centers, including Reproaction's Expose Fake Clinics campaign and Abortion Access Front.[26] Concerned about the dangers of "abortion pill reversal," Colorado became the first state to pass a law restricting this practice. In April of 2023, the Colorado legislature passed a law subjecting healthcare practitioners who perform medication abortion reversal to discipline unless the state's medical licensing boards determined that treatment was a "generally accepted standard of practice." A Catholic medical center promptly challenged the law in federal court.[27] In October 2023, a federal judge entered a preliminary injunction against enforcement of the law as a violation of religious freedom.[28] Meanwhile, abortion opponents introduced "informed consent" laws requiring healthcare providers to notify people taking abortion pills about the option of "abortion pill reversal." As of 2021, fourteen states had these laws, although courts blocked them in several states.[29] These laws were mostly in the Midwest and South, but conservative legislators in progressive states introduced these laws as well.[30]

When the Supreme Court's reversal of *Roe v. Wade* allowed states to ban abortion, advocates expressed concerns that CPCs could share private information about pregnant women seeking abortion with law enforcement. CPCs appeared to be local, but many were part of large anti-abortion, anti-LGBTQ networks, such as Heartbeat International, Care Net, and the National Institute of Family and Life Advocates. Under the direction of these groups, CPCs used sophisticated digital strategies, including geofencing and menstrual apps, to intercept those seeking abortion, and online data platforms to collect client information. Privacy International documented how CPCs used centralized platforms such as eKYROS and Next Level Center Management Solutions to store and share client information. Heartbeat International boasted its software enabled CPCs to share client information with the broader anti-abortion movement.[31]

Many pregnant women provided their medical information to CPCs without understanding that these organizations were not subject to medical records privacy laws and could share their private information with the anti-abortion movement. A group of state-based women's rights advocacy organizations called The Alliance: State Advocates for Women's Equality and Gender Justice published a report in February 2022, "The CPC Industry as a Surveillance Tool of the Post-*Roe* State." According to the report, a "modernized, proliferating and mostly evangelical CPC industry" was collecting "massive amounts of client data including detailed sexual and reproductive histories through in-person 'counseling,' centralized chat platforms, and smartphone apps," stored in a proprietary anti-abortion movement "mega-database."[32] The Alliance warned that the proliferating web of CPCs was positioned to assist with state surveillance of pregnant women and enforcement of abortion bans post-*Roe*.

While there were over 2,500 CPCs in 2022, health clinics providing abortion had diminished precipitously, from 2,749 in 1978 to under 780 in early 2022. In some states, CPCs outnumbered abortion clinics eleven to one. CPCs' attempts to intercept women seeking reproductive health care delayed access until it was too late to use medication abortion or to access abortion care at all in the many states with bans on abortion after a certain number of weeks.[33]

New York-based privacy group Surveillance Technology Oversight Project (S.T.O.P.) released a report in May of 2022 titled "Pregnancy Panopticon: Abortion Surveillance After *Roe*," detailing the digital surveillance threats facing pregnant women who seek abortion information and services, and how these threats could escalate dramatically if the Supreme Court repealed abortion rights and states criminalized abortion. "Police, prosecutors and private anti-abortion litigants will weaponize existing American surveillance infrastructure to target pregnant people and use their health data against them in a court of law," concluded the report. "This isn't speculation—it's already happening."[34]

The report explained how anti-abortion governments and private entities were using cutting-edge digital technologies to surveil women's search history, location data, messages, online purchases, and social media activities by using geofencing,[35] keyword warrants, big data, and more. "Every aspect of pregnant people's digital lives will be put under the microscope, examined for any hints that they sought (successfully or otherwise) to end their pregnancy," stated the report.[36] The report predicted modern surveillance tools would help states to enforce criminal abortion bans on a scale that was technically impossible before *Roe*, posing an unprecedented threat to pregnant women and those helping them access care. Police could use digital keyword warrants to "cast digital dragnets" and identify people seeking abortion information online. They could also purchase data from commercial data brokers—which they could do without any court oversight—and leverage commercial databases that used big data and machine learning to predictively identify pregnant women. Using these technologies, police could track anyone who travels out of state for abortion health care and prosecute them upon their return.

"It will be truly dystopian when police can use modern surveillance to enforce these backwards abortion bans," said Albert Fox Cahn, co-author of the report and executive director of S.T.O.P., which litigated and advocated for privacy and fought excessive local and state-level surveillance. "The Supreme Court may be turning back the clock fifty years on civil rights, but anti-abortion policing will bring us an even darker future," Cahn continued.

> In 1973, police couldn't use the surveillance tools that have become commonplace today. Suddenly, every phone, laptop, and smart device will become a potential policing tool, with pregnant people's location data and search histories mined for evidence. Even when abortion bans stop at the state line, the surveillance will be national, giving anti-abortion police a way to track abortion care coast to coast. Even if the laws are the same as pre-*Roe*, the way they're enforced will be starkly different.[37]

S.T.O.P. was concerned that anti-abortion states would use geofencing to identify people accessing abortion care. Geofence warrants could enable police to force

Google and other companies to identify everyone who comes into a designated area—such as an abortion clinic—during a designated time. As of 2022, only one state—Massachusetts—banned geofencing near abortion clinics. Using these technologies, police could track women who travel out of state for abortion health care and prosecute them upon their return, said advocates. "As it stands, anti-abortion activists already surveil pregnant people to intimidate them out of exercising their legal reproductive rights. Police and prosecutors already surveil pregnant people digitally to pursue cases against them," said S.T.O.P.'s research director Eleni Manis. "We expect a massive escalation of surveillance targeting pregnant people, their reproductive healthcare providers, and anyone helping pregnant people access care, including care for miscarriages and ectopic pregnancies."[38] They also noted that electronic payment records and retail sales data were potent sources for abortion surveillance, and warned that police were already using mass extraction technology to download all data on a user's phone into a searchable file.

Whereas states operated under some limitations, such as probable cause requirements for warrants, private parties do not have to abide by such requirements and could pursue claims under civil bounty-hunter laws prohibiting abortion, with much less evidence than is needed to enforce criminal abortion bans. And while bounty-hunter laws in force in Texas, Idaho, and Oklahoma barred any enforcement action by state officials, private bounty hunters and anti-abortion states would be able to work in tandem to target pregnant women as well as anyone who helped them find abortion health care.

Some states were already tracking menstruation, pregnancy, and abortion. The Missouri state health department director, Dr. Randall Williams, testified at a 2019 state hearing that he kept a spreadsheet monitoring the menstrual periods of Planned Parenthood patients.[39] Oklahoma issued an annual "Abortion Surveillance" report with detailed information about abortions in the state.[40] In January 2022, Oklahoma state senator George Burns introduced Senate Bill 1167, the "Every Mother Matters Act," which would establish a government database of pregnant women looking to get abortions in Oklahoma.[41]

S.T.O.P. recommended that state and federal lawmakers consider steps to protect people's privacy, such as targeted bans on electronic surveillance and bans on private-sector data brokers from buying or selling information about reproductive health. In New York, lawmakers proposed legislation to ban geofence warrants, keyword warrants, and facial recognition technology, as well as ban police from purchasing geolocation data from commercial vendors. S.T.O.P. called on tech giants like Apple, Facebook, and Google to dramatically improve encryption and privacy protections, and to stop allowing mass police surveillance. S.T.O.P. also urged abortion providers and advocates to "harden their digital infrastructure" to ensure the privacy of people seeking their help online by implementing stronger privacy protections into their digital platforms, collecting only data that's absolutely necessary for their services, retaining it only as long as needed, and minimizing third-party sharing. S.T.O.P. recommended that abortion providers and advocates should immediately conduct privacy audits of all electronic communication, including use of third-party social media and messaging services.

To address these privacy concerns, members of Congress introduced the Stop Anti-Abortion Disinformation (SAD) Act on June 23, 2022 to crack down on CPCs. The bill directed the Federal Trade Commission (FTC) to prohibit deceptive or misleading advertising related to the provision of abortion services, and authorized the FTC to enforce these rules by penalizing organizations in violation with fines of up to $100,000 or half of the parent organizations' yearly revenues. The SAD Act required the FTC to make a biannual report to Congress on enforcement actions.[42] A group of senators introduced the My Body, My Data Act—a federal law protecting personal reproductive health data by minimizing the information that companies can collect and retain, for example through period tracking apps. The bill would prevent organizations from disclosing or misusing that information, and create a new national standard to protect reproductive health data, enforced by the FTC.[43] Congressional Republicans blocked both bills.

While Congress did not act, California lawmakers passed AB 1242 to enhance privacy protections. On September 27, 2022, the California governor signed the law barring telecommunications companies incorporated or headquartered in California from providing records of digital communications related to abortion to law enforcement officials seeking to use them in an investigation or prosecution for abortion that is legal under California law.[44] The bill aimed to prevent cases like the Nebraska prosecution of the mother and her seventeen-year-old daughter. "California's AB 1242 could be a huge step forward in protecting people's digital privacy as they navigate abortion access in this post-*Roe* world, especially as people increasingly turn to self-managed abortion," said Elisa Wells. "While self-managed abortion using pills is extremely safe and effective from a medical perspective, we know that people have been unjustly criminalized for managing their own abortions and that digital footprints have been used by prosecutors to build cases against people. Plan C welcomes this effort to strengthen digital privacy. Abortion is normal health care and no one should be investigated or criminalized for it."[45] The law authorized the California attorney general to sue California corporations to compel their compliance with the law, and imposed civil liability if the corporation knew or should have known that the warrant, subpoena, or other legal process was related to an investigation into an abortion or enforcement of a criminal abortion law. With many large tech companies based in California, including Google, Apple, and Meta, which owned Facebook and Instagram, advocates hoped the law would have a nationwide impact because it protected communications occurring between people located outside of California.

California lawmakers proposed another bill in February 2023 to protect people from unconstitutional searches of their data. The law proposed to block police and prosecutors in anti-abortion states from using "reverse warrants" to require technology companies to reveal the names of people who have searched online for abortion or traveled to a location offering abortion services.[46] Normal warrants seek information about a particular person, such as places they've been or the keywords they searched for online. A reverse warrant seeks the identities of all the people who present at a particular location or who searched for a particular keyword. These warrants can be used to conduct broad phishing expeditions for those who seek abortion. Reverse warrants, geofence warrants, or keyword warrants—known as "dragnet surveillance demands"—enabled local law enforcement in states across the country to compel tech companies to search their records and reveal the names and identities of all people whose digital data shows they've spent time at or near an abortion clinic or searched for abortion information online. "Between 2018 and 2020, Google alone received more than 5,700 reverse warrant demands from states that now have anti-abortion and anti-LGBTQ legislation on the books," said Hayley Tsukayama, senior legislative activist at the Electronic Frontier Foundation, which advocates for digital privacy. "As a worldwide leader in technology and innovation, California is uniquely positioned to divest from digital surveillance that would target people for having an abortion or seeking reproductive and gender-affirming care."[47]

The law's introduction came at a critical time, when Republicans in Arkansas and Oklahoma introduced bills allowing authorities to criminally prosecute women who have abortions.[48] "Carrying a smartphone, using social media and allowing apps to know our location has become a part of our daily routines," said Becca Cramer-Mowder, legislative advocate at ACLU California Action, which backed the bill. "But it means that each of us has a vast data trail that is vulnerable to government abuse. Anti-abortion police and prosecutors have used digital data to criminalize people for their abortion long before *Roe v. Wade* was overturned, and law enforcement in other states have already abused reverse warrants to identify people protesting police violence. We need to put a stop to this type of dragnet surveillance."[49]

ANTI-ABORTION CAMPAIGN TO REMOVE MIFEPRISTONE FROM THE MARKET

On November 18, 2022, anti-abortion advocates filed a federal lawsuit—*Alliance of Hippocratic Medicine v. FDA*—challenging the FDA's original approval of the medication mifepristone in 2000, as well as subsequent updates to the approval in 2016, 2019, and 2021. The conservative legal group ADF filed the lawsuit on behalf of four anti-abortion medical organizations, several doctors, and a dentist against the FDA and the HHS. ADF had represented Mississippi in the case that led the Supreme Court to overturn *Roe v. Wade* and they had a history of helping draft anti-abortion laws adopted in many states. In their 113-page complaint, the plaintiffs argued the

FDA unlawfully fast-tracked the approval of mifepristone in 2000 and did not have the required research to prove the safety of the drug under the labeled conditions of use. They argued that mifepristone was a dangerous drug that caused depression and many deaths.[50]

ADF chose to file the case in the Amarillo Division of the Northern District of Texas, where it was assigned to the forty-five-year-old Trump appointee Matthew J. Kacsmaryk. For five years before becoming a federal judge, Kacsmaryk was deputy general counsel for First Liberty Institute, a Christian conservative legal organization that specializes in representing religious groups claiming to have experienced discrimination.[51] In 2015, Kacsmaryk had written an op-ed for the *National Catholic Register* stating his opposition to same-sex marriage, no-fault divorce, birth control, abortion, and sex outside of marriage—and his support for "complementarianism," a religious belief that assigns primary headship roles to men and support roles to women based on the interpretation of certain biblical passages.[52] "He is an anti-LGBT activist and culture warrior who does not respect the equal dignity of all people," said Senator Dianne Feinstein (D-Calif.) during his Senate confirmation hearing, reading from a letter of the Leadership Conference on Civil and Human Rights. "His record reveals a hostility to LGBT equality and to women's health, and he would not be able to rule fairly and impartially in cases involving those issues."[53] Kacsmaryk was the only federal judge in the district where ADF filed the lawsuit, so he was guaranteed to hear the case, leading to charges of judge shopping. Texas was within the Fifth Circuit Court of Appeals, which had a majority of conservative judges—six of whom were appointed by Trump.[54]

The ADF lawsuit asked Kacsmaryk to declare the FDA's 2021 decision to allow healthcare workers to meet with patients by telehealth and mail abortion pills to them a violation of the 1873 Comstock Act. Promoted by anti-vice crusader Anthony Comstock and described as a "chastity" law, the Comstock Act banned sending obscene literature, contraceptives, abortifacients, or any sexual information through US mail. After the Supreme Court ruled in *Griswold v. Connecticut* in 1965 that people had a fundamental right to access and use contraception, Congress removed the language concerning contraception in 1971, but left the part of the law criminalizing mailing abortifacients and information about abortion. Before *Roe v. Wade*, federal courts had ruled this part of the law applied only to "unlawful" abortions. After the *Roe* decision, the Comstock law remained on the books but was not enforced. Since the Supreme Court had reversed *Roe*, ADF hoped to bring the law back into effect. Kirsten Moore described the lawsuit as trying to "put the genie back into the bottle" and "trying to undo progress."[55] Danco, the manufacturer of the brand-name mifepristone Mifeprex, filed a motion to intervene in the lawsuit, which Kacsmaryk granted, but GenBioPro did not join the lawsuit.

After *Dobbs*, in response to a request for clarification from the US Postal Service, the Department of Justice's Office of Legal Counsel issued a legal opinion in late December 2022, stating that the Comstock law does not prohibit mailing abortion pills if the sender does not know that the medications will be used illegally. The Department of Justice opinion, authored by Assistant Attorney General Christopher H. Schroeder, argued the law applied only to "unlawful" abortions, citing a long line of cases. Those sending or delivering pills "typically will lack complete knowledge of how the recipients intend to use them and whether that use is unlawful under relevant law." Abortion was allowed by federal law, Schroeder wrote, and every state allowed abortion in some circumstances, such as to preserve the life of a pregnant woman. Individuals receiving abortion pills had "a constitutional right to travel to another state that has not prohibited that activity and to ingest the drugs there," the opinion stated—so "someone sending a woman these drugs is unlikely to know where she will use them, which might be in a state in which such use is lawful." The opinion concluded, "therefore, even when a sender or deliverer of mifepristone or misoprostol, including USPS, knows that a package contains such drugs—or indeed that they will be used to facilitate an abortion—such knowledge alone is not a sufficient basis for concluding that [the law] has been violated."[56] The decision applied to the US Postal Service and other carriers, such as United Parcel Service and FedEx. While the opinion indicated that federal prosecutors would not use the Comstock law to bring criminal charges against anyone for mailing abortion pills, it did not protect people from charges by state prosecutors under state laws.

By February 2023, tension about an imminent ruling in the Texas case was at fever pitch. On February 16, Senator Ron Wyden (D-Ore.) called on the Biden administration and the FDA to defy any ruling restricting abortion pills. "President Biden and the FDA must ignore it," said Wyden in an impassioned speech on the floor of the Senate. "The FDA should go on just as it has for the last twenty-three years since it first approved mifepristone. The FDA needs to keep this medication on the market without interruption regardless of what the ruling says. Doctors and pharmacies should go about their jobs like nothing has changed."[57]

One reason for defiance, said Wyden, was that the judge was an anti-abortion zealot. Wyden described Kacsmaryk as a "lifelong right-wing activist. A partisan ideologue. An anti-abortion zealot who was hand-picked by Donald Trump and the Federalist Society to feign impartiality on the bench and deliver favorable rulings on the cases his fellow right-wing ideologues funnel his way."[58] Kacsmaryk had made several extreme rulings in other cases. In November 2022, he ruled that the Biden administration wrongly interpreted a provision of the Affordable Care Act as barring healthcare providers from discriminating against LGBTQ+ Americans. Then in December, he ruled that teens must have parental consent to obtain birth control, overturning a decades-long precedent allowing minors to access birth control.[59] "He has issued constitutionally dubious and extraordinarily contentious opinions, has defied precedent on protecting LGBTQ employees, and attacked the right to contraception by restricting minors' access to it," said Wyden, who called Kacsmaryk "the most lawless judge in the country."

Wyden suggested anti-abortion extremists had rigged the system to get an extremist, anti-abortion judge appointed to their abortion pill challenge. "Because of how judges in this federal district in Texas are assigned, the plaintiffs were able to use a procedural loophole and hotwire the judiciary. They could ensure Kacsmaryk was the only judge who could get the case," said Wyden. "This judge is not upholding the oath he took. He is not adhering to the Constitution. He is making a dangerous mockery of the rule of law. Something needs to be done about it," said Wyden.[60]

On the merits, Wyden argued the plaintiffs had no standing to bring the suit because they could not show any actual harm or injury to demonstrate a direct impact by the FDA approval of the drug. He also argued it was too late to challenge the FDA's approval of mifepristone in 2000 because the statute of limitations allowed challenges to FDA procedures for only six years. Finally, Wyden argued the FDA had not unlawfully fast-tracked the approval of mifepristone in 2000 and that they had the required research to prove the safety of the drug that year and in subsequent updates to the approval in 2016, 2019, and 2021, when the agency began allowing clinicians to mail abortion pills to their patients. Wyden cited a 2018 Government Accountability Office report concluding that the FDA had "followed its standard review process when it approved the application…for the drug Mifeprex" and "based its approval on reviews of peer-reviewed published studies, articles, and other information submitted by Mifeprex's sponsor."[61] He noted the FDA also conducted extensive reviews of mifepristone's safety in 2016.

Wyden argued the ADF complaint restated many of the objections anti-abortion groups had already raised to the FDA's 2021 modification of its mifepristone approval. In response, the FDA had published a forty-page rebuttal letter to these objections, which ADF failed to address in their complaint.[62] "Congress long ago empowered the FDA, a body made up of scientists and clinicians, to approve or disapprove the use of new drugs—not states and certainly not activist judges," said Wyden. "The FDA approved Mifepristone twenty-three years ago. For those looking to challenge that approval, well, it's too late. The statute of limitations allows challenges to FDA procedures for only six years."[63] In an impassioned conclusion, Wyden called for defiance of any Texas court ruling restricting mifepristone, noting that the judge had no way to enforce his ruling:

> The power of the judiciary begins and ends with its legitimacy in the eyes of the public. It does not have the military backing of the executive branch or Congress's power of the purse. A judge's rulings stand because elected leaders and citizens have agreed that abiding by them is right and necessary to uphold the rule of law. That's part of the social contract in America. But the judiciary must uphold its end of the social contract too. It must follow the rule of law and earn the confidence of the American people continually, every day, every month, every year. Recently that confidence has eroded, and it's no secret why. Look at the

Dobbs decision overturning *Roe*. Look at what is happening in Texas right now. Parts of the judiciary have morphed into a mob of MAGA ["Make America Great Again"] extremists, conspiring with and willing to do the bidding of every right-wing group or former President that appears before it, no matter the cost to life and liberty. There are moments in history where Americans and their leaders must look at circumstances like this one and say, "Enough." Not "let's see how the appeals process plays out," or "Let's hope Congress can fix this down the road." Just, "Enough."[64]

Other lawmakers, including Rep. Alexandria Ocasio-Cortez, joined Wyden's demand that the FDA ignore the Texas judge's opinion if he tried to remove abortion pills from the market.

Meanwhile, panicked newspaper headlines stated the Texas judge could and likely would end access to mifepristone. A *Washington Post* headline read, "The Texas judge who could take down the abortion pill."[65] *USA Today* feverishly warned, "A Texas judge could soon force a major abortion pill off market nationwide."[66] A *Denver Post* headline ominously declared, "One Texas judge will decide fate of abortion pills used by millions of American women."[67] Legal experts pushed back against these claims, arguing that the Texas judge did not in fact have the power to ban abortion pills nationwide. "Actually, one Texas judge is not the final decision-maker on medication abortion," wrote David Cohen of Drexel Kline School of Law, Greer Donley at University of Pittsburgh School of Law, and Rachel Rebouché of Temple Law School in an article in *Slate* magazine. "Despite the barrage of predictions that this case could ban mifepristone and take it off the market, there are several basic legal principles suggesting that Judge Kacsmaryk's power is limited and that a ruling for the plaintiffs will not necessarily change much at all with medication abortion," wrote Cohen, Donley, and Rebouché.[68]

The experts noted judges could bind only the parties before the court, in this case the FDA and Danco, not GenBioPro. They noted that the plaintiffs were asking only for the judge to declare that approval of mifepristone was unlawful and that there was no mechanism for him to ban a medication. "They can't ask him to take it off the market. That's not in his authority. He can't go into any warehouse and confiscate anything. The FDA can, but that's up to the FDA, just like it's up to a police officer to enforce laws against going fifty-five when I'm driving sixty," said Cohen, who noted that Congress had provided a specific procedure in the Food, Drug, and Cosmetic Act for withdrawing drug approvals. "He may order the FDA to follow the withdrawal process, but that withdrawal process leaves the final decision in the FDA's hands," said Cohen. "So if there's any wiggle room in the judge's order, they could interpret the ruling as a requirement to start this process. And then they start that process. That can be a lengthy process with them as the final decision maker."[69]

Cohen said that if the judge declared the drug was unlawfully approved, it would be an unapproved drug, but it would be up to the FDA to enforce that. Judges couldn't tell the agencies to enforce their laws. The FDA could decide whether they were going to go after the distributor of the unapproved drug, or not. "And if you look at their website, there were multiple documents that talked about unapproved drugs. The FDA had a risk assessment strategy in enforcing their laws. They don't have the capability or the resources to go after every unapproved drug that's out there, just like a police officer goes after someone who's recklessly driving sixty miles an hour, but not me if I'm safely driving sixty miles an hour," said Cohen. The FDA could use their enforcement discretion to not enforce the law against Danco based on the safety of mifepristone. He noted that doctors were not parties to the Texas case, would not be bound by any decision, and that most states allowed doctors to prescribe unapproved drugs as a matter of course. The FDA's authority is to go after the distributor, not doctors. "Unapproved drugs are a part of American medicine. It does raise risks for malpractice lawsuits if you are prescribing unapproved drugs. I'm not saying this is something that is without any legal risk, but it's not against FDA law for doctors to prescribe unapproved drugs. It would be up to their state law." Cohen emphasized that despite newspaper headlines, "this judge does not have the power to ban prescription of the drugs. He does not have the power to actually take it off the shelves."[70]

Meanwhile, advocates reminded the public that misoprostol alone was safe and effective for ending a pregnancy and would remain accessible no matter what happend in the lawsuit. For years studies from around the world had shown self-managed abortion with misoprostol alone to be 93 to 99 percent effective and very safe. Because of the widespread availability of mifepristone, the use of the misoprostol alone for abortion had not been studied in the United States.[71] On February 6, 2023, researchers at the University of Texas at Austin published peer-reviewed research on the use of misoprostol alone for abortion. The research found that misoprostol alone was over 88 percent effective, with few incidents of serious adverse events or signs of potential abortion complications.[72] "This is the first US-based study on misoprostol alone for self-managed abortion and it's coming at this critical time where we don't know what's going to happen with access to mifepristone," said the study's lead author, Dana M. Johnson, a PhD candidate in public policy and demography at the University of Texas at Austin and a senior associate research scientist at Ibis Reproductive Health. "Our contribution with this study is to add to the broad evidence base we have from the international space on how safe and effective misoprostol is."[73]

The research was based on data from Aid Access, which provided telemedicine abortion services with pills in all fifty states. Due to pandemic-related challenges shipping mifepristone, Aid Access prescribed misoprostol alone to over one thousand US-based patients in June of 2020. Aid Access physicians either mailed misoprostol directly to patients or sent prescriptions to local pharmacies for pick-up. "We took a very conservative approach by including just the people who had a totally confirmed, complete abortion at four weeks and didn't get a surgical intervention," said Johnson. "That is why our finding is 88 percent effectiveness, which is much lower than the SAFE Study from Ibis, which showed 98 percent effectiveness."[74]

Published in November of 2021, the SAFE Study—which stands for Studying Accompaniment Feasibility and Effectiveness—showed that 98.8 percent of those who used the misoprostol-alone regimen had a complete abortion without surgical intervention.[75] "Self-managed abortion with misoprostol only is highly effective, and warrants renewed attention," it concluded, calling it "no longer a second-tier method, but one that offers similar effectiveness, and often greater accessibility, than the mifepristone and misoprostol regimen."[76] This research showed that while misoprostol alone was a little less effective than the combination of mifepristone and misoprostol, extra doses of misoprostol could increase efficacy. "We did take this conservative approach, but our findings were really, really good. There were very few people who had a serious adverse event. There were very few people who had any kind of treatment for that or a symptom of a potential complication," added Johnson.[77]

Johnson conducted follow-up interviews with the research participants to understand their experiences of using misoprostol alone, which could be more difficult than the combination of mifepristone and misoprostol because the misoprostol-alone regimen calls for multiple doses of the medication, as opposed to one dose if combined with mifepristone. Those who used misoprostol alone could experience stronger cramping as well as nausea, fever, chills, vomiting, and diarrhea, which can be more severe when taking misoprostol alone because of the higher dosage.

Johnson found in her research that women's experiences of using misoprostol were shaped by their mindset and how prepared they felt. Many found information on Reddit. The abortion subreddit, R/abortion, was curated by OARS (Online Abortion Resource Squad), which trained volunteers to "ensure that every Reddit post asking for abortion-related help gets a quality, accurate, compassionate answer and referral to resources."[78] "People asked a lot of questions and that brought a sense of comfort because if you know that you can prep your hot water bottle or your ibuprofen or your chamomile tea, you're going into it with a little bit more of a mindset that you can manage this pain," said Johnson. Research from other countries had shown that patients can have positive abortion experiences with misoprostol alone when they had access to the information they needed, felt prepared for what they would experience, and were supported through the process.[79]

In response to attempts by abortion opponents to remove mifepristone from the US market, abortion advocates suggested providers could prescribe misoprostol off label to patients in states where abortion remained legal. Many telemedicine abortion providers pledged to do this, including Abortion on Demand, Aid Access, carafem, Choix, Forward Midwifery, Hey Jane, and Just the Pill. Planned Parenthood has also said they would offer this service.[80] NAF's clinical practice guidelines suggested offering misoprostol alone where the mifepristone combination was not accessible. The World

Health Organization also had guidelines for misoprostol alone as a safe and effective option for abortion care.[81] According to these guidelines, women in the first twelve weeks of pregnancy should dissolve four 200 milligrams of misoprostol between their gum and cheek, three times at three-hour intervals.[82] "With clinical options for abortion severely limited post-*Dobbs*, these guidelines are important in affirming self-managed abortion as a safe and essential practice that can be empowering for those seeking to end a pregnancy," concluded the University of Texas at Austin study authors. "There is potential for its use in the U.S. as a method of ensuring reproductive autonomy, especially for populations who have been systematically cut off from safe, affordable and non-coercive reproductive healthcare services."[83] Even in states with legal abortion, people were using misoprostol alone, which they could obtain over the counter at some pharmacies, said Dr. Carolyn Westhoff. "In our community here in Upper Manhattan, lots of people are buying misoprostol basically over the counter from pharmacies and self-administering. They may only come into the clinic if they're not sure whether it worked or not. There are a lot of pharmacies that will sell you whatever you want as long as it's not a scheduled drug, and as long as you're not trying to get insurance to pay for it," reported Westhoff.[84]

Despite the misoprostol-alone contingency plan, reproductive rights advocates fought to keep mifepristone on the market. On February 24, Democratic attorneys general from over a dozen states filed a federal lawsuit in Washington state, asking the court to declare that mifepristone was safe and effective and that the FDA's approval of mifepristone was lawful and valid. The attorneys general asked the court to block the FDA from taking any action to remove mifepristone from the market or reduce its availability, and to require the FDA to remove several current restrictions on the medication. The plaintiffs included attorneys general of Washington, Oregon, Arizona, Colorado, Connecticut, Delaware, Illinois, Michigan, Nevada, New Mexico, Rhode Island, and Vermont.[85] The attorneys general noted the FDA had placed mifepristone in the REMS drug safety program designed to regulate dangerous or addictive drugs, such as fentanyl and other opioids, certain risky cancer drugs, and high-dose sedatives used for patients with psychosis, and had imposed REMS on only sixty medications out of the more than twenty thousand prescription drugs approved for use in the United States. Subjecting mifepristone to the REMS program gave the impression mifepristone was a risky or dangerous drug when, in fact, it was very safe. "The federal government has known for years that mifepristone is safe and effective," said Washington state attorney general Bob Ferguson. "In the wake of the Supreme Court's radical decision overturning *Roe v. Wade*, the FDA is now exposing doctors, pharmacists, and patients to unnecessary risk. The FDA's excessive restrictions on this important drug have no basis in medical science."[86]

The attorneys general noted that the mifepristone REMS program required medical providers prescribing mifepristone to register with the drug manufacturer, required pharmacies to go through a certification process in order to dispense mifepristone, and required patients to sign an agreement attesting that they had chosen to take the medication to terminate a pregnancy, even when they were using the medication for miscarriage. "FDA's decision to continue these burdensome restrictions in January 2023 on a drug that has been on the market for more than two decades with only 'exceedingly rare' adverse events has no basis in science," stated the complaint. "It only serves to make mifepristone harder for doctors to prescribe, harder for pharmacies to fill, harder for patients to access, and more burdensome for the plaintiff states and their healthcare providers to dispense."[87] The plaintiffs argued that the FDA has exceeded its authority by continuing its "unnecessary and extremely burdensome" restrictions on mifepristone, exposing patients to needless anguish and confusion and violating the Fifth Amendment equal protection guarantees of the Constitution. "Through the 2023 REMS, FDA reduces access to a critical and time-sensitive healthcare service needed by pregnant people. And FDA treats providers, pharmacists, and patients who prescribe, dispense, or use mifepristone worse than providers, pharmacists, and patients who prescribe, dispense, or use nearly every other medication. FDA's actions are irrational and violate the Fifth Amendment under any standard of review."[88]

The states also argued that the REMS requirement that providers register with the drug manufacturer could compromise their privacy and safety, and result in them being targeted by anti-abortion violence, noting that abortion opponents made 182 death threats against abortion providers in 2021 alone. The certification requirement for providers and pharmacies might discourage them from offering mifepristone, especially in light of the increased criminalization of providing abortion services in many states. "The certification requirement for providers and pharmacists opens them up to potential liability if they serve patients from other states like Idaho that have restrictive abortion laws, even if the provider is in full compliance with Washington law," according to a press release from Ferguson's office. "In addition, healthcare providers who may move to other states in the future to practice might think twice about completing a certification to prescribe mifepristone, as it may expose them to liability or professional consequences in the future."[89]

Finally, the lawsuit objected to the FDA requirement that patients must fill out a patient agreement form, which must be included in their medical records, and for women from states banning abortion, could be viewed by providers in their home states. "While safeguards exist to protect the privacy of medical records, the patient agreement documentation required by the FDA creates an added risk for patients—particularly for those patients who travel to Washington for medical treatment from states where their abortion is illegal. The documentation of their abortion remains in their medical records, and can be viewed by providers in their home state," said Ferguson.[90]

Ferguson expressed concern about hackers compromising the confidentiality of these patient agreement forms. "Abortion providers have been targets for hackers seeking to steal information about both patients and providers. In 2021, for example, hackers accessed data of roughly 400,000 patients from Planned Parenthood Los Angeles. Providers in Washington report frequent cyberattacks aimed at illegally obtaining information about patients and providers. This is especially concerning because abortion providers and patients can be targeted for harassment and extremist violence."[91] According to the complaint by the attorneys general, "the REMS require burdensome documentation of the patient's use of mifepristone for the purpose of abortion, making telehealth less accessible and creating a paper trail that puts both patients and providers in danger of violence, harassment, and threats of liability amid the growing criminalization and outlawing of abortion in other states."[92] Experts saw the lawsuit as an attempt to produce a contrary ruling from the Texas judge so that the FDA could refuse to remove the medication from the market until the Supreme Court ruled, preserving access to the medication at least until that time.[93]

On Friday, April 7, 2023, federal judges in both Texas and Washington state issued contradictory rulings on mifepristone. Federal judge Matthew Kacsmaryk ruled that the FDA improperly approved mifepristone in 2000 and said he would void the approval, with a stay until April 14 to give the Justice Department an opportunity to appeal. He ruled the FDA had rushed the approval of mifepristone and that the FDA did not have adequate evidence of the drug's safety. He also ruled that the FDA's 2021 decision allowing clinicians to mail abortion pills violated the 1873 Comstock Act. Kacsmaryk cited studies purporting to show negative mental health effects of mifepristone. He cited a study based on several dozen anonymous blog posts from abortionchangesyou.com, a website run by the anti-abortion Institute of Reproductive Grief Care.[94] Kacsmaryk did not mention that bloggers on an anti-abortion website are a self-selected group that is far from a representative sample of women who have obtained abortions. Kacsmaryk also cited a disputed 2002 study by David C. Reardon, an anti-abortion activist associated with the Lozier Institute, claiming that women who had abortions were more likely to experience depression and commit suicide, attributing this to "self-destructive tendencies, depression, and other unhealthy behavior aggravated by the abortion experience."[95] Finally, Kacsmaryk cited a Finnish study he described as finding that the "overall incidence of adverse events is 'fourfold higher' in chemical abortions when compared to surgical abortions." One of the study's authors, gynecology professor Oskari Heikinheimo, later challenged how Kacsmaryk portrayed the study, stating the study showed serious complications from mifepristone were remarkably low and most of the "adverse events" were uterine bleeding.[96]

In his sixty-seven-page decision, Kacsmaryk referred to mifepristone as "chemical abortion" ninety-three times. He used inflammatory and medically inaccurate anti-abortion language, such as repeatedly calling fertilized eggs, zygotes, and embryos "unborn children," and saying the FDA "mandates…mifepristone to kill the unborn human." He called women who had never given birth "mothers" because they were pregnant and he called clinicians "abortionists."[97] He even cited the *Sesame Street* jingle "One of these things is not like the others" to support one of his arguments.[98] The Texas judge ruled the FDA had rushed the approval of mifepristone in 2000. In fact, anti-abortion political interference delayed FDA approval for twelve years. The FDA's review of the drug maker's application for approval of mifepristone took over three times longer than for other drugs: fifty-four months to approve mifepristone, compared to an average wait time of fifteen months for approval of other medications at the time.[99]

Less than one hour after the release of Kacsmaryk's ruling, a federal judge in the Eastern District of Washington, Thomas O. Rice, issued an injunction blocking the FDA from "altering the status quo and rights as it relates to the availability of mifepristone" in the plaintiff states and the District of Columbia.[100] As a result, the FDA was under contradictory federal court orders regarding its approval of mifepristone—with one court saying the FDA approval of mifepristone was invalid, and another saying it must maintain its approval of mifepristone. The Department of Justice immediately appealed Kacsmaryk's ruling and also filed a request for clarification with the Washington state court, describing the court's ruling as in "significant tension" with the Texas abortion ruling.[101]

Despite the Texas ruling, many telemedicine clinicians were determined to continue providing abortion pills, including mifepristone, to patients by mail. "Let me be clear: Mifepristone is extremely safe, effective, and still legally available through Hey Jane," said Kiki Freedman, co-founder and CEO of Hey Jane, a telemedicine abortion provider. "Our focus remains on our patients and delivering the best possible evidence-based, compassionate care and therefore we will continue providing our current medication abortion protocol of mifepristone and misoprostol."[102] In addition, experts said that Aid Access would likely continue to ship generic mifepristone from India to consumers in the United States. "There will still be ways to get the two-pill regimen," said Abigail Aiken at the University of Texas at Austin.[103]

Concerned about abortion pills access, Washington state Governor Jay Inslee bought thirty thousand doses of mifepristone—a three-year supply for that state.[104] Then Massachusetts Governor Maura Healey announced her state had bought fifteen thousand doses of mifepristone—a two-year supply—to "ride out" the legal challenge.[105] In April, Oregon Governor Tina Kotek directed the state to obtain 22,500 doses of mifepristone.[106] In addition, hundreds of pharmaceutical executives, including the CEO of Pfizer, signed a letter objecting to the Texas ruling, arguing it could destabilize the drug market in the United States. "In the face of laws and rulings that aim to undermine the evidence-based and legislatively sanctioned authority of federally mandated institutions such as FDA to protect public interests, and by putting an entire industry focused on medical innovation at risk, we cannot stay quiet," the letter read.[107]

On April 13, 2023, in a divided opinion, the US Court of Appeals for the Fifth Circuit ruled that the Texas plaintiffs had waited too long to challenge the original approval of mifepristone in 2000, but were timely in their challenges to modifications of the approval in 2016, 2019, 2021, and 2023. They ruled the FDA did not have adequate evidence to make these changes, including allowing use of the medication through ten weeks of pregnancy, lowering the recommended dosage to decrease side effects, allowing all qualified clinicians to administer mifepristone, decreasing the number of appointments required to prescribe the medication from three to one, allowing the medication to be prescribed by telemedicine and mail, approving a generic version of mifepristone produced by GenBioPro, and allowing certified pharmacies to dispense the medication. As a result, the ruling only allowed certified physicians to prescribe mifepristone at the higher dosage level for use up to seven weeks of pregnancy, and they could no longer send the medication through the mail nor could pharmacies dispense mifepristone.[108]

The Fifth Circuit decision was written by two Trump-appointed judges—Kurt Engelhardt and Andrew Oldham—and released just after midnight. A third judge—Catharina Haynes, appointed by George W. Bush—would have fully reversed the Texas court's decision. "The Fifth Circuit's latest ruling shows exactly why courts have no place interfering in health care," said Kirsten Moore of EMAA. "This middle-of-the-night ruling, while keeping mifepristone on the market, rolls back years of medical progress by reinstating restrictions that were lifted in 2016 and forcing people to go back to picking up their medications in person, essentially eliminating telehealth access and forcing people to travel, in some cases hundreds of miles, just to receive care."[109] The morning after the Fifth Circuit ruled, Danco filed an emergency appeal of the Fifth Circuit decision to the Supreme Court, arguing that the plaintiffs lacked standing, that the complaint lacked any viable merits claims, and that the 2023 FDA changes were not even before the Fifth Circuit. They also argued that fairness overwhelmingly favored a stay because Danco faced substantial, certain, unrecoverable harm, whereas the plaintiffs faced no irreparable harm from a stay, and that the public interest favored a stay.[110] The next day, the Department of Justice filed an emergency appeal to the Supreme Court. The appeals went to Samuel Alito, who was assigned to handle emergency matters from the New Orleans-based Fifth US Circuit Court of Appeals.[111]

On April 14, the Supreme Court placed a five-day stay on the Fifth Circuit ruling in the mifepristone case, giving the Court until April 19 to rule in the case. The same day, Judge Rice in Washington issued an order requiring the FDA to maintain full access to mifepristone in seventeen states plus Washington, DC, "irrespective" of the Fifth Circuit appeals court. Rice's order applied to the seventeen states that filed the lawsuit: Arizona, Colorado, Connecticut, Delaware, District of Columbia, Illinois, Michigan, Nevada, New Mexico, Oregon, Rhode Island, Vermont, Hawaii, Maine, Maryland, Minnesota, Pennsylvania, and Washington. Rice declined to apply his ruling nationwide.

As the Supreme Court weighed its options on mifepristone, abortion and women's rights supporters across the United States protested the latest efforts to restrict access to abortion. Protests took place in small and large cities, including Amarillo and Dallas, Texas; Chicago; Detroit; Los Angeles and Santa Barbara, California; New York City; Seattle; Sioux Falls, South Dakota; Tallahassee, Florida; and Washington, DC.[112] While 203 House Democrats filed an amicus brief to the Supreme Court urging them to ensure access to medication abortion was based on science not ideology,[113] House Republicans filed a brief urging the Court to uphold Judge Kacsmaryk's decision undermining the FDA and access to medication abortion.[114]

Then on April 18, GenBioPro—the pharmaceutical company that made a generic version of mifepristone—sued the FDA in Maryland federal court, where the agency was headquartered, seeking an order to compel the agency to allow GenBioPro to continue to sell the medication in the United States. GenBioPro estimated their generic medication comprised two-thirds of the mifepristone sold in the United States.[115] The company argued they had the right to preserve the drug's availability under the federal Food, Drug, and Cosmetic Act, the FDA's regulations, and the company's rights guaranteed by the Fifth Amendment of the Constitution. "In the United States, once a drug has been through the rigorous FDA review process and received approval, federal law protects the right to market the drug," said GenBioPro CEO Evan Massingill. "GenBioPro will use all regulatory and legal tools to protect access to mifepristone for patients and providers."[116]

The Supreme Court extended the stay two more days, then in a decision issued late on Friday, April 21, 2023, they blocked the Fifth Circuit ruling from taking effect, allowing mifepristone to remain on the market without any limitations while the case was on appeal, with Clarence Thomas and Samuel Alito dissenting.[117] Reproductive rights advocates expressed frustration that the issue was even before the Court. "While SCOTUS offered temporary relief, the fate of a medication approved by the FDA more than 20 years ago should have never been before the Supreme Court to begin with," said Kirsten Moore of the EMAA Project. "The FDA has the authority and scientific expertise to evaluate and approve medications—not politicians, not activists, and not judges. We must now move forward to ensure access to safe and effective medication abortion care nationwide without any further interference—our freedom to make our own healthcare decisions is on the line."[118] Elisa Wells emphasized the confusion caused by the case: "The longer this court case continues, the further we travel down a path of legitimizing the baseless claims of a small group of extremists as something worthy of the court's attention. A stay is the correct decision but does not erase the chaos, confusion, and fear that this case was designed to cause. And, even though mifepristone can remain on the market for now, access to abortion care is still severely and unjustly restricted in many states."[119]

At the time the courts were hearing this case, over one hundred scientific studies had proven mifepristone to be a safe method for ending a pregnancy. Mifepristone was safer than penicillin and Viagra, which were not subject to any REMS restrictions.[120] Between 2000 and June 2022, the FDA received reports linking mifepristone to twenty-eight deaths out of the 5.6 million people who had used the medication, and information gaps made it impossible to directly attribute the cause of these deaths to mifepristone. In some cases, the deaths involved overdoses and coexisting medical conditions.[121] ACOG, the American Medical Association, the Society for Maternal-Fetal Medicine, and other medical organizations stated in a brief filed in the case, "The risk of death is almost non-existent," citing an analysis by ACOG of hundreds of published studies finding that "serious side effects occur in less than one percent of patients, and major adverse events—significant infection, blood loss, or hospitalization—occur in less than 0.3 percent of patients."[122] According to the brief, "the scientific evidence supporting mifepristone's safety and efficacy is overwhelming. Mifepristone is one of the most studied medications prescribed in the United States and has a safety profile comparable to ibuprofen."[123] ACOG, the American Medical Association, and the American Academy of Family Physicians all issued statements opposing the FDA REMS restrictions and certification requirements for mifepristone because these restrictions had no basis in medicine and created barriers to time-sensitive abortion and miscarriage treatment.[124]

The Supreme Court sent the case back to the Fifth Circuit, where oral arguments were held on May 17, 2023. A lot was at stake in this case. If the Fifth Circuit's ruling had gone into effect, access to mifepristone would have decreased significantly across the country, even in states with legal abortion. Such a ruling would have ended telemedicine abortion with mifepristone, which had expanded significantly since the FDA finally allowed it in 2021, particularly for people living in rural areas who had to travel long distances to find certified doctors. They would have had to make multiple visits over several days to obtain abortion pills. And doctors would have only been able to prescribe mifepristone in the first seven weeks of pregnancy (forty-nine days)—which was just five weeks after conception, since pregnancy was dated from the first day of the last menstrual period. Finally, doctors would have had to prescribe a higher dosage, which would have caused more side effects. The panel of judges selected to hear the appeal included two anti-abortion Trump appointees, James Ho and Cory Wilson. In a 2019 decision, Ho wrote, "abortion is the immoral, tragic and violent taking of innocent human life." As a Mississippi state lawmaker, Wilson voted for a six-week abortion ban. The third judge was a George W. Bush nominee Jennifer Elrod. During the oral arguments, the judges were openly hostile to the two attorneys representing the FDA and Danco—Sarah Harrington and Jessica Ellsworth; and they were friendly to the attorney representing the plaintiffs—Erin Morrow Hawley, who was married to the conservative member of Congress Josh Hawley. Hawley and the three judges were also contributing members of the conservative legal organization The Federalist Society.

During oral arguments, the judges demonstrated their bias against the FDA and their basic misunderstanding of the science behind the case. One of the judges suggested that allowing licensed medical professionals who were not doctors to prescribe mifepristone increased the risk of complications, which is not the case. The judges indicated a belief that ultrasounds were necessary to determine how far along a pregnancy was, which was also not true. The judges repeatedly suggested that mifepristone was unsafe, despite extensive research showing the medication was safer than many over-the-counter medications, including Advil and Tylenol, and far safer than carrying a pregnancy to term. Confronted with this evidence, the judges refused to believe it. Similar to Kacsmaryk, the Fifth Circuit judges used polemical anti-abortion language like "chemical abortion." Elrod repeated an anti-abortion talking point that mifepristone "cuts off nutrition" to an embryo or fetus. The judges also exhibited basic misunderstandings about the role of the FDA. The judges seemed to believe that the FDA should dictate the details of how medical providers should practice medicine, such as how to diagnose how many weeks a patient is pregnant, which is not the role of the FDA. Elrod also suggested that because some patients in states with bans may use mail forwarding to obtain medications from telemedicine providers in other states, the FDA should restrict the use of the medication—a standard that could lead to the removal of almost any drug from the market. Harrington argued that the FDA's role was to determine whether a medication is safe and effective, not whether patients would use the medication in compliance with state law.

The judges did not listen to Harrington and Ellsworth, repeatedly asking them questions that had already been answered. For example, Harrington argued that the plaintiffs had no standing because they were protected by state and federal conscience clause laws from having to provide abortion services they found objectionable. Judge Ho appeared not to hear or listen to her argument, asking the same question again and again, despite her direct answers to his questions. The judges also made scolding comments to Harrington and Ellsworth. Elrod demanded an apology from Ellsworth for a comment in Danco's brief characterizing the district court opinion as an "unprecedented judicial assault on a careful regulatory process" of the FDA. At one point, Judge Ho asked Harrington if the federal government would abide by the court's decision. Sometimes the judges' comments verged on the absurd: one suggested that removing or restricting mifepristone from the market would not harm the drug maker Danco, which markets only that one product. At another point, when Judge Ho was trying to argue that the FDA did not have authority to approve mifepristone under a law authorizing an approval process for drugs to address a "disease, illness or condition," Ho bizarrely asked Harrington, "When we celebrated Mother's Day, were we celebrating illness?" The case got the attention of the pharmaceutical companies, which understood the threat the case posed to the stability and profitability of their industry. Over seven hundred pharmaceutical executives signed an open letter objecting to the Texas ruling, arguing it could destabilize the drug market in the United States. Pharmaceutical companies as well as the pharmaceutical trade association PhRMA also filed amicus curiae briefs in the case.[125]

On August 16, the Fifth Circuit Court of Appeals released a decision in *Alliance for Hippocratic Medicine v. FDA* that dismissed the challenge to the FDA's 2000 approval of mifepristone, but sharply restricted access to medication abortion nationwide and eliminated telemedicine abortion. In a ninety-six-page decision, the Fifth Circuit judges ruled that the plaintiffs had waited too long to challenge the original approval of mifepristone in 2000, but were timely in their challenges to later modifications of the approval in 2016 and 2021. The court ruled the FDA acted improperly in these later modifications in several regards, including allowing the use of mifepristone through ten weeks of pregnancy (from seven weeks approved in 2000), lowering the recommended dosage to decrease side effects, allowing any qualified clinician to administer mifepristone, decreasing the number of appointments required to prescribe the medication from three to one, allowing the medication to be prescribed by telemedicine and mail, and allowing certified pharmacies to dispense mifepristone. The court dismissed the plaintiff's challenge to a 2019 FDA decision to approve a generic version of mifepristone produced by GenBioPro.[126] The plaintiffs and the Department of Justice appealed the ruling, which remained on hold until final review by the US Supreme Court. The Supreme Court denied the plaintiffs' appeal, but agreed to hear the Department of Justice's appeal. Then, at the eleventh hour, the attorneys general of Missouri, Kansas, and Idaho filed a motion to intervene in the case, which Judge Kacsmaryk granted in January 2024, opening the door to ongoing litigation even if the Supreme Court dismissed the lawsuit.[127] During oral arguments on March 26, 2024, several justices expressed skepticism as to whether the plaintiffs had standing to sue.[128] A side effect of the mifepristone lawsuit was that it significantly increased media coverage about abortion pills. Despite the mifepristone misinformation at the heart of the lawsuit, a June 2023 report by NARAL Pro-Choice America found that accurate reporting on medication abortion care outperformed anti-abortion disinformation by 179 percent in the first five and a half months of 2023.[129]

In addition to the Texas case, abortion opponents tried to revive the Comstock law in other ways. In April 2023, the town of Edgewood, New Mexico, passed an ordinance designed to block the mailing of abortion pills and other abortion-related items to Edgewood, citing the Comstock Act. The ordinance allowed residents to sue other residents for violations. The ordinance violated a New Mexico law that expressly forbade local restrictions on abortion.[130] Another town, Eunice, sued the New Mexico Governor Michelle Lujan Grisham and Attorney General Raúl Torrez, arguing that a new state law prohibiting jurisdictions from restricting access to reproductive health care, including abortion, was preempted by the Comstock Act. The lawsuit asked the judge to declare that federal law outlawed all "shipment and receipt of abortion pills and abortion-related paraphernalia throughout the United States," regardless of whether a customer could legally use them where they reside. Local officials and anti-abortion advocates held a news conference in Washington, DC, to announce the filing of the lawsuit.[131] Republican members of Congress introduced a 2024 federal budget with riders revoking the FDA's decision to allow telemedicine abortion and pharmacy dispensing of mifepristone.[132]

In other states, anti-abortion legislators tried to suppress speech about abortion pills. A model bill drafted by the National Right to Life Committee would make it a crime to give "information to a pregnant woman or someone seeking the information on her behalf" about "self-administered abortions or the means to obtain an illegal abortion." In February of 2023, a group of anti-abortion Texas legislators introduced a bill to make it illegal to "provide information on how to obtain an abortion-inducing drug," including making or maintaining websites or creating and distributing apps on the topic. This bill required internet service providers like AT&T, Comcast, Charter, and others to "make every reasonable and technologically feasible effort to block Internet access to information or material intended to assist or facilitate efforts to obtain an elective abortion or an abortion-inducing drug." Because the law clearly violated free speech protections of the First Amendment of the Constitution, the legislators made the bill enforceable by private citizens, similar to Texas's 2021 S.B. 8 bounty-hunter abortion law. The bill encouraged people to notify internet service providers of abortion-related content and "request that the provider block access to the information or material" and granted them "absolute immunity" against lawsuits for agreeing to take down abortion-related information.[133] Other states succeeded in passing laws enhancing the power of the state to enforce abortion bans. In May of 2023, North Carolina adopted a law, over the governor's veto, that imposed a $5,000 fine against any individual or organizations that promote the sale of abortion pills by advertising, hosting, maintaining a website, or providing an internet service "purposefully directed to a pregnant woman who is an NC resident."[134]

Undaunted by legal threats, Mayday Health advertised in states banning abortion. When Mississippi banned abortion shortly after *Dobbs*, Mayday Health put up three billboards saying, "Pregnant? You still have a choice," with a link to their website, which had information about Aid Access and other ways to obtain abortion pills. The Mississippi attorney general subpoenaed Mayday Health and the group put up more billboards.[135] In March of 2023, Mayday drove mobile billboards around college campuses in fourteen states with abortion bans.[136] While these tactics garnered national headlines, they were done without consulting with grassroots activists in Mississippi, who resented Mayday's actions.[137]

Finally, following the Heritage Foundation playbook, an anti-abortion group Life Legal Defense Foundation filed a whistleblower lawsuit against Danco in January 2021 under the False Claims Act, which allows third parties to file challenges on behalf of the US government and claim between 15 and 30 percent of the fine if the action succeeds. On April 12, 2023, in a settlement with the Department of Justice, Danco agreed to pay $765,000 to the United States to resolve allegations that from 2011 to 2019 the company failed to properly label imports of mifepristone as originating in China and to pay customs duties on imports lacking those labels. Under the deal, Danco denied the allegations but stated they were settling the case to "avoid the delay, uncertainty, inconvenience, and expense of protracted litigation." Life Legal received $116,000 of the settlement.[138]

Despite all of these attempts to suppress access to abortion pills, these medications in fact fueled increased access to abortion post-*Dobbs*. In March of 2024, Guttmacher Institute reported that the number of abortions in the formal healthcare system in the United States in 2023 topped one million for the first time since 2012 and had increased 10 percent since 2020 (see Figure 6.1). They attributed this increase to broader availability of telehealth for medication abortion, increased financial support, and state policies improving protections and access to care in some states.[139]

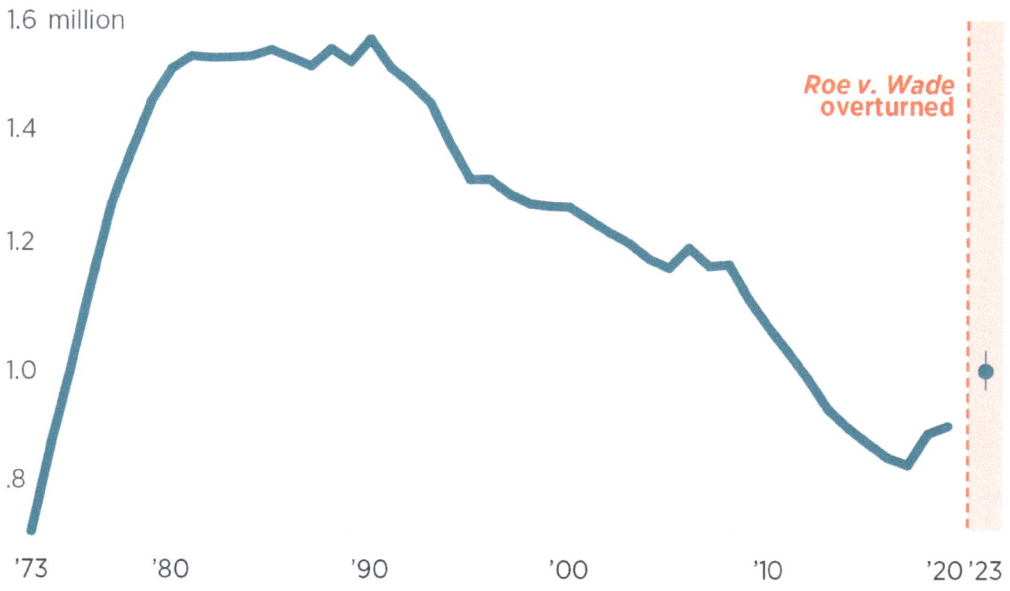

FIGURE 6.1: The estimated number of abortions in the formal healthcare system peaked in the early 1990s and then steadily declined until 2020, when it began to increase, rising sharply in 2023 (courtesy of Guttmacher).

Notes: 2023 estimate shown with accompanying 90% uncertainty interval. No comprehensive data available for 2021 and 2022.

Source: Guttmacher Montly Abortion Provision Study.

In March 2024, the Guttmacher Institute also released research showing that 63 percent of all abortions were done with medications—a fact that raised the stakes in the Supreme Court case.[140] Medication abortion increased from 31 percent of all abortions in 2014 to 63 percent of all abortions in 2023—more than doubling in just ten years (see Figure 6.2).

Another development heralded a continuing increase in use of abortion pills. In March of 2024, CVS and Walgreens announced they would begin dispensing abortion pills at brick-and-mortar pharmacies in some states, with a promise to expand soon to more states.[141]

Telehealth abortion was also increasing. In May of 2024, the Society for Family Planning reported that telehealth abortion accounted for 19 percent of all abortions in the formal healthcare system in December 2023 (see Figure 6.3).[142]

By the spring of 2024, telemedicine abortion providers Aid Access, Abuzz, and Cambridge Reproductive Health Consultants operating in shield states were serving over ten thousand people in states banning abortion each month.[143] Advocates created two new abortion funds to enable these providers to continue to offer a sliding scale fee structure to patients. These funds—Healthcare Across Borders' Abortion Sustainability Fund and Abortion Coalition for Telemedicine's Banned State Abortion Fund—focused only on funding telemedicine abortion serving people in states banning abortion. Most traditional

Medication abortions accounted for more than 60% of all abortions in the formal US health care system in 2023

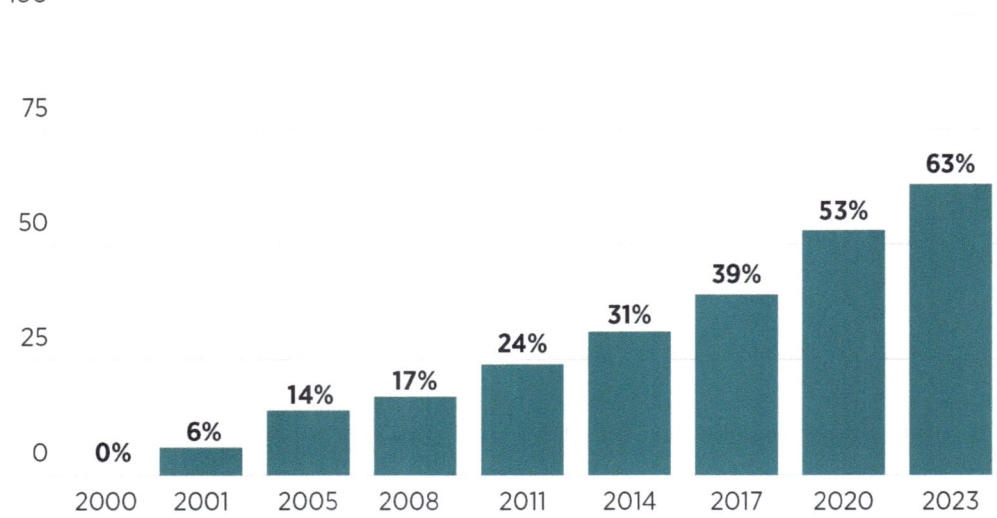

FIGURE 6.2: Use of medication abortion increased steadily over time, but accelerated after the FDA lifted medically unnecessary restrictions in 2016 and 2021 (courtesy of Guttmacher).

Source: Guttmacher Abortion Provider Census and Monthly Abortion Provision Study.

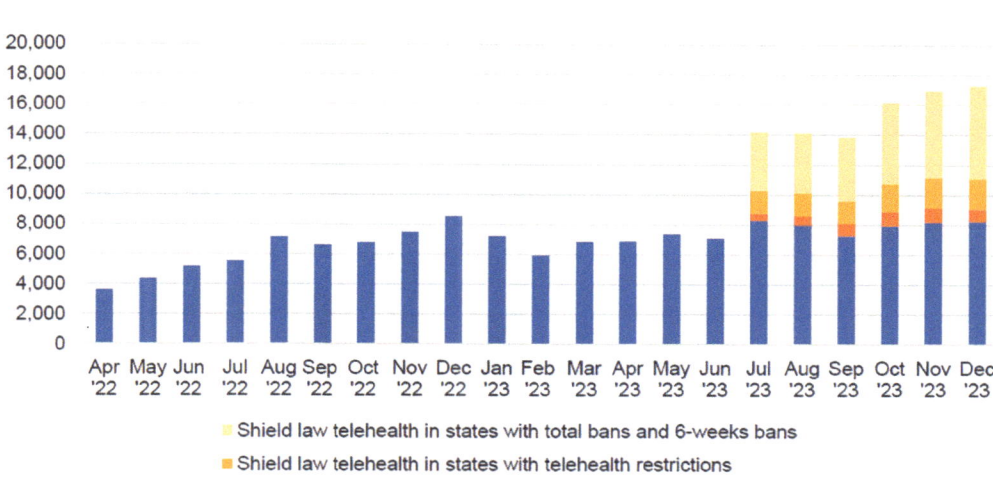

FIGURE 6.3: The dramatic rise in July 2023 is due to the fact that Aid Access shifted from serving patients from outside the country to serving patients from telehealth provider shield states within the United States, so the Society of Family Planning began including their counts (courtesy of Society of Family Planning).

abortion funds were wary of supporting telemedicine abortion in states with bans for fear that anti-abortion politicians might prosecute them under aiding and abetting laws.[144] In April of 2024, Maine passed legislation that included a shield provision for telehealth abortion providers, becoming the seventh state to do so.[145] The next month, Rhode Island adopted a similar law, becoming the eighth state to have a telemedicine abortion provider shield law. A fourth shield law provider opened in June of 2024, Armadillo Clinic, serving six states banning abortion, with providers operating under the California shield law. A fifth shield state provider, We Take Care of Us, began serving all 50 states in late summer 2024, operating as a provider cooperative with a social justice pricing structure.

Meanwhile, self-managed abortion outside of the formal medical system increased significantly. Researchers estimated that the total number of self-managed abortions that took place in the six months after *Dobbs*, from July 1 to December 31, 2022, increased by 26,055 abortions.[146] Most of those pills came from community networks (see Figure 6.4). On May 1, 2024, Red State Access affiliates reported they had served forty thousand clients in twenty-one states and four territories.[147] Plan C played a major part in increasing access to abortion pills. In 2023 alone, the Plan C website received 1.8 million visitors and 20 billion impressions from press and media articles and interviews.[148] Plan C put up billboards in April of 2024 in four states that banned abortion—Texas, Tennessee, Mississippi, and Oklahoma—saying, "Need to be un-pregnant? plancpills.org."[149] New services also developed to support people self-managing abortion, such as Aya

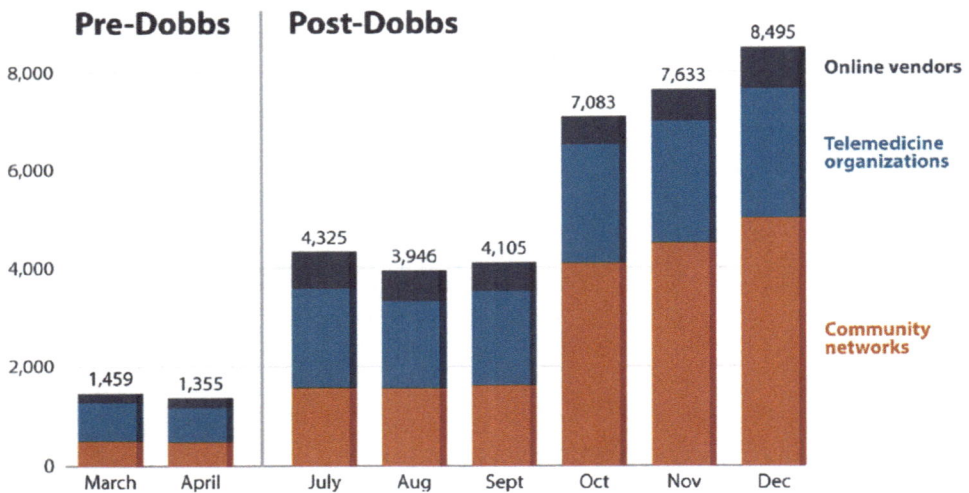

FIGURE 6.4: The first study to comprehensively track self-managed abortion outside of the formal healthcare system showed significant increases in the fall of 2022, especially from community networks in October 2022 when Red State Access began mailing pills (courtesy of Kristin Hopkins).

This figure shows the monthly number of abortion pill packs supplied before and in the 6 months immediately after the June 2022 *Dobbs v. Jackson Women's Organization* decision. Community networks, which are run by volunteers who also provide peer-to-peer support and information, accounted for over half of the total supply of abotion pill packs post-*Dobbs*.

Source: Abortions outside medical system increased sharply after Roe fell, study finds, *Washington Post*, March 25, 2024.

Contigo, which provided Spanish-speaking doulas to support Latinas in the United States.[150]

In June of 2024, the Supreme Court ruled in *FDA v. Alliance for Hippocratic Medicine*, dismissing the lawsuit for lack of standing. In response, anti-abortion advocates and politicians pledged to continue their efforts to remove abortion pills from the market. The Heritage Foundation, a right-wing think tank, released a detailed policy agenda calling for the next conservative president to order the FDA to remove mifepristone from the market and direct the Department of Justice to use the Comstock Act to criminalize mailing abortion medications. Despite anti-abortion efforts to suppress mifepristone, public support for medication abortion remained high. In a survey by Navigator Research, over two-thirds of Americans support "allowing women to legally use prescriptions abortion medication to end an early pregnancy at home."[151] Abortion pills dispensed from both inside and outside the formal medical system continued to play a critical role in maintaining access to safe abortion in the United States post-*Dobbs*.

Conclusion: "Putting Pills Directly in the Hands of Those Who Need Them"

> *Pills have legs. Pills go places. This pill can go places outside of the prescription setting.*
>
> *Cynthia Pearson, recalling a comment made at a meeting on self-managed abortion.*[1]

"Almost no pharmaceutical product has captured the public imagination with the force of mifepristone," said Beverly Winikoff and Carolyn Westhoff in 2015, on the fifteenth anniversary of the FDA's approval of mifepristone. They explained:

> Initially, predictions were both dire and ecstatic: women would run rampant, having more abortions than ever, boyfriends would slip mifepristone into their girlfriends' tea, abortion would become simple and easy, women would have access to abortion without any medical interface, and the politics of abortion would soften. Little of this set of predictions has become reality. On the other hand, medical abortion has now made a profound change in both the experience of abortion and the landscape of abortion provision.[2]

Winikoff and Westhoff predicted that medication abortion "seems poised to become even more important in the next decades."[3] They were right. In the following years, abortion pills became a critical political battleground, especially as the Supreme Court overturned constitutional abortion rights and many states banned healthcare professionals from providing abortion services.

In the face of strident opposition, reproductive rights advocates fought an intense, decades-long battle to establish and expand access to abortion pills in the United States. This movement included a diverse range of people—from medicine, public health, politics, business, and philanthropy. They used innovative strategies to make an important medication available in the United States. Abortion pill access has resulted from the efforts of medical researchers, healthcare providers, and reproductive rights advocates here in the United States and abroad. From the feminist campaign to bring mifepristone to the United States and win FDA approval for the medication in 2000, to the ongoing campaigns to remove medically unnecessary FDA restrictions on abortion pills and to make abortion pills available outside of the formal medical system, many people have fought long and hard to establish and increase access to medication abortion in the United States. Abortion rights supporters drew upon global resources and networks, including international research to support FDA approval of mifepristone in the United States and knowledge from women in Brazil who were using misoprostol to end an unwanted pregnancy. US advocates were inspired by seeing abortion pills available over the counter in Ethiopia, and they turned to organizations based abroad like Aid Access in Austria and Las Libres in Mexico to access pills when restrictive laws in the United States made abortion inaccessible.

Abortion pill policy was advanced by medical research conducted by nonprofits, private companies, and universities—often with private funding from foundations and anonymous donors. This research included the original clinical trials by the Population Council, the groundbreaking TelAbortion study by Gynuity, and studies conducted at ANSIRH, University of Washington Medicine, University of Texas at Austin, and other locations. These studies supported the original approval of mifepristone as well as treatment protocols, the loosening of the FDA REMS, and the rise of self-managed abortion. While the anti-abortion movement produced its own "research" claiming to show the dangers of mifepristone, the sheer volume of research showing the safety and effectiveness of the medication drove the policy agenda forward, kept the medical community informed, and reassured grassroots activists that they could safely share abortion pills with people needing them. Republicans blocked the US government from supporting RU 486 research, which was a serious barrier to developing the medication.[4] As a result, advocates had to seek support for research on mifepristone from private sources. Leading foundations supporting RU 486/mifepristone research and advocacy included the Susan Thompson Buffett Foundation, the David and Lucile Packard Foundation, and the William and Flora Hewlett Foundation, as well as Open Society Institute, the Prentice Foundation, and many anonymous contributors. These donors supported Danco, GenBioPro, the ACLU's Reproductive Freedom Project, Gynuity, and many groups advocating for medication abortion.[5]

On the other hand, the anti-abortion movement fought RU 486 every step of the way with threats of boycotts, lawsuits, and lobbying for legislation restricting abortion pills, as well as misinformation about abortion pills and even terrorist threats and violence. "The anti-abortion movement understood how critical it was to restrict access to this technology," said Coeytaux, "because it would be game over for them if it was in the hands of people without the gatekeepers of the doctors. They were able to scare the FDA."[6] The climate of fear and intimidation abortion opponents created likely influenced the cautious approach the FDA took in their approval of mifepristone in 2000, and ironically contributed to later claims that the FDA acted in violation of the law in *Alliance for Hippocratic Medicine v. FDA*. The anti-abortion movement produced and promoted flawed studies to support inaccurate medical claims that medication abortion was dangerous, so they could frame themselves as protectors of women as they were advocating for laws and policies that endangered women's health and lives. Abortion medications in early pregnancy weakened the anti-abortion movement's strategy of portraying abortion as "baby killing" as both NRLC's president John Willke and their education director Richard Glasow admitted in the 1980s.[7] So the movement pivoted to arguments that "chemical abortion" harmed women's health.

NARAL founder Lawrence Lader explained the intense opposition to abortion medications as motivated by fears about the loss of male power and control over women. Lader argued, "The loss of this power has stirred much of the anger now focused on abortion, but at a deeper level, that anger is aimed at the women's movement and the sexual revolution, which have tested and eroded male dominance."[8] In his 1991 book on RU 486, Lader said "the real agenda of the chastity bloc is not just an attack on abortion but a ban on birth control," noting how the head of the Pro-Life Action League, Joseph Scheidler, described contraception as "disgusting, people using each other for pleasure." In a July 2022 article in the *New Yorker*, Étienne-Émile Baulieu gave his view on why there has been such tremendous opposition to abortion pills from the anti-abortion movement: "A method that makes the termination of pregnancy less physically traumatic for women and less risky to their health has always been rejected by pro-lifers: what they really seek is to harm and punish women."[9]

As abortion opponents have gained political power in recent years, overturned *Roe*, and banned abortion in many states, access to abortion pills has nonetheless expanded in many places by the increasing proliferation of telehealth during the COVID pandemic and the growth of organizations facilitating access to abortion pills outside of the medical system. These contradictory trends have made abortion access geographically uneven across the nation. Many states are banning abortion, but in states maintaining legal abortion access, abortion pills and telemedicine abortion promise to increase access and affordability of abortion health care as well as convenience and privacy. The role that medication abortion plays in states with abortion bans is increasingly clear: it is providing a safe alternative outside of the formal medical system. Before *Roe*, abortion pills did not exist, nor did the internet and social media, where people can now learn about abortion pills and order them online from companies inside or outside the country. A robust network of organizations, healthcare providers, medical researchers, and abortion rights advocates now exists to ensure that people know where to find abortion pills, how to use them safely, and how to find legal help if they are targeted by anti-abortion prosecutors. However, unlike before *Roe*, the United States today has an extensive criminal justice system and increasingly sophisticated digital surveillance systems that may increase the likelihood of criminal prosecutions of those self-managing abortion.

The abortion pill battles in 2023 echoed battles going back over three decades, with advocates using similar legal and political strategies as well as social pressure to achieve their ends. Advocates for and against abortion framed these medications in diametrically opposed ways: as liberating or deadly. They tapped into political opportunities available to them, and they mobilized the resources they had to achieve their political goals. Abortion rights supporters sought to reframe abortion pills as safe and effective, and make them accessible, with support, both inside the medical system and outside of it. They produced research documenting the safety of abortion pills, and communicated their findings to journalists, policymakers, and courts. Abortion opponents, on the other hand, portrayed abortion pills as dangerous and traumatizing. They spread these messages through crisis pregnancy centers and in headlines on lawsuits they filed challenging FDA approval of abortion pills. Abortion opponents resurrected a nineteenth-century law in the twenty-first century. Early abortion restrictions in a time before penicillin were motivated in part by concern for women's health. They were poison control measures designed to restrict the proliferating market of questionable remedies in the 1850s to "restore menstruation."[10] By the mid-twentieth century, anti-abortion advocates focused on fetuses, using Lennart Nilsson's intrauterine hi-res photography released in the mid-1960s to detach the fetus from its environment and declare its full personhood.[11] Medication abortion in early pregnancy threatened this framing of abortion as involving "unborn babies" as people used abortion pills and saw the results. This perhaps motivated the abortion opponents' shift back toward arguments about "chemical abortion" as dangerous to women's health.

These movements took advantage of the political opportunities available to them at different periods of time. Republican presidential administrations clamped down on abortion pills, from George Bush's import alert in 1988, to the Trump administration's refusal to lift in-person distribution requirements on mifepristone during the COVID-19 pandemic and his repeated appeals of the Maryland court decision allowing telemedicine abortion during that time. Democratic administrations, on the other hand, increased access to abortion pills, from the initial approval of mifepristone under the administration of President Bill Clinton, to the FDA's 2016 expansion of access to mifepristone in 2016 under President Barack Obama, to the removal of the in-person distribution requirement in 2021 under President Joseph Biden.

Mifepristone and misoprostol have had a transformative impact on women's access to abortion, offering them the option of ending a pregnancy without the need for an invasive procedure and within the privacy of their own homes. Telemedicine abortion meant women did not have to walk through anti-abortion protesters to get abortion health care and they could more conveniently access this care without driving hundreds of miles. Abortion pills also offered women a safe and effective way to end an unwanted pregnancy outside of the formal medical system—especially important as states began to prohibit clinic-based abortion post-*Dobbs*. While some women might prefer procedural abortion or in-clinic medication abortion, telemedicine abortion and abortion pills outside of the medical system provided options for many women who would not otherwise be able to access abortion at all, especially in the restrictive post-*Dobbs* world.

FDA's reduced restrictions on mifepristone—including allowing pharmacies to dispense the medication—encouraged a wider range of providers to offer medication abortion, increasing access to abortion health care. Dr. Michele Gomez, a family care provider practicing in Burlingame, California, explained why she thought it was important for primary care providers to offer abortion services: "Abortion clinics have done heroic work, but there's no medical reason that abortion needs to be provided in a specialty practice. Early abortion services, both medication abortion and aspiration procedures, can be provided very safely in the privacy of patients' own doctors' offices." Dr. Gomez explained how primary care providers offering this care increases access and enhances patient privacy and safety:

> If more primary care providers offered early abortion services, there would also be increased access—no one should have to drive hours or days to get an abortion. It would also make it harder for abortion services to be targeted by those who want to control pregnant people— what are they going to do, stand outside of every single regular old doctor's office and assume someone might be going in for an abortion? They might just be going in for a check-up, or to follow up on their blood pressure, or for a twisted ankle—it would be impossible to know. It's easy to target Planned Parenthood, but much harder to target every primary care office in the country.[12]

Primary care physician Dr. Emily Godfrey agreed: "The more we isolate abortion as a standalone online service or in a standalone clinic, the more it can get attacked with all this legislation. The more we think about integrating abortion into primary care the same way we've integrated mental health into primary care, we can reduce stigma."[13]

The Reproductive Health Access Project and the MYA Network worked to encourage more primary healthcare providers to offer abortion services, including medication abortion, and to raise public awareness about this option. At the University of Chicago, the Department of Family Medicine formed the Excellence in Providing Access to New Directions in Mifepristone Use (ExPAND Mifepristone) as a learning collaborative to support evidence-based use of mifepristone for early pregnancy loss and/or abortion in primary care settings. Co-directed by Dr. Debra Stulberg, a family physician, and Elizabeth Janiak, ScD, a public health researcher, the learning collaborative provided expert guidance and technical assistance in the form of specialized resources and tools, hands-on training, in-clinic trainings, and individualized administrative coaching. Their goal was to create a network of primary care providers and clinical sites equipped with the resources and training needed to expand and protect access to mifepristone.[14]

In addition to primary care providers offering medication abortion, many medical providers began offering telemedicine abortion because it was more convenient, private, and affordable for their patients. Dr. Deborah Oyer, the medical director of Cedar River Clinics—a brick-and-mortar clinic in the greater Seattle area, explained: "For centuries, we have honored the provider's time, and we have not honored the patient's time. Telemedicine abortion allows patients to be more in control in every way. They're in control of their time. They're in control of how they get their medications." In contrast to the burdens of in-clinic abortion care, telemedicine abortion can happen quickly without the need for taking time off work, finding childcare, and driving long distances. Dr. Oyer also explained how telemedicine abortion enhances privacy: "Telemedicine is even more important with abortion than with other care. Abortion is still a shameful thing in our country, so the fewer people that have to be involved, the better."[15]

Most revolutionary was the proliferation of virtual abortion clinics—where healthcare providers offered fully remote care to patients, quickly and affordably. With low overhead and sophisticated digital platforms, these telehealth providers were able to see patients within a day or two, as opposed to the weeks it often took to get an appointment at a brick-and-mortar clinic. Some required videoconferencing, but many treated patients by phone, text, or online form. All of them offered medication abortion at a significantly reduced cost, sometimes at just a fraction of what the in-clinic care would cost. Telemedicine abortion providers were motivated by wanting to give their patients more options, easier access, and greater control over their experience. Dr. Julie Amaon of Just the Pill explained why she began offering telemedicine abortion:

> While I appreciate our brick-and-mortars and know they need to be there for people, I just felt like abortion care needed to be done a little bit different. We were always getting calls from patients at the clinic asking, "Do I really have to come in for this?" Or comments like, "I don't need counseling. Can I just pick up my pills?" These experiences stuck with us when we started Just the Pill. We asked ourselves, what would it mean to really center the patient and give them what they have been needing in the way that feels most comfortable for them? In the pandemic, it was very obvious that people wanted the security and privacy of doing this in their home. At brick-and-mortar clinics, even for medication abortions, you still have to be in the clinic for several hours because they have to do your counseling, and then they do your ultrasound and lab work, and then you have to wait in between procedures to see the physician. It doesn't have to be that way. We were just trying to think outside the box to make abortion more accessible.[16]

Similarly, Lauren Dubey, a nurse and co-founder of Choix, explained how the model of traditional health care prevented access and often didn't meet the needs of patients:

> Access to abortion health care in California is extremely high compared to other places in the country. And still, it doesn't seem like enough. There are rules and protocols that are rooted more in provider comfort or fear of liability than evidence-based medicine. One of my most heartbreaking things I ever had to do when I was working at Planned Parenthood was someone would come in and they'd be ten weeks and two days in their ultrasound and I would have to turn them away for medication abortion. And they would say, "Well, if I could have just gotten in here two weeks ago when I made the appointment, when I took the pregnancy test…" But my hands were tied. When you do this via telehealth, there's no waiting for an appointment for two weeks.[17]

As some of the first virtual abortion clinics in the country, Just the Pill and Choix courageously pioneered a new, patient-centered model of care that became critical post-*Dobbs*. Between April 2022 and March 2023, virtual-only abortion services increased by 85 percent compared to the pre-*Dobbs* period, from 5 percent of all abortions to 9 percent of all abortions.[18]

Ironically, the overturning of constitutional abortion rights in *Dobbs* and the subsequent state abortion bans played a significant role in expanding access to abortion pills by jumpstarting the movement for self-managed abortion. Abortion bans necessitated bypassing the healthcare system and its tight control over abortion pills, placing them directly into the hands of women needing them. Conflict existed not only between abortion pill supporters and opponents, but also among reproductive health advocates, who had starkly different visions and goals. They divided on how best to help maintain access to abortion after *Dobbs*. Mainstream reproductive healthcare providers and abortion funds, such as Planned Parenthood, National Abortion Federation, Whole Woman's Health, and the National Network of Abortion Funds, took the more conservative approach of strictly obeying abortion restrictions and working to transport people from states with bans to medical providers in states where abortion was still legal. As prime targets for lawsuits and other legal attacks, these large abortion-providing organizations pursued a legally cautious approach and fully complied with a restrictive interpretation of new state abortion bans, making it harder to get abortion medications. One Planned Parenthood affiliate in the Midwest, for example, required patients to take both pills over two days in a state that allows abortions, meaning patients from out of state had to extend their trip. "We needed to protect our staff and protect our organization," said Veronica Jones, the chief operation officer of NAF.[19] Abortion opponents banked on compliance with anti-abortion laws. "Licensed professionals are not in the business of violating the law. You have too much to lose," said Peter Breen, vice president and senior counsel for the Thomas More Society, which represented anti-abortion clients and advised legislators.[20]

Meanwhile, Plan C, Aid Access, many of the new telehealth abortion providers, and abortion pill networks like Las Libres, AccessMA, and WeSaveUs worked to get abortion pills to people where they lived, no matter the law. "There are benefits to taking calculated risks that break new ground, even if otherwise allied people disagree," said Linda Prine.[21] Some reproductive health advocates attacked Plan C, accusing them of placing providers and patients at legal risk. Advocates at Plan C responded that women should be able to make the choice between the legal risks of self-managing an abortion and the risks of being forced to carry an unwanted pregnancy to term. The reality was that half of women needing abortions lived in poverty, and 75 percent were low-income.[22] They often lived in rural areas, already had children, and worked low-wage jobs that didn't give them time off to travel many hours or days to find abortion health care in states where it was legal. Like Kelly from Texas, whose story was described in the introduction, many did not have that option. Because of their radical tactics, Plan C lost their original fiscal sponsor and the organization was eventually ejected from the GLC. Despite opposition from both sides of the political spectrum, Plan C continued to do the critical work of making abortion pills accessible outside of the formal medical system, including working to pass telemedicine provider shield laws that enabled providers in blue states to serve people in states banning abortion.

Mifepristone has remained highly restricted for decades because of a confluence of factors, including the anti-abortion movement, FDA action and inaction, the decisions of the medical and pharmaceutical industries, and entrenched ideas about who should control abortion. The anti-abortion movement created a political climate of misinformation and fear that made the FDA unnecessarily cautious in approving mifepristone, which the agency placed under unusual and discriminatory restrictions. The FDA then repeatedly refused to lift those restrictions, even as medical science conclusively proved the safety of mifepristone. Cynthia Pearson, who knew the head of the FDA committee that approved obstetric and gynecological drugs, Dr. Phillip Corfman,[23] explained what she thinks happened:

> I remember conversations with Dr. Corfman, where he said, we just need to make sure that the first couple of years run really smoothly. No deaths, no bad complications. If we keep it to the most experienced doctors for the first couple of years, and we get a good track record, then it'll go smoothly. That was such a narrow and wrong view because antis were never going to accept that mifepristone was okay because they are opposed to all kinds of abortion. They were always going to foment opposition and try to keep it narrowly contained. And it was really wrong as a bureaucratic tactic, because the FDA didn't loosen those restrictions. They were subpart H restrictions for the first few years but then the FDA invented the REMS program and they just got migrated into REMS and it's very difficult to undo REMS restrictions.[24]

According to Pearson, the FDA justified the restrictions not because the drug was dangerous but because pregnancy was dangerous. As a result, the FDA restrictions, along with the anti-abortion movement's misinformation and threats, created "cognitive dissonance" contributing to the impression that mifepristone itself was dangerous when it was not, and that the FDA had originally restricted the medication because of dangers rather than politics. Sarah Christopherson said these misunderstandings influenced everyone working on the issue. "Not only were the young repro activists working on mife not familiar with the history of the restrictions, the FDA career staff still in place in 2020 weren't either! Even if they supported removing the restrictions, they likely *truly believed* that the restrictions were originally imposed because they were medically necessary, and didn't know the sociopolitical context or the very real fear of violence that guided the FDA in 2000," said Christopherson.[25] Paired with ongoing misinformation and threats, policymakers, medical professionals, and even advocates for loosening restrictions on mifepristone were treating the REMS as if they were based on science when in fact they had always been political.

Christopherson also noted the FDA restrictions coincided with the George W. Bush administration taking office, so the restrictions remained in place. Turnover in the reproductive rights field then led to a loss of institutional knowledge and history, and people came to accept the restrictions. Some even supported them, said Christopherson:

> The restrictions were inconvenient, but we've now built up an infrastructure around managing them. By 2009, when the Obama administration takes over, there is a whole system set up and doctors like having that control of people coming in. And there is a slice of providers that are actually fairly conservative. They don't really trust women. There is an element of paternalism. There were some providers who liked the fact that women had to physically come in to see them and get permission. Some of the lead policy influencers for the movement had a fundamental conservatism about how much to push the envelope, because if you don't trust women, then you don't push for a system that gives them more power.[26]

On removing the in-person dispensing requirement, Christopherson said that some people in the movement feared how telemedicine abortion would impact brick-and-mortar clinics. She said in her advocacy, she had to be clear that the National Women's Health Network did not think mifepristone was a substitute for in-clinic care, but that it was a complement that would take pressure off of clinics in sanctuary states experiencing a mass influx of patients once *Roe* was overturned. "It was something that I felt like I needed to approach with a lot of sensitivity and diplomacy, because there was this sense of defensiveness, like 'It's not the solution. It's not the solution.' And I was always like, 'well, it's part of the broader solution.' "[27]

Barriers to abortion pills were also created by the medical profession, which established a protocol requiring unnecessary ultrasounds and blood tests that drove up the price of medication abortion. These tests discouraged most primary care doctors from offering medication abortion because they did not have access to expensive ultrasound equipment. The high cost was also justified by arguments that medication abortion should be priced the same as procedural abortion so as not to influence lower-income people's choice of service. But the result was that abortion pills were made unaffordable for many low-income and poor women. Some believed that Danco, Planned Parenthood, and NAF, representing independent clinics, did not push for full removal of the FDA restrictions on mifepristone because the REMS allowed them to maintain control over the medication. Others believed that only incremental change was possible. Some abortion providers even resisted alternative modes of care such as telemedicine abortion that are more accessible and convenient for patients, but threatened their business model. Finally, large pharmaceutical companies with the resources for clinical trials, the FDA approval process, and marketing refused to take on mifepristone, forcing it into the hands of a small, inadequately resourced company, which caused delays and may have contributed to the restrictions placed on the medication by the FDA. As a result, the medication ended up entirely in the hands of a small private company, Danco Laboratories, which was able to charge a high price for the medication and maintain a monopoly on mifepristone for fifteen years after its patent expired. Anti-abortion pressure and threats, a risk-averse FDA, and rigid medical and pharmaceutical systems kept mifepristone highly restricted and highly priced for decades after the FDA approved the medication. Paradoxically, *Dobbs* together with the COVID-19 pandemic finally freed mifepristone from the vise grip of the US medical and pharmaceutical industries, making the medication affordably available for the first time through telemedicine providers and community networks.

Even before *Dobbs*, the medical system excessively restricted abortion pills, spurring the creation of organizations to support people needing to access abortion pills outside of the formal medical system. These organizations exposed the medical gatekeeping as unnecessary and harmful. Women realized that abortion pills were safe and easy to use. They realized they could have private and convenient abortions, without having to travel hundreds of miles, cross lines of protestors, pay large sums of money, and put their feet up in stirrups. COVID and *Dobbs* pushed mifepristone out of the medical system in many states and put abortion pills in women's hands much more quickly than ever would have happened through the normal processes of change in FDA policy and medical protocols. People realized they could access abortion pills conveniently and affordably, and use them in the privacy of their own homes. For many people, this was liberating. But even for those who wanted to use pills with a medical professional's involvement, these changes opened up access as primary care providers realized they didn't need ultrasound machines to offer this care, and pharmacies like Honeybee and American Mail Order Pharmacy could send pills quickly and directly to patients. Abortion restrictions motivated people to develop organizations and networks like

SASS, Plan C, MYA Network, and Red State Access, which created pathways around legal bans and medical gatekeepers to re-envision how abortion pills could be accessed and used.

Other organizations like the M+A Hotline, Repro Legal Helpline, Aya Contigo, and the abortion subreddit OARS helped support people self-managing abortion. By July 2023, OARS was receiving four to five thousand views a day.[28] An attorney and OARS volunteer, Nina Henry, said the subreddit provided reassurance and support to people having abortions. "We get a lot of people who are worried that they're too upset, or that they're not upset enough, or that the way they're feeling is totally abnormal," said Henry. "One of the things that I often type is, 'This is normal.' The other thing I type the most is, 'There's no right way to feel about your abortion.'"[29] Henry said her experience working as a volunteer moderator for the abortion subreddit made her feel more hopeful about the future of abortion access: "The closer to working in abortion support that I get, the more optimistic that I feel about people taking care of each other, people sharing their experiences."[30]

While Plan C advocates achieved many of their goals, they had not as of 2024 achieved the kind of access they found at that pharmacy in Ethiopia. There was not an FDA-approved dedicated product: clinicians had to send two prescriptions to patients—one for mifepristone and one for misoprostol (see Figure C.1). The price was still much higher than the $6 or $7 they paid for the MTP (medical termination of pregnancy) kit in Ethiopia. However, Plan C's work was making abortion pills more affordable than ever in the United States. Websites selling pills lowered their prices, provided extra misoprostol, and offered faster shipping in order to be included at the top of the Plan C list of online websites offering abortion pills. "Initially, we said we would test companies that come in with pricing under $200 that have the ability to offer extra misoprostol and fast shipping. We still had so many requests that we said if you're under $140, we'll test you. So, sure enough, we're getting these requests from companies saying they can sell it for less. I'm in conversation right now with three different websites that are gonna come in probably around a hundred dollars and offer extra misoprostol and shipping time of a week or less."[31] By late May of 2023, Plan C had a company offering an MTP kit[32] plus ten extra misoprostol pills with three-day delivery for $100. By mid-July 2023, companies were offering abortion pills for as low as $37 with three-day delivery.[33] "These aren't just regular mail order businesses," said Wells. "These are businesses that are setting up to try and help get abortion pills out there. Some of them are profit driven. But a lot of them are also mission driven. They're taking risks when they're doing this."[34]

The legal future of abortion pills remains uncertain. Most progress on abortion pills has occurred during moments of transition, when Democrats were either gaining control or losing it—in 2000, when the FDA originally approved mifepristone as Clinton was leaving office; in 2016 when the FDA expanded access to mifepristone when Obama was leaving office; and in 2021 when the FDA allowed telemedicine

226 • Abortion Pills

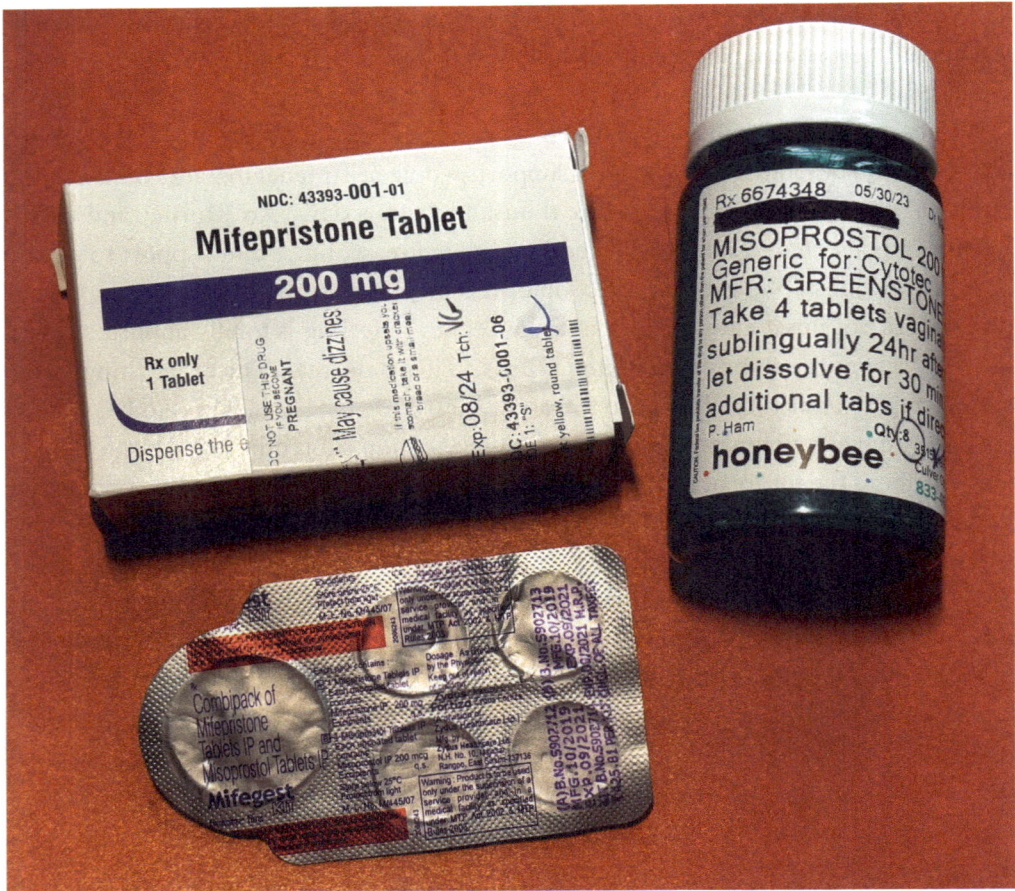

FIGURE C.1: In Europe, mifepristone and misoprostol are combined in one blister pack under the name Mifegest (below). In the United States, mifepristone and misoprostol are packaged separately (above) (photo credit: Carrie N. Baker).

abortion right after Biden became president. The next obvious step forward is removal of the FDA REMS. Danco and GenBioPro have not applied to the FDA for removal of the REMS. The FDA has already rejected advocates' citizen petition to remove the REMS. The lawsuit brought by state attorneys general of seventeen states and DC in a federal court in Washington state is a possible avenue forward, or a presidential executive order requesting the FDA to review the REMS, similar to Biden's executive order issued in May of 2021 for removal of the in-person distribution requirement. Another possibility is a federal lawsuit filed by abortion providers in Virginia, Montana, and Kansas on May 8, 2023, against the FDA, seeking an order to maintain and expand access to mifepristone. Represented by the Center for Reproductive Rights, the plaintiffs spoke from their experiences as abortion providers: "plaintiffs are continuously facing the weaponization of the REMS by anti-abortion activists around the country," they argued. "By making mifepristone seem uniquely dangerous, FDA's continuing restriction of mifepristone stigmatizes medication abortion and contributes to the chaos anti-abortion activists now sow."[35] The plaintiffs, who are independent abortion providers with limited resources in hostile states, argued the REMS restrictions endangered their practices and patients. "These restrictions perpetuate harm, stigma, and create unnecessary barriers to a medication that is safer than penicillin or Tylenol," said Nicole Smith, Executive Director of Blue Mountain Clinic. "It is time to end this ideologically driven government interference in the practice of medicine."[36]

The complaint explained in frank and striking detail why medication abortion access was so important. "Medication abortion allows people to forgo the physical contact and vaginal insertions of a procedural abortion, which may be particularly important for survivors of sexual violence and people experiencing gender dysphoria."[37] Telemedicine abortion could "eliminate the exposure risks inherent in in-person clinic visits, particularly in light of the persistent and escalating violence and harassment at clinics known to provide abortion."[38] The complaint described the harms caused by delayed access to abortion health care: "Each day a person remains pregnant means they continue to experience the symptoms, risks, and potential complications of pregnancy. Pregnancy—even when uncomplicated—stresses the body, causes physiological and anatomical changes, and affects every organ system. Pregnancy can also worsen underlying health conditions, many of which are common, such as diabetes and hypertension."[39] The complaint detailed the harms of forced childbirth, including significant risks resulting from systemic discrimination and inequitable access to health care:

> Every pregnancy-related complication is more common among people having live births than among those having abortions. Vaginal delivery can result in trauma to the pelvic floor and other significant injury. And, for the approximately one-third of pregnancies ending in a caesarean section (C-section), patients will undergo a major abdominal surgery that carries risks of infection, hemorrhage, and damage to internal organs. Pregnancy also has potentially long-term physical, emotional, and mental effects on a person who goes through childbirth, sometimes persisting well after birth.[40]

The complaint noted that the United States had one of the highest maternal mortality rates among wealthy democracies, especially for Black women, who are three to four times more likely to die of a pregnancy-related death in the United States than white women, and Indigenous women, who are 2.3 times more likely to die than white women. Forced pregnancy and childbearing also have long-term impacts on a person's educational and economic futures, and their ability to shape their lives. "People who are denied a wanted abortion are more likely to experience economic insecurity and raise their existing children in poverty," stated the complaint. "The financial impacts of being denied an abortion are as large as or larger than being evicted, losing health insurance, or being hospitalized."[41]

The plaintiffs argued that FDA restrictions on mifepristone also violated women's dignity and autonomy. "The ability to make decisions about whether to continue or end a pregnancy, and by what method, is critical to a person's dignity and autonomy. Continued enforcement of the REMS perpetuates harmful and unnecessary barriers that make it more difficult to access essential health care and interferes with this decision-making."[42] The complaint concluded, "From the very beginning, FDA has overregulated mifepristone in ways that are unjustified and discriminatory. But even as decades of data has accumulated showing mifepristone to be one of the safest medications available in the United States, FDA has continued to subject mifepristone to uniquely burdensome restrictions with increasingly little reason for doing so. These restrictions are already irrational, but in light of the recent chaos surrounding mifepristone, they have also become intolerable and incompatible with Plaintiffs' ability to meet the needs of their patients."[43]

The plaintiffs asked the court to order the FDA to remove the REMS restrictions or, alternatively, to enjoin the FDA from altering the current availability of mifepristone. "We are tired, and we are angry, and we will not compromise or sit idly by as anti-abortion opportunists continue to attempt to block the safest, most effective, and preferred method of medication abortion in this country," said Amy Hagstrom Miller, president and CEO of Whole Woman's Health and Whole Woman's Health Alliance. "Our patients deserve every single option that is available to them as they are making these choices for themselves and their families."[44] On August 21, 2023, a federal court in Virginia denied the Center for Reproductive Rights' preliminary injunction request.[45]

In addition to removal of the REMS, advocates are working toward approval of over-the-counter access to mifepristone, which is justified by medical science but is politically unlikely to happen any time soon. But researchers at ANSIRH are nevertheless pursuing studies to lay the groundwork for this eventual development.[46] Some advocates, like Kirsten Moore of the EMAA Project, continue to work within the system, fighting to improve FDA regulation of mifepristone. Others have become frustrated, and shifted toward working outside of the medical and legal systems. "The more we work with the FDA, the more I feel like we just empower them, embolden them," said Francine Coeytaux "It's just really, really difficult to watch and be a part of continuing to put fingers in holes of a broken system. Our medical system is entirely broken. Our health insurance system is entirely broken. Our human rights system is broken."[47]

Progress on abortion pills has at times been stymied by movement stakeholders with vested interests in the current system, who have resisted change that would have expanded access to abortion pills but endangered the status quo. In the film *Plan C*, an Alabama abortion provider was explicit about their concerns. "All of our first trimester procedures before ten weeks are $700. It's the same, surgical and medical," said Robin Marty, operations director of the West Alabama Women's Center in Tuscaloosa at the time. "It's expensive to run a clinic. Right now, most clinics are doing both procedures and medication abortion. We can operate because we have so much medication abortion and if you take that from us, if we were a state where you could just get medication through the mail and do it far more cheaply, then we would close."[48] Dr. Carolyn Westhoff explained: "Most of those freestanding clinics where all of later abortions take place have a business model where early abortions to some extent are subsidizing the later abortion care. So in these freestanding clinics if people go elsewhere for medication abortion, such as competing clinics that do nothing but medication abortion, it really ruins their business model."[49] In fact, high prices delay access, pushing people into later abortion care.

Similarly, telehealth providers were threatened by the development of even more affordable models of care. Coeytaux gave the example of how some telehealth providers were threatened by the passage of shield laws protecting telehealth providers serving people outside of their state. "They're all worried about how they're going to lose their market share when you can do anything anywhere," said Coeytaux.[50] Marlene Gerber Fried put it another way: "In these moments of horrible repression, the tendency is to protect whatever ground you have right now, however small."[51] She explained: "If you are pushing the radical edge, some advocates fear that you are endangering what exists; that you're endangering other more modest changes that are important, even though they are not the best thing that you can have. And that's what I think you're seeing in this moment. People feel like they have, even if only temporarily, a solution or a stop gap. And at each level, the people who think theirs is the right way are like, 'No, that's gonna shut it all down.'"[52]

Some abortion providers were not willing to take any risks to serve desperate patients from states with bans. After the Supreme Court handed down *Dobbs* in June 2022, the CEO of Planned Parenthood in Montana, Martha Fuller, announced that in order to avoid legal hazards, they would not provide medication abortions to out-of-state patients at all. "As a healthcare provider, we must identify and mitigate risks constantly," she said. "The risks around cross-state provision of services are currently less than clear, with the potential for both civil and criminal action for providing abortions in states with bans."[53] Despite these legal risks, two independent providers—Blue Mountain Clinic in Missoula and All Families Healthcare in Whitefish—offered medication abortion to out-of-state patients. Planned Parenthood eventually agreed to serve people from other states, but only if they were willing to travel all the way to their offices, whereas the independent clinics mailed abortion pills to the state's borders for patients coming from Idaho, Wyoming, and the Dakotas to save them having to travel hundreds of extra miles. Blue Mountain's executive director, Nicole Smith, said their independent clinic was willing to take on some risk to serve their patients who had few alternatives: "I'm not going to be afraid of some hypothetical. For us, we have been trying to find a balance—how do we take on more of the risk as providers versus putting that risk on the patients? There is this level of risk that either gets placed on the patient or on the provider. As much as possible, I think we're trying to take on that risk."[54]

Abortion pill access resulted from the brave, determined, and visionary action of many people across decades, who faced down opposition from the anti-abortion movement, from the medical and legal systems, and sometimes even from allies in the reproductive health movement. They faced an obstacle course of barriers navigating multiple institutions, systems, and stakeholders, including the FDA, federal and state government officials and courts, the medical, pharmaceutical, and insurance industries, some medical providers with vested interests in the status quo, the anti-abortion movement, and other activists with different priorities. As a result medication with many life and health saving potentials was held hostage for years.

The abortion pill movement had advocates who worked within the system taking an incremental approach, such as Marie Bass, Beverly Winikoff, and Kirsten Moore, and people with more radical, confrontational tactics, such as Eleanor Smeal, Lawrence Lader, Francine Coeytaux, Elisa Wells, and Susan Yanow. Groups like RHTP, Population Council, and EMAA Project were reformist, whereas FMF, ARM, and later Plan C used more radical and confrontational tactics that pushed forward abortion pills access at critical points. "People who are on the fringes move things along in their own way," said Winikoff. "I think Larry Lader was a gadfly and provocateur, but an interesting historical character that moved the process along."[55]

Larry Lader and Eleanor Smeal used high-profile publicity stunts. Lader staged the confiscation of a woman's mifepristone by customs agents at JFK airport, then held a press conference and filed a lawsuit. Smeal orchestrated the collection of hundreds of thousands of petitions and delivered them in boxes to the corporate headquarters of Roussel Uclaf in Paris and Hoechst AG in Frankfurt. Meanwhile, Marie Bass and Beverly Winikoff were working behind the scenes to educate and mobilize researchers, doctors, and policymakers about the science of mifepristone. Marie Bass and Joanne Howes formed RHTP to play the important role of bringing people together across multiple divides and creating an inclusive space for conversations among diverse constituents, including physicians, scientists, and activists. Winikoff brought a similarly diverse group of stakeholders to the table with the Coalition to Improve Access to Mifepristone in the United States. Coeytaux explained Winikoff's contribution:

> Beverly [Winikoff] has been at the heart of this whole thing. Her leadership and her work have been critical. Beverly is a visionary and understands better than anybody all the levers and what's needed for change. I believe that from the get-go she was as upset as I was at how the REMS was not evidence-based and we shouldn't put up with it, but she was trying to bring along the people who needed to be brought along—the NAFs, the Planned Parenthoods, and Danco. They needed to trust her. She had to get everybody to the meetings. So she had to

hold her cards close to her chest a lot more than I did. My role was to be open about the fact that the REMS was a mistake. If she had said that, would she have been able to get them to the meetings? She wouldn't have been able to play the role she did if they had sensed that she was judging this to be wrong in the first place.[56]

Bringing together a wide range of stakeholders was a critical step to getting the FDA to loosen its restrictions on mifepristone.

Lawyers also played a critical role by filing lawsuits, including the ACLU's lawsuit to remove the FDA's in-person distribution requirement during the pandemic, the lawsuit by state attorneys general demanding removal of the REMS altogether, and GenBioPro's lawsuit to preempt state restrictions on mifepristone. As self-managed abortion became a reality, groups such as Plan C, SASS, and Reproaction worked to educate people about abortion pills online and in person. "We took small, consistent, bold, unapologetic, direct action," said Pamela Merritt of Reproaction, who described self-managed abortion as an "essential liberating tool."[57]

Activists centering reproductive justice called attention to racial and economic considerations of abortion medications. In the 1980s, they raised concerns about potential dangers and coercive uses of new reproductive technologies. After FDA approval of mifepristone in 2000, they noted the disparate impact of the REMS on women of color. In 2020, the reproductive justice organization SisterSong became a plaintiff lawsuit that removed the in-person distribution requirement on mifepristone for the first time. As access to clinic-based abortion decreased and people increasingly accessed abortion pills outside of the medication system, however, reproductive justice advocates warned about the uneven legal risks of self-managed abortion for women of color and low-income women. This perspective was especially important considering the disproportionate rates of abortion among women of color and low-income women. Several organizations that advocated for abortion pills, including RHTP and the GLC, recognized the importance of race and insisted on creating racially diverse boards. Despite the potentially disproportionate legal risks, the development of alternative supply networks increased access to abortion pills for many low-income women and women of color, who had for years faced steep barriers to clinic-based medication abortion because of the Hyde Amendment. Indigenous women, for example, never had access to abortion medications through the Indian Health Services, and often had to drive hundreds of miles to the nearest abortion clinic offering this service. The overturn of *Roe* spurred the expansion of telemedicine abortion and alternative supply networks that increased access to abortion pills. In these and other ways, reproductive justice activists played a critical role in abortion pill politics.

On the other side of the issue, abortion opponents echoed the politics of the nineteenth century. Hostility to changing sexual norms led to passage of the Comstock Act in 1873, restricting the distribution of "obscene materials" in the US mail, including information about contraception and abortion. Today, anti-abortion advocates' hostility to contemporary sexual norms fuels attempts to revive the Comstock Act. In the early nineteenth century, the first laws restricting abortion were poison control measures designed to protect women from a proliferating array of businesses openly selling abortifacients, some of which were dangerous.[58] With the advent of fetal imaging in the 1960s, abortion opponents came to focus their arguments on the right to life of fetuses.[59] Contemporary abortion opponents, however, have returned to a focus on purported concerns about women's health, but now base these claims about the dangers of "chemical abortion" on pseudoscience. According to Loretta Ross, "the 1980s was when the anti-science wing of the anti-abortion movement got a foothold. They had not weighed in significantly on drug and device approval until RU 486."[60] These anti-science perspectives would later go mainstream on the right across a wide range of issues, especially after the rise to power of Donald Trump. Historian Carol Mason, who studies the influence of the anti-abortion movement on contemporary politics, asks, "Would people have snubbed their noses at Anthony Fauci if physicians hadn't for decades been depicted as quacks and bottom-feeders by anti-abortionists? Would we be seeing reports of medical workers sabotaging COVID-19 vaccinations if so-called 'conscience clauses' hadn't already been written into law? Such clauses allowed and encouraged pharmacists to refuse to fill prescriptions, and employers to refuse to grant health insurance for contraception."[61]

Economics also underpinned abortion politics in both eras. Nineteenth-century restrictions on abortion were pushed by men forming the field of medicine, who sought to "win professional power, control medical practice, and restrict their competitors, particularly homeopaths and midwives."[62] Today's medical system has sought to keep tight control over abortion medications, despite strong evidence that these medications are safe enough to be available over the counter. Historic and contemporary anti-abortion campaigns were both motivated by gender, racial, and class anxieties. Historian Leslie Reagan argues:

> The visible use of abortion by middle-class married women, in conjunction with other challenges to gender norms and changes in the social makeup of the nation, generated anxieties among American men of the same class. Birth rates among the Yankee classes had declined by midcentury while immigrants poured into the country. Anti-abortion activists pointed out that immigrant families, many of them Catholic, were larger and would soon out-populate native-born white Yankees and threaten their political power.[63]

Dr. Horatio R. Storer, who led the campaign against abortion, asked whether the country "shall be filled by our own children or by those of aliens? This is a question our women must answer; upon their loins depends the future destiny of the nation."[64] Reagan argues, "hostility to immigrants, Catholics, and people of color fueled this campaign to criminalize abortion. White male patriotism demanded that maternity be enforced among white Protestant women."[65] Similar hostilities have fueled the contemporary anti-abortion movement. With Catholics now firmly aligned with the white majority, contemporary abortion opponents direct their ire toward current-day immigrants, Jews, and people of color, as documented in the scholarship of Carol Mason, which reveals the deep ties between the anti-abortion and white supremacy movements.[66] "If we continue to abort our babies and import a replacement for them in the form of young violent men, we are supplanting our culture, our civilization," said Rep. Steve King (R-IA) in 2018, an eerie echo of Horatio Storer.[67]

In her book on the history of abortion and the law, legal scholar Mary Ziegler argues that advocates on both side of the abortion issue have increasingly disagreed about the basic facts of abortion.[68] This argument certainly applies to abortion pills. As abortion access dwindled over the first two decades of the twenty-first century, and abortion pills became an increasingly important avenue for American women to end their pregnancies both inside and outside of the formal medical system, the anti-abortion movement increasingly claimed "chemical abortions" were dangerous to pregnant women and advocated the made-up "abortion pill reversal" claim. Meanwhile, abortion supporters produced peer-reviewed medical research supporting the safety and efficacy of these medications, including by telemedicine and in self-managed contexts. Battles over science and facts fundamentally shaped public discussions of abortion pills in the United States from the 1980s to today.

In her book *Pregnancy and Power*, reproductive politics scholar Rickie Solinger explains how since 1970, "many public officials and others have used legislatures, courts, and media to define, advocate, and legislate a complex array of public powers over women's reproductive capacity."[69] She argues that rarely have debates about reproductive politics focused on women but rather focus on how to solve social problems facing the country. For example, governments have proposed scheme after scheme limiting Black women's reproduction to solve poverty, excessive welfare expenditures, teen pregnancy, unwed motherhood, and more. She notes women's reproductive capacity was often considered a national resource, such as providing soldiers or laborers, and women were pressed to reproduce or not in ways that were consistent with a particular version of the country's needs. But women have always resisted. She argues that women engaged in "reproductive misbehavior": "throughout history women have resisted systems of reproductive constraint…through everyday practice." High rates of illegal abortion shaped reproductive politics in the United States leading up to *Roe*, and made legalization an inevitability. She argues single motherhood, for example, has been an "everyday practice" resistive to patriarchal ideology requiring childbirth only in marriage and redefining legitimate motherhood. When women resist reproductive constraints, they violate traditional gender roles. "Today, policies denying individuals reproductive autonomy and health services spring from religious fervor and from old nativist, often racist, and class-based politics that roots its power in revitalizing the vulnerability (or powerlessness) of traditional targets."[70] Solinger wrote these words in 2005. Almost twenty years later, this statement is truer than ever. And women's resistance is as well. Self-managed abortion with pills is today's "everyday practice" of "reproductive misbehavior."

The anti-abortion movement has been successful in making abortion pills seem dangerous. Many people thought the FDA was protecting women by enforcing restrictions on access to mifepristone, but the agency in fact limited access to a safe medication that would have eliminated the need for women to have to travel long distances for abortion care and cross judgmental and often dangerous protestors outside of clinics. But the restrictions often served the interests of those to whom the FDA gave the right to control the medication: abortion providers and the drug manufacturer Danco. According to Coeytaux, Danco, Planned Parenthood, and NAF, providers were "happy that they were the only ones who had access to mifepristone."[71]

After the passage of S.B. 8, abortion providers in Texas refused to share information about ways to obtain abortion pills by mail with their patients, instead insisting upon physically transporting patients to their clinics out of state to obtain abortion pills. They feared they might be sued for "aiding and abetting" abortion in violation of S.B. 8 and held liable for huge sums of money. Lawyers advised abortion providers not to talk about Aid Access or other ways people might get abortion pills, said Coeytaux. "We've got a triumvirate of lawyers, doctors, and organizations who are going to follow the law no matter how unjust," said Coeytaux. "If you make clear that that's what you're going to do, they pass more and more egregious laws. That they probably wouldn't stand doesn't matter."[72] Plan C members shared information about Aid Access with people in Texas and urged others there to do so, but they received hostile reactions from abortion providers in Texas. When the *Atlantic* magazine published an article, "The Abortion Backup Plan No One is Talking About," quoting Coeytaux, a Texas abortion provider tweeted, "I don't need a Plan C. I'd rather dismantle white supremacy," instigating a flood of vicious tweets directed at Coeytaux.[73]

After *Dobbs*, many abortion providers continued to insist on transporting people hundreds of miles to far-away states to get abortion pills, sometimes pushing patients past twelve weeks so medication abortion was no longer an option, despite the easy availability of abortion pills through the mail and supportive services like the M+A Hotline. "It's been so difficult to get people to really embrace medication abortion," said Coeytaux. "There was never any evidence that mifepristone wasn't safe and effective, but it doesn't matter. They were just really, really worried about medication abortion, and not wanting to move it forward. There was a lot of fear, but the REMS are not evidence-based restrictions. It's still so political."[74] Coeytaux concluded, "It wasn't ever really about giving women power. It was about which doctors were going to be allowed to do what and defending the doctors."[75]

The anti-abortion movement created a climate of danger that fundamentally shaped the behavior of policymakers, medical providers, insurance companies, and even many activists, making them overly cautious and resistant to expanded access. They stayed within the bounds of the law, even if those laws were clearly unconstitutional like S.B. 8, and they conformed to the most conservative interpretation of laws out of fear they might be charged with violating them. Yale historian Timothy Snyder, a scholar of authoritarianism, explains, "most of the power of authoritarianism is freely given. In times like these, individuals think ahead about what a more repressive government will want, and then offer themselves without being asked. A citizen who adapts in this way is teaching power what it can do."[76]

The dream of early advocates has not been achieved. They envisioned a combined product of mifepristone and misoprostol, easily and affordably accessible on pharmacy shelves for a few dollars. Abortion pills are a long way from over the counter, or even behind the counter. They've only just arrived at pharmacies—or at least certified pharmacies in states without abortion bans. We do not yet have a combined product, as exists in many countries around the world. In the United States, clinicians still have to give patients two prescriptions—one for mifepristone and one for misoprostol. And while telemedicine is making the medications available for around $150, most medical providers still charge on average $550 for medication abortion services in clinic. We still have a long way to go.

No matter what happens in the future, abortion pills are fundamentally changing the abortion landscape in the United States post-*Roe*. Abortion pills offer a safe, affordable way to end a pregnancy outside of the formal medical system and beyond the law. COVID began the process of dislodging abortion pills from rigid medical systems that kept them highly restricted. The overturn of *Roe v. Wade* removed abortion pills from the medical system in many states and spurred the development of informal networks of pill distribution and support for using them. Rather than moving patients to providers, advocates worked to move pills to people. As a result, more and more people became aware of abortion pills and realized they were safe and easy to use. The future of abortion pills in the medical system is uncertain, but one thing is sure: abortion pills are not going away.

How is it that a medication that is so safe and effective for abortion and has many other potential uses could be so heavily restricted for so long? Politics, bureaucracy, vested interests, profits, white supremacy, and misogyny all played a role in keeping this medication so inaccessible for so long. Betrayals abounded, including the FDA's vise grip on mifepristone years after it had been shown to be safer than many over-the-counter medications, the profit motives behind the pharmaceutical industry's refusal to take on RU 486 in the 1980s, doctors' cautious practices that required unnecessary tests and burdensome procedures for patients to obtain the medication, and the fears of people within the reproductive health movement who slow-walked expanding access to mifepristone. After the FDA approved mifepristone, the failure to push for lifting all the restrictions placed on the medication or to push for increased access from a wider range of providers despite the restrictions was a betrayal of the women needing this medication for abortion and other medical conditions.

But the movement also had many successes, including the relentless work by FMF, RHTP, ARM, and the Population Council to get mifepristone to market in the United States, the determined campaign to lessen the FDA restrictions on mifepristone led by Gynuity Health Projects, ANSIRH, and the EMAA Project, the small number of bold, creative healthcare providers who pioneered telemedicine abortion, the organizations and community support networks that supported self-managed abortion, especially after *Dobbs*, and the smart, determined women, such as Kelly, who spoke out about the need for increased access to medication abortion. These people were able to de-medicalize abortion and put abortion pills directly in women's hands.[77]

Diana Lugo-Martinez, co-director of the reproductive justice organization Forward Together, argues that community care is part of a long and important tradition in the United States:

> People in the United States have lost connection to the traditional elements of community care. Folks had these traditions in their communities for a long time, in the Puritan communities to the enslaved communities. But with the privatization and professionalization of the health care, we've lost access to the possibilities of community care and community wellness and that's led us to a very dangerous place where our survival, our well-being, is tied to the State and the government in a way that is often fatal to so many of our community members. We are so dependent on the State and the government for everything, including access to health care. That makes it easier to tear away access from those who need it most. We have to have other systems of care, not just for abortion access, but also just in general. It's in the tradition of the Black Panthers and The Young Lords and the work that they did to establish community clinics.[78]

After *Dobbs*, as many states banned abortion and medical systems were no longer willing or able to help people access abortion health care, advocates created their own systems of community care. Despite anti-abortion threats, women's resilient spirit remained undaunted. "They thought they were going to break us, but they've done nothing but make us stronger," said Michelle Cohen of SHERo. "They made us develop new relationships, mentor and train the next generation of the movement. History has shown that women have helped women for eons with childbirth, with abortion, with family care. That's not going to stop now."[79]

At a time when many nations have decriminalized abortion, including Mexico, Argentina, Thailand, and Ireland, the United States is going in the opposite direction, but advocates are learning from women in those countries. In Ireland, the unenforceability of a longstanding abortion ban—the Eighth Amendment of the Irish Constitution— was a factor that contributed to the legalization of abortion in that country in 2018. "Pills had made restrictions obsolete and unenforceable, undermining the totality of the 8th Amendment legal regime," argued British scholar of abortion politics Sydney Calkin.[80] In the United States, abortion pills may in the future play a role in once again decriminalizing abortion. But in the meantime, they provide a critical avenue to abortion for tens of thousands of people, while simultaneously revolutionizing abortion in the United States by making it more accessible, affordable, and private than ever before. The new pathways to abortion pills spurred by COVID-19 and *Dobbs* finally freed mifepristone from the vise grip of medically unnecessary FDA restrictions on mifepristone as well as the overmedicalization of medication abortion that together have for decades made abortion medications hard to access and expensive. COVID-19, *Dobbs*, a bit of ingenuity and a lot of determination by reproductive health advocates ripped away decades of political red tape and finally placed abortion pills directly in the hands of the people who need them.

By August 2024, interstate telemedicine abortion and robust alternative supply networks for abortion pills meant that people living in states banning abortion had many more options than Kelly did in spring of 2022. Rather than having to use mail forwarding, they could order pills directly from five different telemedicine abortion clinics located in states where abortion was legal, and get abortion pills in just a few days. They could also get free pills from community networks or order them online for under $50. If they weren't sure what to do, Charley the Chatbot could walk them through their options. After they obtained their medications, they could call on the M+A Hotline or Aya Contigo for confidential advice from medical professionals or obtain emotional support from the Reprocare Healthline. If they had any legal questions, they could call the Repro Legal Helpline for free legal advice. Surprisingly, states did not criminalize self-managed abortion in the first two years after *Dobbs*, and no one using pills in early pregnancy had been arrested or prosecuted as of August of 2024. The future was uncertain, but advocates had made safe abortion much more widely available than before *Roe*—and in some respects even during *Roe*.

Appendix A: Abortion Pill Timeline

1980	Roussel Uclaf patents mifepristone.
1988	The French government approves use of mifepristone for abortion.
1994	Roussel Uclaf donates its US patent rights for mifepristone to the Population Council, which begins clinical trials.
1996	On July 19, 1996, the FDA Advisory Committee on Reproductive Health Drugs recommends the FDA approve mifepristone and misoprostol for abortions up to seven weeks gestation, but recommends close medical supervision of mifepristone administration. On September 18, 1996, the FDA issues an "approvable letter" for mifepristone for early abortion, but notes that additional information is needed on the manufacturing process and labeling before a final decision will be made.
1999	The FDA authorizes the Feminist Majority Foundation to administer the "compassionate use program" for use of mifepristone to treat meningioma and other cancers.
2000	The FDA approves mifepristone for abortion under the brand name Mifeprex made by Danco Laboratories. The FDA recommends a dosage of 600 milligrams of mifepristone and 400 micrograms of misoprostol for use during the first forty-nine days of pregnancy, but allows only certified physicians to dispense the medications directly to patients. The FDA does not allow pharmacies to dispense mifepristone.
2004	South Carolina authorities arrest a twenty-two-year-old undocumented migrant farm worker, Gabriella Flores, for taking misoprostol to end a sixteen-week pregnancy. Her sister in Mexico sent her the pills.
2005	The FDA issues a public health warning about mifepristone/misoprostol-induced abortion and its association with clostridium sordellii-related deaths.
2007	Authorities in Massachusetts arrest a teenaged immigrant woman, Amber Abreu, for using misoprostol she had obtained from her sister in the Dominican Republic. Abreu is indicted for procuring a miscarriage.
2010	Ohio passes a law requiring medical providers to follow the FDA dosing recommendations, despite research showing a lower dosage of mifepristone is safer and has fewer side effects.
2011	FDA places mifepristone in the Risk Evaluation and Mitigation Strategy (REMS) drug safety program, continuing the previous restrictions.
2012	FDA approves mifepristone for treatment of Cushing syndrome under the brand name Korlym made by Corcept Therapeutics. Korlym is not placed within a REMS, even though the dosage is much higher than the dosage approved to end a pregnancy.

2016	The FDA modifies the Mifeprex label, recommending 200 milligrams of mifepristone and 800 micrograms of misoprostol for use through ten weeks of gestation. The FDA modifies the REMS to allow any certified medical provider to prescribe mifepristone and approves the TelAbortion research project.
2019	The FDA approves a generic form of mifepristone, produced by GenBioPro.
2020	Because of COVID-19 concerns, a Maryland federal court partially enjoins the REMS, allowing providers to mail abortion pills to patients. The online pharmacy Honeybee Health begins dispensing mifepristone and is later joined by the American Mail Order Pharmacy.
2021	In January the Supreme Court reverses the Maryland injunction and reinstates the REMS. In April, the FDA removes the in-person dispensing requirement for the duration of the COVID-19 pandemic. In May, President Joseph Biden orders the FDA to review the REMS. In December the FDA modifies the REMS, permanently removing the in-person distribution requirement and allowing healthcare providers to mail abortion pills. The FDA also announces they will allow certified pharmacies to dispense mifepristone.
2022	On June 24, 2022, the Supreme Court rules in *Dobbs v. Jackson Women's Health Organization* that there is no constitutional right to abortion, overturning the forty-nine-year-old precedent of *Roe v. Wade*. In July, Massachusetts passes a provider shield law protecting telemedicine abortion providers serving patients located in any state. In November 2022, a community support network Red State Access forms with the mission of facilitating the provision of free abortion pills to people in states banning abortion. In the first nine months, Red State Access affiliates mail abortion pills to over fifteen thousand people.
2023	In January, the FDA announces the certification process for pharmacies. On April 7, a federal district court judge in Texas issues a nationwide stay on the FDA approval of mifepristone, ruling the agency improperly approved mifepristone in 2000. On April 13, the Fifth Circuit reverses in part, but orders the pre-2016 restrictions back in place. On April 21, the Supreme Court issues a stay until final resolution of the case. In 2023, five more states pass telemedicine abortion provider shield laws: Washington, Colorado, Vermont, New York, and California. In June, Aid Access begins providing telemedicine abortion services from shield states to patients in all fifty states. Abuzz Health forms with plans to eventually offer similar services in all fifty states, operating from shield states. In October 2023, Cambridge Reproductive Health Consultants forms The Massachusetts Medication Abortion Access Project (The MAP), offering telemedicine abortion to patients in all fifty states.
2024	In June 2024, the Supreme Court dismissed in *FDA v. Alliance for Hippocratic Medicine*. Two more states pass telemedicine abortion provider shield laws: Maine and Rhode Island. In June, Armadillo Clinic forms and begins offering telemedicine abortion to people living in six states with abortion bans, operating from shield states. In August, a fifth shield state provider, We Take Care of Us, begins serving people in all 50 states.

Appendix B: Glossary

Abortion pills: Medications that cause abortion, including mifepristone, misoprostol, and methotrexate.

Antiprogesterone (antiprogestin): A class of drug that prevents absorption of the hormone progesterone, blocking its biological effects. Also known as progesterone antagonists or progesterone blockers.

Emergency contraception: Methods of contraception that can prevent pregnancy after sexual intercourse. Brand names emergency contraceptives include Plan B (over the counter) and Ella (by prescription), which function by preventing fertilization of an ovum. Also known as "morning after pills," emergency contraception can be effective up to 120 hours (five days) after having unprotected sex. Emergency contraceptives do not affect established pregnancies.

Geofencing: A virtual boundary that triggers an ad on a mobile device when a user enters or exits that boundary.

Harm reduction: Strategies to lessen the negative consequences associated with criminalized behaviors, such as needle and syringe programs for drug users or condoms for sex workers.

Korlym: A form of mifepristone approved by the FDA for treatment of Cushing disease. Corcept Therapeutics distributes the medication in 300-milligram tablets.

Medication abortion or medical abortion: An abortion caused by medications. The "gold standard" for medication abortion in the United States is use of a combination of mifepristone and misoprostol, but misoprostol alone is also very effective.

Methotrexate: An FDA-approved cancer medication that is used off label in conjunction with misoprostol for treatment of ectopic pregnancies (a dangerous condition of a fertilized egg growing outside the uterus). Methotrexate stops fetal cells from growing by blocking the folic acid needed to maintain an early pregnancy.

Mifeprex: The brand-name mifepristone manufactured by Danco Laboratories.

Mifepristone: An antiprogesterone that blocks the hormone progesterone that sustains a pregnancy. The FDA has approved mifepristone for use in early abortion as well as for treatment of Cushing syndrome. The FDA also allows use of mifepristone for meningioma (non-cancerous tumors near the brain) in limited circumstances (under their "compassionate use" program). Research has shown mifepristone is effective for treating fibroids, endometriosis, breast cancer, and depression, and can be used as an emergency or monthly contraceptive.

Misoprostol: A synthetic prostaglandin approved by the FDA and developed by Searle for the treatment of ulcers in 1988. Used in conjunction with mifepristone, misoprostol causes uterine contractions to expel pregnancy tissue. Misoprostol is also used off label for miscarriage management and to assist labor during childbirth. Misoprostol alone is safe and effective to cause an abortion and is used widely around the world for that purpose.

Plan B: A brand-name emergency contraceptive.

Procedural abortion (surgical abortion): An abortion done by suction or manual removal of pregnancy tissue from the uterus.

Progesterone: A hormone that prepares the lining of the uterus (called the endometrium) for a fertilized egg to implant and grow. If an egg is fertilized, progesterone increases to support a pregnancy. If there is no fertilized egg present, the endometrium lining sheds as a menstrual period.

Prostaglandins: A hormone-like substance that affects several bodily functions, including inflammation, pain, and uterine contractions. Healthcare providers use synthetic forms of prostaglandins to treat several conditions. They also use medications to block the effects of prostaglandins. Prostaglandins used with mifepristone for abortion have included injections of sulprostone and a vaginal suppository of gemeprost in the 1980s, and now misoprostol, which can be taken orally, buccally (in the cheek pouch), or vaginally.

REMS: The Risk Evaluation and Management Strategy program that allows the FDA to restrict and closely monitor medications considered to have serious safety concerns in order to help ensure the benefits of the medication outweigh its risks.

Self-managed abortion: When a person obtains and uses abortion pills outside of the formal medical system. Researchers have identified a spectrum of self-managed abortion, from a person obtaining and using abortion pills wholly independently of the formal medical system, to partial self-management, such as taking medications at home instead of inside of a clinic, but still under the supervision of a medical professional.[1]

Telemedicine abortion: When a clinician screens a patient by videoconferences, telephone, or online form, then prescribes abortion pills to be mailed to the patient.

Appendix C: Interviews

The people interviewed for this book are listed below, identified by their affiliation at the time of their work on abortion pills.

Anonymous, GenBioPro
Anonymous, Red State Access
Phoebe Abramowitz, Reprocare
Billy Adam (Alias), Private Emma
Cindy Adam, Choix
Julie Amaon, Just the Pill
Abigail R.A. Aiken, University of Texas at Austin
Amy Allina, National Women's Health Project and Generative Learning Community
Sarah Baruch, Reproductive Health Technologies Project
Marie Bass, Reproductive Health Technologies Project
Antonia Biggs, ANSIRH
Maggie Carpenter, Aid Access, Abortion Coalition for Telemedicine Access
Alison Case, Whole Woman's Health
Sarah Christopherson, National Women's Health Network
Francine Coeytaux, Plan C
David Cohen, Drexel Kline School of Law
Michelle Colon, SHERo (Sisters Helping Every Woman Rise and Organize) Mississippi
Peggy Cooke, Reproaction
Leah Coplon, Maine Family Planning
Mitchell D. Creinin, University of California Davis Medical Center
Teresa DePiñeres, Period Pills
Farah Diaz-Tello, If/When/How: Lawyering for Reproductive Justice
Greer Donley, University of Pittsburgh School of Law
Lauren Dubey, Choix
Emme Edmunds, Researcher
Steven Eisinger, University of Rochester Medical Center
Catherine Euvrard, Roussel Uclaf
Kevin Fiscella, University of Rochester
Jessica Sarah Flaum, Filmmaker
Marlene Gerber Fried, Hampshire College

duVergne Gaines, Feminist Majority Foundation
Sylvia Ghazarian, Women's Reproductive Rights Assistance Fund
Roopan Gill, Vitala Global Foundation
Emily Godfrey, University of Washington Medical School
Michele Gomez, Family Care Associates and MYA Network
Rebecca Gomperts, Aid Access
Melissa Grant, carafem
Daniel Grossman, ANSIRH, University of California, San Francisco
Nina Henry, Online Abortion Resource Squad (OARS)
Lara Islinger, Visiting Student Researcher, University of California, Berkeley
Jennifer Jackman, Feminist Majority Foundation
Jodi Jacobson, Healthcare Across Borders
Dana Johnson, Ibis Reproductive Health
Dr. Beth Jordan, Medical Director, Compassionate Use Program, Feminist Majority Foundation
Julia Kaye, ACLU Reproductive Freedom Project
Julie F. Kay, Abortion Coalition for Telemedicine
Hanna Kim, Hey Jane
Diana Lugo-Martinez, National Latina Institute for Reproductive Justice and Forward Together
April Lockley, M+A Hotline
Abby Long, Director of Public Affairs and Marketing, Danco Laboratories
Morgan Love, Reprocare
Kara Mailman, Reproaction
Luz Alvarez Martinez, National Latina Health Organization
Erin Matson, Reproaction; Abortion On Our Own Terms
Jenifer McKenna, The Alliance: State Advocates for Women's Rights and Gender Equality
Amy Merrill, Plan C
Pamela Merritt, Reproaction; Medical Students for Choice
Ariella Messing, Online Abortion Resource Squad (OARS)
Kirsten Moore, EMAA (Expanding Medication Abortion Access) Project
Judith Norsigian, Our Bodies, Ourselves
Deborah Oyer, Cedar River Clinics
Lynn Paltrow, National Advocates for Pregnant Women
Cynthia Pearson, National Women's Health Network
Jamila Perritt, Physicians for Reproductive Health
Skye Perryman, Democracy Forward
Jamie Phifer, Abortion on Demand
Christie Pitney, Forward Midwifery
Linda Prine, Reproductive Health Access Project, Aid Access, Abortion Coalition for Telemedicine Access
Razel Ramen, Pills by Post
Rachel Rebouché, Temple University School of Law
Paula Rita Rivera, Telefem
Loretta Ross, SisterSong: Women of Color Reproductive Justice Collective
Tara Shochet, TelAbortion Project, Gynuity Health

Eleanor Smeal, Feminist Majority Foundation

Tracy Droz Tragos, Filmmaker

Robin Tucker, Metro Advanced Practice Healthcare

Ushma Upadhyay, ANSIRH

Steven Vladeck, University of Texas School of Law

Aisha Wagner, Choix

Rebecca Wang, If/When/How: Lawyering for Reproductive Justice

Tracy Weitz, Director for the Susan Thompson Buffett Foundation and co-founder and Director of the Advancing New Standards in Reproductive Health

Elisa Wells, Plan C

Carolyn Westhoff, Columbia University Irving Medical Center

Beverly Winikoff, Population Council and Gynuity Health Projects

Susan Yanow, SASS (Self-Managed Abortion, Safe and Supported)

Miriam Yeung, National Asian Pacific American Women's Forum

Acknowledgments

This book grew out of my public writing on abortion pills over the last six years, primarily for *Ms.* magazine. In that reporting, I came to know many of the people featured in this book—activists, researchers, medical providers, people seeking abortion pills, and more. I am grateful to all the people who shared their memories, their perspectives, and their personal records, especially Francine Coeytaux and Elisa Wells of Plan C. I am also grateful to Kathy Spillar, Roxy Szal, and Carmen Rios at *Ms.* magazine, who encouraged me to do this work.

Thanks to the many people who read drafts of the manuscript and provided me with feedback, including Marilyn Schuster, Elisa Wells, Francine Coeytaux, Laura Briggs, Lara Islinger, Susan Faludi, Andrea Zarafshon Moore, Emily Wojcik, Sarah Evans, Emmaline Kenney, Tallulah Costa, Lauren Thompsen, Anya Rozario, and two anonymous readers.

I'd especially like to thank Beth Bouloukos at Amherst College Press, who inspired me to write this book and encouraged me along the way. I am also grateful to Hannah Brooks-Motl at Amherst College Press for her helpful guidance.

My thanks and love to my family and friends who have supported me throughout the process of researching and writing this book.

The book is dedicated to the many abortion pill advocates who fought tirelessly for decades to increase access to these important medications.

Endnotes

Introduction

1   Kelly, interview by Carrie N. Baker, March 26, 2022 (full name and identifying details are withheld for safety reasons). An edited version of the interview is published at Carrie N. Baker, "Kelly's Story: Overcoming S.B. 8 and a 'Crisis Pregnancy Center' to Have an Abortion in Texas," *Ms. Magazine*, April 4, 2022, https://msmagazine.com/2022/04/04/texas-s-b-8-crisis-pregnancy-center-medication-abortion-pills/.

2   Plan C (@plancpills), "Mifepristone Is Still Available," *Instagram*, April 20, 2023, https://www.instagram.com/p/CrO48_OIq70/.

3   Angela Hume, *Deep Care: The Radical Activists Who Provided Abortions, Defied the Law, and Fought to Keep Clinics Open* (Chico, CA: AK Press, 2023); Mary Ziegler, *Abortion in America: A Legal History from Roe to the Present* (New York: Cambridge University Press, 2020); Rickie Solinger, *Pregnancy and Power: A History of Reproductive Politics in the United States*, rev. ed. (New York: New York University Press, 2019); Leslie J. Reagan, *When Abortion Was a Crime: Women, Medicine, and Law in the United States, 1867–1973* (Berkeley: University of California Press, 1997); Laura Kaplan, *The Story of Jane: The Legendary Underground Feminist Abortion Service*, 1st ed. (New York: Pantheon Books, 1995).

4   Naomi Braine, *Abortion beyond the Law: Building a Global Feminist Movement for Self-Managed Abortion* (New York: Verso Books, 2023); Sydney Calkin, *Abortion Pills Go Global: Reproductive Freedom across Borders* (Oakland: University of California Press, 2023).

5   Appendix B is a glossary of terms.

6   "Food and Drug Administration: Information on Mifeprex Labeling Changes and Ongoing Monitoring Efforts" (Washington, DC: US Government Accountability Office, March 2018), https://www.gao.gov/assets/gao-18-292.pdf.

7   World Health Organization, "Abortion Care Guidance" (Geneva, Switzerland: World Health Organization, 2022), https://www.who.int/publications/i/item/9789240039483.

8   Jessica L. Morris et al., "FIGO's Updated Recommendations for Misoprostol Used Alone in Gynecology and Obstetrics," *International Journal of Gynecology & Obstetrics* 138, no. 3 (2017): 363–66, https://doi.org/10.1002/ijgo.12181.

9   World Health Organization, "Abortion Care Guidance."

10 Abigail R.A. Aiken et al., "Effectiveness, Safety and Acceptability of No-Test Medical Abortion (Termination of Pregnancy) Provided via Telemedicine: A National Cohort Study," *BJOG: An International Journal of Obstetrics & Gynaecology* 128, no. 9 (August 2021): 1464–74, https://doi.org/10.1111/1471-0528.16668.

11 Ushma D. Upadhyay et al., "Incidence of Emergency Department Visits and Complications after Abortion," *Obstetrics & Gynecology* 125, no. 1 (January 2015): 175–83, https://doi.org/10.1097/AOG.0000000000000603.

12 Dana M. Johnson et al., "Safety and Effectiveness of Self-Managed Abortion Using Misoprostol Alone Acquired from an Online Telemedicine Service in the United States," *Perspectives on Sexual and Reproductive Health* 55, no. 1 (March 2023): 4–11, https://doi.org/10.1363/psrh.12219.

13 Rebecca Chalker and Carol Downer, *A Woman's Book of Choices: Abortion, Menstrual Extraction, RU-486*, 1st ed. (New York: Four Walls Eight Windows, 1992).

14 Carrie N. Baker, "Abortion Pill Effective for Treating Fibroids, but Anti-abortion Politics Stymie Access," *Ms. Magazine*, July 26, 2021, https://msmagazine.com/2021/07/26/mifepristone-abortion-pill-fibroids-endometriosis-depression-fda-rems-biden/.

15 Carrie N. Baker and Carly Thomsen, "The Importance of Talking about Women in the Fight against Abortion Bans," *Ms. Magazine*, June 23, 2022, https://msmagazine.com/2022/06/23/women-abortion-bans-inclusive-language-pregnant-people/.

16 Linda Gordon, *The Moral Property of Women: A History of Birth Control Politics in America*, First Illinois paperback edition (Urbana and Chicago: University of Illinois Press, 2007).

17 Ibis Reproductive Health, "Feminist Medication Abortion Accompaniment 101" (Cambridge, MA, November 2021), https://www.ibisreproductivehealth.org/sites/default/files/files/publications/Abortion%20accompaniment%20101.pdf; Naomi Braine, *Abortion beyond the Law: Building a Global Feminist Movement for Self-Managed Abortion* (New York: Verso Books, 2023); Sydney Calkin, *Abortion Pills Go Global: Reproductive Freedom across Borders* (Oakland: University of California Press, 2023).

18 Leslie J. Reagan, *When Abortion Was a Crime: Women, Medicine, and Law in the United States, 1867–1973* (Berkeley: University of California Press, 1997).

19 Susan Rinkunas, "Nebraska Mom Pleads Guilty to Giving Abortion Pills to Her Teen Daughter," *Jezebel*, July 10, 2023, https://jezebel.com/nebraska-mom-pleads-guilty-to-giving-abortion-pills-to-1850621217.

20 "#WeCount Report April 2022 to June 2023" (The Society of Family Planning, October 24, 2023), https://doi.org/10.46621/218569qkgmbl.

21 Loretta J. Ross and Rickie Solinger, *Reproductive Justice: An Introduction* (Oakland: University of California Press, 2017).

22 See Appendix A for a timeline of major events.

23 Carrie N. Baker, "No-Test Medication Abortion Increases Safety and Access during COVID-19," *Ms. Magazine*, May 13, 2020, https://msmagazine.com/2020/05/13/no-test-medication-abortion-increases-safety-and-access-during-covid-19/.

24 International family planning programs had for years promoted medication abortion in global South countries with high maternal mortality rates due to unsafe, often illegal abortion. Rebecca F. Baggaley, Joanna Burgin, and Oona M.R. Campbell, "The Potential of Medical Abortion to Reduce Maternal Mortality in Africa: What Benefits for Tanzania and Ethiopia?," *PLOS ONE* 5, no. 10 (October 11, 2010): e13260, https://doi.org/10.1371/journal.pone.0013260.

25 Carrie N. Baker, "'Plan C' Film Documents Campaign for Universal Abortion Pill Access in the U.S.," *Ms. Magazine*, February 1, 2023, https://msmagazine.com/2023/02/01/plan-c-abortion-pills-movie-film-sundance/.

Chapter 1

1 Étienne-Émile Baulieu and Mort Rosenblum, *The "Abortion Pill": RU-486, a Woman's Choice* (New York: Simon & Schuster, 1991), 129.

2 Steven Greenhouse, "A New Pill, a Fierce Battle," *New York Times Magazine*, February 12, 1989, 23.

3 Baulieu and Rosenblum, *The "Abortion Pill,"* 17.

4 Lauren Collins, "The Complicated Life of the Abortion Pill," *New Yorker*, July 5, 2022, https://www.newyorker.com/science/annals-of-medicine/emile-baulieu-the-complicated-life-of-the-abortion-pill.

5 Baulieu and Rosenblum, *The "Abortion Pill,"* 18.

6 Étienne-Émile Baulieu, "Steroid Receptors and Hormone Receptivity," *Journal of the American Medical Association* 125, no. 2 (August 15, 1976): 1049. Other researchers at Roussel Uclaf included Alain Belanger, Beatrice Couzinet, and Gilber Schaison.

7 Lawrence Lader, *A Private Matter: RU 486 and the Abortion Crisis* (New York: Prometheus Books, 1995), 121.

8 Lader, 120.

9 Clinicians at first used the synthetic prostaglandin sulprostone administered intramuscularly by injection, but after several serious reactions they switched to the vaginal suppository gemeprost, which worked but was relatively expensive and required refrigeration. Misoprostol eventually became the preferred prostaglandin because it was stable at room temperature, active orally, buccally (in the cheek pouch), and vaginally, and is available in an inexpensive generic. Eric A. Schaff, "Mifepristone: Ten Years Later," *Contraception* 81, no. 1 (January 2010): 1–7, https://doi.org/10.1016/j.contraception.2009.08.004.

10 Marc Bygdeman, "Progesterone Receptor Blockage," *Contraception* 32, no. 1 (July 1985): 45.

11 "The Case for Antiprogestins: A Report of the Reproductive Health Technologies Project" (Washington, DC: Reproductive Health Technologies Project, 1992), 23.

12 Department of Health and Human Services, Public Health Service, Food and Drug Administration, Center for Drug Evaluation and Research, "Application Number 20–687: Statistical Reviews," February 14, 2000.

13 R. Alta Charo, "A Political History of RU486," in *Biomedical Politics* (Washington, DC: National Academy Press, 1991), 43–93.

14 Charo, 43–93.

15 Charo, 43–93.

16 Greenhouse, "A New Pill, A Fierce Battle."

17 Charo, "A Political History of RU486," 57.

18 Greenhouse, "A New Pill, a Fierce Battle."

19 Greenhouse.

20 Schaff, "Mifepristone," 2. In 1998, the ministry of health allowed gynecologists and general practitioners to administer medication abortion in private medical offices.

21 "The Case for Antiprogestins," 23.

22 W. Brennan, "Chemical Warfare on the Unwanted: The I.G. Farben-Hoechst Connection," *National Right to Life News*, January 8, 1991.

23 "Upjohn Drops Research on Drug Criticized by Anti-abortion Groups," *AP News*, October 29, 1986, sec. Archive, https://apnews.com/article/72cbafa2cdbddabda2a4a3163607b548; Michael Klitsch, *RU 486: The Science and the Politics* (New York: The Alan Guttmacher Institute, 1989), 16.

24 Rebecca Chalker and Carol Downer, *A Woman's Book of Choices: Abortion, Menstrual Extraction, RU-486*, 1st ed. (New York: Four Walls Eight Windows, 1992), 216.

25 Charo, "A Political History of RU486," 61–62.

26 Greenhouse, "A New Pill, a Fierce Battle."

27 Charo, "A Political History of RU486," 60–61.

28 Pamela Belluck, "The Father of the Abortion Pill," *New York Times Magazine*, January 17, 2023, https://www.nytimes.com/2023/01/17/health/abortion-pill-inventor.html.

29 Charo, "A Political History of RU486," 61.

30 Greenhouse, "A New Pill, a Fierce Battle."

31 This conference was sponsored by the World Health Organization and the International Federation of Gynecology and Obstetrics.

32 "Abortion Pill Creator Calls for Action to Get It on the Market," *Reuters Library Report*, October 27, 1988.

33 Greenhouse, "A New Pill, a Fierce Battle."

34 Marie Bass, "Toward Coalition: The Reproductive Health Technologies Project," in *Abortion Wars: A Half Century of Struggle, 1950–2000*, ed. Rickie Solinger (Los Angeles: University of California Press, 1998), 258.

35 Charo, "A Political History of RU486," 63–64.

36 Charo, 64.

37 Greenhouse, "A New Pill, a Fierce Battle."

38 Greenhouse.

39 Rone Tempest, "France Orders Company to Distribute Abortion Pill," *Los Angeles Times*, October 29, 1988. Some at the time suggested that the French government and Roussel Uclaf may have collaborated in order to take pressure off of the company. Charo, "A Political History of RU 486," 67. A French court later ruled that Evin did not have the statutory authority to force Roussel Uclaf to keep RU 486 on the market.

40 "The Case for Antiprogestins: A Report of the Reproductive Health Technologies Project," 7.

41 "The Case for Antiprogestins: A Report of the Reproductive Health Technologies Project," 25.

42 Chalker and Downer, *A Woman's Book of Choices*, 219.

43 Bass, "Toward Coalition: The Reproductive Health Technologies Project," 261.

44 Webster v. Reproductive Health Services, 492 U.S. 490 (1989).

45 Hoechst AG, "Drug Induced Termination of Pregnancy with Mifepristone (RU 486)" (Memo prepared by the Health Policy Department of the Pharmaceuticals Division, October 1991).

46 "The Case for Antiprogestins: A Report of the Reproductive Health Technologies Project," 24.

47 Baulieu and Rosenblum, *The "Abortion Pill,"* 129.

48 Baulieu and Rosenblum.

49 This section draws on several primary and secondary sources, including the papers of Planned Parenthood and Lawrence Lader at the Sophia Smith Collection, Smith College, Northampton, Massachusetts; Jennifer Jackman, "Anatomy of a Feminist Victory: Winning the Transfer of RU 486 Patent Rights to the United States, 1988–1994," *Women & Politics* 24, no. 3 (June 2002): 81–99, https://doi.org/10.1300/J014v24n03_05; Charo, "A Political History of RU486"; Julie A. Hogan, "The Life of the Abortion Pill in the United States" (Cambridge, MA: Harvard University, 2012), https://core.ac.uk/display/28938892.

50 Melissa Haussman, *Reproductive Rights and the State: Getting the Birth Control, RU-486, Morning-After Pills and the Gardasil Vaccine to the U.S. Market*, Reproductive Rights and Policy (Santa Barbara, CA: Praeger, 2013), 98.

51 In the 1970s, researchers tested synthetic prostaglandins as an abortifacient. While they found them to be effective, about half the women studied experienced nausea, severe cramps, or diarrhea, so the research ended. Klitsch, *RU 486: The Science and the Politics*.

52 "The Case for Antiprogestins: A Report of the Reproductive Health Technologies Project," 13.

53 David A. Grimes et al., "Predictors of Failed Attempted Abortion with the Antiprogestin Mifepristone (RU 486)," *American Journal of Obstetrics and Gynecology* 162, no. 4 (April 1990): 910–17, https://doi.org/10.1016/0002-9378(90)91291-J.

54 Lawrence Lader, *RU 486: The Pill That Could End the Abortion Wars and Why American Women Don't Have It* (Reading, MA: Addison-Wesley Pub. Co, 1991).

55 Jennifer Jackman, "Blue Smoke, Mirrors, and Mediators: The Symbolic Contest over RU 486," in *Cultural Strategies of Agenda Denial: Avoidance, Attack, and Redefinition* (Lawrence: University Press of Kansas, 1997), 112–38.

56 Mindy J. Lees, "I Want a New Drug: RU 486 and the Right to Choose," *Southern California Law Review* 63 (1990): 113.

57 Megan Rosenfeld, "Conception of a Controversy: The French Doctor and His Pill to Prevent Pregnancy," *Washington Post*, December 18, 1986.

58 Laura Fraser, "Pill Politics," *Mother Jones*, June 1988, 33.

59 Margaret Talbot, "The Little White Bombshell," *New York Times Magazine*, July 11, 1999, sec. 6.

60 Richard Glasow and John Wilkie, "Omen of the Future? The Abortion Pill RU 486" (Washington, DC: National Right to Life Committee, 1990).

61 Jackman, "Blue Smoke, Mirrors, and Mediators: The Symbolic Contest over RU 486."

62 Feminist Majority Foundation, "Feminist Majority Foundation Demonstrates against Operation Rescue," June 18, 1992.

63 David A. Grimes et al., "An Epidemic of Antiabortion Violence in the United States," *American Journal of Obstetrics and Gynecology* 165, no. 5 (November 1991): 1263–68, https://doi.org/10.1016/0002-9378(91)90346-S.

64 "Violence to Abortion Providers," *Feminist Majority Foundation* (blog), accessed August 21, 2023, https://feminist.org/our-work/national-clinic-access-project/violent-attacks-on-abortion-providers-murders-attempted-murders-kidnapping/.

65 "Freedom of Access to Clinic Entrances Act," 18 U.S. § 248 (1994), https://www.law.cornell.edu/uscode/text/18/248.

66 Carol Mason, *Killing for Life: The Apocalyptic Narrative of Pro-Life Politics* (Ithaca, NY: Cornell University Press, 2002).

67 Collins, "The Complicated Life of the Abortion Pill."

68 Marie Bass and Joanna Howes, "A Report on RU 486 and Its Prospects for Use in the United States" (Washington, DC: Bass and Howes, 1987), 37–39.

69 Jean Reith Schroedel and Tanya Buhler Corbin, "Gender Relations and Institutional Conflict over Mifepristone," *Women & Politics* 24, no. 3 (June 2002): 41, https://doi.org/10.1300/J014v24n03_03; "The Case for Antiprogestins: A Report of the Reproductive Health Technologies Project," 23.

70 Feminist Majority Foundation, "A Brief Chronology in the Fight to Make RU 486 Available in the US," n.d., https://feminist.org/our-work/mifepristone/timeline/.

71 US Food and Drug Administration, "Regulatory Procedures Manual Chapter 9-71-30(C)," February 1, 1989.

72 Haussman, *Reproductive Rights and the State*, 104.

73 *RU 486: The Import Ban and Its Effect on Medical Research: Hearing before the Subcomm. on Regulation, Bus. Opportunities, and Energy of the H.R. Comm. on Small Bus.*, 101st Cong. 31 (1990), at 4–6, 18 (testimony of William Regelson, MD, professor of medicine, Medical College of Virginia; testimony of George P. Chrousos, MD, senior investigator and section chief, Pediatric Endocrinology, National Institute of Child Health and Human Development, National Institutes of Health).

74 Schroedel and Corbin, "Gender Relations and Institutional Conflict over Mifepristone," 35–60, 40.

75 "The Case for Antiprogestins: A Report of the Reproductive Health Technologies Project," 24.

76 Chalker and Downer, *A Woman's Book of Choices*, 217.

77 "The Case for Antiprogestins: A Report of the Reproductive Health Technologies Project," 25.

78 Lader, *RU 486*, 132.

79 "The Case for Antiprogestins: A Report of the Reproductive Health Technologies Project," 14.

80 Tempest, "France Orders Company to Distribute Abortion Pill"; "The Case for Antiprogestins: A Report of the Reproductive Health Technologies Project," 13.

81 Charo, "A Political History of RU486," 55–56; "The Case for Antiprogestins: A Report of the Reproductive Health Technologies Project," 15.

82 Carol Pogash, "Does the Abortion Pill Have a Future in America?," *San Francisco Examiner*, April 14, 1991, 14–15.

83 Lou Finter, "French Abortion Drug RU 486: U.S. Research Battle Heats Up," *Journal of the National Cancer Institute*, March 6, 1991, 316.

84 Terri Kapsalis, "Mastering the Female Pelvis: Race and the Tools of Reproduction," in *In Skin Deep, Spirit Strong: The Black Female Body in American Culture* (Ann Arbor: University of Michigan Press, 2002), 263–300.

85 Laura Briggs, *Reproducing Empire: Race, Sex, Science, and U.S. Imperialism in Puerto Rico* (Berkeley: University of California Press, 2002), 11.

86 Dorothy E. Roberts, *Killing the Black Body: Race, Reproduction, and the Meaning of Liberty*, Vintage Books 2nd ed. (New York: Vintage Books, 2017).

87 Janice G. Raymond, Renate Klein, and Lynette J. Dumble, *RU 486: Misconceptions, Myths and Morals* (Cambridge, MA: Institute on Women and Technology, 1991), 112.

88 Carrie N. Baker, "Abortion How-To: The Ms. Q&A on Menstrual Extraction with Carol Downer," *Ms.* magazine, July 14, 2022, https://msmagazine.com/2022/07/14/abortion-how-to-carol-downer-menstrual-extraction/.

89 Raymond, Klein, and Dumble, *RU 486: Misconceptions, Myths and Morals*, 117.

90 Raymond, Klein, and Dumble, 120.

91 Raymond, Klein, and Dumble, 122.

92 Alexandra Minna Stern, *Eugenic Nation: Faults and Frontiers of Better Breeding in Modern America* (Berkeley: University of California Press, 2005); Betsy Hartmann, "Everyday Eugenics," ZNetwork, September 22, 2006, https://znetwork.org/znetarticle/everyday-eugenics-by-betsy-hartmann/.

93 Charo, "A Political History of RU486," 48, 56–57.

94 Janice G. Raymond, Renate Klein, and Lynette J. Dumble, "RU 486: No," *Ms.* magazine, January 10, 1993.

95 Janet Callum and Rebecca Chalker, "RU 486: Yes," *Ms.* magazine, January 10, 1993.

96 Bass and Howes, "A Report on RU 486 and Its Prospects for Use in the United States," 58.

97 Bass and Howes, 30.

98 Bass and Howes, 41.

99 Bass and Howes, 48–49.

100 Bass and Howes, 61.

101 Bass and Howes.

102 Bass, "Toward Coalition: The Reproductive Health Technologies Project," 260.

103 Bass, 260.

104 Judy Norsigian, interview by Carrie N. Baker, June 29, 2023.

105 Cynthia Pearson, interview by Carrie N. Baker, July 5, 2023.

106 Bass, "Toward Coalition: The Reproductive Health Technologies Project," 261.

107 Bass, 262.

108 Amy Allina, interview by Carrie N. Baker, May 16, 2023.

109 Linda Gordon, *The Moral Property of Women: A History of Birth Control Politics in America*, First Illinois paperback edition (Urbana and Chicago: University of Illinois Press, 2007).

110 Baker, "Abortion How-To: The Ms. Q&A on Menstrual Extraction with Carol Downer."

111 Carol Downer, interview by Carrie N. Baker, October 19, 2023.

112 "The Case for Antiprogestins: A Report of the Reproductive Health Technologies Project," 24.

113 Bass, "Toward Coalition: The Reproductive Health Technologies Project," 261.

114 "Review of Programs, 1995–1996" (Washington, DC: Reproductive Health Technologies Project, 1996), 3.

115 Rickie Solinger, ed., *Abortion Wars: A Half Century of Struggle, 1950–2000* (Berkeley: University of California Press, 1998), 252.

116 Luz Alvarez Martinez, interview by Carrie N. Baker, June 29, 2023.

117 Reproductive Health Technologies Project [oral history] interview 4A with Amy Allina, Susan Wood, Jessica Arons, Kimberly Inez Maguire, and Susannah Baruch. 2017. Records of Reproductive Health Technologies Project, 1992–2017, MC 934: T-542: CD-115: Vt-288: DVD-138, E.9. Schlesinger Library, Radcliffe Institute.

118 After working in international reproductive health and family planning for many years, in 1993 Coeytaux founded the Pacific Institute for Women's Health, a data-driven advocacy organization focused on women's sexual and reproductive health in the United States and abroad, with a focus on applied research, advocacy, community involvement, consultation, and training.

119 Francine Coeytaux, interview by Carrie N. Baker, April 3, 2023.

120 "The Case for Antiprogestins: A Report of the Reproductive Health Technologies Project."

121 Marie Bass, interview by Carrie N. Baker, April 3, 2023.

122 Reproductive Health Technologies Project [oral history] interview 1A, 1B, 1C, and 2A with Marie Bass, Sharon Camp, and Joanna Howes. 2017. Records of Reproductive Health Technologies Project,

1992–2017, MC 934: T-542: CD-115: Vt-288: DVD-138, E.9. Schlesinger Library, Radcliffe Institute, https://id.lib.harvard.edu/ead/c/sch01590c00401/catalog. Accessed March 21, 2023; Marie Bass, interview by Carrie N. Baker, April 3, 2023.

123 "The Case for Antiprogestins: A Report of the Reproductive Health Technologies Project," 4.
124 "The Case for Antiprogestins: A Report of the Reproductive Health Technologies Project," 6.
125 "The Case for Antiprogestins: A Report of the Reproductive Health Technologies Project," 25.
126 Eleanor Smeal, interview with Carrie N. Baker, June 16, 2023. Smeal said Yorkin was a major funder of the campaign and that she "always thought big" and "kept people focused."
127 "Peg Yorkin, Feminist Leader and Philanthropist, Dies at 96," *AP News*, June 26, 2023, sec. U.S. News, https://apnews.com/article/feminist-peg-yorkin-dead-c8fc328b380396c3413b295acd643438.
128 Charo, "A Political History of RU486," 72.
129 Eleanor Smeal, interview by Carrie N. Baker, June 16, 2023.
130 Eleanor Smeal, interview by Carrie N. Baker, June 16, 2023.
131 Eleanor Smeal, interview by Carrie N. Baker, June 16, 2023.
132 Lader, *RU 486*, 111.
133 Lader, 131.
134 Feminist Majority Foundation, "Feminist Majority Foundation Delegation to Roussel Uclaf, Paris France, 1990," Facebook, September 25, 2015, https://www.facebook.com/photo/?fbid=10154247228827571&set=making-history-in-1990-a-feminist-majority-foundation-delegation-comprised-of-fe&locale=ar_AR.
135 Eleanor Smeal, interview by Carrie N. Baker, June 16, 2023.
136 Eleanor Smeal, interview by Carrie N. Baker, June 16, 2023.
137 Jennifer Jackman, interview by Carrie N. Baker, April 5, 2023.
138 Catherine Euvrard, interview by Carrie N. Baker, May 1, 2023.
139 Feminist Majority Foundation, "A Brief Chronology in the Fight to Make RU 486 Available in the US."
140 Jennifer Jackman, interview by Carrie N. Baker, April 5, 2023.
141 "The Case for Antiprogestins: A Report of the Reproductive Health Technologies Project," 25.
142 Lader, *RU 486*, 19.
143 Lader, 97.
144 Eleanor Smeal, interview by Carrie N. Baker, June 16, 2023.
145 Eleanor Smeal, interview by Carrie N. Baker, June 16, 2023.
146 *RU 486: The Import Ban and Its Effect on Medical Research: Hearing before the Subcomm. on Regulation, Bus. Opportunities, and Energy of the H.R. Comm. on Small Bus.*, 101st Cong. 31 (1990); *The Safety and Effectiveness of the Abortifacient RU486 in Foreign Markets: Opportunities and Obstacles to U.S. Commercialization: Hearing before the Subcomm. on Regulation, Bus. Opportunities, and Energy of the H.R. Comm. on Small Bus.*, 102nd Cong. 11 (1991); *The Effect of Federal Ban of RU 486 on Medical Research, New Drug Development, and Pharmaceutical Manufacturers: Hearing before the Subcomm. on Regulation, Bus. Opportunities, and Energy of the H.R. Comm. on Small Bus.*, 102nd Cong. 76 (1992).
147 *RU 486: The Import Ban and Its Effect on Medical Research: Hearing before the Subcomm. on Regulation, Bus. Opportunities, and Energy of the H.R. Comm. on Small Bus.*, 101st Cong. 31 (1990), at 2.
148 Schroedel and Corbin, "Gender Relations and Institutional Conflict over Mifepristone," 41.
149 *The Safety and Effectiveness of the Abortifacient RU486 in Foreign Markets: Opportunities and Obstacles to U.S. Commercialization: Hearing before the Subcomm. on Regulation, Bus. Opportunities, and Energy of the H.R. Comm. on Small Bus.*, 102nd Cong. 11 (1991) (testimony of Eleanor Smeal).
150 *The Effect of Federal Ban of RU 486 on Medical Research, New Drug Development, and Pharmaceutical Manufacturers*, at 2 (testimony of Ron Wyden).
151 *The Effect of Federal Ban of RU 486 on Medical Research, New Drug Development, and Pharmaceutical Manufacturers*, at 12–15 (testimony of David J. Grow).
152 H.R. 875, 102nd Cong. (1991).
153 Lader, *A Private Matter*.
154 Lader, 129.

155 Benten v. Kessler, No. CV-92–3161(CPS) (U.S. District Court for the Eastern District of New York 1992).

156 Rachael N. Pine, "Benten v. Kessler: The RU 486 Import Case," *Law, Medicine and Health Care* 20, no. 3 (1992): 238–42, https://doi.org/10.1111/j.1748-720X.1992.tb01196.x.

157 Lader, *A Private Matter*, 139.

158 Lader, 149.

159 Lader, 146–47.

160 Lader, 147.

161 Farah Nayeri, "An Abortion Pill May Soon Be on the Market in France," *United Press International*, March 28, 1989, https://www.upi.com/Archives/1987/03/28/Abortion-pillNEWLNAn-abortion-pill-may-soon-be-on-the-market-in-France/4751543906000/. Research has shown mifepristone is effective for emergency and regular contraception, but no drug company has pursued FDA approval for these uses.

162 Baulieu and Rosenblum, *The "Abortion Pill,"* 47.

163 "The Case for Antiprogestins: A Report of the Reproductive Health Technologies Project," 21.

164 Jill Smolowe, "New, Improved and Ready for Battle," *Time*, June 14, 1993.

165 Jackman, "Anatomy of a Feminist Victory," 92.

166 Charo, "A Political History of RU486," 43–93.

167 Alliance for Hippocratic Medicine v. U.S. Food and Drug Administration, No. 2:22-cv-00223-Z (U.S. District Court for the Northern District of Texas, Amarillo Division April 7, 2023).

168 Christopher M. Gacek, "Politicized Science: The Manipulated Approval of RU-486 and Its Dangers to Women's Health" (Washington, DC: Family Research Council, 2007), https://downloads.frc.org/EF/EF07A29.pdf; Life Issues Institute, "FDA Panel Moves on RU 486," September 1996, https://lifeissues.org/1996/09/fda-panel-moves-on-ru-486/.

169 William Clinton, "Letter to Donna Shalala on Importation of RU 486," January 22, 1993.

170 Ann Devroy, "Clinton Cancels Abortion Restrictions of Reagan–Bush Era," *The Washington Post*, January 23, 1993, https://www.washingtonpost.com/archive/politics/1993/01/23/clinton-cancels-abortion-restrictions-of-reagan-bush-era/0e145a5a-0b37-4908-8c4d-44643f62b0a0/.

171 Cynthia Pearson of NWHN reported she heard Kessler did this because he wanted to stay on as FDA commissioner and knew that Clinton wanted mifepristone approved. Cynthia Pearson, interview by Carrie N. Baker, July 5, 2023.

172 Catherine Euvrard, interview by Carrie N. Baker, May 1, 2023.

173 Francine Coeytaux, interview by Carrie N. Baker, April 3, 2023.

174 Beverly Winikoff, interview by Carrie N. Baker, May 22, 2023.

175 William E. Leary, "Maker of Abortion Pill Reaches Licensing Pact with U.S. Group," *The New York Times*, April 21, 1993.

176 Feminist Majority Foundation, "A Brief Chronology in the Fight to Make RU 486 Available in the US."

177 Tamar Lewin, "British Offering Abortion Drug to U.S. Women," *The New York Times*, February 18, 1994.

178 *RU-486, Status Report on the U.S. Commercialization Project, Transfer of Anti-progestin Technology to the United States*, 103rd Cong. 6 (1994) at 16 (testimony of Lester Hyman, representing Roussel Uclaf).

179 Edouard Sakiz, letter to Eleanor Smeal, May 30, 1995.

180 Eleanor Smeal, interview by Carrie N. Baker, May 8, 2023.

181 AFP-Extel News, "Roussel Uclaf Dismisses Planned U.S. Anti-abortion Groups' Boycott," June 2, 1994.

182 Gannett News Service, "RU 486 Company Faces Boycott," *Marin Independent Journal*, June 2, 1994, A3.

183 T.J. Raphael, "The Pill Plot," *Cover Up*, episode 6 at 5:10, 7:23, accessed August 15, 2023, https://podcasts.apple.com/us/podcast/cover-up-the-pill-plot/id1621750804.

184 Robert O'Harrow, Jr, "Drug's U.S. Marketer Remains Elusive," *The Washington Post*, October 12, 2000, https://www.washingtonpost.com/archive/politics/2000/10/12/drugs-us-marketer-remains-elusive/8b7b732b-0f23-4c96-9051-714cd3d9f6f8/.

185 "Status of Mifepristone in the United States" (New York: Population Council, April 1996).

186 Carolyn Ryan, "Clinic Stops Distributing Abortion Pill Brookline Killings Prompt Move," *Patriot Ledger*, January 31, 1995.

187 "Review of Programs, 1995–1996," 3.

188 Richard U. Hausknecht, "Methotrexate and Misoprostol to Terminate Early Pregnancy," *New England Journal of Medicine* 333, no. 9 (August 31, 1995): 537–40, https://doi.org/10.1056/NEJM199508313330901.

189 "The Abortion Drug Arrives," *The Washington Post*, September 2, 1995, sec. A.

190 "Harassment-Free Abortions," *The New York Times*, September 1, 1995, sec. A.

191 Elyse Tanouye, "Combined Use of Cancer, Ulcer Drugs to Cause Abortion Stirs Controversy," *The Wall Street Journal*, August 31, 1995.

192 Eric A. Schaff et al., "Combined Methotrexate and Misoprostol for Early Induced Abortion," *Archives of Family Medicine* 4, no. 9 (n.d.): 774–79.

193 Russell Sabin, "Abortion-Rights Group Asks to Test RU-486 Copy/UCSF Scientists Also Trying Another Version of Pill," *San Francisco Chronicle*, March 14, 1996. Later research revealed that methotrexate caused fetal abnormalities so it was never developed as an abortifacient. Dr. Hausknecht later became the medical director at Danco.

194 Steven Eisinger, interview with Carrie N. Baker, July 6, 2023. Mitchell Creinin said that methotrexate works best in the first seven weeks of pregnancy, but is less effective than mifepristone after that. Mitchell Creinin, interview with Carrie N. Baker, September 12, 2023.

195 Schaff, "Mifepristone," 2.

196 Tracy Weitz, interview by Carrie N. Baker, May 25, 2023.

197 US Food and Drug Administration Reproductive Health Advisory Committee, "New Drug Application for the Use of Mifepristone for Interruption of Early Pregnancy," July 19, 1996; Bass, "Toward Coalition: The Reproductive Health Technologies Project," 267.

198 Sheryl Stolberg, "FDA Panel Call for OK of Abortion Pill," *Los Angeles Times*, July 20, 1996.

199 Cynthia Pearson, interview by Carrie N. Baker, July 5, 2023.

200 Carolyn Westhoff, interview by Carrie N. Baker, August 9, 2023.

201 Mitchell Creinin, interview by Carrie N. Baker, September 12, 2023.

202 Mitchell Creinin, interview by Carrie N. Baker, September 12, 2023.

203 T.J. Raphael, "The Pill Plot," *Cover Up*, episode 6 at 11:05, accessed August 15, 2023, https://podcasts.apple.com/us/podcast/cover-up-the-pill-plot/id1621750804.

204 T.J. Raphael, "The Pill Plot," *Cover Up*, episode 6 at 13:30, accessed August 15, 2023, https://podcasts.apple.com/us/podcast/cover-up-the-pill-plot/id1621750804.

205 Tamar Lewin, "Group Is Intensifying Its Campaign to Distribute Abortion Pill," *The New York Times*, July 2, 1997, sec. U.S., https://www.nytimes.com/1997/07/02/us/group-is-intensifying-its-campaign-to-distribute-abortion-pill.html.

206 Steven Eisinger, interview by Carrie N. Baker, July 6, 2023.

207 Eric A. Schaff et al., "Low-Dose Mifepristone 200 Mg and Vaginal Misoprostol for Abortion," *Contraception* 59, no. 1 (January 1999): 1–6, https://doi.org/10.1016/S0010-7824(98)00150-4.

208 Andrea Tone, *Devices and Desires: A History of Contraceptives in America*, 1st ed. (New York: Hill and Wang, 2001).

209 Klitsch, *RU 486: The Science and the Politics*, 15.

210 Haussman, *Reproductive Rights and the State*, 103.

211 Bass, "Toward Coalition: The Reproductive Health Technologies Project," 256.

212 Tamar Lewin, "FDA Approval Sought for French Abortion Pill," *The New York Times*, April 1, 1996.

213 Redstone Strategy Group and David and Lucile Packard Foundation, "Mission Investments at the Packard Foundation," October 2015, https://www.packard.org/wp-content/uploads/2015/10/Packard_MIR_2015OCT51.pdf.

214 Hannah Levintova, "The Abortion Pill's Secret Money Men," *Mother Jones*, April 2023, https://www.motherjones.com/politics/2023/01/abortion-pill-mifepristone-mifeprex-roe-dobbs-private-equity/.

215 Carlyle Murphy and Kathleen Day, "Abortion Pill's U.S. Debut Snagged by Business Dispute; Sponsor Seeks to Oust Associate for Not Disclosing Disbarment," *The Washington Post*, January 12, 1997.

216 Tamar Lewin, "Legal Hurdle Cleared in Sale of French Abortion Pill in U.S.," *The New York Times*, February 13, 1997.

217 Julie Rovner, "US Antiabortionists Boycott Allergy Drug," *The Lancet*, April 12, 1997.

218 "'Army of God' Claims It Bombed Alabama Clinic," *The Washington Post*, February 3, 1998.

219 Kathleen Day, "Protest Fears Spur Effort to Keep Name of Abortion Pill's Maker Secret," *The Washington Post*, September 21, 1996.

220 Irving M. Spitz et al., "Early Pregnancy Termination with Mifepristone and Misoprostol in the United States," *New England Journal of Medicine* 338, no. 18 (April 30, 1998): 1241–47, https://doi.org/10.1056/NEJM199804303381801.

221 Schroedel and Corbin, "Gender Relations and Institutional Conflict over Mifepristone," 46.

222 Lader, *RU 486*.

223 Feminist Majority Foundation, "Feminist Majority Foundation Declares Victory in 12-Year Campaign to Bring RU 486 to the United States" (Arlington, VA: Feminist Majority Foundation, September 28, 2000), https://feminist.org/news/press/feminist-majority-foundation-declares-victory-in-12-year-campaign-to-bring-ru-486-to-the-united-states/.

224 Eleanor Smeal, interview by Carrie N. Baker, June 16, 2023.

225 Feminist Majority Foundation, "Compassionate Use Program," accessed March 4, 2023, https://feminist.org/our-work/mifepristone/compassionate-use-program/.

226 Eleanor Smeal, interview by Carrie N. Baker, May 8, 2023.

227 Eleanor Smeal, interview by Carrie N. Baker, May 8, 2023.

228 Sheryl Gay Stolberg, "FDA Adds Hurdles in Approval of Abortion Pill," *The New York Times*, June 8, 2000.

229 Schroedel and Corbin, "Gender Relations and Institutional Conflict over Mifepristone," 49.

230 Beverly Winikoff, interview by Carrie N. Baker, May 22, 2023.

231 Feminist Majority Foundation, "A Brief Chronology in the Fight to Make RU 486 Available in the US."

232 Haussman, *Reproductive Rights and the State*, 103.

233 FDC Reports, "Searle Cytotec Pregnancy Reminder Issued As RU-486 Action Nears," The Pink Sheet, August 28, 2000.

234 "Abortion Pill Maker Revealed," *CBS News*, October 13, 2000, https://www.cbsnews.com/news/abortion-pill-maker-revealed/.

235 Robert O'Harrow, Jr, "Drug's U.S. Marketer Remains Elusive."

236 O'Harrow, Jr.

237 Department of Health and Human Services, Public Health Service, Food and Drug Administration, Center for Drug Evaluation and Research, "Memorandum," September 28, 2000.

238 Haussman, *Reproductive Rights and the State*.

239 Kirsten Moore, interview by Carrie N. Baker, May 4, 2023.

240 This claim was made in the lawsuit *Alliance for Hippocratic Medicine v. FDA*, filed in November of 2022 (see discussion in Chapter 6).

241 Haussman, *Reproductive Rights and the State*.

242 Eleanor Smeal, interview by Carrie N. Baker, May 8, 2023.

243 Beverly Winikoff, interview by Carrie N. Baker, May 22, 2023.

244 Beverly Winikoff, interview by Carrie N. Baker, May 22, 2023.

245 Cynthia Pearson, interview by Carrie N. Baker, July 5, 2023.

246 Emily Langer, "Philip Corfman, Advocate for Women's Reproductive Health, Dies at 92," *The Washington Post*, March 2, 2019, https://www.washingtonpost.com/local/obituaries/philip-corfman-advocate-for-womens-reproductive-health-dies-at-92/2019/02/28/78305ab6-3aa3-11e9-a06c-3ec8ed509d15_story.html.

247 Kirsten Moore, interview by Carrie N. Baker, May 4, 2023.

248 Amy Allina, interview by Carrie N. Baker, May 16, 2023.

249 Amy Allina, interview by Carrie N. Baker, May 16, 2023.

250 Eleanor Smeal, interview by Carrie N. Baker, June 16, 2023.

251 Schroedel and Corbin, "Gender Relations and Institutional Conflict over Mifepristone."

252 Enav Z. Zusman et al., "Dispensing Mifepristone for Medical Abortion in Canada: Pharmacists' Experiences of the First Year," *Canadian Pharmacists Journal* 156, no. 4 (August 2023): 204, https://doi.org/10.1177/17151635231176270.

253 Carole Joffe and Susan Yanow, "Advanced Practice Clinicians as Abortion Providers: Current Developments in the United States," *Reproductive Health Matters* 12, no. 24 Suppl (November 2004): 198–206, https://doi.org/10.1016/s0968-8080(04)24008-3.

254 Talbot, "The Little White Bombshell."

255 Lader, *RU 486*, 114–15.

256 Lader, *A Private Matter*, 225.

257 Chalker and Downer, *A Woman's Book of Choices*, 209.

258 Klitsch, *RU 486: The Science and the Politics*, 13.

259 Talbot, "The Little White Bombshell."

Chapter 2

1 Jean Reith Schroedel, "Assessing Medical Abortion in the US: One Year after the FDA Approval of Mifepristone," *Women & Politics* 24, no. 3 (June 2002): 3, https://doi.org/10.1300/J014v24n03_01.

2 "National Survey of Gynecologists and Family Practice Physicians: Few Offering Mifepristone One Year after FDA Approval; Indications That Number May Increase in Next Year" (news release) (San Francisco: Kaiser Family Foundation, September 24, 2001).

3 Rachel Jones and Jenna Jerman, "Abortion Incidence and Service Availability in the United States," *Perspectives on Sexual and Reproductive Health* 46 (2014): 3–14.

4 Beverly Winikoff and Carolyn Westhoff, "Fifteen Years: Looking Back and Looking Forward," *Contraception* 92, no. 3 (September 2015): 177, https://doi.org/10.1016/j.contraception.2015.06.019.

5 Felicia H. Stewart et al., "Early Medical Abortion: Issues for Practice" (San Francisco: UCSF Center for Reproductive Health Research & Policy, 2001).

6 Elisa Wells, interview by Carrie N. Baker, May 24, 2023.

7 Tracy Weitz, interview by Carrie N. Baker, May 25, 2023.

8 Tracy Weitz, interview by Carrie N. Baker, May 25, 2023.

9 "Our Impact. RHEDI," accessed May 26, 2023, https://rhedi.org/our-impact/.

10 Emily Godfrey, interview by Carrie N. Baker, May 5, 2023.

11 Emily Godfrey, interview by Carrie N. Baker, May 5, 2023.

12 Tracy Weitz, interview by Carrie N. Baker, May 25, 2023.

13 Carolyn Westhoff, interview by Carrie N. Baker, August 9, 2023.

14 Susan Yanow, interview by Carrie N. Baker, May 25, 2023.

15 Wells had worked with a wide range of organizations, including the global health equity non-profit PATH and the Association of Reproductive Health Professionals.

16 Elisa Wells, interview by Carrie N. Baker, May 24, 2023.

17 Trace Weitz, interview by Carrie N. Baker, May 25, 2023.

18 Carolyn Westhoff, interview by Carrie N. Baker, August 9, 2023.

19 Francine Coeytaux, Kirsten Moore, and Lillian Gelberg, "Convincing New Providers to Offer Medical Abortion: What Will It Take?," *Perspectives on Sexual and Reproductive Health* 35, no. 1 (January 2003): 44–47, https://doi.org/10.1363/3504403.

20 Coeytaux, Moore, and Gelberg.

21 Coeytaux, Moore, and Gelberg.

22 Coeytaux, Moore, and Gelberg.

23 Emily M. Godfrey et al., "Factors Associated with Successful Implementation of Telehealth Abortion in 4 United States Clinical Practice Settings," *Contraception* 104, no. 1 (July 2021): 82–91, https://doi.org/10.1016/j.contraception.2021.04.021.

24 Marcel P. Gemperli et al., "A Qualitative Study of Insurers' Coverage for Mifepristone-Induced Abortion," *Managed Care Interface* 18, no. 3 (March 2005): 26–30, 32. Tracy Weitz worked with malpractice carriers to put medication abortion on the family practice page for coverage but they refused to. Tracy Weitz, interview by Carrie N. Baker, May 25, 2023.

25 Tracy Weitz, interview by Carrie N. Baker, May 25, 2023.

26 Francine Coeytaux, interview by Carrie N. Baker, April 3, 2023.

27 Beverly Winikoff, interview by Carrie N. Baker, May 22, 2023.

28 Beverly Winikoff, interview by Carrie N. Baker, May 22, 2023.

29 Clyde Wilcox and Julia Riches, "Pills in the Public's Mind: RU 486 and the Framing of the Abortion Issue," *Women & Politics* 24, no. 3 (June 2002): 61–80, https://doi.org/10.1300/J014v24n03_04.

30 Schroedel and Corbin, "Gender Relations and Institutional Conflict over Mifepristone," 50.

31 Schroedel, "Assessing Medical Abortion in the US," 5.

32 Kati Schindler, Anna E. Jackson, and Charon Asetoyer, "Indigenous Women's Reproductive Rights: The Indian Health Service and Its Inconsistent Application of the Hyde Amendment" (Native American Women's Health Education Resource Center, October 2002), 5, https://www.prochoice.org/pubs_research/publications/downloads/about_abortion/indigenous_women.pdf.

33 Feminist Majority Foundation, "Abortion Rights Group Challenges Law Restricting Mifepristone" (Arlington, VA, March 2, 2001), https://feminist.org/news/abortion-rights-group-challenges-law-restricting-mifepristone/.

34 Schroedel, "Assessing Medical Abortion in the US," 6.

35 California Health & Safety Code sec. 439.905 (2001).

36 Schroedel, "Assessing Medical Abortion in the US," 7.

37 Feminist Majority Foundation, "NAF to Launch $2M Public Ed Campaign on Mifepristone" (Arlington, VA, May 25, 2001), https://feminist.org/news/naf-to-launch-2m-public-ed-campaign-on-mifepristone/.

38 "Letter to Dr. Mark McClellan, Commissioner of the FDA, from Cynthia Peterson, Executive Director of the National Women's Health Network, and Dr. Sidney Wolfe, Director of the Public Citizens' Health Research Group," January 21, 2004.

39 "Letter to Members of the Committee on Emerging Clostridial Disease, from Gynuity, Ipas, NAF, NWHN and RHTP," May 11, 2006.

40 Amy Allina, email to Carrie N. Baker, May 17, 2023.

41 Elissa Meites, Suzanne Zane, and Carolyn Gould, "Fatal Clostridium Sordellii Infections after Medical Abortions," *New England Journal of Medicine* 363, no. 14 (September 30, 2010): 1382–83, https://doi.org/10.1056/NEJMc1001014; Beverly Winikoff, "Clostridium Sordellii Infection in Medical Abortion," *Clinical Infectious Diseases* 43, no. 11 (December 1, 2006): 1447–48, https://doi.org/10.1086/508895.

42 Centers for Disease Control and Prevention, "Abortion Surveillance—United States, 2007," Morbidity and Mortality Weekly Report, Surveillance Summaries, Vol. 60, No. 1 (Washington, DC: Centers for Disease Control and Prevention, February 25, 2011), https://www.cdc.gov/mmwr/pdf/ss/ss6001.pdf.

43 Anna Popinchalk and Gilda Sedgh, "Trends in the Method and Gestational Age of Abortion in High-Income Countries," *BMJ Sexual & Reproductive Health* 45, no. 2 (April 2019): 95–103, https://doi.org/10.1136/bmjsrh-2018-200149.

44 Michelle Cohen, interview by Carrie N. Baker, June 8, 2023.

45 Michelle Cohen, interview by Carrie N. Baker, June 8, 2023.
46 Michelle Cohen, interview by Carrie N. Baker, June 8, 2023.
47 Michelle Cohen, interview by Carrie N. Baker, June 8, 2023.
48 "Food and Drug Administration Amendments Act of 2007," Pub. L. No. 110–85, 121 Stat. 823 (2007), https://www.congress.gov/bill/110th-congress/house-bill/3580.
49 US Food and Drug Administration, "Risk Evaluation and Mitigation Strategy for Mifeprex," June 2011, https://www.fda.gov/media/164648/download.
50 Schaff, "Mifepristone."
51 Elizabeth G. Raymond et al., "First-Trimester Medical Abortion with Mifepristone 200 Mg and Misoprostol: A Systematic Review," *Contraception* 87, no. 1 (January 2013): 26–37, https://doi.org/10.1016/j.contraception.2012.06.011.
52 Schaff, "Mifepristone," 2.
53 Dina Abbas, Erica Chong, and Elizabeth G. Raymond, "Outpatient Medical Abortion Is Safe and Effective through 70 Days Gestation," *Contraception* 92, no. 3 (September 2015): 197–99, https://doi.org/10.1016/j.contraception.2015.06.018.
54 Ilana Dzuba et al., "Outpatient Mifepristone–Misoprostol Medical Abortion through 77 Days of Gestation," *Contraception* 94, no. 4 (October 2016): 389, https://doi.org/10.1016/j.contraception.2016.07.027.
55 World Health Organization, "Abortion Care Guidance" (Geneva, Switzerland: World Health Organization, 2022), https://www.who.int/publications/i/item/9789240039483.
56 Emily Godfrey, interview by Carrie N. Baker, May 5, 2023.
57 Schaff, "Mifepristone," 3.
58 Schaff, 3.
59 Eric A. Schaff et al., "Vaginal Misoprostol Administered 1, 2, or 3 Days after Mifepristone for Early Medical Abortion: A Randomized Trial," *JAMA* 284, no. 15 (October 18, 2000): 1948, https://doi.org/10.1001/jama.284.15.1948.
60 Elizabeth G. Raymond et al., "Reaching Women Where They Are: Eliminating the Initial In-Person Medical Abortion Visit," *Contraception* 92, no. 3 (September 2015): 190–93, https://doi.org/10.1016/j.contraception.2015.06.020; Marji Gold and Erica Chong, "If We Can Do It for Misoprostol, Why Not for Mifepristone? The Case for Taking Mifepristone out of the Office in Medical Abortion," *Contraception* 92, no. 3 (September 2015): 194–96, https://doi.org/10.1016/j.contraception.2015.06.011.
61 Gold and Chong, "If We Can Do It for Misoprostol, Why Not for Mifepristone?"; Erica Chong et al., "A Prospective, Non-randomized Study of Home Use of Mifepristone for Medical Abortion in the U.S.," *Contraception* 92, no. 3 (September 1, 2015): 215–19, https://doi.org/10.1016/j.contraception.2015.06.026.
62 María Mercedes Lafaurie et al., "Women's Perspectives on Medical Abortion in Mexico, Colombia, Ecuador and Peru: A Qualitative Study," *Reproductive Health Matters* 13, no. 26 (January 2005): 75–83, https://doi.org/10.1016/S0968-8080(05)26199-2; Diana Lara et al., "Pharmacy Provision of Medical Abortifacients in a Latin American City," *Contraception* 74, no. 5 (November 2006): 394–99, https://doi.org/10.1016/j.contraception.2006.05.068.
63 Schaff, "Mifepristone," 2.
64 Cui-Lan Li et al., "Effectiveness and Safety of Lower Doses of Mifepristone Combined with Misoprostol for the Termination of Ultra-early Pregnancy: A Dose-Ranging Randomized Controlled Trial," *Reproductive Sciences* 22, no. 6 (June 2015): 706–11, https://doi.org/10.1177/1933719114557897.
65 Daniel Grossman et al., "Effectiveness and Acceptability of Medical Abortion Provided through Telemedicine," *Obstetrics & Gynecology* 118, no. 2 (August 2011): 296–303, https://doi.org/10.1097/AOG.0b013e318224d110; Kate Grindlay, Kathleen Lane, and Daniel Grossman, "Women's and Providers' Experiences with Medical Abortion Provided through Telemedicine: A Qualitative Study," *Women's Health Issues* 23, no. 2 (March 2013): e117–22, https://doi.org/10.1016/j.whi.2012.12.002.
66 Angel M. Foster et al., "From Qualified Physician to Licensed Health Care Professional: The Time Has Come to Change Mifepristone's Label," *Contraception* 92, no. 3 (September 2015): 200–202, https://doi.org/10.1016/j.contraception.2015.06.022.

67 Daniel Grossman and Philip Goldstone, "Mifepristone by Prescription: A Dream in the United States but Reality in Australia," *Contraception* 92, no. 3 (September 2015): 186–89, https://doi.org/10.1016/j.contraception.2015.06.014.

68 Richard J. Rovelli, Nicole E. Cieri-Hutcherson, and Timothy C. Hutcherson, "Systematic Review of Oral Pharmacotherapeutic Options for the Management of Uterine Fibroids," *Journal of the American Pharmacists Association* 62, no. 3 (May 2022): 674–682.e5, https://doi.org/10.1016/j.japh.2022.02.004; Ally Murji et al., "Selective Progesterone Receptor Modulators (SPRMs) for Uterine Fibroids," ed. Cochrane Gynaecology and Fertility Group, *Cochrane Database of Systematic Reviews* 2017, no. 4 (April 26, 2017), https://doi.org/10.1002/14651858.CD010770.pub2; Julietta Fiscella et al., "Distinguishing Features of Endometrial Pathology after Exposure to the Progesterone Receptor Modulator Mifepristone," *Human Pathology* 42, no. 7 (July 2011): 947–53, https://doi.org/10.1016/j.humpath.2010.11.003.

69 Steven Eisinger, interview by Carrie N. Baker, July 6, 2023.

70 Kevin Fiscella, interview by Carrie N. Baker, July 25, 2023.

71 Steven Eisinger, interview by Carrie N. Baker, July 6, 2023.

72 Kevin Fiscella, interview by Carrie N. Baker, July 25, 2023.

73 Steven Eisinger, email to Carrie N. Baker, July 9, 2023.

74 Kevin Fiscella, interview by Carrie N. Baker, July 25, 2023.

75 Kevin Fiscella, interview by Carrie N. Baker, July 25, 2023.

76 Steven Eisinger, interview by Carrie N. Baker, July 6, 2023.

77 Carrie N. Baker, "Anti-abortion Politics Hinder Access to Important Fibroid Treatment: Mifepristone," *Ms.* magazine, July 14, 2023, https://msmagazine.com/2023/07/14/mifepristone-fibroids/.

78 Kevin Fiscella, interview by Carrie N. Baker, July 25, 2023.

79 Kevin Discella, interview by Carrie N. Baker, July 25, 2023.

80 Y.X. Zhang, "Effect of Mifepristone in the Different Treatments of Endometriosis," *Clinical and Experimental Obstetrics & Gynecology* 43, no. 3 (2016): 350–53.

81 Thaddeus S. Block et al., "Combined Analysis of Mifepristone for Psychotic Depression: Plasma Levels Associated with Clinical Response," *Biological Psychiatry* 84, no. 1 (July 2018): 46–54, https://doi.org/10.1016/j.biopsych.2018.01.008.

82 Jocelyn Solis-Moreira, "Banning the Abortion Pill Would Harm Veterans, Cancer Patients, and Many Others," *Popular Science* (blog), May 1, 2023, https://www.popsci.com/health/abortion-pill-ban-other-treatments/.

83 Francisco Díaz-Castro et al., "Mifepristone for Treatment of Metabolic Syndrome: Beyond Cushing's Syndrome," *Frontiers in Pharmacology* 11 (2020): 429, https://doi.org/10.3389/fphar.2020.00429.

84 Nathalie Chabbert-Buffet et al., "Selective Progesterone Receptor Modulators and Progesterone Antagonists: Mechanisms of Action and Clinical Applications," *Human Reproduction Update* 11, no. 3 (May 1, 2005): 293–307, https://doi.org/10.1093/humupd/dmi002.

85 Baker, "Abortion Pill Effective for Treating Fibroids, but Anti-abortion Politics Stymie Access."

86 Diane S. Aschenbrenner, "FDA Approves First Drug for Endogenous Cushing's Syndrome," *American Journal of Nursing* 112, no. 6 (June 2012): 26, https://doi.org/10.1097/01.NAJ.0000415123.61735.8e.

87 Sarah Jane Tribble, "How a Drugmaker Turned the Abortion Pill into a Rare-Disease Profit Machine," *Washington Post*, April 10, 2018, https://www.washingtonpost.com/national/health-science/how-a-drugmaker-turned-the-abortion-pill-into-a-rare-disease-profit-machine/2018/04/10/af989610-3c9f-11e8-955b-7d2e19b79966_story.html.

88 Sarah Christopherson and Olivia Snavely, "The FDA's Convoluted Stance on Abortion Pills Doesn't Protect Patients—It Endangers Them," National Women's Health Network, May 8, 2020, https://nwhn.org/the-fdas-convoluted-stance-on-abortion-pills-doesnt-protect-patients-it-endangers-them/.

89 "States Enact Record Number of Abortion Restrictions in 2011" (New York: Guttmacher Institute, January 2012), https://www.guttmacher.org/article/2012/01/states-enact-record-number-abortion-restrictions-2011.

90 Francine Coeytaux and Elisa Wells, "A Tale of Two Methods: Applying the Lessons Learned from Emergency Contraception to Misoprostol for Early Abortion, Briefing Paper Commissioned by the Reproductive Health Technologies Project" (Washington, DC: Reproductive Health Technologies Project, July 2016), 4–5.

91 Morgani Guzzo, "Brasil: As Regras Que Puseram o Misoprostol 'Na Cadeia,'" *Futuro Do Cuidado* (blog), August 25, 2021, https://futurodocuidado.org/o-misoprostol-esta-na-cadeia/. By 1998, the government had criminalized misoprostol in most circumstances and it was unavailable in Brazil. The government later blocked the dissemination of information about misoprostol as well.

92 H.L.L. Coêlho et al., "Misoprostol and Illegal Abortion in Fortaleza, Brazil," *The Lancet* 341, no. 8855 (May 1993): 1261–63, https://doi.org/10.1016/0140-6736(93)91157-H; Ilana Löwy and Marilena Cordeiro Dias Villela Corrêa, "The 'Abortion Pill' Misoprostol in Brazil: Women's Empowerment in a Conservative and Repressive Political Environment," *American Journal of Public Health* 110, no. 5 (May 2020): 677–84, https://doi.org/10.2105/AJPH.2019.305562.

93 Mariana Carbajal, "Meet the Latin American Women Who Launched the Global Day for Safe Abortion," *Open Democracy*, September 28, 2021, https://www.opendemocracy.net/en/5050/safe-abortion-day-brazil-argentina/.

94 M.A. Rosing and C.D. Archbald, "The Knowledge, Acceptability, and Use of Misoprostol for Self-Induced Medical Abortion in an Urban US Population," *Journal of the American Medical Women's Association (1972)* 55, no. 3 Suppl (2000): 183–85.

95 K. Blanchard, B. Winikoff, and C. Ellertson, "Misoprostol Used Alone for the Termination of Early Pregnancy. A Review of the Evidence," *Contraception* 59, no. 4 (April 1999): 209–17, https://doi.org/10.1016/s0010-7824(99)00029-3.

96 *Vessel*, 2014, https://vesselthefilm.com/.

97 "Abortion Pills in U.S. Women's Hands: Bold Action to Meet Women's Needs, Report on Meeting Held on 12/4/2013 in Washington, D.C." (Public Health Institute, Ipas, and National Women's Health Network, December 2013), 2–3 (describing the Working Group); Susan Yanow, interview by Carrie N. Baker, May 25, 2023.

98 Elisa Wells et al., "Surfing for Abortion: An Assessment of the Online Availability of Information about Misoprostol," June 29, 2014, 2 (unpublished report).

99 N.L. Moreno-Ruiz et al., "Alternatives to Mifepristone for Early Medical Abortion," *International Journal of Gynecology & Obstetrics* 96, no. 3 (March 2007): 212–18, https://doi.org/10.1016/j.ijgo.2006.09.009.

100 Research published in 2006 revealed that in one Latin American city, pharmacists often prescribed misoprostol, but their knowledge about proper dosing regimens was low. Researchers interviewed staff at a random sample of 102 pharmacies in the Latin American city and dispatched mystery clients to the same pharmacies to ascertain prescribing practices and counseling. Sixty percent of pharmacists reported recommending misoprostol and 39 percent of the mystery client encounters resulted in a misoprostol prescription, but few of the pharmacists (6 percent in the survey and 17 percent in the mystery client encounters) recommended a misoprostol dosing regimen that was potentially effective. Lara et al., "Pharmacy Provision of Medical Abortifacients in a Latin American City."

101 Eleanor J. Bader, "A Miscarriage of Justice for Dominican Immigrant," *The Indypendent*, April 13, 2007, https://indypendent.org/2007/04/a-miscarriage-of-justice-for-dominican-immigrant/.

102 Yadira Betances, "Lawrence Teen Accused of Inducing Abortion Given Pretrial Probation," *Eagle-Tribune*, June 3, 2008, https://www.eagletribune.com/news/local_news/lawrence-teen-accused-of-inducing-abortion-given-pretrial-probation/article_babe78b6-70f5-5aab-9bd7-5ba79c630942.html; Susan Yanow, interview by Carrie N. Baker, May 25, 2023.

103 Susan Yanow, "The Best Defense Is a Good Offense: Misoprostol, Abortion, and the Law, Conference Summary and Strategic Recommendations" (New York: Gynuity Health Projects and the Reproductive Health Technologies Project, August 2009), https://gynuity.org/assets/resources/Goldman_best_defense_web.pdf; Susan Yanow, interview by Carrie N. Baker, May 25, 2023.

104 Yanow.

105 Beverly Winikoff, interview by Carrie N. Baker, May 22, 2023.

106 Daniel Grossman et al., "Self-Induction of Abortion among Women in the United States," *Reproductive Health Matters* 18, no. 36 (January 2010): 136–46, https://doi.org/10.1016/S0968-8080(10)36534-7; "Abortion Pills in U.S. Women's Hands: Bold Action to Meet Women's Needs, Report on Meeting Held on 12/4/2013 in Washington, D.C.," 3–4.

107 Susan Yanow, interview by Carrie N. Baker, May 25, 2023.

108 Susan Yanow, interview by Carrie N. Baker, May 25, 2023.

109 Rachel K. Jones, "How Commonly Do US Abortion Patients Report Attempts to Self-Induce?," *American Journal of Obstetrics & Gynecology* 204, no. 1 (January 1, 2011): 23.e1–23.e4, https://doi.org/10.1016/j.ajog.2010.08.019.

110 Emily Bazelon, "A Mother in Jail for Helping Her Daughter Have an Abortion," *The New York Times*, September 22, 2014, sec. Magazine, https://www.nytimes.com/2014/09/22/magazine/a-mother-in-jail-for-helping-her-daughter-have-an-abortion.html.

111 Helen Davidson, "Texas Abortion Bill Defeated by Wendy Davis Filibuster and Public Protest," *The Guardian*, June 26, 2013, sec. US news, https://www.theguardian.com/world/2013/jun/26/texas-abortion-vote-defeated-deadline-wendy-davis.

112 Diana Lugo-Martinez, interview by Carrie N. Baker, July 24, 2023.

113 Erik Eckholm, "A Pill Available in Mexico Is a Texas Option for Abortion," *The New York Times*, July 13, 2013, sec. U.S., https://www.nytimes.com/2013/07/14/us/in-mexican-pill-a-texas-option-for-an-abortion.html.

114 Diana Lugo-Martinez, interview by Carrie N. Baker, July 24, 2023.

115 Marlene Gerber Fried, interview by Carrie N. Baker, May 18, 2023.

116 "Abortion Pills in U.S. Women's Hands: Bold Action to Meet Women's Needs, Report on Meeting Held on 12/4/2013 in Washington, D.C.," 1. The states involved were California, Georgia, Massachusetts, North Carolina, New York, Oklahoma, Tennessee, Texas, Washington, and the District of Columbia.

117 Some women saw the process of using misoprostol as more natural than procedural abortion, likening it to miscarriage.

118 Francine Coeytaux noted that when mifepristone was first introduced in the United States, many providers believed the medication was an inferior method to evacuation abortion.

119 Wells et al., "Surfing for Abortion."

120 "Abortion Pills in U.S. Women's Hands: Bold Action to Meet Women's Needs, Report on Meeting Held on 12/4/2013 in Washington, D.C."

121 Francine Coeytaux et al., "Facilitating Women's Access to Misoprostol through Community-Based Advocacy in Kenya and Tanzania," *International Journal of Gynecology & Obstetrics* 125, no. 1 (April 2014): 53–55, https://doi.org/10.1016/j.ijgo.2013.10.004.

122 Elisa Wells, interview by Carrie N. Baker, May 24, 2023.

123 Elisa Wells, email to Carrie N. Baker, June 9, 2023.

124 Barbara Pillsbury, Francine Coeytaux, and Andrea Johnston, "From Secret to Shelf: How Collaboration Is Bringing Emergency Contraception to Women" (Los Angeles: Pacific Institute Health, 1999), 24.

125 Pillsbury, Coeytaux, and Johnston, 24.

126 Pillsbury, Coeytaux, and Johnston, 28.

127 DKT is one of the largest private providers of family planning products in the world.

128 Elisa Wells, interview by Carrie N. Baker, May 24, 2023.

129 Francine Coeytaux, interview by Carrie N. Baker, January 23, 2023.

130 Francine Coeytaux, interview by Carrie N. Baker, April 3, 2023.

131 Coeytaux and Wells, "A Tale of Two Methods: Applying the Lessons Learned from Emergency Contraception to Misoprostol for Early Abortion, Briefing Paper Commissioned by the Reproductive Health Technologies Project," 33.

132 Francine Coeytaux, Leila Hessini, and Amy Allina, "Bold Action to Meet Women's Needs: Putting Abortion Pills in U.S. Women's Hands," *Women's Health Issues* 25, no. 6 (November 2015): 608–11, https://doi.org/10.1016/j.whi.2015.08.004.

133 Coeytaux, Hessini, and Allina.

134 Francine Coeytaux, interview by Carrie N. Baker, April 3, 2023.

135 Jenifer McKenna, interview by Carrie N. Baker, July 18, 2023.

136 Coeytaux and Wells, "A Tale of Two Methods: Applying the Lessons Learned from Emergency Contraception to Misoprostol for Early Abortion, Briefing Paper Commissioned by the Reproductive Health Technologies Project," 2.

137 Coeytaux and Wells, 4.

138 Coeytaux and Wells, 24–30.

139 Coeytaux and Wells, 31.

140 "Introducing the SIA Legal Team" (Berkeley, CA: UC Berkeley School of Law, 2015), www.law.berkeley.edu/wp-content/uploads/2016/01/SIA-Legal-Team-Brochure.pdf.

141 "About Reproaction | Reproaction," accessed June 16, 2023, https://reproaction.org/about/.

142 Pamela Merritt, interview by Carrie N. Baker, June 14, 2023.

143 Pamela Merritt, interview by Carrie N. Baker, June 14, 2023.

144 Later published as Coeytaux and Wells, "A Tale of Two Methods: Applying the Lessons Learned from Emergency Contraception to Misoprostol for Early Abortion, Briefing Paper Commissioned by the Reproductive Health Technologies Project."

145 Amy Allina, interview by Carrie N. Baker, May 16, 2023.

146 Elisa Wells, personal correspondence, November 13, 2023.

147 Amy Allina, interview by Carrie N. Baker, May 16, 2023.

148 Chelsea Conaboy, "She Started Selling Abortion Pills Online. Then the Feds Showed Up," *Mother Jones*, April 2019, https://www.motherjones.com/politics/2019/02/she-started-selling-abortion-pills-online-then-the-feds-showed-up/; Sydney Calkin, *Abortion Pills Go Global: Reproductive Freedom across Borders* (Oakland: University of California Press, 2023), 73.

149 Conaboy.

150 Department of Justice, "New York Woman Sentenced for Selling Abortion-Inducing Pills Illegally Smuggled into US," July 10, 2020, https://www.justice.gov/usao-wdwi/pr/new-york-woman-sentenced-selling-abortion-inducing-pills-illegally-smuggled-us.

151 Schaff et al., "Low-Dose Mifepristone 200 Mg and Vaginal Misoprostol for Abortion."

152 Agata Bodie, "Off-Label Use of Prescription Drugs," Summary (Washington, DC: Congressional Research Service, February 23, 2021), https://sgp.fas.org/crs/misc/R45792.pdf; Schaff, "Mifepristone," 3.

153 Rachel K. Jones and Heather D. Boonstra, "The Public Health Implications of the FDA Update to the Medication Abortion Label" (Washington, DC: Guttmacher Institute, June 2016).

154 Ushma D. Upadhyay et al., "Comparison of Outcomes before and after Ohio's Law Mandating Use of the FDA-Approved Protocol for Medication Abortion: A Retrospective Cohort Study," ed. Joel G. Ray, *PLOS Medicine* 13, no. 8 (August 30, 2016): e1002110, https://doi.org/10.1371/journal.pmed.1002110.

155 Ushma D. Upadhyay et al., "Sociodemographic Characteristics of Women Able to Obtain Medication Abortion before and after Ohio's Law Requiring Use of the Food and Drug Administration Protocol," *Health Equity* 2, no. 1 (July 2018): 122–30, https://doi.org/10.1089/heq.2018.0002.

156 Francine Coeytaux, interview by Carrie N. Baker, April 3, 2023.

157 Beverly Winikoff, interview by Carrie N. Baker, May 22, 2023.

158 Beverly Winikoff, interview by Carrie N. Baker, May 22, 2023.

159 Kirsten Moore, interview by Carrie N. Baker, May 4, 2023. On the other hand, Tracy Weitz suggested that removal of the REMS maybe would have decreased advocates' efforts to encourage the development of a generic. Tracy Weitz, interview by Carrie N. Baker, May 25, 2023.

160 Carolyn Westhoff, interview by Carrie N. Baker, August 9, 2023.

161 Cynthia Pearson, interview by Carrie N. Baker, July 14, 2023.

162 Carolyn Westhoff, interview by Carrie N. Baker, August 9, 2023.

163 Mitchell Creinin, interview by Carrie N. Baker, September 12, 2023.

164 Mitchell Creinin, interview by Carrie N. Baker, September 12, 2023.

165 Center for Drug Evaluation and Research, "Medical Review(s) for Application 020687Orig1s020" (Washington, DC: US Food and Drug Administration, March 29, 2016), https://www.accessdata.fda.gov/drugsatfda_docs/nda/2016/020687Orig1s020MedR.pdf.

166 Joint Stipulation of Facts, *Chelius v. Becerra*, Civ. No. 1:17-cv-00493-JAO-RT, April 15, 2021, https://www.aclu.org/sites/default/files/field_document/dkt._140_-_joint_stipulations_of_facts_with_exhibits_april_15_2021.pdf.

167 Beverly Winikoff and Carolyn Westhoff, "Fifteen Years: Looking Back and Looking Forward," *Contraception* 92, no. 3 (September 2015): 177–78, https://doi.org/10.1016/j.contraception.2015.06.019.

168 US Food and Drug Administration, "Risk Evaluation and Mitigation Strategy for Mifeprex," March 2016, https://www.fda.gov/media/164649/download.

169 Kirsten Moore, interview by Carrie N. Baker, May 4, 2023.

170 Christopherson and Snavely, "The FDA's Convoluted Stance on Abortion Pills Doesn't Protect Patients—It Endangers Them."

171 Elizabeth Raymond et al., "TelAbortion: Evaluation of a Direct to Patient Telemedicine Abortion Service in the United States," *Contraception* 100, no. 3 (September 2019): 173–77, https://doi.org/10.1016/j.contraception.2019.05.013.

172 Carolyn Westhoff, interview by Carrie N. Baker, August 9, 2023.

173 Rachel K. Jones et al., "Medication Abortion Now Accounts for More Than Half of All US Abortions" (Washington, DC: Guttmacher Institute, February 2022), https://www.guttmacher.org/article/2022/02/medication-abortion-now-accounts-more-half-all-us-abortions.

174 Chloe Murtagh et al., "Exploring the Feasibility of Obtaining Mifepristone and Misoprostol from the Internet," *Contraception* 97, no. 4 (April 2018): 287–91, https://doi.org/10.1016/j.contraception.2017.09.016.

175 Francine Coeytaux, interview by Carrie N. Baker, April 3, 2023.

176 Elisa Wells, interview by Carrie N. Baker, May 31, 2023.

177 Elisa Wells and Francine Coeytaux, "Mail-Order Abortion: The Future Is Now," *Rewire News Group*, November 8, 2016, https://rewirenewsgroup.com/2016/11/08/mail-order-abortion-future-now/.

178 ACLU Hawaii, Chelius v. Azar, United States District Court for the District of Hawaii, October 3, 2017, https://www.acluhi.org/en/cases/chelius-v-azar.

179 Kirsten Moore, interview by Carrie N. Baker, May 10, 2021.

180 "Ending the Risk Evaluation and Mitigation Strategy (REMS) Policy on Mifepristone (Mifeprex), Policy H-100.948" (American Medical Association, 2018), https://www.ama-assn.org/sites/ama-assn.org/files/corp/media-browser/public/hod/a18-resolutions.pdf.

181 Kirsten Moore, interview by Carrie N. Baker, May 10, 2021.

182 "Food and Drug Administration, Information on Mifeprex Labeling Changes and Ongoing Monitoring Efforts" (Washington, DC: United States Government Accountability Office, March 2018), https://www.gao.gov/assets/gao-18-292.pdf.

183 Courtney A. Schreiber et al., "Mifepristone Pretreatment for the Medical Management of Early Pregnancy Loss," *The New England Journal of Medicine* 378, no. 23 (June 7, 2018): 2161–70, https://doi.org/10.1056/NEJMoa1715726.

184 "Improving Access to Mifepristone for Reproductive Health Indications, Position Statement" (Washington, DC: American College of Obstetricians and Gynecologists, June 2018), https://www.acog.org/clinical-information/policy-and-position-statements/position-statements/2018/improving-access-to-mifepristone-for-reproductive-health-indications.

185 "Removing REMS Categorization on Mifepristone, Res. R1-401" (Kansas City, MO: American Academy of Family Physicians, August 2018), https://www.aafp.org/dam/AAFP/documents/events/nc/congress/nc18-ncfmr-actions-referrals.pdf.

186 Francine Coeytaux, Elisa Wells, and Sophia Yen, "Reproductive Health Care by Mail," *Stanford Social Innovation Review* 16, no. 2 (Spring 2018): 61–62, https://doi.org/10.48558/JNW3-2E38.

187 Coeytaux, Wells, and Yen.

188 Francine Coeytaux, interview by Carrie N. Baker, April 11, 2023.

189 Carrie N. Baker, "Why Order Abortion Pills Online? Affordability, Privacy and Convenience, Says New Study," *Ms.* magazine, May 27, 2021, https://msmagazine.com/2021/05/27/order-abortion-pills-medication-abortion-online-affordability-privacy-convenience-aid-access/.

190 Rebecca Gomperts, interview by Carrie N. Baker, February 11, 2022.

191 Abigail R.A. Aiken, Jennifer E. Starling, and Rebecca Gomperts, "Factors Associated with Use of an Online Telemedicine Service to Access Self-Managed Medical Abortion in the US," *JAMA Network Open* 4, no. 5 (May 21, 2021): e2111852, https://doi.org/10.1001/jamanetworkopen.2021.11852.

192 Elisa Wells, email to Carrie N. Baker, June 29, 2023.

193 Francine Coeytaux, interview by Carrie N. Baker, April 11, 2023.

194 Abigail R.A. Aiken et al., "Safety and Effectiveness of Self-Managed Medication Abortion Provided Using Online Telemedicine in the United States: A Population Based Study," *The Lancet Regional Health—Americas* 10 (June 2022): 100200, https://doi.org/10.1016/j.lana.2022.100200.

195 Abigail Aiken, interview by Carrie N. Baker, February 23, 2022.

196 Abigail Aiken, interview by Carrie N. Baker, February 23, 2022.

197 Carrie N. Baker and Emily Bellanca, "Safe and Supported: Inside the DIY Abortion Movement," *Ms.* magazine, January 26, 2018, https://msmagazine.com/2018/01/26/safe-supported-inside-diy-abortion-movement/.

198 Francine Coeytaux, interview by Carrie N. Baker, April 11, 2023; SASS, *Safe Abortion with Pills, What Everyone Should Know about Medical Abortion*, June 2019.

199 Cherel, "Abortion without Provider Involvement: Exercising Autonomy beyond Partisan Politics," *The Women's Health Activist*, April 2017.

200 Cherel.

201 Lauren Ralph et al., "Prevalence of Self-Managed Abortion among Women of Reproductive Age in the United States," *JAMA Network Open* 3, no. 12 (December 18, 2020): e2029245, https://doi.org/10.1001/jamanetworkopen.2020.29245.

202 Ushma D. Upadhyay, Alice F. Cartwright, and Daniel Grossman, "Barriers to Abortion Care and Incidence of Attempted Self-Managed Abortion among Individuals Searching Google for Abortion Care: A National Prospective Study," *Contraception* 106 (February 2022): 49–56, https://doi.org/10.1016/j.contraception.2021.09.009.

203 Anonymous, interview by Carrie N. Baker, July 10, 2023.

204 Elizabeth G. Raymond, Margo S. Harrison, and Mark A. Weaver, "Efficacy of Misoprostol Alone for First-Trimester Medical Abortion: A Systematic Review," *Obstetrics & Gynecology* 133, no. 1 (January 2019): 137–47, https://doi.org/10.1097/AOG.0000000000003017.

205 FDA, Personal Importation, accessed April 11, 2023, https://www.fda.gov/industry/import-basics/personal-importation.

206 If/When/How: Lawyering for Reproductive Justice, "Fulfilling Roe's Promise: 2019 Update," 2019, https://www.ifwhenhow.org/resources/roes-unfinished-promise-2019-update/.

207 If/When/How: Lawyering for Reproductive Justice, "If/When/How and the SIA Legal Team Unite: Introducing the New Leading Edge in Lawyering for Reproductive Justice," March 13, 2019, https://www.ifwhenhow.org/sia-legal-team-merger-announcement-if-when-how/.

208 If/When/How: Lawyering for Reproductive Justice, "Fulfilling Roe's Promise: 2019 Update."

209 April Lockley, interview by Carrie N. Baker, March 2, 2022.

210 Deborah Oyer, email to Carrie N. Baker, July 1, 2023.

211 Godfrey et al., "Factors Associated with Successful Implementation of Telehealth Abortion in 4 United States Clinical Practice Settings."

212 Emily M. Godfrey et al., "Family Medicine Provision of Online Medication Abortion in Three US States during COVID-19," *Contraception* 104, no. 1 (July 2021): 54–60, https://doi.org/10.1016/j.contraception.2021.04.026.

213 Francine Coeytaux, interview by Carrie N. Baker, April 3, 2023.

214 Susheela Singh et al., "The Incidence of Abortion and Unintended Pregnancy in India, 2015," *The Lancet Global Health* 6, no. 1 (January 2018): e111–20, https://doi.org/10.1016/S2214-109X(17)30453-9.

215 Guttmacher Institute, "National Estimate of Abortion in India Released," News Release, December 11, 2017, https://www.guttmacher.org/news-release/2017/national-estimate-abortion-india-released.

216 Raymond et al., "TelAbortion."

217 Ushma D. Upadhyay, Alice F. Cartwright, and Nicole E. Johns, "Access to Medication Abortion among California's Public University Students," *Journal of Adolescent Health* 63, no. 2 (August 2018): 249–52, https://doi.org/10.1016/j.jadohealth.2018.04.009; Melody Gutierrez, "Abortion Medication to Be Available at California's College Health Centers under New Law," *Los Angeles Times*, October 11, 2019, sec. California, https://www.latimes.com/california/story/2019-10-11/abortion-medication-california-college-health-centers-legislation.

218 "About GenBioPro Prescriber," GenBioPro, accessed October 24, 2023, https://genbiopro.com/about-genbiopro-prescriber/.

219 Kirsten Moore, interview by Carrie N. Baker, May 4, 2023.

220 US Food and Drug Administration, "Risk Evaluation and Mitigation Strategy, Single Shared System for Mifepristone," April 2019, https://www.fda.gov/media/164650/download.

221 Francine Coeytaux, interview by Carrie N. Baker, April 3, 2023.

222 Kirsten Moore, email to Carrie N. Baker, July 10, 2023.

223 Mitchell Creinin, interview by Carrie N. Baker, September 12, 2023.

224 US Food and Drug Administration, "Warning Letter to AidAccess.Org," March 8, 2019, https://www.fda.gov/inspections-compliance-enforcement-and-criminal-investigations/warning-letters/aidaccessorg-575658-03082019.

225 Carrie N. Baker, "Telemedicine Abortion Provider Rebecca Gomperts Gets Abortion Pills into the Hands of Those Who Need Them: 'It's a Privilege,'" *Ms.* magazine, February 23, 2023, https://msmagazine.com/2022/02/23/telemedicine-abortion-rebecca-gomperts-abortion-pills/.

226 Gomperts v. Azar, Verified Complaint, United States District Court for the District of Ohio, September 8, 2019, https://www.documentcloud.org/documents/6390359-Access-Aid-Verified-Complaint-With-Exhibits.html.

227 "Missouri Forcing Invasive Pelvic Exam on Women Seeking Abortions," *Rachel Maddow Show*, NBC, June 6, 2019, https://www.msnbc.com/rachel-maddow/watch/missouri-forcing-invasive-pelvic-exam-on-women-seeking-abortion-61462597599.

228 Michael B. Thomas, "Missouri Health Director Tracked Menstrual Periods of Planned Parenthood Patients," *NBC News*, October 29, 2019, https://www.nbcnews.com/news/us-news/missouri-health-director-tracked-menstrual-periods-planned-parenthood-patients-n1073701.

229 Pamela Merritt, interview by Carrie N. Baker, June 14, 2023.

230 "US States Have Enacted 1,381 Abortion Restrictions Since Roe v. Wade Was Decided in 1973," Guttmacher Institute, June 28, 2022, https://www.guttmacher.org/infographic/2022/us-states-have-enacted-1381-abortion-restrictions-roe-v-wade-was-decided-1973.

231 Jones et al., "Medication Abortion Now Accounts for More Than Half of All US Abortions."

Chapter 3

1 Carrie N. Baker, "Telemedicine Abortion: What It Is and Why We Need It Now More Than Ever," *Ms.* magazine, March 26, 2020, https://msmagazine.com/2020/03/26/telemedicine-abortion-what-it-is-and-why-we-need-it-now-more-than-ever/.

2 "DEA's Response to COVID-19" (Washington, DC: US Department of Justice Drug Enforcement Administration, March 20, 2020), https://www.dea.gov/press-releases/2020/03/20/deas-response-covid-19; Kirsten Moore, interview by Carrie N. Baker, May 10, 2021.

3 Elizabeth G. Raymond et al., "Commentary: No-test Medication Abortion: A Sample Protocol for Increasing Access during a Pandemic and beyond," *Contraception* 101, no. 6 (June 2020): 361–66, https://doi.org/10.1016/j.contraception.2020.04.005.

4 Emily Godfrey, interview by Carrie N. Baker, May 5, 2023.

5 Elizabeth G. Raymond et al., "Simplified Medical Abortion Screening: A Demonstration Project," *Contraception* 97, no. 4 (April 2018): 292–96, https://doi.org/10.1016/j.contraception.2017.11.005.

6 Jamila Perritt, interview by Carrie N. Baker, May 11, 2022.

7 Baker, "Telemedicine Abortion: What It Is and Why We Need It Now More Than Ever."

8 Baker.

9 Elisa Wells, email to Carrie N. Baker, June 29, 2023.

10 ACOG, *COVID-19 FAQs for Obstetrician–Gynecologists, Gynecology*, March 30, 2020. Washington, DC: ACOG.

11 Carrie N. Baker, "Feminist Multi-Front Battle to End FDA's Abortion Pill Restriction," *Ms.* magazine, May 20, 2020, https://msmagazine.com/2020/05/20/feminist-multi-front-battle-to-end-fdas-abortion-pill-restriction/.

12 Baker.

13 Baker.

14 Baker.

15 Xavier Bacerra, "Letter to Secretary Alex M. Azar II and Commissioner Stephen Hahn," March 30, 2020, https://ag.ny.gov/sites/default/files/final_ag_letter_hhs_medication_abortion_2020.pdf.

16 "Attorney General James Pushes to Increase Abortion Access by Medication during Coronavirus Pandemic," Press Release (Office of the New York Attorney General, March 30, 2020), https://ag.ny.gov/press-release/2020/attorney-general-james-pushes-increase-abortion-access-medication-during.

17 National Women's Health Network et al., "Letter to Dr. Stephen Hahn," April 6, 2020, https://www.nwhn.org/wp-content/uploads/2020/04/2020-04-06-FDA-mifepristone-REMS-letter-FINAL-1.pdf.

18 Susan F. Wood and Cynthia F. Pearson, "The UK Allows Home Use of the Abortion Pill—the US Should Do the Same," *The Hill*, April 27, 2020, https://thehill.com/opinion/healthcare/494914-the-uk-allows-home-use-of-the-abortion-pill-the-us-should-do-the-same/.

19 Baker, "Telemedicine Abortion: What It Is and Why We Need It Now More Than Ever."

20 Cynthia Pearson, interview by Carrie N. Baker, July 14, 2023.

21 Elizabeth Warren, "Letter to FDA Commissioner Stephen Hahn," April 14, 2020, https://www.warren.senate.gov/imo/media/doc/2020.04.14%20Letter%20to%20FDA%20re%20Medication%20Abortion.pdf.

22 Diana DeGette, "Letter to FDA Commissioner Stephen Hahn," June 16, 2020, https://pressley.house.gov/sites/pressley.house.gov/files/Mifepristone%20Letter%20to%20FDA_6.16.2020.pdf.

23 Sarah Christopherson, interview by Carrie N. Baker, August 9, 2023.

24 Francine Coeytaux, interview by Carrie N. Baker, April 11, 2023.

25 Anna E. Fiastro et al., "Remote Delivery in Reproductive Health Care: Operation of Direct-to-Patient Telehealth Medication Abortion Services in Diverse Settings," *The Annals of Family Medicine* 20, no. 4 (July 2022): 336–42, https://doi.org/10.1370/afm.2821.

26 University of Washington and Plan C, "Access, Delivered: A Toolkit for Providers Offering Medication Abortion" (Seattle: University of Washington, 2020).

27 Elisa Wells, interview by Carrie N. Baker, May 24, 2023.

28 "ACOG Suit Petitions Court to Remove FDA's Burdensome Barriers to Reproductive Care during COVID-19" (American College of Obstetricians and Gynecologists, May 27, 2020), https://www.acog.org/news/news-releases/2020/05/acog-suit-petitions-the-fda-to-remove-burdensome-barriers-to-reproductive-care-during-covid-19.

29 Carrie N. Baker, "The Abortion Pill Mifepristone Just Became Easier to Get," *Ms.* magazine, July 21, 2020, https://msmagazine.com/2020/07/21/the-abortion-pill-mifepristone-just-became-easier-to-get/.

30 Patrick Adams, "Amid Covid-19, a Call for M.D.s to Mail the Abortion Pill," *The New York Times*, May 12, 2020, https://www.nytimes.com/2020/05/12/opinion/covid-abortion-pill.html.

31 Elisa Wells, interview by Carrie N. Baker, May 10, 2020.

32 Jones et al., "Medication Abortion Now Accounts for More Than Half of All US Abortions."

33 Memorandum Opinion, ACOG v. FDA, Civil Action No. TDC-20-1320, July 13, 2020, https://www.aclu.org/cases/american-college-obstetricians-and-gynecologists-v-us-food-and-drug-administration?document=preliminary-injunction-granted.

34 Baker, "The Abortion Pill Mifepristone Just Became Easier to Get."

35 "American College of Obstetricians and Gynecologists v. U.S. Food and Drug Administration," *American Civil Liberties Union* (blog), accessed July 8, 2023, http://www.aclu.org/cases/american-college-obstetricians-and-gynecologists-v-us-food-and-drug-administration.

36 Julie Amaon, interview by Carrie N. Baker, November 11, 2020.

37 Cindy Adam, interview by Carrie N. Baker, November 12, 2020.

38 Julie Amaon, interview by Carrie N. Baker, November 11, 2020.

39 Lauren Dubey, interview by Carrie N. Baker, November 12, 2020.

40 Lauren Dubey, interview by Carrie N. Baker, November 12, 2020.

41 Aisha Wagner, interview by Carrie N. Baker, November 12, 2020.

42 Aisha Wagner, interview by Carrie N. Baker, November 12, 2020.

43 Aisha Wagner, interview by Carrie N. Baker, November 12, 2020.

44 Cindy Adam and Lauren Dubey, interview by Carrie N. Baker, December 30, 2021.

45 Morgan Love, interview by Carrie N. Baker, November 11, 2020.

46 Phoebe Abramowitz, interview by Carrie N. Baker, November 11, 2020.

47 Morgan Love, interview by Carrie N. Baker, November 11, 2020.

48 Melissa Grant, interview by Carrie N. Baker, January 18, 2022; Leah Coplon, interview by Carrie N. Baker, January 6, 2021.

49 Melissa Grant, interview by Carrie N. Baker, November 12, 2020.

50 Shelly Kaller et al., "Abortion Service Availability during the COVID-19 Pandemic: Results from a National Census of Abortion Facilities in the U.S.," *Contraception: X* 3 (2021): 100067, https://doi.org/10.1016/j.conx.2021.100067; Ushma D. Upadhyay et al., "Outcomes and Safety of History-Based Screening for Medication Abortion: A Retrospective Multicenter Cohort Study," *JAMA Internal Medicine* 182, no. 5 (May 1, 2022): 482, https://doi.org/10.1001/jamainternmed.2022.0217.

51 Order, ACOG v. FDA, Civil Action No. TDC-20-1320, United States District Court, District of Maryland, August 19, 2020 (Judge Theodore J. Chuang).

52 Elisa Wells, email to Carrie N. Baker, June 9, 2023.

53 Abigail Abrams, "Meet the Pharmacist Expanding Access to Medication Abortion," *Time*, June 13, 2022, https://time.com/6183395/abortion-pills-honeybee-health-online-pharmacy/.

54 Carrie N. Baker, "U.S.-Based Online Pharmacy First to Ship Abortion Pills to Patients inside the U.S.," *Ms.* magazine, September 30, 2020, https://msmagazine.com/2020/09/30/honeybee-health-us-based-online-pharmacy-first-to-ship-abortion-pills-to-patients-inside-the-u-s/.

55 Abrams, "Meet the Pharmacist Expanding Access to Medication Abortion."

56 Baker, "U.S.-Based Online Pharmacy First to Ship Abortion Pills to Patients inside the U.S."

57 Elisa Wells, interview by Carrie N. Baker, November 5, 2020.

58 Plan C at www.plancpills.org (accessed November 15, 2020).

59 Carrie N. Baker, "People Are Getting Creative Obtaining Abortion Pills Online," *Ms.* magazine, February 7, 2022, https://msmagazine.com/2022/02/07/how-to-get-abortion-pills-online-telemedicine-abortion/.

60 University of Washington and Plan C, "Access, Delivered: A Toolkit for Providers Offering Medication Abortion."

61 Melissa Grant, interview by Carrie N. Baker, November 12, 2020.
62 Ted Cruz, "Letter to Stephen Hahn," September 1, 2020, https://www.cruz.senate.gov/files/documents/Letters/2020.09.01%20--%20Pro-Life%20Mifeprex%20Letter%20to%20FDA%20-%20FSV.pdf.
63 FDA v. ACOG, 592 U.S. ___ (2021), https://www.supremecourt.gov/opinions/20pdf/20a34_3f14.pdf.
64 FDA v. ACOG, 592 ___ (2021), at 12.
65 FDA v. ACOG, 592 ___ (2021), at 8.
66 Carrie N. Baker, "SCOTUS Blocks Access to Abortion Pill by Mail during Pandemic. Advocates Look to Biden Administration to Reverse Trump Policy," *Ms.* magazine, January 13, 2021, https://msmagazine.com/2021/01/13/supreme-court-abortion-pill-trump-biden/.
67 Baker.
68 Baker.
69 Baker.
70 Baker.
71 Julie Amaon, interview by Carrie N. Baker, January 14, 2022.
72 Emily Bazelon, "Risking Everything to Offer Abortions across State Lines," *The New York Times*, October 4, 2022, sec. Magazine, 32, https://www.nytimes.com/2022/10/04/magazine/abortion-interstate-travel-post-roe.html.
73 Hanna Kim, interview by Carrie N. Baker, March 16, 2022; Christie Pitney, interview by Carrie N. Baker, January 17, 2022.
74 Tara Shochet, interview by Carrie N. Baker, January 12, 2021.
75 Rachel K. Jones et al., "Long-Term Decline in US Abortions Reverses, Showing Risking Need for Abortion as Supreme Court Is Poised to Overturn Roe v. Wade" (Washington, DC: Guttmacher Institute, June 15, 2022), https://www.guttmacher.org/article/2022/06/long-term-decline-us-abortions-reverses-showing-rising-need-abortion-supreme-court.
76 Jones et al.
77 Rosalyn Schroeder et al., "Trends in Abortion Care in the United States, 2017–2021" (San Francisco: Advancing New Standards in Reproductive Health, 2022), https://www.dropbox.com/s/30ziy4nl1o0wclf/ANSIRH_trends-in-abortion-care-report-v3.pdf?dl=0.
78 Schroder et al.
79 Carrie N. Baker, "Abortion on Our Own Terms: 'Supreme Court Justices Can't Put Abortion Pills Back in the Bottle,'" *Ms.* magazine, June 16, 2022, https://msmagazine.com/2022/06/16/abortion-pills-abortion-on-our-own-terms-supreme-court/; Amy Allina, interview by Carrie N. Baker, May 16, 2023.
80 "GLC Membership Documents" (Generative Learning Community, December 2020), 1.
81 "GLC Membership Documents," 1.
82 Francine Coeytaux, interview by Carrie N. Baker, May 3, 2023.
83 Kirsten Moore, interview by Carrie N. Baker, May 3, 2023.
84 Kirsten Moore, interview by Carrie N. Baker, November 13, 2020.
85 "First Priorities: Executive and Agency Actions Blueprint for Sexual and Reproductive Health, Rights, and Justice" (Reproductive Blueprint, September 2020), https://reproblueprint.org/wp-content/uploads/2020/09/First-Priorities-Executive-Agency-Actions-Incoming-Administration-Blueprint.pdf.
86 Herminia Palacio and Daniel Grossman, "How the Biden Administration Should Stand Up for Abortion Rights," *The Washington Post*, January 27, 2021, https://www.washingtonpost.com/opinions/2021/01/27/biden-abortion-rights-orders-healthcare/.
87 Sarah Christopherson, interview by Carrie N. Baker, August 9, 2023.
88 Dr. Woodcock took over as acting head of the FDA hours after Biden took office.
89 Carolyn Maloney et al., "Letter to Janet Woodcock, Acting Director of the FDA," February 9, 2021.
90 ACLU et al., "Letter to Honorable Joseph R. Biden, Jr.," March 18, 2021, https://www.aclu.org/letter/reproductive-health-rights-and-justice-groups-letter-biden-administration-mifepristone.

91 US Food and Drug Administration, "Risk Evaluation and Mitigation Strategy, Single Shared System for Mifepristone," April 2021, https://www.fda.gov/media/164651/download.

92 Janet Woodcock, "Letter to Maureen G. Phipps and William Grobman," April 12, 2021, https://www.aclu.org/letter/fda-response-acog-april-2021.

93 American College of Obstetricians and Gynecologists, "ACOG Applauds the FDA for Its Action on Mifepristone Access during the COVID-19 Pandemic," April 12, 2021, https://www.acog.org/news/news-releases/2021/04/acog-applauds-fda-action-on-mifepristone-access-during-covid-19-pandemic.

94 Sarah Christopherson, interview by Carrie N. Baker, August 9, 2023.

95 Carrie N. Baker, "FDA Allows Telemedicine Abortion during Pandemic," *Ms.* magazine, April 19, 2021, https://msmagazine.com/2021/04/19/fda-telemedicine-abortion-pill-mifepristone/.

96 Elisa Wells, interview by Carrie N. Baker, April 13, 2021.

97 Baker, "FDA Allows Telemedicine Abortion during Pandemic."

98 Joint Motion to Stay Case Pending Agency Review, Chelius v. Becerra, United States District Court for the District of Hawaii, Civ. No. 1:17-00493 JAO-RT, May 7, 2021, https://www.aclu.org/cases/chelius-v-becerra?document=joint-motion-stay-case-pending-agency-review.

99 Dr. Jamie Phifer, interview by Carrie N. Baker, May 18, 2021.

100 Dr. Razel Ramon, interview by Carrie N. Baker, February 22, 2022.

101 Hanna Kim, interview by Carrie N. Baker, March 16, 2022.

102 Christie Pitney, interview by Carrie N. Baker, January 17, 2022.

103 Robin Tucker, interview by Carrie N. Baker, December 24, 2021.

104 Dr. Deborah Oyer, interview by Carrie N. Baker, December 29, 2021.

105 Michele Gomez, interview by Carrie N. Baker, December 29, 2021.

106 Alison Case, interview by Carrie N. Baker, February 2, 2022.

107 Emily M. Godfrey et al., "Patient Perspectives Regarding Clinician Communication during Telemedicine Compared with In-Clinic Abortion," *Obstetrics & Gynecology* Publish Ahead of Print (May 4, 2023), https://doi.org/10.1097/AOG.0000000000005192.

108 Godfrey et al., 13.

109 Emily Godfrey, email to Carrie N. Baker, May 5, 2023.

110 Michele Gomez, interview by Carrie N. Baker, December 29, 2021.

111 "Availability of Telehealth Services for Medication Abortion in the U.S., 2020–2022," Issue Brief (Advancing New Standards in Reproductive Health, June 2023).

112 Katherine Ehrenreich, M. Antonia Biggs, and Daniel Grossman, "Making the Case for Advance Provision of Mifepristone and Misoprostol for Abortion in the United States," *BMJ Sexual & Reproductive Health* 48, no. 4 (October 2022): 238–42, https://doi.org/10.1136/bmjsrh-2021-201321.

113 Carrie N. Baker, "Abortion Pills in Your Medicine Cabinet? Advance Provision Medication to End Early Pregnancies," *Ms.* magazine, December 14, 2021, https://msmagazine.com/2021/12/14/abortion-pill-end-early-pregnancy-at-home/.

114 Baker.

115 M. Antonia Biggs et al., "Support for and Interest in Alternative Models of Medication Abortion Provision among a National Probability Sample of U.S. Women," *Contraception* 99, no. 2 (February 2019): 118–24, https://doi.org/10.1016/j.contraception.2018.10.007.

116 Ehrenreich, Biggs, and Grossman, "Making the Case for Advance Provision of Mifepristone and Misoprostol for Abortion in the United States."

Chapter 4

1 Elizabeth Nash and Lauren Cross, "2021 Is on Track to Become the Most Devastating Antiabortion State Legislative Session in Decades" (New York: Guttmacher Institute, April 2021), https://www.guttmacher.org/article/2021/04/2021-track-become-most-devastating-antiabortion-state-legislative-session-decades.

2 Abigail R. A. Aiken et al., "Demand for Self-Managed Online Telemedicine Abortion in the United States during the Coronavirus Disease 2019 (COVID-19) Pandemic," *Obstetrics & Gynecology* 136, no. 4 (October 2020): 835–37, https://doi.org/10.1097/AOG.0000000000004081.

3 Elisa Wells, interview by Carrie N. Baker, May 15, 2021.

4 S.B. 8, Texas 87th Legislature, 2021–2022, https://legiscan.com/TX/text/SB8/id/2395961.

5 Carrie N. Baker, "Educating Texans on How to Get Abortion Pills Online: 'Your Nearest Provider Is in Your Pocket,'" *Ms.* magazine, August 31, 2021, https://msmagazine.com/2021/08/31/how-to-get-abortion-pills-online-texas/.

6 Baker.

7 Elisa Wells, interview by Carrie N. Baker, August 19, 2021.

8 Elisa Wells, interview by Carrie N. Baker, August 19, 2021.

9 Whole Woman's Health v. Jackson, 594 U.S. ___ (2021), https://www.supremecourt.gov/opinions/20pdf/21a24_8759.pdf.

10 Elisa Wells, interview by Carrie N. Baker, September 25, 2021.

11 Carrie N. Baker, "Texas Law Prohibiting Mailing Abortion Pills Won't Stop Texans Seeking Pills Online," *Ms.* magazine, October 11, 2021, https://msmagazine.com/2021/10/11/texas-mail-abortion-pills-online-plan-c-sb4/.

12 Abigail R. A. Aiken et al., "Association of Texas Senate Bill 8 with Requests for Self-Managed Medication Abortion," *JAMA Network Open* 5, no. 2 (February 25, 2022): e221122, https://doi.org/10.1001/jamanetworkopen.2022.1122.

13 Abigail Aiken, interview by Carrie N. Baker, February 26, 2022.

14 Aiken et al., "Association of Texas Senate Bill 8 with Requests for Self-Managed Medication Abortion."

15 Aiken et al.

16 Aiken et al.

17 Michelle Cohen, interview by Carrie N. Baker, June 8, 2023.

18 Abigail Aiken, interview by Carrie N. Baker, February 26, 2022.

19 Baker, "Texas Law Prohibiting Mailing Abortion Pills Won't Stop Texans Seeking Pills Online."

20 Elisa Wells, interview by Carrie N. Baker, October 9, 2021.

21 Abigail Aiken, interview by Carrie N. Baker, February 26, 2022.

22 Abigail Aiken, interview by Carrie N. Baker, May 25, 2021.

23 Abigail Aiken, interview by Carrie N. Baker, May 25, 2021.

24 Abigail Aiken, interview by Carrie N. Baker, May 25, 2021.

25 Aiken, Starling, and Gomperts, "Factors Associated with Use of an Online Telemedicine Service to Access Self-Managed Medical Abortion in the US."

26 Abigail Aiken, interview by Carrie N. Baker, May 25, 2021.

27 Abigail Aiken, interview by Carrie N. Baker, May 25, 2021.

28 Abigail Aiken, interview by Carrie N. Baker, May 25, 2021.

29 Abigail Aiken et al., "Effectiveness, Safety and Acceptability of No-test Medical Abortion (Termination of Pregnancy) Provided via Telemedicine: A National Cohort Study," *BJOG: An International Journal of Obstetrics & Gynaecology* 128, no. 9 (August 2021): 1464–74, https://doi.org/10.1111/1471-0528.16668.

30 Abigail Aiken, interview by Carrie N. Baker, February 17, 2021.

31 Abigail Aiken et al., "Effectiveness, Safety and Acceptability of No-test Medical Abortion (Termination of Pregnancy) Provided via Telemedicine."

32 Abigail Aiken, interview by Carrie N. Baker, February 17, 2021.

33 Aiken et al., "Effectiveness, Safety and Acceptability of No-test Medical Abortion (Termination of Pregnancy) Provided via Telemedicine."

34 Abigail Aiken, interview by Carrie N. Baker, February 17, 2021.

35 Abigail R. A. Aiken et al., "Demand for Self-Managed Online Telemedicine Abortion in Eight European Countries during the COVID-19 Pandemic: A Regression Discontinuity Analysis," *BMJ Sexual & Reproductive Health* 47, no. 4 (October 2021): 238–45, https://doi.org/10.1136/bmjsrh-2020-200880.

36 Abigail Aiken, interview by Carrie N. Baker, February 17, 2021.

37 Holly A. Anger et al., "Clinical and Service Delivery Implications of Omitting Ultrasound before Medication Abortion Provided via Direct-to-Patient Telemedicine and Mail in the U.S," *Contraception* 104, no. 6 (December 2021): 659–65, https://doi.org/10.1016/j.contraception.2021.07.108; Erica Chong et al., "Expansion of a Direct-to-Patient Telemedicine Abortion Service in the United States and Experience during the COVID-19 Pandemic," *Contraception* 104, no. 1 (July 2021): 43–48, https://doi.org/10.1016/j.contraception.2021.03.019.

38 Ushma D. Upadhyay, Leah R. Koenig, and Karen R. Meckstroth, "Safety and Efficacy of Telehealth Medication Abortions in the US during the COVID-19 Pandemic," *JAMA Network Open* 4, no. 8 (August 24, 2021): e2122320, https://doi.org/10.1001/jamanetworkopen.2021.22320.

39 Ushma Upadhyay, interview by Carrie N. Baker, August 19, 2021.

40 Ushma Upadhyay, interview by Carrie N. Baker, August 19, 2021.

41 Kelly Cleland et al., "Contraception Special Issue on the Mifepristone Risk Evaluation and Mitigation Strategy (REMS)," *Contraception* 104, no. 1 (July 2021): 1–3, https://doi.org/10.1016/j.contraception.2021.05.012.

42 Julia Kaye, Rachel Reeves, and Lorie Chaiten, "The Mifepristone REMS: A Needless and Unlawful Barrier to Care," *Contraception* 104, no. 1 (July 2021): 12–15, https://doi.org/10.1016/j.contraception.2021.04.025.

43 Kirsten Moore, interviewed by Carrie N. Baker, May 10, 2021.

44 "Expressing the Sense of the House of Representatives That Policies Governing Access to Medication Abortion Care in the United States Should Be Equitable and Based on Science," Pub. L. No. H. Res. 589 (2021), https://www.congress.gov/bill/117th-congress/house-resolution/589/cosponsors?r=2&s=3.

45 "Pressley, Maloney, Degette and Lee Announce Resolution in Support of Equitable, Science-Based Access to Medication Abortion Care," Press Release (Office of Congresswoman Ayanna Pressley, August 19, 2021), https://pressley.house.gov/2021/08/19/pressley-maloney-degette-lee-and-pressley-announceresolution-support-equitable/.

46 Daniel Grossman et al., "Medication Abortion with Pharmacist Dispensing of Mifepristone," *Obstetrics & Gynecology* 137, no. 4 (April 2021): 613–22, https://doi.org/10.1097/AOG.0000000000004312.

47 Carrie N. Baker, "FDA Lifts Some Abortion Pill Restrictions, Leaves Others in Place: 'Ignores the Science and Smacks of Political Interference,'" *Ms.* magazine, December 17, 2021, https://msmagazine.com/2021/12/17/fda-abortion-pill-medication-biden-mifepristone/.

48 Baker.

49 Baker.

50 Baker.

51 Baker.

52 Baker.

53 Kathryn Kolbert and Julie F. Kay, *Controlling Women: What We Must Do Now to Save Reproductive Freedom*, 1st ed. (New York: Hachette Books, 2021), 189.

54 Baker, "FDA Lifts Some Abortion Pill Restrictions, Leaves Others in Place: 'Ignores the Science and Smacks of Political Interference.'"

55 Baker.

56 Emily Godfrey, interview by Carrie N. Baker, May 5, 2023.

57 Baker, "FDA Lifts Some Abortion Pill Restrictions, Leaves Others in Place."

58 "Medication Abortion" (Guttmacher Institute, March 2022).

59 Elizabeth Nash, Lauren Cross, and Joerg Dreweke, "2022 State Legislative Sessions: Abortion Bans and Restrictions on Medication Abortion Dominate." (New York: Guttmacher Institute, March 2022).

60 "Potential Legal Flaws in State Restrictions Targeting Mifepristone" (New York: American Civil Liberties Union, 2022), https://www.aclu.org/other/potential-legal-flaws-state-restrictions-targeting-mifepristone.

61 Carrie N. Baker, "Self-Managed Abortion Pill Ads Launch in 250 NYC Subway Stations," *Ms.* magazine, April 15, 2022, https://msmagazine.com/2022/04/15/self-managed-abortion-pill-ads-nyc-subway-plan-c-medication-abortion/.

62 Elisa Wells, interview by Carrie N. Baker, April 13, 2022.

63 Elisa Wells, interview by Carrie N. Baker, April 13, 2022.

64 Elisa Wells, interview by Carrie N. Baker, April 13, 2022.

65 April Lockley, interview by Carrie N. Baker, March 14, 2022.

66 Kara Mailman, interview by Carrie N. Baker, November 28, 2021.

67 Kara Mailman, interview by Carrie N. Baker, November 28, 2021.

68 SASS, Instagram post, September 2, 2021, https://www.instagram.com/p/CTV2IktggMG/?utm_medium=copy_link.

69 Peggy Cooke, interview by Carrie N. Baker, November 28, 2021.

70 Peggy Cooke, interview by Carrie N. Baker, November 28, 2021.

71 Center for Countering Digital Hate, "Petition," accessed November 30, 2021, https://act.counterhate.com/page/89325/petition/1.

72 Reproaction, "Facebook and Instagram: Stop Hiding Abortion Information," accessed November 30, 2021, https://reproaction.org/action/tell-facebook-and-instagram-to-stop-hiding-fact-based-abortion-information/.

73 Carrie N. Baker and Carly Thomsen, "Facebook Profits from Anti-Abortion Misinformation While Suppressing Medically Accurate Abortion Facts," *Ms.* magazine, November 30, 2021, https://msmagazine.com/2021/11/30/facebook-anti-abortion-misinformation-abortion-pill-reversal/.

74 Francine Coeytaux, interview by Carrie N. Baker, April 7, 2023.

75 Elisa Wells, interview by Carrie N. Baker, March 29, 2022.

76 Beverly Winikoff, interview by Carrie N. Baker, March 29, 2022.

77 Carrie N. Baker, "Is It Legal to Order Abortion Pills Online?," *Ms.* magazine, December 22, 2021, https://msmagazine.com/2021/12/22/is-it-legal-to-order-medication-abortion-pills-online/.

78 Layal Liverpool, "'Abortion Tests' Developed in Poland Spark Concern," *Nature*, October 11, 2023, https://doi.org/10.1038/d41586-023-03129-9.

79 Nash and Cross, "2021 Is on Track to Become the Most Devastating Antiabortion State Legislative Session in Decades."

80 US Food and Drug Administration, "Is It Legal for Me to Personally Import Drugs?" (FDA, June 28, 2021), https://www.fda.gov/about-fda/fda-basics/it-legal-me-personally-import-drugs.

81 Elisa Wells, interview by Carrie N. Baker, September 25, 2021.

82 If/When/How: Lawyering for Reproductive Justice, "Fulfilling Roe's Promise: 2019 Update."

83 McCormack v. Hiedeman, Nos. 11-36010 (9th Circuit, September 11, 2012), https://caselaw.findlaw.com/us-9th-circuit/1611625.html.

84 Paltrow, "*Roe v Wade* and the New Jane Crow."

85 Carrie N. Baker, "New Repro Legal Defense Fund Supports Self-Managed Abortion," *Ms.* magazine, June 16, 2021, https://msmagazine.com/2021/06/16/repro-legal-defense-fund-if-when-how-supports-self-managed-abortion-medication-abortion-pill-lawyer-lawsuit/.

86 Tina Vásquez, "American Bar Association's Resolution Opposes Criminalization of Abortion or Miscarriage," *Prism*, March 9, 2021, https://prismreports.org/2021/03/09/american-bar-associations-resolution-opposes-criminalization-of-abortion-or-miscarriage/.

87 Baker, "New Repro Legal Defense Fund Supports Self-Managed Abortion."

88 American College of Obstetricians and Gynecologists, "Opposition to Criminalization of Individuals during Pregnancy and the Postpartum Period, Statement of Policy" (Washington, DC: American College of Obstetricians and Gynecologists, 2020), https://www.acog.org/clinical-information/policy-and-posit

ion-statements/statements-of-policy/2020/opposition-criminalization-of-individuals-pregnancy-and-postpartum-period.

89 Elisa Wells, interview by Carrie N. Baker, December 19, 2021.

90 Pamela Merritt, interview by Carrie N. Baker, June 14, 2023.

91 Carrie N. Baker, "Woman Arrested for Abortion in Texas, Held on Half-Million-Dollar Bond: 'This Arrest Is Inhumane,'" *Ms.* magazine, April 9, 2022, https://msmagazine.com/2022/04/09/woman-arrested-abortion-texas-mexico-murder-lizelle-herrera/.

92 Carrie N. Baker, "Texas Woman Lizelle Herrera's Arrest Foreshadows Post-Roe Future," *Ms.* magazine, April 16, 2022, https://msmagazine.com/2022/04/16/texas-woman-lizelle-herrera-arrest-murder-roe-v-wade-abortion/.

93 Stephen Vladeck, interview by Carrie N. Baker, April 7, 2022.

94 Lynn Paltrow, interview by Carrie N. Baker, April 14, 2022.

95 Lynn Paltrow, interview by Carrie N. Baker, April 14, 2022.

96 Paltrow, "*Roe v Wade* and the New Jane Crow."

97 Lynn Paltrow, interview by Carrie N. Baker, April 14, 2022.

98 Lynn Paltrow, interview by Carrie N. Baker, April 14, 2022.

99 Lynn Paltrow, interview by Carrie N. Baker, April 14, 2022.

100 Stephen Vladeck, interview by Carrie N. Baker, April 13, 2022.

101 "Abortion in America: How Legislative Overreach Is Turning Reproductive Rights into Criminal Wrongs" (Washington, DC: National Association of Criminal Defense Lawyers, 2021), 2, https://www.nacdl.org/getattachment/ce0899a0-3588-42d0-b351-23b9790f3bb8/abortion-in-america-how-legislative-overreach-is-turning-reproductive-rights-into-criminal-wrongs.pdf.

102 Elisa Wells, interview by Carrie N. Baker, June 1, 2022.

103 Elisa Wells, interview by Carrie N. Baker, June 1, 2022.

104 Abrams, "Meet the Pharmacist Expanding Access to Medication Abortion."

105 Jessica Sarah Flaum, interview by Carrie N. Baker, May 25, 2022; Carrie N. Baker, "'Abortion: Add to Cart' Envisions a Future for Safe Self-Managed Abortion Post-Roe," *Ms.* magazine, May 27, 2022, https://msmagazine.com/2022/05/24/abortion-add-to-cart-documentary-film-abortion-pills/.

106 Carrie N. Baker, "Abortion on Our Own Terms: 'Supreme Court Justices Can't Put Abortion Pills Back in the Bottle,'" *Ms.* magazine, June 16, 2022, https://msmagazine.com/2022/06/16/abortion-pills-abortion-on-our-own-terms-supreme-court/.

107 Erin Matson, interview by Carrie N. Baker, June 13, 2022.

108 Erin Matson, interview by Carrie N. Baker, June 13, 2022.

109 Sylvia Ghazarian, interview by Carrie N. Baker, May 27, 2022.

110 Sylvia Ghazarian, interview by Carrie N. Baker, May 27, 2022.

111 Upadhyay et al., "Outcomes and Safety of History-Based Screening for Medication Abortion."

112 Aiken et al., "Safety and Effectiveness of Self-Managed Medication Abortion Provided Using Online Telemedicine in the United States."

113 World Health Organization, "Abortion Care Guidance."

114 M. Antonia Biggs et al., "A Cross-Sectional Survey of U.S. Abortion Patients' Interest in Obtaining Medication Abortion over the Counter," *Contraception* 109 (May 2022): 25–31, https://doi.org/10.1016/j.contraception.2022.01.010.

115 Antonia Biggs, interview by Carrie N. Baker, February 7, 2022.

116 Karlin et al., "Greasing the Wheels."

117 Biggs et al., "A Cross-Sectional Survey of U.S. Abortion Patients' Interest in Obtaining Medication Abortion over the Counter."

118 Antonio Biggs, interview by Carrie N. Baker, February 7, 2022.

119 Antonio Biggs, interview by Carrie N. Baker, February 7, 2022.

120 Antonio Biggs, interview by Carrie N. Baker, February 7, 2022.

Chapter 5

1 Linda Prine, interview by Carrie N. Baker, January 17, 2023.

2 Harmeet Kaur, "Why Tribal Lands Are Unlikely to Become Abortion Sanctuaries," *CNN*, June 26, 2022, https://www.cnn.com/2022/06/26/us/tribal-lands-abortion-safe-havens-roe-cec/index.html.

3 The White House, "Executive Order on Protecting Access to Reproductive Healthcare Services," The White House, July 8, 2022, https://www.whitehouse.gov/briefing-room/presidential-actions/2022/07/08/executive-order-on-protecting-access-to-reproductive-healthcare-services/.

4 Office for Civil Rights (OCR), "HHS Issues Guidance to the Nation's Retail Pharmacies Clarifying Their Obligations to Ensure Access to Comprehensive Reproductive Health Care Services," HHS.gov, July 13, 2022, https://www.hhs.gov/about/news/2022/07/13/hhs-issues-guidance-nations-retail-pharmacies-clarifying-their-obligations-ensure-access-comprehensive-reproductive-health-care-services.html.

5 The White House, "Executive Order on Securing Access to Reproductive and Other Healthcare Services," The White House, August 3, 2022, https://www.whitehouse.gov/briefing-room/presidential-actions/2022/08/03/executive-order-on-securing-access-to-reproductive-and-other-healthcare-services/.

6 "#WeCount Report April to August 2022 Findings" (Society of Family Planning, October 28, 2022), https://doi.org/10.46621/UKAI6324.

7 Aatish Bhatia, Claire Cain Miller, and Margot Sanger-Katz, "A Surge of Overseas Abortion Pills Blunted the Effects of State Abortion Bans," *The New York Times*, November 1, 2022, sec. The Upshot, https://www.nytimes.com/2022/11/01/upshot/abortion-pills-mail-overseas.html.

8 Abigail R. A. Aiken et al., "Requests for Self-Managed Medication Abortion Provided Using Online Telemedicine in 30 US States before and after the *Dobbs v Jackson Women's Health Organization* Decision," *JAMA* 328, no. 17 (November 1, 2022): 1768, https://doi.org/10.1001/jama.2022.18865.

9 Carrie N. Baker, "Self-Managed Abortions Soar Post-Dobbs," *Ms.* magazine, November 7, 2022, https://msmagazine.com/2022/11/07/abortion-pills-roe-v-wade-dobbs/.

10 Charlotte Alter, "This Group Wants to Teach You How to Get Abortions Even Where They're Banned," *Time*, December 9, 2022, https://time.com/6239573/mayday-health-abortion-pills/.

11 Baker, "Self-Managed Abortions Soar Post-Dobbs."

12 Aiken et al., "Requests for Self-Managed Medication Abortion Provided Using Online Telemedicine in 30 US States before and after the *Dobbs v Jackson Women's Health Organization* Decision."

13 Abigail R.A. Aiken, interviewed by Carrie N. Baker, November 5, 2022.

14 Carrie N. Baker, "Mexican Telehealth Abortion Provider Now Serves U.S. Women: 'We Are Here for You!'," *Ms.* magazine, July 26, 2022, https://msmagazine.com/2022/07/26/mexico-abortion-pills-us-border-telefem-telehealth/.

15 Paula Rita Rivera, interviewed by Carrie N. Baker, July 24, 2022.

16 Carrie N. Baker, "What Clinicians Want You to Know about Getting Abortion Pills in Anti-Abortion States," *Ms.* magazine, March 14, 2023.

17 Baker.

18 Baker.

19 Baker.

20 Baker.

21 Baker.

22 Baker.

23 Laura Huss, Farah Diaz-Tello, and Goleen Samari, "Self-Care, Criminalized: August 2022 Preliminary Findings" (If/When/How: Lawyering for Reproductive Justice, 2022), https://www.ifwhenhow.org/download/?key=vL43kFFaxm.

24 Purvaja S. Kavattur et al., "The Rise of Pregnancy Criminalization: A Pregnancy Justice Report" (Washington, DC: Pregnancy Justice, September 2023), https://www.pregnancyjusticeus.org/rise-of-pregnancy-criminalization-report/.

25 Linda Prine, interview by Carrie N. Baker, March 12, 2023.

26 Eleanor Klibanoff, "Three Texas Women Are Sued for Wrongful Death after Allegedly Helping Friend Obtain Abortion Medication," *The Texas Tribune*, March 10, 2023, https://www.texastribune.org/2023/03/10/texas-abortion-lawsuit/.

27 Poppy Noor, "Republicans Push Wave of Bills That Would Bring Homicide Charges for Abortion," *The Guardian*, March 10, 2023, sec. US news, https://www.theguardian.com/us-news/2023/mar/10/republican-wave-state-bills-homicide-charges.

28 Rebecca Wang, interview by Carrie N. Baker, March 13, 2023.

29 Patrick Adams, "Opinion | In Poland, Testing Women for Abortion Drugs Is a Reality. It Could Happen Here," *The New York Times*, September 14, 2023, sec. Opinion, https://www.nytimes.com/2023/09/14/opinion/abortion-pills-testing-poland.html; Liverpool, "'Abortion Tests' Developed in Poland Spark Concern."

30 Ibis Reproductive Health, "Feminist Medication Abortion Accompaniment 101" (Cambridge, MA, November 2021), https://www.ibisreproductivehealth.org/sites/default/files/files/publications/Abortion%20accompaniment%20101.pdf.

31 Heidi Moseson et al., "Effectiveness of Self-Managed Medication Abortion with Accompaniment Support in Argentina and Nigeria (SAFE): A Prospective, Observational Cohort Study and Non-inferiority Analysis with Historical Controls," *The Lancet Global Health* 10, no. 1 (January 2022): e105–13, https://doi.org/10.1016/S2214-109X(21)00461-7; Caitlin Gerdts et al., "Effect of a Smartphone Intervention on Self-Managed Medication Abortion Experiences among Safe-Abortion Hotline Clients in Indonesia: A Randomized Controlled Trial," *International Journal of Gynaecology and Obstetrics: The Official Organ of the International Federation of Gynaecology and Obstetrics* 149, no. 1 (April 2020): 48–55, https://doi.org/10.1002/ijgo.13086.

32 Heidi Moseson et al., "Effectiveness of Self-Managed Medication Abortion between 13 and 24 Weeks Gestation: A Retrospective Review of Case Records from Accompaniment Groups in Argentina, Chile, and Ecuador," *Contraception* 102, no. 2 (August 2020): 91–98, https://doi.org/10.1016/j.contraception.2020.04.015; Caitlin Gerdts et al., "Second-Trimester Medication Abortion outside the Clinic Setting: An Analysis of Electronic Client Records from a Safe Abortion Hotline in Indonesia," *BMJ Sexual & Reproductive Health* 44, no. 4 (July 18, 2018): 286–91, https://doi.org/10.1136/bmjsrh-2018-200102.

33 "Red Compañera," accessed November 12, 2023, https://redcompafeminista.org/; "MAMA Network," accessed November 12, 2023, https://mamanetwork.org/.

34 Lara Islinger, interview with Carrie N. Baker, November 12, 2023.

35 Ibis Reproductive Health, "Feminist Medication Abortion Accompaniment 101."

36 Stephania Taladrid, "The Post-Roe Abortion Underground," *The New Yorker*, October 10, 2022, https://www.newyorker.com/magazine/2022/10/17/the-post-roe-abortion-underground.

37 "Find Abortion Pill Access in Your State | Plan C," accessed April 18, 2023, https://www.plancpills.org/find-pills.

38 Francine Coeytaux, interviewed by Carrie N. Baker, April 11, 2023.

39 "An Act Expanding Protections for Reproductive and Gender Affirming Care," Chapter 127 of the Acts of 2022, https://malegislature.gov/Laws/SessionLaws/Acts/2022/Chapter127.

40 Massachusetts General Assembly, "An Act Expanding Protections for Reproductive and Gender-Affirming Care" (2022), https://malegislature.gov/Laws/SessionLaws/Acts/2022/Chapter127.

41 Carrie N. Baker, "Groundbreaking Massachusetts Abortion Law Repeals Parental Consent for Older Teens," *Ms.* magazine, December 29, 2020, https://msmagazine.com/2020/12/29/massachusetts-abortion-law-roe-act/.

42 David S. Cohen, Greer Donley, and Rachel Rebouché, "The New Abortion Battleground," *Columbia Law Review* 123, no. 1 (2022): 1–100, 35, 82.

43 Elisa Wells, interview by Carrie N. Baker, May 31, 2023.

44 The White House, "Readout of Vice President Kamala Harris's Meeting with Governor Baker, Massachusetts State Legislators, and Advocates on Reproductive Rights," The White House, August 5,

2022, https://www.whitehouse.gov/briefing-room/statements-releases/2022/08/04/readout-of-vice-president-kamala-harriss-meeting-with-governor-baker-massachusetts-state-legislators-and-advocates-on-reproductive-rights/.

45 Linda Prine, interview by Carrie N. Baker, August 16, 2022.

46 "SB-345 Health Care Services: Legally Protected Health Care Activities," accessed April 18, 2023, https://leginfo.legislature.ca.gov/faces/billNavClient.xhtml?bill_id=202320240SB345.

47 Carrie N. Baker, "New York Shield Law Would Protect Clinicians Mailing Abortion Pills to Patients in Red States," *Ms.* magazine, January 19, 2023, https://msmagazine.com/2023/01/19/new-york-shield-law-abortion-pills/.

48 Linda Prine, interview by Carrie N. Baker, January 17, 2023.

49 "Tell NYS Legislators to Protect Telemab," Reproductive Health Access Project, accessed April 18, 2023, https://www.reproductiveaccess.org/get-involved/12-22-nys-legislator-letter/.

50 Linda Prine, interview by Carrie N. Baker, January 17, 2023.

51 Bazelon, "Risking Everything to Offer Abortions across State Lines," 28.

52 Linda Prine, interview by Carrie N. Baker, January 17, 2023.

53 Linda Prine, interview by Carrie N. Baker, January 17, 2023.

54 Elisa Wells, interview by Carrie N. Baker, May 31, 2023.

55 "An Act Relating to Protecting Access to Reproductive Health Care Services and Gender-Affirming Treatment in Washington State, 68th Legislature" (2023), https://legiscan.com/WA/text/HB1469/2023.

56 Francine Coeytaux, interview by Carrie N. Baker, May 2, 2023.

57 Elisa Wells, interview by Carrie N. Baker, May 31, 2023.

58 Pamela Belluck and Emily Bazelon, "New York Passes Bill to Shield Abortion Providers Sending Pills into States with Bans," *The New York Times*, June 20, 2023, sec. Health, https://www.nytimes.com/2023/06/20/health/abortion-shield-law-new-york.html.

59 Carrie N. Baker, "California Becomes the Sixth State to Legally Protect Telehealth Abortion and Gender-Care Providers," *Ms.* magazine, October 3, 2023, https://msmagazine.com/2023/10/03/california-shield-law-telehealth-abortion-pills-trans-gender-affirming-care/.

60 Caroline Kitchener et al., "A Fragile New Phase of Abortion in America," *The Washington Post*, accessed June 23, 2023, https://www.washingtonpost.com/politics/interactive/2023/roe-v-wade-ruling-one-year-anniversary/.

61 "Blue-State Doctors Launch Abortion Pill Pipeline into States with Bans," Washington Post, July 20, 2023, https://www.washingtonpost.com/politics/2023/07/19/doctors-northeast-launch-abortion-pill-pipeline-into-states-with-bans/.

62 Anonymous, interview by Carrie N. Baker, July 20, 2023.

63 Julie F. Kay, interview by Carrie N. Baker, July 20, 2023.

64 Elisa Wells, interview by Carrie N. Baker, May 31, 2023. Abuzz Health at https://www.abuzzhealth.com/.

65 Michelle Cohen, interview by Carrie N. Baker, June 8, 2023.

66 Julie F. Kay, email to Carrie N. Baker, October 2, 2023.

67 Hey Jane, "One Year since Dobbs: How Medication Abortion Has Changed Post-Roe | Hey Jane," accessed June 21, 2023, https://www.heyjane.com/articles/abortion-changes-post-roe.

68 "Medication Abortion Access Project," Cambridge Reproductive Health Consultants, accessed October 4, 2023, https://www.cambridgereproductivehealthconsultants.org/map.

69 Maggie Carpenter, interview with Carrie N. Baker, October 10, 2023.

70 Maggie Carpenter, interview with Carrie N. Baker, October 10, 2023.

71 Cohen, Donley, and Rebouché, "The New Abortion Battleground," 3.

72 Bazelon, "Risking Everything to Offer Abortions across State Lines," 30.

73 Julie F. Kay, interview by Carrie N. Baker, July 20, 2023.

74 Julie F. Kay, interview by Carrie N. Baker, July 20, 2023.

75 Julie F. Kay, interview by Carrie N. Baker, July 20, 2023.

76 Cohen, Donley, and Rebouché, "The New Abortion Battleground," 44–45.

77 The Associated Press, "Judge Temporarily Blocks Wyoming's 1st-in-the-Nation Abortion Pill Ban," *NPR*, June 23, 2023, sec. National, https://www.npr.org/2023/06/23/1183924567/judge-temporarily-blocks-wyomings-1st-in-the-nation-abortion-pill-ban.

78 "Medication Abortion," Guttmacher Institute, June 1, 2023, https://www.guttmacher.org/state-policy/explore/medication-abortion.

79 Greer Donley, interview by Carrie N. Baker, June 1, 2022.

80 Zogenix, Inc. v. Patrick, Civil Action No. 14-11689-RWZ (July 8, 2014).

81 Cohen, Donley, and Rebouché, "The New Abortion Battleground," 43–59; Rachel Rebouché, interview by Carrie N. Baker, May 31, 2022.

82 "Attorney General Merrick B. Garland Statement on Supreme Court Ruling in Dobbs v. Jackson Women's Health Organization, Department of Justice, Office of Public Affairs," June 24, 2022, https://www.justice.gov/opa/pr/attorney-general-merrick-b-garland-statement-supreme-court-ruling-dobbs-v-jackson-women-s.

83 GenBioPro, Inc. v. Dobbs, No. 3:2020cv00652, accessed April 25, 2023.

84 GenBioPro v. Sorsaia and Morrisey, No. 2:23-cv-11111 (US District Court for the Southern District of West Virginia, Huntington Division January 25, 2023).

85 Carrie N. Baker, "Two New Lawsuits Challenge State Restrictions on Abortion Pill Access, Arguing Federal Law Preempts State Laws," *Ms.* magazine, January 25, 2023, https://msmagazine.com/2023/01/25/lawsuits-state-law-abortion-pill-federal-fda/.

86 GenBioPro v. Raynes and Morrisey, Civil Action No.: 3:23-cv-00058 (S.D. West Va., 2023).

87 Baker, "Two New Lawsuits Challenge State Restrictions on Abortion Pill Access, Arguing Federal Law Preempts State Laws."

88 Baker.

89 Amy Friedrich-Karnik, Emma Stoskopf-Ehrlich, and Rachel K. Jones, "Medication Abortion within and outside the Formal US Health Care System: What You Need to Know," Guttmacher Institute, February 2024, https://www.guttmacher.org/2024/02/medication-abortion-within-and-outside-formal-us-health-care-system-what-you-need-know.

90 Memorandum and Order, Amy Bryant v. Joshua H. Stein, 1:23-CV-77, United States District Court for the Middle District of North Carolina, April 30, 2024.

91 Emails to author from Kirsten Moore and Francine Coeytaux, May 1, 2024.

92 Gutierrez, "Abortion Medication to Be Available at California's College Health Centers under New Law."

93 Carrie N. Baker, "Increasing Gender Equity through Abortion Pills on Campus," *Ms.* magazine, July 7, 2021, https://msmagazine.com/2021/07/07/abortion-pill-college-campus-university-massachusetts/.

94 Carrie N. Baker and Julia Mathis, "Barriers to Medication Abortion among Massachusetts Public University Students," *Contraception* 109 (May 2022): 32–36, https://doi.org/10.1016/j.contraception.2021.12.010.

95 Tessa Holtzman et al., "Reproductive Health and Community College Students: Building Momentum toward Holistic Approaches to Student Success," *IWPR* (blog), November 4, 2019, https://iwpr.org/media/in-the-lead/reproductive-health-and-community-college-student-success/; Mary Prentice, Chelsey Storin, and Gail Robinson, "Make It Personal: How Pregnancy Planning and Prevention Help Students Complete College" (Washington, DC: American Association of Community Colleges, 2012); Lawrence B. Finer et al., "Reasons U.S. Women Have Abortions: Quantitative and Qualitative Perspectives," *Perspectives on Sexual and Reproductive Health* 37 (September 1, 2005): 110–18.

96 Carrie N. Baker, "Groundbreaking Massachusetts Law Protects Telemedicine Abortion Providers Serving Patients Located in States Banning Abortion," *Ms.* magazine, August 18, 2022, https://msmagazine.com/2022/08/18/massachusetts-abortion-law/.

97 Carrie N. Baker, "Students Rally for Medication Abortion at University Health Centers in N.Y.: 'Direct, Unfettered and Accessible,'" *Ms.* magazine, December 21, 2022, https://msmagazine.com/2022/12/21/abortion-pills-new-york-college-university-health/.

98 Baker.
99 Baker.
100 Baker.
101 Baker.
102 Baker.
103 Baker.
104 Kayla Bamberger, "New York Takes Steps to Assure Access to Abortion Pills on Public College Campuses," New York Daily News, April 28, 2023, https://www.nydailynews.com/new-york/education/ny-new-york-posed-to-offer-abortion-pills-on-public-college-campuses-20230428-ducrtnlwwbdy5ipqsdbjbypda4-story.html.
105 Baker, "Students Rally for Medication Abortion at University Health Centers in N.Y.: 'Direct, Unfettered and Accessible.'"
106 "On Eve of Dobbs Decision Anniversary, Governor Hochul Signs Legislation Strengthening Access to Reproductive Health Care," June 23, 2023, https://www.governor.ny.gov/news/eve-dobbs-decision-anniversary-governor-hochul-signs-legislation-strengthening-access.
107 Carrie N. Baker, "Citizen Petition to FDA Requests Lifting Restrictions on Mifepristone for Miscarriage Use," Ms. magazine, October 20, 2022, https://msmagazine.com/2022/10/20/fda-mifepristone-miscarriage/.
108 Kirsten Moore, interview by Carrie N. Baker, October 18, 2022.
109 Schreiber et al., "Mifepristone Pretreatment for the Medical Management of Early Pregnancy Loss."
110 "Alabama HB261 | TrackBill," accessed April 18, 2023, https://trackbill.com/bill/alabama-house-bill-261-abortion-ban-non-surgical-chemical-abortions-criminal-penalties-alabama-chemical-abortion-prohibition-act/2217015/; "HB2811 Unlawful Abortion Medication, Arizona State Legislature" (2022), https://www.azleg.gov/legtext/55leg/2r/bills/hb2811p.htm.
111 Carrie N. Baker, "Citizen Petition to FDA Requests Lifting Restrictions on Mifepristone for Miscarriage Use," Ms. magazine, October 20, 2022, https://msmagazine.com/2022/10/20/fda-mifepristone-miscarriage/.
112 Kirsten Moore, interview by Carrie N. Baker, October 18, 2022.
113 Kirsten Moore, interview by Carrie N. Baker, October 18, 2022.
114 Danielle Calloway, Debra B. Stulberg, and Elizabeth Janiak, "Mifepristone Restrictions and Primary Care: Breaking the Cycle of Stigma through a Learning Collaborative Model in the United States," Contraception 104, no. 1 (July 2021): 24–28, https://doi.org/10.1016/j.contraception.2021.04.002; Sara Neill, Alisa Goldberg, and Elizabeth Janiak, "Medication Management of Early Pregnancy Loss: The Impact of the U.S. Food and Drug Administration Risk Evaluation and Mitigation Strategy [A289]," Obstetrics & Gynecology 139 (May 2022): 83S, https://doi.org/10.1097/01.AOG.0000825716.77939.40.
115 ACOG et al., "Citizen Petition to Lauren Roth, Associate Commissioner for Policy, U.S. Food and Drug Administration," October 4, 2022, https://emaaproject.org/wp-content/uploads/2022/10/Citizen-Petition-from-the-American-College-of-Obstetrician-and-Gynecologists-et-al-10.3.22-EMAA-website.pdf.
116 Kirsten Moore, interview by Carrie N. Baker, October 18, 2022.
117 Patritzia Cavazzoni, "Agency Response Letter from FDA CDER to American College of Obstetricians and Gynecologists," January 5, 2023, https://www.regulations.gov/document/FDA-2022-P-2425-0003.
118 "Open Letter to the Senior Leadership and Board of Directors of Danco Laboratories, LLC from Senators Mazie K. Hirono, Margaret Wood Hassan, Elizabeth Warren, Richard Blumenthal, Jeanne Shaheen, Ron Wyden, Kirsten Gillibrand and Alex Padilla," February 1, 2023, https://www.hirono.senate.gov/imo/media/doc/2023.02.01_FINAL_Miscarriage%20Management%20Mifepristone%20Label.pdf.
119 "Open Letter to the Senior Leadership and Board of Directors of Danco Laboratories, LLC from Senators Mazie K. Hirono, Margaret Wood Hassan, Elizabeth Warren, Richard Blumenthal, Jeanne Shaheen, Ron Wyden, Kirsten Gillibrand and Alex Padilla."

120 Elise W. Boos et al., "Trends in the Use of Mifepristone for Medical Management of Early Pregnancy Loss from 2016 to 2020," *JAMA* 330, no. 8 (August 22, 2023): 766–68, https://doi.org/10.1001/jama.2023.13628.

121 Kirsten Moore, interview by Carrie N. Baker, February 1, 2023.

122 Patritzia Cavazzoni, "Letter from Director of the Center for Drug Evaluation and Research of the U.S. Food and Drug Administration to Graham Chelius of the Society of Family Planning," December 16, 2021.

123 Kirsten Moore, interview by Carrie N. Baker, January 4, 2023.

124 Carrie N. Baker, "FDA Allows Pharmacies to Sell Abortion Pills—but Requires Unnecessary and Burdensome Certification Process," *Ms.* magazine, January 6, 2023, https://msmagazine.com/2023/01/06/fda-pharmacies-abortion-pills/.

125 Kirsten Moore, interview by Carrie N. Baker, January 4, 2023.

126 Baker, "FDA Allows Pharmacies to Sell Abortion Pills—but Requires Unnecessary and Burdensome Certification Process."

127 Carrie N. Baker, "Anti-Abortion Groups Try to Intimidate Pharmacies Planning to Dispense Abortion Pills," *Ms.* magazine, January 31, 2023, https://msmagazine.com/2023/01/31/anti-abortion-protest-pharmacies-abortion-pills/.

128 duVergne Gaines, interview by Carrie N. Baker, January 29, 2023.

129 Baker, "Anti-Abortion Groups Try to Intimidate Pharmacies Planning to Dispense Abortion Pills."

130 The White House, "Memorandum on Further Efforts to Protect Access to Reproductive Healthcare Services," The White House, January 22, 2023, https://www.whitehouse.gov/briefing-room/presidential-actions/2023/01/22/memorandum-on-further-efforts-to-protect-access-to-reproductive-healthcare-services/.

131 duVergne Gaines, interview by Carrie N. Baker, January 29, 2023.

132 Carrie N. Baker, "After Backlash, Walgreens Re-pledges to Sell Abortion Pill Mifepristone," *Ms.* magazine, March 3, 2023, https://msmagazine.com/2023/03/03/fda-pharmacies-abortion-pills/.

133 Baker.

134 Carrie N. Baker, "Brick-and-Mortar Pharmacies Begin Dispensing Abortion Pills across the U.S.," *Ms.* magazine, October 11, 2023, https://msmagazine.com/2023/10/11/pharmacies-abortion-pill-mifepristone/.

135 Caroline Lewis, "NYC's Public Hospitals to Offer Abortion Pills via Mail and Telehealth," Gothamist, October 2, 2023, https://gothamist.com/news/nyc-public-hospitals-to-offer-abortion-pills-via-telehealth-despite-uncertainty-in-courts.

136 As of July 11, 2023, AccessMA served Alabama, all US Territories, Louisiana, Missouri, Texas, Wisconsin, Utah; WeSaveUs served Indiana, Kentucky, Ohio; IdahoAccess served Idaho, Nebraska, North and South Dakota; ARTogether served Arkansas; and OKAccess served Oklahoma.

137 Anonymous, interview by Carrie N. Baker, July 11, 2023.

138 In July of 2023, Las Libres served Georgia, Mississippi, North Carolina, Puerto Rico, South Carolina, Tennessee, and West Virginia.

139 Alhelí Calderón-Villarreal et al., "Accompaniment on the Edge: What Can the US Learn from Latin America about Contested Abortion Care?," ed. Julia Robinson, *PLOS Global Public Health* 3, no. 5 (May 22, 2023): e0001922, https://doi.org/10.1371/journal.pgph.0001922.

140 Decca Muldowney, "Inside the Secretive Network of Abortion Pill Vigilantes," *The Daily Beast*, May 23, 2023, sec. us-news, https://www.thedailybeast.com/abortion-pill-vigilantes-are-operating-a-covert-network-from-mexico-to-republican-states.

141 Lorena Ríos and Daniela Dib, "How Feminist Groups in Mexico Are Aiding Abortion Seekers in the U.S.," Rest of World, May 8, 2023, https://restofworld.org/2023/mexican-women-help-us-abortion-seekers/. Las Libres served Georgia, Mississippi, North Carolina, Puerto Rico, South Carolina, Tennessee, and West Virginia.

142 Alhelí Calderón-Villarreal et al., "Accompaniment on the Edge: What Can the US Learn from Latin America about Contested Abortion Care?," ed. Julia Robinson, *PLOS Global Public Health* 3, no. 5 (May 22, 2023): e0001922, https://doi.org/10.1371/journal.pgph.0001922.

143 Lara Islinger, interview with Carrie N. Baker, November 13, 2023.
144 Lara Islinger, interview with Carrie N. Baker, November 11, 2023.
145 Lara Islinger, interview with Carrie N. Baker, November 11, 2023.
146 Email from Red State Access, October 19, 2023 (on file with author).
147 Pam Belluck, "Religious Freedom Arguments Underpin Wave of Challenges to Abortion Bans," *The New York Times*, June 28, 2023, sec. Health, https://www.nytimes.com/2023/06/28/health/abortion-religious-freedom.html.
148 Allison McCann, "Inside the Online Market for Overseas Abortion Pills," *The New York Times*, April 13, 2023, sec. U.S., https://www.nytimes.com/interactive/2023/04/13/us/abortion-pill-order-online-mifepristone.html.
149 Elisa Wells, interview by Carrie N. Baker, July 13, 2023.
150 Elisa Wells, interview by Carrie N. Baker, July 13, 2023.
151 Elisa Wells, interview by Carrie N. Baker, July 13, 2023. These companies were located in a range of countries, including the Canada, UK, Russia, and the United States.
152 Anonymous, interview by Carrie N. Baker, July 14, 2023.
153 Elisa Wells, interview by Carrie N. Baker, May 24, 2023.
154 Francine Coeytaux, interview by Carrie N. Baker, May 23, 2023.
155 Allison McCann, "Inside the Online Market for Overseas Abortion Pills," *The New York Times*, April 13, 2023, sec. U.S., https://www.nytimes.com/interactive/2023/04/13/us/abortion-pill-order-online-mifepristone.html.
156 Susan Yanow, interview by Carrie N. Baker, May 25, 2023.
157 Kitchener et al., "A Fragile New Phase of Abortion in America."
158 Michelle Cohen, interview by Carrie N. Baker, June 8, 2023.
159 Pamela Merritt, interview by Carrie N. Baker, June 14, 2023.
160 Pamela Merritt, interview by Carrie N. Baker, June 14, 2023.
161 Pamela Merritt, interview by Carrie N. Baker, June 14, 2023.
162 Pamela Merritt, interview by Carrie N. Baker, June 14, 2023.
163 Pamela Merritt, interview by Carrie N. Baker, June 14, 2023.
164 "#WeCount Report April 2022 to June 2023" (The Society of Family Planning, October 24, 2023), https://doi.org/10.46621/218569qkgmbl.
165 Leah R. Koenig et al., "The Role of Telehealth in Promoting Equitable Abortion Access in the United States: Spatial Analysis," *JMIR Public Health and Surveillance* 9, no. 1 (November 7, 2023): e45671, https://doi.org/10.2196/45671.
166 Michelle Cohen, interview by Carrie N. Baker, June 8, 2023.
167 "The Issue of Tissue | Myanetwork," accessed April 18, 2023, https://myanetwork.org/the-issue-of-tissue/.
168 Michele Gomez, interviewed by Carrie N. Baker, November 2, 2022.
169 Michele Gomez, interviewed by Carrie N. Baker, November 2, 2022.
170 Michele Gomez, interviewed by Carrie N. Baker, November 2, 2022.
171 Michele Gomez, interviewed by Carrie N. Baker, November 2, 2022.
172 "The Issue of Tissue | Myanetwork."
173 @auntiekilljoy, #greenscreen they need to show these images at every political debate about abortion #feminism #abortion #fyp ♫ original sound – Jessica Valenti; @whitneywithheart Replying to @this.is.my.brain.69 ♫ Cornfield Chase – Dorian Marko.
174 Michele Gomez, interviewed by Carrie N. Baker, November 2, 2022.
175 Mary Ann Castle et al., "Listening and Learning from Women about Mifepristone: Implications for Counseling and Health Education," *Women's Health Issues* 5, no. 3 (September 1995): 132–33, https://doi.org/10.1016/1049-3867(95)00044-5.
176 Teresa DePiñeres, interviewed by Carrie N. Baker, October 18, 2022.
177 Wendy R. Sheldon et al., "Exploring Potential Interest in Missed Period Pills in Two US States," *Contraception* 102, no. 6 (December 2020): 414–20, https://doi.org/10.1016/j.contraception.2020.08.014.

178 Teresa DePiñeres, interviewed by Carrie N. Baker, October 18, 2022.

179 Sheldon et al., "Exploring Potential Interest in Missed Period Pills in Two US States," 20.

180 Carrie N. Baker, "Period Pills: Another Option for Fertility Control," *Ms.* magazine, October 20, 2022, https://msmagazine.com/2022/10/20/missed-period-pills-fertility-control/.

181 "National Working Group on Period Pills in the United States," Period Pills, n.d., https://www.periodpills.org/national-working-group-on-period-pills.

182 Baker, "Period Pills."

183 Teresa DePiñeres, interviewed by Carrie N. Baker, October 18, 2022.

184 Carrie N. Baker, "A Once-a-Week Contraceptive Pill, without Side Effects? Yes, Mifepristone," *Ms.* magazine, February 8, 2024, https://msmagazine.com/2024/02/08/contraceptive-pill-mifepristone/; Erin Snodgrass, "Mifepristone in Moldova: Women on Waves Founder Wants to Use the Abortion Pill as Contraception in the Wake of Roe v. Wade Reversal," *Business Insider*, June 30, 2022, https://www.businessinsider.com/women-on-waves-founder-abortion-pill-roe-v-wade-overturned-2022-6.

185 "Medication Abortion among Asian Americans, Native Hawaiians, and Pacific Islanders: Knowledge, Access, and Attitudes" (National Asian Pacific American Women's Forum and Ibis Reproductive Health, May 2023), https://www.napawf.org/assets/download/med-abortion-aanhpi-study.pdf.

186 "About," RHITES, accessed June 10, 2023, https://www.rhites.org/about.

187 Carrie N. Baker and Ramona Flores, "Jex Blackmore Swallows Abortion Pill on Fox News: 'It's Literally This Easy,'" *Ms.* magazine, February 1, 2022, https://msmagazine.com/2022/02/01/jex-blackmore-abortion-pill-live-tv-fox-news-medication-abortion/.

188 Amy Allina, interview by Carrie N. Baker, May 16, 2023.

189 Tracy Droz Tragos, interview by Carrie N. Baker, Sundance Film Festival, Park City, Utah, January 23, 2023.

190 Francine Coeytaux, interview by Carrie N. Baker, Sundance Film Festival, Park City, Utah, January 23, 2023.

191 Elisa Wells, interview by Carrie N. Baker, Sundance Film Festival, Park City, Utah, January 23, 2023.

192 Amy Merrill, interview by Carrie N. Baker, Sundance Film Festival, Park City, Utah, January 23, 2023.

193 Elisa Wells, interview by Carrie N. Baker, Sundance Film Festival, Park City, Utah, January 23, 2023.

194 Amy Merrill, interview by Carrie N. Baker, January 23, 2023.

195 Red State Access, *Instagram*, https://www.instagram.com/p/Cwgk4jPJs6I/.

196 Red State Access, *Instagram*, https://www.instagram.com/p/CkwZoqEJuI9/.

Chapter 6

1 "Tracking the States Where Abortion Is Now Banned," *The New York Times*, April 14, 2023, sec. U.S., https://www.nytimes.com/interactive/2022/us/abortion-laws-roe-v-wade.html.

2 "#WeCount Report April to December 2022 Findings" (Society of Family Planning, April 11, 2023), https://doi.org/10.46621/143729dhcsyz.

3 Paul Dans and Steven Groves, eds., *Mandate for Leadership: The Conservative Promise*, 9th ed. (Heritage Foundation, 2023), 458–59.

4 Shaila Dewan and Sheera Frenkel, "A Mother, a Daughter and an Unusual Abortion Prosecution in Nebraska," *The New York Times*, August 18, 2022, https://www.nytimes.com/2022/08/18/us/abortion-prosecution-nebraska.html. The mother and daughter eventually pled guilty. Susan Rinkunas, "Nebraska Mom Pleads Guilty to Giving Abortion Pills to Her Teen Daughter," *Jezebel*, July 10, 2023, https://jezebel.com/nebraska-mom-pleads-guilty-to-giving-abortion-pills-to-1850621217.

5 "People in Alabama Can Be Prosecuted for Taking Abortion Pills, State Attorney General Says," *CBS News*, January 11, 2023, https://www.cbsnews.com/news/abortion-pills-alabama-prosecution-steve-marshall/.

6 "Texas Lawmakers Neglect Preborn Children in First Legislative Session after Roe, Yet Improve Protections for Vulnerable Patients," May 29, 2023, https://mailchi.mp/texasrighttolife/052923-session-recap?e=9b71165fb9.

7 Lorena O'Neil, "Louisiana Lawmakers Move to Criminalize Possession of Abortion Pills," *Rolling Stone*, May 1, 2024, https://www.rollingstone.com/politics/politics-features/louisiana-criminalize-possession-abortion-pills-1235013039/.

8 Huss, Diaz-Tello, and Samari, "Self-Care, Criminalized: August 2022 Preliminary Findings."

9 Abigail R. A. Aiken et al., "Factors Associated with Knowledge and Experience of Self-Managed Abortion among Patients Seeking Care at 49 US Abortion Clinics," *JAMA Network Open* 6, no. 4 (April 18, 2023): e238701, https://doi.org/10.1001/jamanetworkopen.2023.8701.

10 Mary Szoch, "The Next Abortion Battleground: Chemical Abortion" (Family Research Council, February 2022), https://downloads.frc.org/EF/EF19L05.pdf.

11 American College of Obstetricians and Gynecologists, "Induced Abortion and Breast Cancer Risk," June 2009, https://www.acog.org/clinical/clinical-guidance/committee-opinion/articles/2009/06/induced-abortion-and-breast-cancer-risk.

12 "Restricting Access to Abortion Likely to Lead to Mental Health Harms, APA Asserts," American Psychological Association, accessed April 20, 2023, https://www.apa.org/news/press/releases/2022/05/restricting-abortion-mental-health-harms; Diana Greene Foster, *The Turnaway Study: Ten Years, a Thousand Women, and the Consequences of Having—or Being Denied—an Abortion* (New York: Scribner, 2020), https://www.goodreads.com/book/show/49680209-the-turnaway-study.

13 "Safety and Effectiveness of First-Trimester Medication Abortion in the United States" (Advancing New Standards in Reproductive Health, June 2021), https://www.ansirh.org/sites/default/files/2021-06/medication-abortion-safety_2021_FINAL.pdf.

14 Kristi Hamrick, "SFL Action & SFLA Launch a Campus, State, & Federal Campaign Asking, 'What's In the Water?,'" November 23, 2022, https://studentsforlife.org/2022/11/23/sflaction-sfla-launch-a-campus-state-federal-campaign-asking-whats-in-the-water/.

15 Kristan Hawkins and Hamrick Kristi, "Students for Life Citizen Petition to the FDA," April 19, 2023, https://thisischemicalabortion.com/wp-content/uploads/2023/04/Citizen-Petition-3-ESA-AS-FILED.pdf; Alice Miranda Ollstein, "Anti-abortion Group Launches New Pill Challenge as SCOTUS Mulls Sweeping Restrictions," POLITICO, April 19, 2023, https://www.politico.com/news/2023/04/19/students-for-life-abortion-scotus-00092771.

16 "Crisis Pregnancy Center Map & Finder," CPC Map, accessed June 26, 2023, https://crisispregnancycentermap.com/.

17 Sonya Borrero, Susan Frietsche, and Christine Dehlendorf, "Crisis Pregnancy Centers: Faith Centers Operating in Bad Faith," *Journal of General Internal Medicine* 34, no. 1 (January 1, 2019): 144–45, https://doi.org/10.1007/s11606-018-4703-4.

18 American College of Obstetricians and Gynecologists, "Medication Abortion 'Reversal' Is Not Supported by Science," accessed April 20, 2023, https://www.acog.org/advocacy/facts-are-important/medication-abortion-reversal-is-not-supported-by-science.

19 Daniel Grossman et al., "Continuing Pregnancy after Mifepristone and 'Reversal' of First-Trimester Medical Abortion: A Systematic Review," *Contraception* 92, no. 3 (September 2015): 206–11, https://doi.org/10.1016/j.contraception.2015.06.001.

20 American College of Obstetricians and Gynecologists, "Medication Abortion 'Reversal' Is Not Supported by Science."

21 "Endangering Women for Profit" (Center for Countering Digital Hate, 2021), https://counterhate.com/research/endangering-women-for-profit/.

22 Pamela Merritt, interview by Carrie N. Baker, June 19, 2023.

23 Tara Murta and Jenifer McKenna, "Designed to Deceive: A Study of the Crisis Pregnancy Center Industry in Nine States" (The Alliance: State Advocates for Women's Equality and Gender Justice, February 1, 2022), https://alliancestateadvocates.org/wp-content/uploads/sites/107/Alliance_CPC_Report_FINAL2-1-22.pdf.

24 American College of Obstetricians and Gynecologists, "Induced Abortion and Breast Cancer Risk."

25 Murta and McKenna, "Designed to Deceive: A Study of the Crisis Pregnancy Center Industry in Nine States."

26 Carrie N. Baker and Juliet Schulman-Hall, "Feminists Fight Fake Abortion Clinics: 'No One Should Be Lied to,'" *Ms.* magazine, August 8, 2021, https://msmagazine.com/2021/08/08/feminists-fight-fake-abortion-clinics-no-one-should-be-lied-to/.

27 Brendan Pierson, "Judge Declines to Block Colorado from Banning Medication Abortion Reversal," *Reuters*, April 28, 2023, sec. Legal, https://www.reuters.com/legal/judge-declines-block-colorado-banning-medication-abortion-reversal-2023-04-28/.

28 John Ingold, "Federal Judge Blocks Colorado's New Law Banning Abortion Pill 'Reversal,'" *The Colorado Sun*, October 22, 2023, http://coloradosun.com/2023/10/22/judge-blocks-colorado-abortion-pill-reversal/.

29 Sara K. Redd et al., "Medication Abortion 'Reversal' Laws: How Unsound Science Paved the Way for Dangerous Abortion Policy," *American Journal of Public Health* 113, no. 2 (February 2023): 202–12, https://doi.org/10.2105/AJPH.2022.307140.

30 "H.1783 An Act Relative to Abortion Pill Reversal; Informed Consent," Massachusetts Citizens for Life, accessed April 30, 2023, https://www.masscitizensforlife.org/hd_1383_an_act_relative_to_abortion_pill_reversal_informed_consent.

31 Carrie N. Baker and Carly Thomsen, "The Anti-Abortion Movement's Digital Strategies to Track Pregnant Women—Women's Media Center," December 15, 2021, https://womensmediacenter.com/news-features/the-anti-abortion-movements-digital-strategies-to-track-pregnant-women; "Privacy and Sexual and Reproductive Health in the Post-Roe World" (Privacy International, July 2022), http://privacyinternational.org/long-read/4937/privacy-and-sexual-and-reproductive-health-post-roe-world.

32 "The CPC Industry as a Surveillance Tool of the Post-Roe State" (The Alliance: State Advocates for Women's Equality and Gender Justice, February 2022), https://alliancestateadvocates.org/wp-content/uploads/sites/107/Alliance_CPC_Report_Feb2022_UrgentBrief2-10-22.pdf.

33 "The CPC Industry as a Surveillance Tool of the Post-Roe State."

34 Albert Fox Cahn and Eleni Manis, "Pregnancy Panopticon: Abortion Surveillance after Roe" (New York: Surveillance Technology Oversight Project, May 24, 2022), https://www.stopspying.org/pregnancy-panopticon.

35 Geofencing is a virtual boundary that triggers an ad on a mobile device when a user enters or exits that boundary.

36 Cahn and Manis, "Pregnancy Panopticon: Abortion Surveillance after Roe."

37 Carrie N. Baker, "Enforcing Criminal Abortion Bans Post-Roe: 'A Massive Escalation of Surveillance,'" *Ms.* magazine, June 7, 2022, https://msmagazine.com/2022/06/07/police-abortion-bans-roe-v-wade-surveillance/.

38 Baker.

39 Thomas, "Missouri Health Director Tracked Menstrual Periods of Planned Parenthood Patients."

40 "Abortion Surveillance in Oklahoma 2002–2021" (Oklahoma Department of Health, August 5, 2022).

41 "Every Mother Counts Act," Pub. L. No. 1167 (n.d.), http://www.oklegislature.gov/BillInfo.aspx?Bill=sb1167&Session=2200.

42 Carrie N. Baker, "Democrats in Congress Introduce Bill to Crack Down on Fake Clinics and Anti-abortion Disinformation," *Ms.* magazine, June 28, 2022, https://msmagazine.com/2022/06/28/democrats-congress-sad-act-fake-clinics-anti-abortion-cpc-disinformation/.

43 Carrie N. Baker, "Senators Introduce Bill to Protect Reproductive Health Data: 'My Body, My Data,'" *Ms.* magazine, June 23, 2022, https://msmagazine.com/2022/06/23/reproductive-health-my-body-my-data-act/.

44 Carrie N. Baker, "New California Law Protects Digital Privacy of Abortion Seekers Nationwide," *Ms.* magazine, September 12, 2022, https://msmagazine.com/2022/09/12/california-law-digital-privacy-abortion-seekers/.

45 Elisa Wells, interviewed by Carrie N. Baker, September 10, 2022.

46 Carrie N. Baker, "Proposed California Law Would Block Digital Surveillance of People Seeking Abortion and Gender-Affirming Care," *Ms.* magazine, February 17, 2023, https://msmagazine.com/2023/02/17/california-law-digital-surveillance-abortion-gender-affirming-care/.

47 Baker.

48 Alanna Vagianos, "2 States Introduce Radical Bills to Prosecute Pregnant People for Abortions," *Huffington Post*, January 20, 2023, https://www.huffpost.com/entry/states-introduce-radical-bills-to-prosecute-pregnant-people-for-abortions_n_63cad58be4b0c2b49ad52898.

49 Baker, "New California Law Protects Digital Privacy of Abortion Seekers Nationwide."

50 Carrie N. Baker, "Anti-abortion Groups Ask Trump-Appointed Judge to Ban Mailing Abortion Pills," *Ms.* magazine, November 23, 2022, https://msmagazine.com/2022/11/23/texas-lawsuit-abortion-pills-mifepristone-fifth-circuit-court/.

51 Stephen Young, "Trump-Nominated Plano Religious Hardliner One Step away from North Texas Federal Bench," January 19, 2018, https://www.dallasobserver.com/news/anti-lgbtq-lawyer-matthew-kacsmaryk-nominated-by-trump-one-step-from-federal-bench-10275809.

52 Matthew Kacsmaryk, "The Abolition of Man…and Woman | National Catholic Register," *National Catholic Register*, June 24, 2015, https://www.ncregister.com/news/the-abolition-of-man-and-woman-tpnrdgjq.

53 Young, "Trump-Nominated Plano Religious Hardliner One Step away from North Texas Federal Bench."

54 Baker, "Anti-abortion Groups Ask Trump-Appointed Judge to Ban Mailing Abortion Pills."

55 Kirsten Moore, interview by Carrie N. Baker, November 21, 2022.

56 General Counsel, United States Postal Service, "Application of the Comstock Act to the Mailing of Prescription Drugs That Can Be Used for Abortions," December 23, 2022, https://www.justice.gov/olc/opinion/file/1560596/download.

57 Ron Wyden, "Wyden Delivers Floor Speech Calling on President Biden and the FDA to Keep Mifepristone on the Market, Regardless of Outcome in Texas Case," February 16, 2023, https://www.wyden.senate.gov/news/press-releases/wyden-delivers-floor-speech-calling-on-president-biden-and-the-fda-to-keep-mifepristone-on-the-market-regardless-of-outcome-in-texas-case.

58 Wyden.

59 Carrie N. Baker, "Lawmaker Urges Biden to 'Ignore' Texas Judge Who May Order FDA to Ban Mifepristone and Abortion Pill by Mail," *Ms.* magazine, February 24, 2023, https://msmagazine.com/2023/02/24/abortion-pills-mifepristone-texas-judge/.

60 Wyden, "Wyden Delivers Floor Speech Calling on President Biden and the FDA to Keep Mifepristone on the Market, Regardless of Outcome in Texas Case."

61 "Food and Drug Administration: Information on Mifeprex Labeling Changes and Ongoing Monitoring Efforts."

62 US Food and Drug Administration, "Response Letter to American Association of Pro-Life Obstetricians and Gynecologists and American College of Pediatricians," December 17, 2021, https://www.regulations.gov/document/FDA-2019-P-1534-0016.

63 Wyden, "Wyden Delivers Floor Speech Calling on President Biden and the FDA to Keep Mifepristone on the Market, Regardless of Outcome in Texas Case."

64 Wyden.

65 Carolyn Kitchener and Ann E. Marimow, "The Texas Judge Who Could Take Down the Abortion Pill," *The Washington Post*, February 25, 2023, https://www.washingtonpost.com/politics/2023/02/25/texas-judge-abortion-pill-decision/.

66 Christine Fernando, "A Texas Judge Could Soon Force a Major Abortion Pill off the Market Nationwide," *USA Today*, February 9, 2023, https://eu.usatoday.com/story/news/nation/2023/02/09/texas-judge-fda-abortion-pill-medication-abortion-mifepristone/11203396002/.

67 Kaiser Health News, "One Texas Judge Will Decide Fate of Abortion Pill Used by Millions of American Women," *The Denver Post* (blog), March 1, 2023, https://www.denverpost.com/2023/03/01/texas-abortion-pill-case-lawsuit-mifepristone/.

68 David S. Cohen, Greer Donley, and Rachel Rebouché, "Actually, One Texas Judge Is Not the Final Decision-Maker on Medication Abortion," *Slate*, February 28, 2023, https://slate.com/news-and-politics/2023/02/texas-judge-abortion-case-actually-limited-mifepristone.html.

69 David Cohen, interview by Carrie N. Baker, March 2, 2023.

70 David Cohen, interview by Carrie N. Baker, March 2, 2023.

71 "Misoprostol-Alone Medication Abortion Is Safe and Effective" (Cambridge, MA: Ibis Reproductive Health, November 2021), https://www.ibisreproductivehealth.org/sites/default/files/files/publications/Misoprostol-alone%20medication%20abortion%20is%20safe%20and%20effective.pdf.

72 Johnson et al., "Safety and Effectiveness of Self-managed Abortion Using Misoprostol Alone Acquired from an Online Telemedicine Service in the United States."

73 Dana Johnson, interview by Carrie N. Baker, February 12, 2023.

74 Dana Johnson, interview by Carrie N. Baker, February 12, 2023.

75 Heidi Moseson et al., "Effectiveness of Self-Managed Medication Abortion with Accompaniment Support in Argentina and Nigeria (SAFE): A Prospective, Observational Cohort Study and Non-inferiority Analysis with Historical Controls," *The Lancet Global Health* 10, no. 1 (January 2022): e105–13, https://doi.org/10.1016/S2214-109X(21)00461-7.

76 Dana Johnson, interview by Carrie N. Baker, February 12, 2023.

77 Dana Johnson, interview by Carrie N. Baker, February 12, 2023.

78 Online Abortion Resource Squad at https://www.abortionsquad.org/.

79 Laura E. Jacobson et al., "Understanding the Abortion Experiences of Young People to Inform Quality Care in Argentina, Bangladesh, Ethiopia, and Nigeria," *Youth & Society* 54, no. 6 (September 2022): 957–81, https://doi.org/10.1177/0044118X211011015.

80 Susan Rinkunas, "If the Main Abortion Pill Is Banned This Week, Providers Are Prepared to Go Off-Label," *Jezebel*, February 7, 2023, https://jezebel.com/mifepristone-ban-misoprostol-only-abortions-in-the-us-1850083070.

81 "Clinical Policy Guidelines for Abortion Care" (Washington, DC: National Abortion Federation, 2022), https://prochoice.org/wp-content/uploads/2022-CPGs.pdf.

82 "Abortion Care Guidance" (Geneva, Switzerland: World Health Organization, 2022), https://srhr.org/abortioncare/.

83 Johnson et al., "Safety and Effectiveness of Self-managed Abortion Using Misoprostol Alone Acquired from an Online Telemedicine Service in the United States."

84 Carolyn Westhoff, interview by Carrie N. Baker, August 9, 2023.

85 Carrie N. Baker, "Democratic AGs File Counter-Lawsuit to Expand Access to Abortion Pills," *Ms.* magazine, February 27, 2023, https://msmagazine.com/2023/02/27/democratic-attorney-general-lawsuit-abortion-pills-mifepristone-fda/.

86 Baker.

87 Complaint, Washington et al. v. FDA, No. 1:23-cv-03026 (United States District Court for the Eastern District of Washington February 23, 2023).

88 Complaint, Washington et al. v. FDA.

89 "AG Ferguson Challenges FDA over Unlawful, Unnecessary Restrictions on Medication Abortion Drug | Washington State," accessed April 26, 2023, https://www.atg.wa.gov/news/news-releases/ag-ferguson-challenges-fda-over-unlawful-unnecessary-restrictions-medication.

90 "AG Ferguson Challenges FDA over Unlawful, Unnecessary Restrictions on Medication Abortion Drug | Washington State."

91 "AG Ferguson Challenges FDA over Unlawful, Unnecessary Restrictions on Medication Abortion Drug | Washington State."

92 Complaint, Washington et al. v. FDA.

93 Baker, "Democratic AGs File Counter-Lawsuit to Expand Access to Abortion Pills."

94 Katherine A. Rafferty and Tessa Longbons, "#AbortionChangesYou: A Case Study to Understand the Communicative Tensions in Women's Medication Abortion Narratives," *Health Communication* 36, no. 12 (October 15, 2021): 1485–94, https://doi.org/10.1080/10410236.2020.1770507.

95 David C. Reardon et al., "Deaths Associated with Pregnancy Outcome: A Record Linkage Study of Low Income Women," *Southern Medical Journal* 95, no. 8 (August 2002): 834–41.

96 Lauren Weber et al., "Unpacking the Flawed Science Cited in the Texas Abortion Pill Ruling," *The Washington Post*, April 14, 2023, https://www.washingtonpost.com/health/2023/04/13/abortion-pill-safety/.

97 Alliance for Hippocratic Medicine v. U.S. Food and Drug Administration.

98 Alliance for Hippocratic Medicine v. U.S. Food and Drug Administration at 43.

99 Baker, "Supreme Court Blocks Fifth Circuit Ruling, Allowing Mifepristone to Stay on the Market as Case Proceeds," *Ms.* magazine, April 14, 2023, https://msmagazine.com/2023/04/14/abortion-pill-washington-supreme-court-fda/.

100 Washington et al. v. U.S. Food and Drug Administration et al., No. 1:23-cv-03026-TOR (U.S. District Court for the Eastern District of Washington April 7, 2023).

101 Carrie N. Baker, "Federal Courts in Texas and Washington Release Contradictory Rulings. Abortion Pills Remain on the Market—for Now," *Ms.* magazine, April 7, 2023, https://msmagazine.com/2023/04/07/texas-washington-abortion-pill-rulings/.

102 Baker.

103 Baker.

104 Sarah McCammon, "Washington State Stockpiles Thousands of Abortion Pills," *NPR*, April 4, 2023, sec. National, https://www.npr.org/2023/04/04/1167867948/washington-state-stockpiles-thousands-of-abortion-pills.

105 Matt Stout and Mike Damiano, "Healey, in Bid to 'Ride out' Legal Challenge, Moves to Stockpile 15,000 Mifepristone Doses in Massachusetts," *Boston Globe*, April 10, 2023, https://www.bostonglobe.com/2023/04/10/metro/abortion-pill-ruling-healey-plan-protect-access-massachusetts/.

106 "Oregon Secures 3-Year Supply of Abortion-Inducing Medication," *AP News*, April 21, 2023, sec. Medication, https://apnews.com/article/oregon-abortion-pills-mifepristone-05b7d00601cd3d431a0c43034ca55729.

107 "In Support of FDA's Authority to Regulate Medicines," n.d., https://docsend.com/view/2ahvmwy8djzxax3g.

108 Alliance for Hippocratic Medicine et al. v. U.S. Food and Drug Administration et al., No. No. 23-10632 (Fifth Circuit Court of Appeals April 12, 2023).

109 Carrie N. Baker, "Circuit Court Rules Abortion Pill Can Remain on the Market, but with Limitations That Could Restrict Access," *Ms.* magazine, April 13, 2023, https://msmagazine.com/2023/04/13/mifepristone-abortion-pill-fifth-circuit-court/.

110 Emergency Application for a Stay of Preliminary Injunction Pending Appeal in Alliance of Hippocratic Medicine v. FDA (Supreme Court of the United States April 14, 2023).

111 Baker, "Circuit Court Rules Abortion Pill Can Remain on the Market, but with Limitations That Could Restrict Access."

112 Carrie N. Baker and Roxy Szal, "As Supreme Court Weighs Next Steps on Abortion Pill, Protesters Rally in Support of Abortion Rights," *Ms.* magazine, April 17, 2023, https://msmagazine.com/2023/04/17/supreme-court-abortion-pill-protest-rally-march/.

113 "Democratic Women's Caucus Joins House and Senate Dems to File Amicus Brief Urging Appeals Court to Prevent Dangerous Ruling Threatening Access to Mifepristone from Taking Effect,"

Democratic Women's Caucus, April 12, 2023, http://democraticwomenscaucus-frankel.house.gov/media/press-releases/democratic-womens-caucus-joins-house-and-senate-dems-file-amicus-brief-urging.

114 Stephen Neukam, "69 Republicans Ask Appeals Court to Allow Ban on Abortion Pill to Go Forward," *The Hill*, April 12, 2023, https://thehill.com/policy/healthcare/3945256-republicans-appeals-court-abortion-pill-texas/.

115 Carrie N. Baker, "GenBioPro Sues FDA to Keep Generic Mifepristone on the Market," *Ms.* magazine, April 20, 2023, https://msmagazine.com/2023/04/20/genbiopro-sues-fda-mifepristone-abortion-pill/.

116 Baker.

117 Danco Laboratories v. Alliance for Hippocratic Medicine et al.; U.S. Food and Drug Administration et al. v. Alliance for Hippocratic Medicine at al., 598 U.S. __ (United States Supreme Court 2023).

118 Carrie N. Baker, "Supreme Court Blocks Fifth Circuit Ruling, Allowing Mifepristone to Stay on the Market as Case Proceeds."

119 Elisa Wells, Plan C Statement: SCOTUS preserves status quo for now, but access to abortion is still lacking in the US, email dated April 22, 2023.

120 Amy Schoenfeld Walker et al., "Are Abortion Pills Safe? Here's the Evidence," *The New York Times*, April 1, 2023, sec. Health, https://www.nytimes.com/interactive/2023/04/01/health/abortion-pill-safety.html.

121 Center for Drug Evaluation and Research, "Questions and Answers on Mifepristone for Medical Termination of Pregnancy through Ten Weeks Gestation," *FDA*, January 19, 2023, https://www.fda.gov/drugs/postmarket-drug-safety-information-patients-and-providers/questions-and-answers-mifepristone-medical-termination-pregnancy-through-ten-weeks-gestation.

122 Brief of *Amici Curiae* Medical and Public Health Societies in Opposition to Plaintiffs' Motion, Alliance for Hippocratic Medicine v. FDA, Civil Action No. 2:22-cv-00223-Z, United States District Court for the Northern District of Texas, Amarillo Division, February 10, 2023, https://www.acog.org/-/media/project/acog/acogorg/files/advocacy/amicus-briefs/mifepristone-amicus-brief-21023.pdf.

123 Brief of *Amici Curiae* Medical and Public Health Societies in Opposition to Plaintiffs' Motion.

124 "Improving Access to Mifepristone for Reproductive Health Indications, Position Statement" (Washington, DC: American College of Obstetricians and Gynecologists, June 2018), https://www.acog.org/clinical-information/policy-and-position-statements/position-statements/2018/improving-access-to-mifepristone-for-reproductive-health-indications; American Medical Association, "H-100.948 Supporting Access to Mifepristone (Mifeprex)," accessed April 28, 2023, https://policysearch.ama-assn.org/policyfinder/detail/mifepristone?uri=%2FAMADoc%2FHOD.xml-H-100.948.xml; American Academy of Family Physicians, "Summary of Actions of the 2018 National Congress of Family Medicine Residents," 2018.

125 Carrie N. Baker, "Far-Right Fifth Circuit Judges Appear Determined to Remove Access to Abortion Pill Mifepristone," *Ms.* magazine, May 18, 2023, www.msmagazine.com/2023/05/18/fifth-circuit-abortion-mifepristone/.

126 Alliance for Hippocratic Medicine v. U.S. Food and Drug Administration, No. 23-10362 (Fifth Circuit Court of Appeals August 16, 2023).

127 Chris Geidner, "Three GOP AGs Seek to Join Medication Abortion Lawsuit, Raising SCOTUS Questions," August 8, 2023, https://www.lawdork.com/p/gop-ags-seek-intervention-mifeprisone-case; Order, Alliance for Hippocratic Medicine v. U.S. Food and Drug Administration, 2:22-CV-223-Z, January 1, 2024, https://fingfx.thomsonreuters.com/gfx/legaldocs/zgvokmqdovd/abortion%20pill%20intervention%20order%201-12.pdf.

128 Ann E. Marimow and Caroline Kitchener, "Supreme Court Skeptical of Efforts to Restrict Access to Abortion Pill," *The Washington Post*, March 26, 2024, https://www.washingtonpost.com/politics/2024/03/26/supreme-court-abortion-pill-mifepristone/.

129 NARAL Pro-Choice America, "Medication Abortion Disinformation Trends Surrounding Alliance for Hippocratic Medicine v. FDA," June 15, 2023, https://reproductivefreedomforall.org/wp-content/uploads/2023/06/Medication-Abortion-Disinformation-Trends-Surrounding-Alliance-for-Hippocratic-Medicine-v.-FDA.pdf.

130 Sarah McCammon, "In New Mexico, Anti-abortion Activists Take Abortion Restrictions Local," *NPR*, April 29, 2023, sec. Law, https://www.npr.org/2023/04/29/1172918575/in-new-mexico-anti-abortion-activists-take-abortion-restrictions-local.

131 Elise Kaplan and Dan Boyd, "A Small Southeastern New Mexico City Passed an Ordinance Restricting Abortion Access. Now It's Suing the AG, Gov.," *Albuquerque Journal*, April 17, 2023, https://www.abqjournal.com/2591584/eunice-new-mexico-city-passed-an-ordinance-restricting-abortion-access-now-its-suing-the-attorney-general-governor.html.

132 Sharon Zhang, "Republicans Are Quietly Moving to Limit Mifepristone Access Nationwide," Truthout, May 22, 2023, https://truthout.org/articles/republicans-are-quietly-moving-to-limit-mifepristone-access-nationwide/.

133 "HB 2690, Texas House of Representatives, 2023," 26, accessed May 17, 2023, https://capitol.texas.gov/BillLookup/History.aspx?LegSess=88R&Bill=HB2690.

134 Carrie N. Baker, "North Carolina Legislature Overrides Governor's Veto of 12-Week Abortion Ban," *Ms.* magazine, May 17, 2023, https://msmagazine.com/2023/05/17/north-carolina-abortion/.

135 Bazelon, "Risking Everything to Offer Abortions across State Lines," 62.

136 Maya Miller, "These Billboards Want You to Know How to Get Abortion Pills—Even If Your State Banned Abortions," Mississippi Public Broadcasting, March 2, 2023, https://www.mpbonline.org/blogs/news/these-billboards-want-you-to-know-how-to-get-abortion-pills-even-if-your-state-banned-abortions/.

137 Michelle Cohen of SHERo in Mississippi explained: "What Mayday does not get, nor do I believe they care about, is that during that process, they're going to fuck shit up for those of us, like myself, who are here in Mississippi, who are barely getting by, all because they want to be lauded as this liberal, progressive group. I don't partner with Mayday. They're problematic. The simple fact is that they don't respect local people. They're here basically for their own notoriety." Michelle Cohen, interview by Carrie N. Baker, June 8, 2023.

138 Jennifer Habercorn and Josh Gerstein, "Abortion Pill Manufacturer to Pay $765K to U.S. to Settle Suit over Incorrect Labeling," POLITICO, April 17, 2023, https://www.politico.com/news/2023/04/17/abortion-pill-manufacturer-settlement-00092448.

139 Isaac Maddow-Zimet and Candice Gibson, "Despite Bans, Number of Abortions in the United States Increased in 2023," Guttmacher Institute, March 2024, https://www.guttmacher.org/2024/03/despite-bans-number-abortions-united-states-increased-2023.

140 Rachel K. Jones and Amy Friedrich-Karnik, "Medication Abortion Accounted for 63% of All US Abortions in 2023—An Increase from 53% in 2020," Guttmacher Institute, March 2024, https://www.guttmacher.org/2024/03/medication-abortion-accounted-63-all-us-abortions-2023-increase-53-2020.

141 Carrie N. Baker, "Abortion Pill Revolution: CVS and Walgreens Now Selling Abortion Pills, While Telehealth Abortion Soars," *Ms.* magazine, March 6, 2024, https://msmagazine.com/2024/03/06/pharmacy-mifepristone-abortion-pills-cvs-walgreens-order-abortion-online/.

142 Society of Family Planning, "#WeCount Public Report, April 2022 to December 2023," May 14, 2024, https://doi.org/10.46621/970371hxrbsk.

143 Email from Elisa Wells, May 14, 2024.

144 Carrie N. Baker, "Healthcare Across Borders: Funding Telemedicine Abortion for People in Abortion-Ban States," *Ms.* magazine, February 22, 2024, https://msmagazine.com/2024/02/22/pay-abortion-pills-telemedicine-abortion-ban-states-shield-law/.

145 Maine State Legislature, "An Act Regarding Legally Protected Health Care Activity in the State, April 22, 2024," https://legislature.maine.gov/bills/getPDF.asp?paper=HP0148&item=3&snum=131.

146 Abigail R.A. Aiken et al., "Provision of Medications for Self-Managed Abortion before and after the Dobbs v Jackson Women's Health Organization Decision," *Journal of the American Medical Association*, March 25, 2024 (advance publication online), https://jamanetwork.com/journals/jama/article-abstract/2816817; Abigail R.A. Aiken et al., "The Supply of Pill Packs for Self-managed Abortion Increased Substantially after the U.S. Supreme Court Eliminated the Constitutional Right to Choose Abortion," University of Texas at Austin Population Research Center Research Brief 9, no. 2, https://doi.org/10.26153/tsw/51546.

147 Email to author from Red State Access, May 1, 2024.

148 Email to author from Plan C, December 2023.

149 Email to author from Plan C, May 4, 2024.

150 Interview with Roopan Gill, May 1, 2024 and May 13, 2024; see https://hola.ayacontigo.org/.

151 Navigator Research, "Public Opinion on Medication Abortion," March 26, 2024, 2, https://navigatorresearch.org/wp-content/uploads/2024/03/Navigator-Interested-Parties-Memo-Medication-Abortion-03.26.2024.pdf.

Conclusion

1 Cynthia Pearson, interview by Carrie N. Baker, July 14, 2023.

2 Winikoff and Westhoff, "Fifteen Years."

3 Winikoff and Westhoff, "Fifteen Years."

4 Klitsch, *RU 486: The Science and the Politics*, 14.

5 The David and Lucile Packard Foundation, "Grants and Mission Investments," accessed May 26, 2023, https://www.packard.org/grants-and-investments/grants-database/; Hewlett Foundation, "Grants," *Hewlett Foundation* (blog), March 20, 2023, https://hewlett.org/grants/; Tracy Weitz, interview by Carrie N. Baker, May 24, 2023.

6 Francine Coeytaux, interview by Carrie N. Baker, May 24, 2023.

7 Rosenfeld, "Conception of a Controversy: The French Doctor and His Pill to Prevent Pregnancy"; Fraser, "Pill Politics."

8 Lader, *RU 486*, 97.

9 Collins, "The Complicated Life of the Abortion Pill."

10 Reagan, *When Abortion Was a Crime*.

11 Lynn M. Morgan and Meredith W. Michaels, *Fetal Subjects, Feminist Positions* (Philadelphia: University of Pennsylvania, 1999).

12 Carrie N. Baker, "Online Abortion Provider and 'Activist Physician' Michele Gomez Is Expanding Early Abortion Options into Primary Care," *Ms. Magazine*, January 19, 2022, https://msmagazine.com/2022/01/19/online-abortion-primary-care-doctor-michele-gomez-mya-network/.

13 Emily Godfrey, interview by Carrie N. Baker, May 5, 2023.

14 "ExPAND Mifepristone, Department of Family Medicine, The University of Chicago," accessed May 14, 2023, https://familymedicine.uchicago.edu/research/expand-mifepristone-learning-collaborative.

15 Carrie N. Baker, "Telemedicine Abortion Provider Dr. Deborah Oyer Supports Patient Autonomy and Control: 'No Different Than When They're in Clinic,'" *Ms. Magazine*, January 12, 2022, https://msmagazine.com/2022/01/12/telemedicine-abortion-deborah-oyer-cedar-river-clinics-seattle-washington-idaho/.

16 Carrie N. Baker, "Online Abortion Provider Julie Amaon of Just the Pill Is 'Making Abortion as Easy as Possible for People,'" *Ms. Magazine*, January 26, 2022, https://msmagazine.com/2022/01/26/online-abortion-provider-julie-amaon-just-the-pill/.

17 Carrie N. Baker, "Online Abortion Providers Cindy Adam and Lauren Dubey of Choix: "We're Really Excited About the Future of Abortion Care,'" *Ms. Magazine*, January 14, 2022, https://msmagazine.com/2022/01/14/abortion-pills-california-colorado-illinois-online-abortion-cindy-adam-lauren-dubey-choix/.

18 "#WeCount Report April to March 2023 Findings" (Society of Family Planning, June 20, 2023), https://doi.org/10.46621/XBAZ6145.

19 Bazelon, "Risking Everything to Offer Abortions across State Lines," 33.
20 Bazelon, 33.
21 Bazelon, 33.
22 Jenna Jerman, Rachel K. Jones, and Tsuyoshi Onda, "Characteristics of U.S. Abortion Patients in 2014 and Changes since 2008" (New York: Guttmacher Institute, May 10, 2016), https://www.guttmacher.org/report/characteristics-us-abortion-patients-2014.
23 Langer, "Philip Corfman, Advocate for Women's Reproductive Health, Dies at 92."
24 Cynthia Pearson, interview by Carrie N. Baker, July 5, 2023.
25 Email from Sarah Christopherson, August 9, 2023.
26 Sarah Christopherson, interview by Carrie N. Baker, August 9, 2023.
27 Sarah Christopherson, interview by Carrie N. Baker, August 9, 2023.
28 Ariella Messing, interview by Carrie N. Baker, July 20, 2023.
29 Nina Henry, interview by Carrie N. Baker, August 10, 2023.
30 Nina Henry, interview by Carrie N. Baker, August 10, 2023.
31 Elisa Wells, interview by Carrie N. Baker, May 24, 2023.
32 An MTP kit includes one 200-milligram mifepristone pill and four 200-microgram misoprostol pills.
33 Plan C, "Websites That Sell Pills," July 12, 2023, https://www.plancpills.org/websites-that-sell-pills.
34 Elisa Wells, interview by Carrie N. Baker, May 31, 2023.
35 "Complaint, Whole Woman's Health Alliance v. FDA, U.S. District Court for the Western District of Virginia" (Case 3:23-cv-00019-NKM, May 8, 2023), 3, https://reproductiverights.org/wp-content/uploads/2023/05/WWH-v-FDA-Complaint.pdf.
36 Carrie N. Baker, "Healthcare Providers File Federal Lawsuit to Expand Abortion Pill Access," *Ms. Magazine*, May 9, 2023, https://msmagazine.com/2023/05/09/fda-lawsuit-abortion-pill-mifepristone/.
37 "Complaint, Whole Woman's Health Alliance v. FDA, U.S. District Court for the Western District of Virginia," 17.
38 "Complaint, Whole Woman's Health Alliance v. FDA, U.S. District Court for the Western District of Virginia," 17–18.
39 "Complaint, Whole Woman's Health Alliance v. FDA, U.S. District Court for the Western District of Virginia," 18.
40 "Complaint, Whole Woman's Health Alliance v. FDA, U.S. District Court for the Western District of Virginia," 18–19.
41 "Complaint, Whole Woman's Health Alliance v. FDA, U.S. District Court for the Western District of Virginia," 19.
42 "Complaint, Whole Woman's Health Alliance v. FDA, U.S. District Court for the Western District of Virginia," 21–22.
43 "Complaint, Whole Woman's Health Alliance v. FDA, U.S. District Court for the Western District of Virginia," 22.
44 Baker, "Healthcare Providers File Federal Lawsuit to Expand Abortion Pill Access."
45 Memorandum Opinion, Whole Woman's Health Alliance v. FDA, No. Civil Action No.: 3:23-cv-00019 (U.S. District Court for the Western District of Virginia, August 21, 2023).
46 Biggs et al., "A Cross-Sectional Survey of U.S. Abortion Patients' Interest in Obtaining Medication Abortion over the Counter."
47 Francine Coeytaux, interview by Carrie N. Baker, May 2, 2023.
48 *Plan C*. Directed by Tracy Droz Tragos. Dinky Pictures, 2023, at 23:16.
49 Carolyn Westhoff, interview by Carrie N. Baker, August 9, 2023.
50 Francine Coeytaux, interview by Carrie N. Baker, May 2, 2023.
51 Marlene Gerber Fried, interview by Carrie N. Baker, May 18, 2023.
52 Marlene Gerber Fried, interview by Carrie N. Baker, May 18, 2023.
53 Eyal Press, "The Planned Parenthood Problem," *New Yorker*, May 15, 2023, 34.
54 Press, 44.

55 Beverly Winikoff, interview by Carrie N. Baker, May 22, 2023.

56 Francine Coeytaux, interview by Carrie N. Baker, May 23, 2023.

57 Pamela Merritt, interview by Carrie N. Baker, June 19, 2023.

58 Reagan, *When Abortion Was a Crime*, 10.

59 Reagan.

60 Loretta Ross, interview by Carrie N. Baker, June 13, 2023.

61 Carol Mason, "How Trumpism Fostered Anti-Choice Violence," *Ms. Magazine*, February 9, 2021, https://msmagazine.com/2021/02/09/trump-capitol-riots-women-abortion-anti-choice-violence-anti-abortion-extremists-propaganda/.

62 Reagan, *When Abortion Was a Crime*, 10.

63 Reagan, 11.

64 Reagan, 11.

65 Reagan, 13.

66 Mason, "How Trumpism Fostered Anti-Choice Violence"; Alex DiBranco, "The Long History of the Anti-Abortion Movement's Links to White Supremacists," February 3, 2020, https://www.thenation.com/article/politics/anti-abortion-white-supremacy/; Carol Mason, *Killing for Life: The Apocalyptic Narrative of Pro-Life Politics*.

67 Ari M. Brostoff, "How White Nationalists Aligned Themselves with the Antiabortion Movement," *The Washington Post*, June 22, 2020, https://www.washingtonpost.com/outlook/2019/08/27/how-white-nationalists-aligned-themselves-with-antiabortion-movement/; Tom McCarthy, "'He's So Openly Racist': Why Does Iowa Keep Electing Steve King to Congress?," *The Guardian*, October 27, 2018, sec. US news, https://www.theguardian.com/us-news/2018/oct/26/hes-so-openly-racist-why-does-iowa-keep-electing-steve-king-to-congress.

68 Mary Ziegler, *Abortion in America: A Legal History from Roe to the Present* (New York: Cambridge University Press, 2020).

69 Rickie Solinger, *Pregnancy and Power: A History of Reproductive Politics in the United States*, rev. Ed. (New York: New York University Press, 2019), 3.

70 Solinger, 4.

71 Francine Coeytaux, interview by Carrie N. Baker, May 25, 2023.

72 Francine Coeytaux, interview by Carrie N. Baker, May 25, 2023.

73 Olga Khazan, "The Abortion Backup Plan No One Is Talking About," *The Atlantic*, October 12, 2021, https://www.theatlantic.com/politics/archive/2021/10/plan-c-secret-option-mail-order-abortion/620324/; Francine Coeytaux, interview by Carrie N. Baker, May 25, 2023.

74 Francine Coeytaux, interview by Carrie N. Baker, May 25, 2023.

75 Francine Coeytaux, interview by Carrie N. Baker, May 25, 2023.

76 Timothy Snyder, *On Tyranny: Twenty Lessons from the Twentieth Century* (New York: Crown, 2017).

77 A scholar of the Irish decriminalization of abortion, Sydney Calkins, has expressed concerns that liberalization of abortion laws may in fact decrease access to abortion pills by institutionalizing medical control of abortion pills. Kath Browne and Sydney Calkin, eds., *After Repeal: Rethinking Abortion Politics* (London: Zed Books, 2019), 81, 88.

78 Diana Lugo-Martinez, interview by Carrie N. Baker, July 24, 2023.

79 Michelle Cohen, interview by Carrie N. Baker, June 8, 2023.

80 Browne and Calkin, *After Repeal: Rethinking Abortion Politics*, 87.

Appendix B: Glossary

1 Monica Dragoman et al., "Integrating Self-Managed Medication Abortion with Medical Care," *Contraception* 108 (April 2022): 1–3, https://doi.org/10.1016/j.contraception.2021.12.003.